EVERYTHING YOU ALWAYS WANTED TO KNOW ABOUT WINE
(but were afraid to ask the wine steward)

Do supercilious French waiters press you into ordering wines you don't recognize? Does the local wine seller give you the old fish-eye when you question him about a particular vintage or vineyard? Take heart, this fascinating book not only rates over 20,000 wines, it also gives pertinent facts about vineyards, distributors, and different vintages for the same wine which may differ in quality. All you need do is look up the prominent word on the label of any bottle of wine, and *voilà*—you become a connoisseur!

THE SIGNET ENCYCLOPEDIA OF WINE

SIGNET Books for Your Reference Shelf

THE
SIGNET
ENCYCLOPEDIA
OF WINE

E. Frank Henriques

A SIGNET BOOK
NEW AMERICAN LIBRARY
TIMES MIRROR

For

Alicia, my wife, without whom this book would never have been written, for she supported me physically—bought things like food (and wine)—during the many years this book has been in the writing . . .

And for Jon, my brother-priest, who supported me spiritually by assuming my own "bounden duty and service," the spiritual care of the St. Matthias Episcopal Church, and who has absolutely no need for this book, for Jon came to us, like John (Jon?) the Baptist, "neither eating bread nor drinking wine" (Luke 7:33) . . . but we've managed to corrupt him a little . . .

And for Jacky who, with no compensation whatever, gave a year of her life and labors to this book . . . And for Doug and Loretta who loaned her to us . . .

And for Leonard and Evie who gave of their home so that this book might have a place to be born . . .

And for the people of St. Matthias, who allowed their shepherd to neglect the sheep in favor of the vineyards—and who sorely need this book, for they still favor Carmel Concord Grape for their altar wine!

ALL YE CITIZENS OF THE EARTH—
NOW HEAR THIS WORD OF THE LORD:

Thou dost cause the grass to grow for the cattle,
    and plants for man to cultivate,
        that he may bring forth food from the earth,
    and wine to gladden the heart of man.
                            Psalm 104:14-15

Go, eat your bread with enjoyment, and drink your wine
with a merry heart.
                                 Ecclesiastes 9:7

ALL YE DISCIPLES OF JESUS CHRIST—
NOW HEAR THIS WORD OF THE LORD:

No longer drink only water, but use a little wine for the sake of
your stomach and your frequent ailments.
                                 1 Timothy 5:23

serve at cool room temperature, with hamburgers, barbecued meats, pasta ...

ness and richness, but Beringer's product is not overly long in bottle ... it's best with roast ... and ... dark game. All ... be ...

Key to Coding of Wines

* * * * *	Exceptional
* * * *	Very Good
* * *	Good
* *	Fair
*	Passable

A Note to the Reader:

The prices listed herein will obviously
vary depending upon your locale, your
liquor store, and price fluctuations in
the market since this book was compiled.

MOST OF YE DISCIPLES OF JESUS CHRIST*
NOW HEAR THIS WORD OF THE LORD:

Wine puts life into a man,
if he drinks it in moderation.
What is life to a man deprived of wine?
Was it not created to warm men's hearts?
Wine brings gaiety and high spirits,
if a man knows when to drink and when to stop;
but wine in excess makes for bitter feelings
and leads to offense and retaliation.

Ecclesiasticus 31:27-29

* Most, not all, Christians will accept this Word of the Lord because it is from Ecclesiasticus, one of the Apocryphal Books of Scripture. The vast majority of Christians—all those of the "Catholic" tradition—ascribe at least partial authority to the Apocrypha.

Introduction

The book you hold in your hands is certainly one of the most audacious, most presumptuous, most brazen books in the history of American publishing. I almost said *the* most audacious and presumptuous. Which, quite literally, might well be the case. But that would be audacious and presumptuous.

This book, in essence, tells you what you should like—and that's pretty presumptuous—not to say dangerous. Its purview is the realm of food and drink, tastes and preferences. But the Romans said twenty centuries ago, *"De gustibus non est disputandum"*—"There's no arguing about tastes."

This book presumes to tell you exactly how good—or bad —virtually every fine wine in the world is, down to the last 25 cents worth. Further, it forthrightly proclaims precisely when every wine will be at its best, almost down to the day and hour. Finally, this book tells you exactly how you should drink every one of the thousands of bottles of wines listed herein: in what company, with what food, in what clime. Yet all these matters are largely subjective areas of personal taste, delectation, predilection.

Our only, and yet our *complete* response is that this book is a guide, and guides don't equivocate. A guidebook is nothing if not definite, authoritative. There are few "perhaps" and no "???" in guidebooks. A famous critic once said that there are no good wines, there are only good bottles of wine. If that were wholly, 100 percent true, there would be no need for a book such as this. Perish that thought forever! But the statement is true in this sense, that wine from the very same barrel sometimes differs from one bottle to another because of the way in which the wine was stored. Thus there occurs that occasional "bad bottle" which you have every right—nay, it is your duty—to send back to your sommelier or wine merchant. But 99 percent of the time what is true of one bottle of wine is true of the next bottle with the identical label.

This book is for anyone who has ever bought or will ever buy a bottle of wine. And that's not said to sell books. That's said to tell the whole truth. With this trusty volume in hand, behold, you are an instant authority. And we challenge anyone to gainsay that. Incredibly, you are.

Thus armed, you can walk with confidence through the most kaleidoscopic and bewildering array of wines in the most splendid wine shop in the world, and you will know what you are about.

This book is also for the advanced wine lover, for the seasoned enophile, even for the true connoisseur, for this is an authoritative guide. He may compare his own judgments against these "universal" evaluations. More importantly, it is a guide to lead him onward and upward into new, exciting uncharted lands.

But in all these instances this book is only a first step. It is you, novice or expert, who will take the second and third and hundredth step, and make your own evaluations and judgments. In a true sense, it is you who will be writing your own wine guide, whether inscribed on your cerebellum or laboriously written out in longhand in your own notebook.

Which brings us to the most important principle of all wine evaluation. The ultimate norm, the final dictum, the supreme principle, which deserves to be inscribed at the head of every page of this guide, is this—that YOU ARE THE ULTIMATE CONNOISSEUR, the final expert. If you like the wine, drink it! It is good wine.

Penultimately, this book is not simply one man's appraisal of the world's finest wine. This volume represents the accumulated wisdom of wine lovers, wine experts, winemakers, the world round, over the past century. Between these two covers you hold in your hands the distilled truth of thousands of evaluations, wine tastings, professional appraisals.

Finally, as an active minister of the Christian Church, I am compelled to say a brief word about wine and religion. The true mainstream Christian tradition of almost two thousand years has never seen any conflict between wine and the Gospel of Jesus Christ. In fact, the opposite has been true: there has been a positive identification between wine and the Christian religion.

As Will Rogers used to say, "Let's look at the record." What saith the Bible? There are exactly 271 references in Sacred Scripture to wine and strong drink. Not a single one of these references condemns the use of alcoholic drink per se. God's Written Word clearly distinguishes, over and over again, between the use and the abuse of alcohol. The use is sanctioned, even blessed by God—the abuse is severely condemned.

Most important of all: what was Jesus' own attitude toward wine? He obviously used wine himself. On one occasion He worked a prodigious miracle to provide an enormous amount of wine—120 to 180 gallons, scholars tell us—for a party when the supply had run low. Most significant of all, He chose two of mankind's staples, bread and wine—wine, not grape juice—to be the ongoing symbol of His Presence among us, to the end of time.

The man who knows and loves wine will not abuse it. It's too celestial, not to say costly, to be wasted or abused. The man who drinks fine wine because he appreciates and enjoys it so, will not drink too much of it, for the simple reason that the wine will become distasteful to him before it becomes paralyzing!

Wine is for enjoyment, not intoxication. The man who only wants to get drunk will opt for distilled spirits, not wine. Wine is a food and a relaxant, not an intoxicant. Wine is of God—spirits all too often are of Satan. It was a wise man who said, "It was whiskey that made you shoot at the landloard . . . And what's worse, it was whiskey that made you miss!"

Hilaire Belloc said it beautifully:

> Wherever a Christian sun does shine,
> There's always laughter and good red wine—
> At least I've always found it so—
> *Benedicamus Domino!*

But perhaps Sir Walter Scott said it best of all:

> God in his goodness sent the grapes
> To cheer both great and small;
> Little fools will drink too much
> And great fools none at all!

God gave man wine to gladden his heart, to brighten his days, to lighten his burden. Enjoy it sanely, soberly, slowly, as one of God's best gifts. Bless and praise Him for his loving kindness!

THE
SIGNET
ENCYCLOPEDIA
OF WINE

A

ABBEY, ASSUMPTION: See ASSUMPTION ABBEY.

AERATION OF WINE: See AIRING OF WINE.

AIRING OF WINES There's a simple rule here: Air all wine. Almost every bottle of wine—except, obviously, sparkling wines—will improve with a little "breathing time." Even white wines, and especially young reds. The younger and more tannic (or astringent—tannin is what puckers the mouth) the wine, the more the need for airing, for the exposure to air softens and, in effect, matures the wine. Some general norms:

Dry white wines: Air 15 to 30 minutes.

Sweet white wines: Air 30 minutes.

Very old red wines (20 to 40 years): No air.

Old red wines (10 to 20 years old): Air 15 minutes.

Fairly old red wines (5 to 10 years): Air 30 minutes.

Young red wines (to 5 years of age): Air 1 hour.

Young strong red wines: Air 2 to 4 hours.

If you neglected to air your wine ahead of time, and it's simply too hard, too astringent for human consumption—you'll know if your guests have turned blue or their mouths are stuck together in a permanent pucker —then you can accelerate the airing process and so soften the wine simply by pouring it back and forth from one container to another.

ALBERINI LAMBRUSCO: See LAMBRUSCO.

ALIANCA ROSÉ A nice little Portuguese rosé—leaning to the dry side, with some fruitiness, totally trustworthy, fair value, $2.70. How to serve rosé: See under the general heading ROSÉ.

ALMADÉN VINEYARDS (San Francisco, Calif.) Almadén is the largest producer of premium wines in California—and one of the largest in the world. The statistics are rather incomprehensible: 4 million vines, 20,000 cases of wine per day, 24-million-gallon storage capacity. But such statistics are relevant here only if they affect the quality of the wines. Which they do.

Largeness is a mixed blessing when it comes to wine production. Bigness usually makes for consistency and dependability, but it also makes for mediocrity. When you buy your *second* bottle of Almadén Burgundy (or whatever), you can be certain that it will be precisely the same as the first bottle of Almadén Burgundy you bought. It certainly will not be any worse, but unfortunately, neither will it ever be any better. Better batches of wine do come along, but here they simply disappear in the huge, amorphous blending process.

Unless you read something to the contrary below, know that

all Almadén wines are ready to drink when purchased and they should be consumed within two or three years.

It is perhaps true that Almadén has never made a truly *great* wine, but it is equally true that Almadén's prices are never anything but *great*. Not a single Almadén wine has a price tag over $3—other than its sparkling wines—a remarkable feat in today's grossly inflated wine market. Further, Almadén's Le Domaine (see) brand of sparkling wines are among the world's best values in bubbly wines.

Beaujolais: See GAMAY BEAUJOLAIS.

Blanc de Blancs**** Almadén makes lots of bubbly wine, none of it poor, most of it good, some of it excellent. This is numbered among the excellent. Serve this wine well chilled, as an aperitif or toasting wine—it's too delicate to accompany even light foods. Champagne traditionally lives for seventeen years, but to enjoy most of them at their sparkly best, drink them within seven or eight years of their vintage date. Fair value—well, almost fair: $6.50.

Blanc Fumé*** and aspiring to******** A new wine for Almadén, happily inaugurated in 1972, it won a gold medal its first time out. Most wineries call this Sauvignon Blanc, and when well made, as Almadén's is, it is a fresh, sprightly white wine with a touch of earthiness—that's good. Connoisseurs—and you're one with this "infallible" guide in your hot little grasp—will enjoy sipping this wine on its own, before dinner. It's on the dry side. But it will also go beautifully with fowl, veal, ham, even lobster, says Almadén—if

your oil well's still gushy. Ready for drinking when you buy it, and it will keep for three or four years. An excellent value at $3.

Burgundy** Be circumspect here: Almadén makes two Burgundies: this one and a Mountain Red Burgundy, a somewhat cheaper wine. Both are offered in half-gallons and gallons. This one is a quite adequate *vin ordinaire*, a reliable hamburger and hot dog wine. Won't do you much good, won't do you much harm. Fair value, $2 ($3.80 half-gallon).

Burgundy, Mountain Red: See MOUNTAIN RED BURGUNDY.

Cabernet Sauvignon** A decade ago this classic red wine of Almadén's invariably received high commendation from wine experts. Today the reviews are almost 100 percent bad; it has not placed well in a single recent tasting. Some special bottlings (Lot 1081, 109068, plus some vintaged bottles) have been equally disappointing. For a Cabernet, the price ($3) is good, but the wine is less than great.

Chablis*** If you'll look carefully at the label, you'll see that the full name of this wine is California Mountain Chablis. Confusingly enough, Almadén also makes a Mountain White Chablis (see), a somewhat cheaper wine ($1.70 vs. $1.90) which is as good as this wine. Both wines are good values.

Chablis, Mountain White: See MOUNTAIN WHITE CHABLIS.

Champagne, Brut** to ******* This is not a vintaged (dated) wine and it has varied considerably over the years. Some batches have had the critics muttering disconsolately in their beards. The Extra Dry (see below) is a more consistent and better wine. However, if you already possess a bottle or some dear soul gives you some of the Brut, serve it well chilled, as as aperitif or after-dinner "settler." Rather unfair value, $5.25 to $5.60.

Champagne, Extra Dry*** This is a bit sweeter than the Brut (see preceding wine) and a bit better to most American tastes, with its slight touch of sweetness. Serve it well chilled —best on its own—savor it tenderly. Fair value, $5.25 to $5.60.

Champagne, Pink and **Champagne, Rosé**** Both are medium sweet, pleasant enough, but lack any real character. It would take an expert, tasting them blind, to distinguish between them. They are festive, however, and pretty, and will fit in anywhere: before, during, after meals. Serve well chilled. Fair price—well, not really, but it's what you'll have to pay: $5.25 to $5.60.

Chardonnay: See PINOT CHARDONNAY.

Chenin Blanc*** A soft, fruity white wine with a touch of sweetness. Ideal for cool sipping of an evening, around fireplace or pool. It will also fit well with a not too sweet dessert or with fresh fruit. It's a wine to be drunk young and fresh: within two years of purchase. A good value at $2.25 to $2.40.

Chianti** Quite average, Italian-type (far removed!) red wine. But if you can find it in gallons, at $6.40 to $7, you could do worse—that price figures out to something like $1.30 per fifth. Some Chiantis, even in Italy, are not this good and cost more. Serve at cool room temperature.

Claret: See MOUNTAIN RED CLARET.

Cocktail Sherry*** Sherries are one of Almadén's strong suits. They're made in the true Spanish manner with true Spanish grapes, and it shows. This is their driest, and as the name proclaims, it's ideal as a cocktail wine. Almadén says to serve it chilled. A good value at $1.90.

Cream Sherry*** Soft and sweet, for after dinner. A good value at $1.90.

Dry Sémillon Sauterne*** Here's an inexpensive little white wine to keep on hand to serve with any light food, but especially fish and seafood. It's got a good earthy flavor. It will improve slightly in the bottle, though it's perfectly ready to be consumed when you buy it, and it will keep for at least five years after purchase. Serve chilled. A good value at $2.25 to $2.40.

Flor Fino Sherry*** Almadén's newest sherry—introduced in '73—and perhaps their finest. The "Flor" refers to a special yeast that gives the wine its special flavor. "Fino" is the lightest, palest, driest of the grades of sherry. Serve it chilled, or, says Almadén, on the rocks—but some wine lovers (snobs?) may demand your life in forfeiture for such sacrilegious action. Once opened, sherry will keep for days if you refrigerate it and especially if you put it in a smaller container, thus eliminating its air exposure. One critic says this wine could become habit-forming for connoisseurs! An excellent value at $2.

Gamay Beaujolais*** Beaujolais is probably the world's most delightful young red wine.

Gamay is an Americanized version of the same. Almadén's product falls noticeably short of its French counterpart, but it's nonetheless a sound and pleasant young wine. It goes with almost any food: hamburgers, steaks, pasta, fowl, casseroles. Serve it at cool room temperature. Drink it young, within three years of purchase. Fair value, $3.

Gewürztraminer**** This fine white wine is spicy, tasty, and soft. It has a touch of sweetness, making it a wine to savor on its own, chilled, before dinner. It's ready to drink when purchased and will be at its best for at least three years thereafter. A good value at $3.

Golden Sherry**** This is Almadén's medium sherry, which makes it all-purpose: a before-dinner (aperitif) wine, with the soup course, after dinner. It's golden, light, crisp, and clean. Serve it chilled or at cool room temperature. A good value at $1.90.

Grenache Rosé*** This is America's most popular rosé and probably the best-selling premium wine in the U.S. Here, for once, Americans have displayed their wine expertise, for this is one of America's better rosés. It is not overly sweet and has an abundance of flavor and character. Drink it chilled and young, within a year or two of purchase. A good rosé fits anywhere, as an aperitif, with almost any food, even after dinner with not too sweet desserts. A good value at $1.90 to $2. It even comes, at further savings, in half-gallons, $3.80 to $4.10, and gallons, $6.40 to $7.

Grenoir Original*** A new and unusual wine, designed for beginning wine drinkers. The name says it's an original, which it is. "Grenoir" is from the name of the grape: the Grenache Noir. Almadén planned this wine as a bridge between a rosé and a standard full-bodied red. And that's where it is and what it's like: fresh, light, soft, slightly sweet. Veteran wine lovers may not be overly impressed, but lots of others will love this wine. It will fit almost anywhere: on a picnic, with grilled hamburgers, at a buffet luncheon, or you can serve it as a before-dinner drink. Serve it at cool room temperature or slightly chilled. Drink it young, within two or three years of purchase. Fair value, $2.25 to $2.40.

Grey Riesling*** A pleasant, flowery white wine, it will go well with fish or fowl, in fair weather or foul. It may not set anyone to writing poetry, or even reciting it, but be grateful for what it is, at a reasonable $2.25 to $2.40. Serve it chilled, ready for present drinking; don't keep it more than a couple of years.

Johannisberg Riesling*** A tasty dry white wine, with a zingy flavor, ideal with fish and shellfish. Ready to drink when you buy it, at its best when young, within three years of purchase. Serve chilled. Fair value, $3.

Mountain Nectar Vin Rosé*** This is not one of Almadén's Mountain jug wines, though it is relatively inexpensive ($1.90). Most Americans will like this wine, especially wine novices, as it's fresh, light, fragrant, with an edge of sweetness. It's a good sipping wine for a summer's evening. It's not as dry as Almadén's best-selling Grenache Rosé. Serve chilled.

Mountain Red Burgundy** This everyday wine is just a smidgen heavier-bodied than the Mountain Red Claret (see following wine) and a mite better, but that's not exactly extravagant adulation! If nothing better's available, you have a reluctant okay. Fair value, ca. $1.70 ($3.40 half-gallon).

Mountain Red Claret** This wine is lighter than Almadén's Mountain Red Burgundy (see preceding wine) and not as good. It's inexpensive all right, but even at its modest price ($3.20 half-gallon) it's no bargain.

Mountain Rhine* It's sweet, but so's sugared water, and a lot cheaper.

Mountain White Chablis*** The best of Almadén's Mountain wines, serve it chilled with fish, chicken, cold cuts. Dollar for dollar, you may prefer this wine to Almadén's "straight" Chablis. A good value, indeed, at ca. $1.70.

Mountain White Sauterne* Drier and softer than the Mountain White Chablis (see preceding wine). Best—if you must—chilled with light foods and fish. Fair value, ca. $1.70 ($3.40 half-gallon).

Nectar Vin Rosé: See MOUNTAIN NECTAR VIN ROSÉ.

Pinot Blanc*** A dry white wine, with good flavor, ideal to accompany fish, poultry. Serve chilled. It's ready to drink when you purchase it and will be at its freshest and best for two years thereafter. Fair value, ca. $2.90.

Pinot Chardonnay*** Chardonnay is the great classic grape of the great white Burgundies of France. Some California Chardonnays approach those great French wines, but Almadén's product does not realize the full potential of this grape. It is, however, a flavorful and well-balanced wine, on the dry side, best used to accompany fish, shellfish, fowl. This wine is at its best when you buy it, and for about four years thereafter. Serve it chilled. Fair value, $3.

Pinot Chardonnay, 1971*** This was a special bottling, but it wasn't worth the extra effort —it's standard Almadén Chardonnay at a special price— $4.15.

Pinot Chardonnay, Special Selection, 1972—**** Flavorful with a touch of sweetness. Fine drinking, now and through 1977 at least.

Pinot Noir*** This is Almadén's third Burgundy-type wine (others, "plain" Burgundy and Mountain Burgundy) and by far the best—and most expensive, ca. $3. Serve it at cool room temperature, with your steaks, hamburgers, roast turkey, barbecued chicken.

Rhine Wine, Mountain: See MOUNTAIN RHINE.

Ruby Cabernet*** A brand-new wine for Almadén, and well begun—good flavor, well balanced. Air it at least a half hour, a good value at less than $2.

Sauterne: See DRY SÉMILLON SAUTERNE and MOUNTAIN WHITE SAUTERNE.

Sauvignon Blanc** A dry white wine without much depth or flavor. If you're looking for a wine to accompany your broiled fish, shrimp dish, holiday ham, prefer Almadén's Pinot Blanc, Johannisberg Riesling or Grey Riesling. Fair value, $2.90.

Sémillon: See DRY SÉMILLON SAUTERNE.

Sherry: See COCKTAIL SHERRY —CREAM SHERRY—FLOR FINO SHERRY—GOLDEN SHERRY.

Solera Sherry: See COCKTAIL SHERRY; CREAM SHERRY; GOLDEN SHERRY.

Sparkling Burgundy** Has showed poorly in tastings. Like most sparkling wines, it fits in almost anywhere. Serve it well chilled. Fair value, $5.40.

Sylvaner* Somebody said it tastes like cleaning fluid—that's rather unkind, but it *is* exceedingly average. Fair value, $2.35.

Vin Rosé: See MOUNTAIN NECTAR VIN ROSÉ.

Zinfandel** "Z" is California's own special invention—it's made nowhere else in the world; Almadén's version is about average. It's a bit thin but will still enhance your hamburgers, steaks, barbecued spare ribs. Serve at cool room temperature—or cool patio temperature. Fair value, $2.40.

ALOXE-CORTON A unique French Burgundy wine in that it comes in both red and white versions, equally renowned, though the red is more commonly available. It is an excellent, though never great wine, well balanced and soft, yet full and powerful, with marvelous perfume. It is a fast-maturing wine, and is generally at its best when it is between three and six years old. Aloxe-Corton will usually merit ****, and occasionally even *****. Some reliable shippers: Bichot, Louis Latour, Michel Voarick, Joseph Drouhin, Doudet-Naudin, Sichel, Tollot-Beaut. These wines will range in price from $7 to $9. Air Aloxe-Corton an hour and serve it at cool room temperature.

ALSACE WILLM: See WILLM RIESLING.

ALSACE—WINES This little nation, half French, half German, makes a lot of good wine, mostly white, all of it selling at reasonable prices. As French wine prices have zoomed heavenward, Alsatian wines have gained steadily in popularity in the U.S. Notice that these are virtually the only European wines that go by the name of the grape, as so many fine American wines do, not by some geographic or invented name. The principal wines (to be found in this book under their own names) are Gewürztraminer and Riesling. Some recent Alsace vintages:

1966—Very good—Lesser wines are now over the hill.

1967—Excellent—Best wines now at their peak.

1968—Poor—Eschew!

1969—Very good—Drink soon; cheaper wines are past their peak.

1970—Very good—Drink soon, especially the cheaper wines.

1971—Exceptional—Lesser wines now at their peak, the big ones will be at their best, 1976–1980.

AMARONE: See RECIOTO DELLA VALPOLICELLA.

AMERICA—WINES: See UNITED STATES—WINES.

AMONTILLADO: A particular type of sherry. For general information, see under SHERRY. For evaluation of a particular bottle, see under the name of the producer of the wine.

(LES) AMOUREUSES: See CHAMBOLLE-MUSIGNY, LES AMOUREUSES.

ANDRÉ CHAMPAGNE* It may sound vaguely like a French Champagne but that's where the similarity ends. André Champagne is as American as E. & J. Gallo of Modesto California, because they're the ones who make it. André is Gallo's second line of sparkling wines, selling for around $2. Their "top of the line" is labeled simply Gallo, and sells for around $3. The Gallo brand is at least a dollar's worth better than the André.

Unquestionably, it is a remarkable feat to produce *any* sparkling wine for a mere $2, especially considering the U.S. taxes on these bubblers. As Sam Johnson (or whoever it was) said of the dancing dog and the lady-preacher (before the days of female priests and girl altar boys), the remarkable thing wasn't that they did these things well, but that they did them at all. When a winery makes a sparkling wine for $2, you, the consumer, had better know full well that you're dealing, by definition, with a wine base reduced to its lowest common denominator. It's just barely wine.

André is very popular—Gallo makes more than a million cases of bubbly wine a year—but its secret of success can only be its lowly price and familiar label. These wines—there are four under this label: Champagne (Extra Dry), Pink Champagne, Sparkling Burgundy, Cold Duck —are unbelievably nondescript —they possess no individuality, no substance, indeed, no flavor. Beneath the bubbles there is only the faintest whisp of wine. They sparkle and that's all. But they're easy drinking, and if you're not interested in flavor, André wines look and even sound festive—be careful, the plastic corks can be explosive.

ANGELICA Without question this is one of the world's worst wines—99 percent of the time. Standard Angelica, a purely American invention, said to be named after the City of Los Angeles (which is an honor akin to having a disease or a plague named after you), is one of the staples of Skid Row. Almost all Angelica is a sickly-sweet blend of partially fermented grape juice laced with cheap brandy. There is only one word for it: ghastly. But only 99 percent is bad. That remaining 1 percent consists mainly of Heitz's Angelica****, a luscious after-dinner wine. Novitiate (see) also makes a palatable Angelica.

ANHEUSER & FEHRS JOHANNISBERGER: See JOHANNISBERGER.

ANJOU ROSÉ: See under name of shipper or brand name: CRUSE, NECTAROSÉ, ROSÉ DES ANGES etc.

ANNIE GREEN SPRINGS Even if the wines aren't much— they're not!—the names are sheer genius: Country Cherry, Berry Frost, Peach Creek, Plum Hollow. Who wouldn't try at least one at least once? The kids, it seems, try them a bunch more than once, for these are among the most popular of America's "Pop" wines. Perhaps these are not wines at all in the proper sense: the simple fruit of the grape, but they've accounted in large part for the tremendous "wine boom" in America since the late 60s, and they're serving to bridge the gap, for the Pepsi generation, from Coke and Hi-C to good wine. These are simple, sweet, pleasant, fruit-flavored wines, fruit nectar with alcohol— bottled wine punch, really, but as Aristotle (or was it Charlie Brown?) said: "Wine punch is wine punch." These wines, incidentally, are made by Italian Swiss Colony of Asti, California, though the name is nowhere on the label. They all sell for around $1.09 per fifth—antifreeze costs more than that and doesn't taste nearly as good.

ANTICHI PODERI DEI MARCHESI DI BAROLO: See MARCHESI DI BAROLO.

ANTINORI, MARCHESI: See under the name of the particular wine, e.g., VALPOLICELLA.

ANTINORI, MARCHESI CHIANTI: See VILLA ANTINORI.

AQUERIA, CHÂTEAU D'*** This is the name of one of the best known and best of Tavel's (France) rosés. It's a typical Tavel rosé: dry, almost austere, yet delicate and fresh. It's a dubious value—or more exactly, a poor value—however, at ca. $5.20. You can do better with American rosé (see the "Comparative Standings" under ROSÉ), or if you insist on a Tavel, try Chapoutier's. How to serve it: See under ROSÉ.

ASSUMPTION ABBEY This is the brand name for some of the best wines of Brookside Winery of Southern California. The name comes from the winery's long-time association with the Benedictine monks of North Dakota—the label even bears a papal coat of arms. But Protestants are allowed to drink the wines. These are inexpensive wines, by no means great or complex, but many of them are unusually good buys. The best are listed.

Dido Noir*** "Dido" comes from Escondido, California, where the grapes are grown, and "noir" is French for "black." So there you have it: a black dido. Well, anyhow this is the best red wine Assumption Abbey produces; it's

a flavorful, full-bodied red table wine that will go well with any red meat (grilled, roasted, whatever) or with stews, pasta, casseroles. Serve at cool room temperature. A good value at $2.50.

Emerald Riesling*** This is a light and pleasant white wine from new vines in the Temecula area north of San Diego, a very promising grape-growing region. The winery suggests you take a bottle with you on a picnic or enjoy it at a Sunday brunch. A good value at $2.50. It won gold medals at the Los Angeles County Fair in both 1973 and 1974.

Haute Sauterne** It took a silver medal at the 1974 Los Angeles County Fair. Fair value, $2.15.

Johannisberg Riesling*** White table wine of substance, dry, with good depth. Many good Johannisberg Rieslings are made in California, but since the grape is light-bearing, the wine is almost always expensive. This is doubtlessly the most inexpensive Johannisberger you're going to find across the breadth of this land, or any other land. An excellent value at $2.80 to $3.

Petite Sirah*** The Petite Sirah grape produces a hearty red wine in California, largely overlooked by the citizenry. More's the pity. The Assumption Abbey version is representative of the breed. It's dry, tasty, and full-bodied. It's the perfect complement to steaks, hamburgers, pasta, roasts. Serve at cool room temperature. Fair value, $3.

Pinot Chardonnay* Very forgettable. Fair value—well, the winery thinks it's fair: $3.25.

Sherry de Oro*** This medium sherry has to be one of

the best sherry-values in America—or anywhere. It's fittin' before dinner, during (with the soup), or after dinner. An excellent value at $2.30.

Sherry Palido** "Palido" means "pale" in Spanish, and this dry sherry is that all right, but not much more. Fair value, $2.30.

Vertdoux Blanc*** The name, pronounced "Veerdough," is the French name for the grape from which the wine is made, the Golden Chasselas. It's a Sauterne-type wine, quite nice. Serve it, chilled, with light foods. Fair value, $2.50.

ASTI SPUMANTE Just about every country on earth has its own sparkling wine, and in Italy just about every district and town has its own. Italy's most famous Spumante (sparkling wine) is the one that comes from the town of Asti, in northern Italy. It's soft, aromatic, decidedly sweet; women usually like it, but many Americans and all connoisseurs will find it overly sweet. It has the unmistakable scent and flavor of the Muscat grape and it is best served as a dessert wine. Serve it well chilled, 40°F. Because of the high federal tax on sparkling wines, Asti Spumante has to be considered a dubious value at $5.50 to $7. Avoid cheap Asti Spumante, anything under $4; all the expense has gone into the tax and the freight. The following are reliable shippers: Bersano; Cella; Cinzano (the '71 took a British gold medal); Gancia; Martini & Rossi (one of the most expensive: $6.85); Mirafiore; Opera Pia; Perlino; Ponti; Riccadonna; Vallarino.

AUSLESE This is a good word to find on a German wine label—especially if you're not paying for the wine. It means the wine is from a "special picking" (that's what Auslese means) of grapes that had been attacked—blest—by the "noble rot," a fungus that sometimes occurs and which gives the grapes additional flavor and richness. Auslese on a label will boost a wine's price by two or three times that of the "plain" version of that particular wine. Auslesen (the German plural) are dessert wines to be sipped tenderly, with fruit cake or Riz à L'Impératrice, or perhaps even better, on their own, in the company, not of food, but of other wine-happy souls.

AUSONE, CHÂTEAU One of the very greatest of all red Bordeaux (France) wines, though it has been under something of a cloud over the past several decades. Ausone is a full and hearty wine, one which beginners can readily appreciate. The vineyard is small, less than eighteen acres, and the wines, like all first growths, are extremely expensive. Ausone will be best appreciated on its own, with bits of bread and cheese, or at the dinner table with lamb simply cooked, roast turkey (a holiday bonanza!), or roast beef. Serve at cool room temperature.

1880—A famous wine, it *was* a Classic.

1900—A legendary wine, it sold some years ago for $180 for 24 ounces.

1906—Originally Near-Classic, but long gone.

1913*****—Still holding on, but not worth the $50 it was bringing in 1973.

1938—Remarkable wine in an off-year: *****

1947—Near-Classic, but may be fading.

1950—Fine wine, *****, and still good—You may just find a bottle lying around somewhere for $10.

1951—R.I.P.

1953—Passing fair, best drink it soon.

1956—Remarkably fine for a poor vintage: ****

1959—A fine wine from a great vintage: *****—It's been grossl, overpriced, however, at $50 to $70.

1961—Near-Classic—Try it, starting in 1980—Fair or not, it's been selling for $50 and more.

1962—*****—Best drinking, 1975–1985, fair value, $25.

1964—Not great despite a $40 price tag: ****

1966—*****—It's been selling for around $40, but $25 would be more like a fair price.

1967—****, or ***** at most—Not very enthusiastically recommended at $25.

1970—Great wine: Near-Classic—Fair or not, it's selling for $40 and better.

1971—Early reports say it's going to be marvelous.

AYALA One of France's great Champagne houses. See under CHAMPAGNE.

AYL(ER) KUPP Ayl is the name of a village of Germany's Saar Valley; Kupp is the name of the vineyard—a great wine, said to be a connnoisseur's wine. Like all Saar wines it needs lots of sunshine and can be magnificent in hot years, but hard in poor ones. For a general estimate of some recent vintages, see SCHARZHOFBERGER, a neighboring vineyard. How to drink this wine: See under MOSELLE.

B

BALI HAI: See ITALIAN SWISS COLONY.

BANDA AZUL: See (FEDERICO) PATERNINA.

BARBARESCO A fine red Italian wine, first cousin to the great Barolo, and considerably cheaper. It's a lighter wine than Barolo, does not live as long, and is faster-maturing. Because of Barolo's fame, Barbaresco is often a better value, and at times, even a better wine. It's a kind of Burgundy-type wine, rich and fragrant, velvety dry. It is especially suited to accompany roast beef, goes well with lamb, and, like any good red wine, shows to its very best when it accompanies cheeses. Barbaresco ages well and is at its best when it is between four and fifteen years old. Some vintages:

1961 Prunotto: Not recommended.

1962 Pio Cesare: Not recommended.

1964 Marchesi di Barolo: *****

    Beccaro: Not recommended.

    Prunotto: Not recommended.

1965 Prunotto: ***

    Bersano: ***

    Contratto: *****

1966 Prunotto: ***

    Minuto: ***

    Marchesi di Barolo: ***

1967 Carnevale: ****

    Galarey: ***

1968 Cantina del Parroco de Neive: ***

1969 Casa del Vino di Alba: ****—Very tannic, lay it away until 1977.

BARBERA A rich and bold red wine produced primarily in Italy and California. You can drink it young or old. It's sometimes a little rough when it's young—"tannic" is the correct word (tannin is what puckers the mouth). It goes well with grilled meats (hamburgers, steaks, chicken), stews, casseroles, pasta, game, even spicy dishes. Serve it at cool room temperature (65 to 72°F), having aired it about one hour.

Italian Barbera, as imported into the U.S., is a dependable middle-class wine, big and rather heavy. "Good, not fine," says one authority. It's quite dry, the classic accompaniment of roasts. Most of the time the label will say simply Barbera (the accent is on the second syllable: Bar-*bear*-ah), sometimes Barbera d' Asti, Barbera di Monferrato, or Barbera di Alba. It's relatively inexpensive, ranging from $3 to $5, and is usually a good value. The very best Barberas will say on the label either Barbera Riserva or Barbera Extra.

Reliable Italian firms importing into the U.S. include: Bersano; Borgogno; Marchesi di Barolo; and Beccaro.

Recent vintages for Italian Barbera:

11

1968: Good—drink during 1975.

1969: Very good—drink during 1975.

1970: Good—at their best in 1975.

1971: Very good—at their best, 1975 through 1977.

California Barbera is often a better wine and a better value than its Italian namesake. Here are the best, listed in descending order of excellence. When two wines have identical ratings, the least expensive is listed first.

California Barberas—
Comparative Standings
****
Very Good
  Sebastiani Barbera ($3.05)
  Martini Barbera, 1968 ($4)
  Buena Vista Barbera ($5)
  Sebastiani Barbera, 1967 (Bin 15) ($5)
  Martini Barbera, 1966 ($6)
  Martini Barbera, 1956 and 1962 and 1964 ($7 to $10)
***
Good
  Gallo Barbera ($1.85)
  La Mont Barbera ($2)
  Martini Barbera, 1969 ($3)
  Bynum Barbera ($3.25)
  Sutter Home Barbera ($3.50)
  Bargetto Barbera ($3.75)
  Heitz Barbera ($4)
  Martini Barbera, 1967 ($5)
  Martini Barbera, 1961 Private Reserve ($7)
**
Fair
  Martini Barbera, 1965
BARBIER, RENÉ: See RENÉ BARBIER.
BARDOLINO Delicious and delightful red Italian table wine, never great, never bad (at least not as imported to the U.S.). It's just faintly sweet, and at times, just a trifle *frizzante.* Drink it young: one to three years old. It can serve

beautifully at the barbecue grill, and, the Italians say, with fish and fowl. Vintages are not important except to tell you how old your wine is. Shippers' names *are* important—here are some of the most reliable: Bertani; Bolla; Bosca; Cantina Sociale di Soave; Fabiano; Gancia; Lamberti; Masi; Pasqua; Ricasoli; Ruffino; Santa Sofia; Sanzeno.

BARGETTO WINERY (Soquel, Calif.) This winery is the most oceanward of any California winery—it's just out of Santa Cruz, on the Pacific Coast. It's family-owned and -operated. A curiosity is Bargetto's Chaucer Mead, the classic drink of the gods, made from wild honey. It's not really *wine,* however, for it's not the fruit of the grape—but do try it if you ever chance by one of Bargetto's tasting rooms; one's on Monterey's famed Cannery Row (cf. John Steinbeck).

Barbera*** This Italian-type wine is the kind of thing that Bargetto, one of those little ol' Italian winemakers, does best. It's a full-bodied, full-flavored red, ready to drink when purchased, but it ages well. You can keep it ten years beyond its vintage date, and it will be better on its tenth birthday than it was on its first. Air at least one hour, serve at cool room temperature. Let it accompany any red meat, pasta, stew, Italian-style dishes. Fair value, $3.50 to $3.75.

Burgundy** Won't do you any good, won't do you any harm. Fair value, $2.50.

Chablis** Ho, hum . . .

Chenin Blanc*** Slightly on the sweet side, cool, refreshing. Good, chilled, of a summer's evening. It took a gold medal at the Los Angeles County Fair, 1973. Fair value, $3.

Chianti*** The winery bestows extra care on its Italian-style wines, and the Bargettos are particularly fond of their Chianti which they say compares with the real Chianti Classico of Italy. And that's not wholly hyperbolic propaganda. It's certainly superior to most California jug Chiantis, and a good value at ca. $2.50. Perfect with hamburgers, steaks, pasta, Italian dishes. Air at least one hour, serve at cool room temperature (65°F).

Claret** One critic says it has a "flat cooked nose." That wouldn't be a compliment for a person—much less a wine. But that refers to the bouquet —the taste is not all that bad.

Grenache Rosé: See ROSÉ.

Haut Sauterne*** It took a silver medal at the 1973 Los Angeles County Fair and a gold medal at the 1974 Fair.

Moscato Amabile*** It's won a lot of medals and if you like sweet wines you'll like this wine; and if you also like the Muscat flavor, you'll *love* this wine. It's strictly for after-dinner consumption, well chilled. Once opened, you can keep it for several weeks if you put it in a smaller bottle, thus eliminating air space. Fair value, $3.

Pinot Chardonnay*** The Chardonnay is the noble grape of the great white Burgundies of France. Beginning wine drinkers don't usually take immediately to this wine because of its dryness and austerity. It's the perfect table wine to accompany light food, especially fish and seafood. Serve it chilled. Fair value, $5.

Rosé** Bargetto makes three

rosés: Grenache Rosé, Zinfandel Rosé, and Vin Rosé Dolce: none of them as yet demanding huge plaudits. Nor are they especially inexpensive for rosés: $2.50 to $2.90; most American rosés hover around $2.25. Rosés are well known as "universal" wines, may be served anywhere, anytime. Which is largely true, but these wines would be most enjoyed chilled, sipped companionably, of a summer's eve. Almost all rosé should be consumed young: within a year or two of purchase.

Ruby Cabernet* This wine will do just as much for you as their Burgundy (see above).

Vin Rosé Dolce: See ROSÉ.

Zinfandel*** Bargetto makes a lot of this wine, which is good, because it's good. And a good value: $2.75.

Zinfandel Rosé: See ROSÉ.

BAROLO Just about everybody agrees that this is Italy's greatest wine. It's a big, full-bodied red, the king of Italian table wines; it improves considerably with age, and is at its best when it is between eight and fifteen years old. (It's already been aged a minimum of three years when you buy it.) Barolo is noted for its huge bouquet, said to be violet-scented. Few wines need airing more than this one—figure on a minimum of three hours, and twelve would be more like it. Just once try day-long airing: it's a different wine. Barolo is totally dry, an ideal table wine: marvelous with red meats (especially roasts), game, robust fare of any kind, cheeses. Check it for sediment, decanting if necessary. Look for these names on the label; most of them will be regularly **** or better: Abbazzia Dell'

Annunziata (Renato Ratti);
Beccaro; Bersano: Conti Della
Creosina; Borgogno; Giorgio
Carnevale; Cella; Conterno;
Guiseppe Contratto; Cossetti;
Fontanafredda; Fracassi; Gala-
rey; Graziola; Guido Giri;
Marchese Villa Doria; Opera
Pia; Alfredo Prunotto.

BARON: The word means
what it says: a Baron—and if
it's the first word of your wine
label, go to the next important
word, such as "Pichon."

BAROQUE: See under (PAUL)
MASSON.

BARSAC See SAUTERNES. The
two wines are virtually identical and everything said there
applies, *ipsissimis verbis,* to any
wine labeled Barsac. The two
best vineyards, and they are
very good, are Château
Climens and Château Coutet.

BÂTARD - MONTRACHET
The name means precisely what
you suspected: the Bastard—
but it's a royal bastard! This is
one of the world's greatest dry
white wines—many say second
only to Le Montrachet (see),
the queen of white wines. In
fact, some experts believe that
since World War II, Bâtard has
even surpassed Montrachet.
Like all the great Montrachets,
Bâtard is in extremely short
supply and very expensive, $20
to $35 per 24 ounces, and it's
clear that at such outlandish
prices it sometimes constitutes
a very poor value. It's at its
best when it's five to ten years
old. Some notable bottles:

1966 Ramonet-Prudhon:
*****—Now at its best.

1967 Leflaive: Near-Classic

1970 Ramonet-Prudhon:
*****

1971 Ramonet-Prudhon:
*****

1971 Henri Clerc: Near-Classic

BEAR MOUNTAIN: See LA-
MONT, M.

BEAUJOLAIS Here's one of
the most beloved names in all
of winedom! There are wines
similar to Beaujolais, and California even makes a Gamay
Beaujolais (see), a nice little
wine, but there is only one
Beaujolais and it comes from
France. A small amount of
Beaujolais is actually white,
Beaujolais Blanc (see), but in
these pages the name standing
alone means red Beaujolais.

Beaujolais is simply the best
fresh young red wine in the
world. If you want to know
what wine people mean by
"fruitiness" in a red wine, get
yourself a good bottle of Beaujolais and you'll know. It's not
depth of flavor one looks for
here, but freshness and fruitiness

It is said that Beaujolais is not
for sipping but for quaffing,
and it does consume right easily, but Scripture says: "Woe to
you who drink wine by the
bowlful . . ." (Amos 6:6). No
wine is for gulping or quaffing
—all wine worthy of the name
is for sipping, and if it's not
worthy of the name, then it's
for discarding—down the
hatch, no, not yours, the sink's.
There are hundreds of brands
of Beaujolais to be found in
American wine shops—at least
two hundred. Amid the bewildering array, and the gaudy display, there is only one safe
course: look to neither right
nor left, be blind to the luring
crates and racks and bins, see
not the distracting signs and
sales and specials. Hold a
steady course, however sore be-
set, and buy your Beaujolais
only from these major, reliable
shippers: Paul Bocuse; Bouchard Père et Fils; Caves de

Charnay Bellevue (G.S. Sumner Selections); Chanson, St. Vincent; Cruse; Joseph Drouhin; Dufour; Dulong; Louis Jadot; Jaffelin; J. Lapalus; Louis Latour; Alexis Lichine; Marquisat; Proper Maufoux; Pierre Olivier (G. S. Sumner Selections); Patriarche; Piat; St. André; Frank Schoonmaker; J.Thorin; Frederick Wildman. Avoid cheap Beaujolais—it may be phony and even if it isn't, it will probably be bad. Again, stick to the list.

Half of the Beaujolais you see on retail shelves will say "Beaujolais Supérieur" or "Beaujolais-Villages" on the label. To all intents and purposes these are exactly the same as "plain" Beaujolais.

Increasingly you will be finding bottles calling themselves "Beaujolais Primeur" or "Beaujolais Nouveau." These are what the names say: First or New Beaujolais, brand-new wine, only months old. Paris waits each year for the Nouveau to arrive—in barrels, so new it's not even bottled—in mid-November, when it's only weeks, not months, old. Now shippers are beginning to bottle and air-freight this Beaujolais Nouveau to the U.S. in time for Christmas. Perhaps such wine should be tried once —it's extremely light, sappy, grapey. It's barely wine! And like most infants, it doesn't travel well. So restrain yourself, save your money, fly to Paris, and try your Beaujolais Nouveau in a Lyon or Paris bistro.

Beaujolais has only one fault: it's become rather expensive. Not really, but relatively—relative to its once humble bourgeois price range. Beaujolais, once the poor man's red table

wine, can rise today to $8 and $10, and even "standard" Beaujolais from a major shipper sells between $3.50 and $5. Beaujolais vintages are unimportant in one sense, all-important in another: they're unimportant as regards the quality of the wine in the bottle—but the vintage-date is all-important in that it tells you how old your wine is. And that you want to know, because Beaujolais must be drunk young. Old Beaujolais is bad Beaujolais. Never buy a bottle of ordinary Beaujolais that is more than three years old. If you own some, drink it before it's four years of age.

Beaujolais is one of those versatile wines that goes well with most foods, but it's particularly adaptable to light meats (pork, veal, poultry) and smoked ham; it will also be appreciated at the barbecue grill. Cheese and wine, of course, is the world's greatest food-beverage combination, and Beaujolais goes especially well with these cheeses: Cantal, Gouda, Hervé, Port-Salut, Tilsiter, Edam, Brie, Cheddar.

Beaujolais is one of the few red wines that should be served *cool*—not icy, but slightly chilled, ca. 55°F. Beaujolais does not need to be aired.

The best Beaujolais of all often does not have the name Beaujolais on the label. It comes from eight villages in the northern part of the Beaujolais area and is allowed to go simply by the name of the village. It will cost you a dollar or so more than "plain" Beaujolais. Different rules regarding age and quality apply to these wines, and you will find all of them in their proper place in this book. In roughly descending order of quality (and usually, price) these are the names to look for: Moulin-à-Vent; Juliénas; Fleurie; Brouilly and Côte de Brouilly; Saint-Amour; Morgon; Chénas; Chiroubles.

BEAUJOLAIS BLANC Not a great deal of this white Beaujolais is made, and maybe that's a mistake, for it's a good little wine and a good value. It can take the place of a Pouilly-Fuissé or Chablis almost any day of the week, and it goes particularly well with fish, shellfish, and smoked ham. Drink Beaujolais Blanc while it's young: between two and four years old. Some reliable brands and shippers: Bouchard; Louis Jadot; Chanson (St. Vincent); Marquisat (see). Drink Beaujolais Blanc chilled, 45 to 50°F. It is rarely less than***.

BEAUJOLAIS BROUILLY: See BROUILLY.

BEAUJOLAIS NOUVEAU: See BEAUJOLAIS.

BEAUJOLAIS PRIMEUR: See BEAUJOLAIS.

BEAUJOLAIS SUPÉRIEUR: See BEAUJOLAIS.

BEAUJOLAIS - VILLAGES: See BEAUJOLAIS.

BEAULIEU VINEYARDS (Rutherford, Calif.) Beaulieu's familiar BV insignia is one you can trust. Under it you won't be buying any poor wine, and you can buy some very good wine. In some of their Cabernet Sauvignons you will be buying great wine: their Georges de Latour Private Reserve is world-renowned. Beaulieu was recently purchased by the giant conglomerate of Heublein, Inc., but no dire things have happened thus far to the qualit*y* of BV wines. Several wines have fallen upon poor vintages recently, but some have improved. The winery's very capable winemakers are still allowed a free hand, and the wines generally show it.

Beauclair, Johannisberg Riesling "Beauclair" is a name invented by Beaulieu. Johannisberg Riesling is the grape responsible for the best of those marvelous German Rhine wines. Beaulieu does a good job with it also, though a few recent vintages were disappointing. This rather dry white wine goes well with seafood, fish, fowl, pork, veal.

1969***—Not up to BV standards; drink immediately.

1970**—Drink soon—at the latest. A poor value at ca. $4.60.

1971****—Marvelous, deep, lingering flavors. Too good to allow it to accompany food, even light food; deserves to be enjoyed on its own. Best drinking through 1975.

1972—*****—In the style of a true German Rhine wine—which is to say: light and flowery. Great for sipping, chilled. There is also a '72 Spätlese (from late-picked grapes) at $5 ******.

1973—Looks like another beauty, but it's_ too early for final word. Watch and pray!

Beaufort, Pinot Chardonnay "Beaufort": another of those brand names invented by Beaulieu. Pinot Chardonnay is the noble grape of the great white French Burgundies. Beaulieu generally does right by it, and is justifiably proud of its Beaufort. They say it has the taste of sage. It's certainly one of California's best Chardonnays, an ideal wine to accompany fish, shellfish, poultry.

1968**** — Drink immediately.

1969**—This wine has fared very poorly in a number of

blind tastings; it is below Beaulieu's standards. Not recommended at $4.50 and more.

1970****—Just now reaching maturity and will be at its best through '77. Fair value, $5.

1971***—Very dry. Will be at its best, 1975 through 1978. Fair value, $4.50 to $4.75.

1972***—Best drinking, 1975 through 1977.

1973—It promises well.

Beaumont, Pinot Noir "Beaumont" is one of Beaulieu's invented trade names. Pinot Noir is the name of the illustrious grape of Burgundy (France) which produces some of the greatest red wines in the world. Generally speaking, the Pinot Noir doesn't do quite *that* well in California, but Beaulieu demonstrates *how* well it can do. Serve it at cool room temperature with your finest roast or best steaks.

1945, 1946, 1947*****—These wines, if you can find them, will cost you dearly—at least $50, and the '46 around $75, but they're majestic. Better not keep these much longer.

1962****—Drink now and through 1976.

1964***—Drink now and through 1976.

1965**—Drink now and through 1976.

1966***—Good drinking now and through the rest of the 70s. Fair value, $6.

1967**—Present drinking and through 1978.

1968*****—Already quite drinkable and will improve through the 70s. Fair value, $6.

1969****—Quite ready for present consumption but will be a lot better from 1976 through 1982. With a few more years of bottle age this wine could possibly merit *******.

Good wine to lay down. Fair value, $5.

1970***—Drink, 1975–1980. One must question, however, whether this wine is worth its present asking price of $7 and more.

1971 and *1972*****—Already good drinking, but will be even better, 1976 through 1980.

Beaurosé*** A relatively dry rosé, well made and well priced ($2.25 to $2.50). It'll go well with your grilled hamburgers in the backyard or roasted hot dogs on a picnic. Or for entertaining. You can trust all the recent vintages ('70 through '73) and the '71 might even merit ****. Ready to drink when purchased, consume within five years of the vintage date. Serve chilled.

Brut Champagne Beaulieu makes four Champagnes, all high-quality products, all made by the classic "Champagne method" (by hand), all vintage-dated. Their Brut (the word means "dry") is not their driest; Private Reserve is that. But this is clearly one of California's finest Brut Champagnes, and most people will prefer it to the Private Reserve, as it has the slightest touch of sweetness.

Beaulieu's sparkling wines—they call them all Champagne, but the French can get bellicose at the term—are elegant, fine wines, best reserved for festive and holiday consumption, preferably as aperitif wines, because their delicacy and finesse would be sinfully lost if they are consumed with anything but the blandest of foods. Fair value, $6.25.

1962 and *1964*****—Mostly for the record book now—although these wines are still in good condition, if you can find 'em. It's said that Champagnes live seventeen years . . . which gives these two a few to go.

1966****—A special Growers Lot this year probably deserves *******.

1967***
1969****

Burgundy*** In California, Burgundy can mean almost any red alcoholic beverage, from the veriest swill to a heavenly potion. BV's product is somewhere in between, clearly meriting *** and sometimes even ****. At $2.50 or $2.75, certainly a fine value. It's ready to drink when you bring it home and will keep for a good five years after its vintage date. Serve at cool room temperature.

1968 Special Bottling****— An unusual wine—it's rare that a batch of "generic wine" (the grapes from which it was made are not specified) is set aside for "special handling." In this case it was worth the effort, and the wine has become something of a collector's item. It will be at its peak 1975 through 1980. It bears a special descriptive label. Fair value, $5 to $6.25.

1969***, 1970**** — Best drinking, 1975 through 1979. Very good values at $2.50 to $2.75.

1971****—Will be at its best, 1975 through 1979. Excellent value at $2.50 to $2.75.

Cabernet Sauvignon This noble red wine—California's answer to France's famous Clarets—was in great measure the making of the Beaulieu vineyards. The wine achieved early fame—deservedly—and it has never since lost it. It's produced each year in two "editions": a Regular Bottling and a special bottling, named after the winery's founder, Georges de Latour Private Reserve. The regular is released when it is about two years old; the Private Reserve comes from special grapes grown on choice plots of land, and gets extra aging—and love. Beaulieu's Georges de Latour Private Reserve is probably America's most illustrious single wine. It is frequently a collector's item, and for this reason it often fetches exorbitant prices and is not a good value. Good drinking, yes—good value, no. It is always in demand and difficult to find. If you do come upon it, and your blood doesn't run cold at the sight of the price tag, you might want to try a wee bottle. But if it's too expensive for you to drink in good conscience, you can simply store your wine and show it off to impressionable friends. Just caress it periodically.

All the following wines should be aired at least one hour. The older vintages (40s, 50s, 60s) should be checked for sediment; if present, stand the bottle upright for twenty-four hours, then decant.

1940s Georges de Latour Private Reserve—Some famous vintages here, especially the '41 (Near-Classic) and the '47 (*****) and you'll pay dearly for them—if you can find them. The '41 a few years ago sold for $50 in a Berkeley, California, restaurant. It's probably $100 now. If you own any of these, don't just stand there —start pulling some corks— these wines are just now at the top of their bent.

1951 Georges de Latour Private Reserve—Near-Classic— Now at its peak and will hold there well into the next decade. Fair (?) value, $50 . . . well, it may not be fair, but it's what you can expect to pay.

1955 Georges de Latour Private Reserve****—Best drinking, now through 1980.

1958, 1960 Georges de Latour Private Reserve*****—These are just now reaching their best and they'll hold until 1990. Fair (?) value, $36.

1960, 1961 Regular Bottling***—Unfortunately now bringing ca. $30.

1961 Georges de Latour Private Reserve*****—Now at its best, will hold at least through 1985. Last time it was seen around, it was bringing ca. $40, brrrrr . . .

1962 Georges de Latour Private Reserve*****—Drink anytime before 1980. If not too rich for your blood, a good value at $30.

1963 Georges de Latour Private Reserve****—Drink before 1976.

1964 Georges de Latour Private Reserve*****—Best drinking, 1975 through 1980. Fair value, $18.

1965 Regular Bottling****—Now at its best and will remain so until 1981. Fair value, $9.50.

1965 Georges de Latour Private Reserve****—Just reaching its peak and will remain in top form for another decade. Fair value, $15.

1966 Regular Bottling****—Just reaching its peak and will remain there at least until 1984. If sediment is present, stand the bottle upright for twenty-four hours, then decant. Fair value, $8.

1966 Georges de Latour Private Reserve*****—Best drinking, 1975 through 1984. Fair value, $14.

1967 Regular Bottling****

—Goodly drinking now and through 1979.

1967 Georges de Latour Private Reserve****—It's almost ready—drink 1976 through 1985. Some would rate this wine only ***. It's selling for about $11.

1968 Regular Bottling****—Ah, this ol' "plain" Cabernet Sauvignon is better than some of the Private Reserves. If you find it, don't hesitate; buy it! Fair value, ca. $9.

1968 Georges de Latour Private Reserve*****—Outstanding wine but may already be overpriced; a *fair* value would be around $15. Some say it's the greatest BV has ever produced. Already good drinking and will improve at least to 1980 and will keep until 1990.

1969 Regular Bottling*****—"Spectacular," says one critic. An exceptional value at $5, even $10. Look for it, lay it away in a cool dark nook at least until 1979, and drink it anytime before 1985.

1969 Georges de Latour Private Reserve****—According to some experts, this is not as good as the Regular bottling of this year. Others rate it *****. Best drinking, 1975–1982. Fair value, $7.

1970 Regular Bottling*****—Already smooth and tasty but will develop further, through the decade. It'll keep even longer. One critic says this was the greatest wine bargain in the world in 1973. A very good value, $7 to $8.

1970 Georges de Latour Private Reserve—Near-Classic—It may seem presumptuous to rate such a young wine so highly, but this one has all the earmarks of greatness. It will be both big and great, a wine to lay down for that special anniversary in 1985 or 1990. A panel of fifteen experts recently rated this wine highest among 101 foreign and domestic wines, ahead of a great Mouton-Rothschild of the same vintage, selling for around $40. An exceptional value at $8 to $9.

1971 Regular Bottling***— Already good drinking but will be much better, 1978–1988. An excellent value at $4.50, look for it.

1971 Georges de Latour Private Reserve—According to the Beaulieu winemakers, it will be very good. We shall see.

1972 Regular Bottling ***

1973 Georges de Latour Private Reserve—It's too early for a definitive assessment, but the reigning enologist at Beaulieu is enthusiastic about this wine —of course, they almost always are. But he says it will be a giant, powerful and long-lived. And a lot of people seem to agree with him, for a 50-gallon barrel recently sold for $4,000, which figures out to something like $17 per bottle (24 ounces).

Chablis*** A vast amount of what is sold in the U. S. as "California Chablis" is the closest thing to water one can find this side of a babbling brook. Here's a happy exception. It's not a real Chablis, of course— those don't come these days with $2.50 price tags—but this is a medium-dry white wine with some character and real flavor—of all things in a California Chablis! Very good value at $2.50 to $2.75. P. S. Avoid the '69 . . . blah. All other recent vintages: ***

Château Beaulieu (Sauvignon Blanc)*** Looking for something to go with your dessert: pie, cake, pudding? Look no further. Here's an economical perfumed white wine to fill the bill. Also fine for casual summer sipping. Serve well chilled (40˚F). Fair value, $3.50.

Cream Sherry: See SHERRY.

Dry Sauternes (Sémillon)** A dry white wine of no great dimension; would go well with fish, poultry, cheese dishes. Fair value, $2.75.

Extra Dry Champagne**** —Despite the name, this is one of Beaulieu's sweetest Champagnes, but that still doesn't make it Cold Duck! It will probably be more to the taste of most Americans than will the Private Reserve, which is extremely dry. Fair value, $6.25.

Gamay Beaujolais*** Soft young red wine, suitable almost anywhere, anytime, but especially with those grilled hamburgers, steaks, shish kebab. Or on a picnic, with hot dogs. Drink within four years of its vintage date. Fair value, $3.10.

Grenache Rosé*** Slightly sweeter than their Beaurosé, equally consistent. Perfect for luncheon in the patio. You can trust any of the recent vintages: '70, '71, '72. Consume within five years of vintage date. Fair value, $2.25 to $2.45.

Haut Sauternes (Sweet Sémillon)** "Haut" means "high," but, for some unknowable reason, to Californians it usually means "sweet." Thus, this is a rather sweet "Sauterne," though Beaulieu's Château Beaulieu is a bit sweeter and more expensive. The better vintages make good summer sipping (chilled, of course). Or enjoy your "High Sauternes" with fresh fruit, sippingly. It's ready to drink when you buy it and it will keep for about five years beyond its vintage date. Current vintages: '70, '71, '72: **. Fair value, $2.75.

Johannisberg Riesling: See BEAUCLAIR.

Muscat de Frontignan*** If one appreciates the distinctive flavor of the Muscat grape— and lots of folks do—one will appreciate and enjoy this sweet dessert wine. There are better ones made in California, but Beaulieu's is a good and tasty wine. Serve it well chilled. Fair value, $2.

Pale Dry Sherry: See SHERRY.

Pinot Chardonnay: See BEAUFORT.

Pinot Noir: See BEAUMONT.

Private Reserve Champagne ****—Beaulieu's most prestigious and driest Champagne. It's their *crème de la crème*, an elegant wine, crisp and brilliant, a wine that connoisseurs delight in. Even wine beginners, however, can appreciate this exquisite wine if they will sip it carefully—they'll have to at the price: $7.25.

Riesling (Sylvaner)*** This white German-type wine will make an excellent accompaniment to almost any light food —it's got character and flavor. Recent vintages can be trusted. For maximum freshness drink it within four years of its vintage date. Fair value, $3 to $3.20.

Rouge Champagne****— This wine is more commonly called "sparkling Burgundy." Perhaps the more elegant name is to denote its superiority, for that it has. This could well be America's finest sparkling Burgundy. Fair value, $6.25.

Sherry*** Beaulieu makes the three standard grades, all good wines, and at ca. $2, all good values: *Pale Dry:* the driest of the three, crisp and clean; excellent aperitif wine; *Sherry:* "Plain," no modifiers: this is a medium sherry, very versatile:

for before meals, during meals (with soup), and after meals; *Cream:* an after-dinner sherry. All three wines may be served slightly chilled, or at cool room temperature.

BEAUNE A lot of French Burgundies have the name Beaune somewhere on their labels—it's pronounced "Bone," like a dog's—but not very many have the name standing by itself. When they do, they are among the lowliest of red Burgundies from this area, but can still be very nice wines, not cheap, not terribly expensive, but worthy of examination. These are "village" or "commune" wines, and they can vary markedly from label to label. Look for the names of these shippers on the bottle: Barolet; Schroder & De Constans; Louis Latour; Chanson; Bouchard; Le Baron; Piat; Thorin; Drouhin. This wine goes well with beef, lamb, fowl, game (especially venison). It's a little too elegant to accompany hamburgers and the like, and the best bottles deserve to be appreciated on their own or with cheeses, nuts, fruit. This wine is at its best when it is between three and seven years old. Air it one hour and serve at cool room temperature.

Just a notch below these Beaune wines are those labeled Côte de Beaune-Villages. The same principles regarding maturity and serving (above) apply to these. Moreover they can be better bargains than the simple Beaunes. Especially trustworthy are those under the aegis of these shippers: Drouhin; Jouvet; Jadot; Chanson (St. Vincent); Monot;   Poulet;   Bouchard; Crispin.

BEAUNE, HOSPICE DE: See HOSPICES OF BEAUNE.

BEAUNE Ier CRÛ The *Ier Crû* is *Premier* in French, "first": this is a "first growth" red Burgundy wine. That doesn't mean that it is at the very top of the heap, but it does denote an excellent wine. (The very best wines of this area go by their vineyard names: Clos des Mouches, Clos de l' Ecu, etc.) A *1964 Leroy* was ****, but it is probably past its peak. The *1966 Chanson* deserves *****. The '66 Leroy, ***, is silky soft but lacks body. A *'71 Remoissenet* is **** but needs a little more age; try it in '76. *1973 Bouchard:* ****. These wines should cost $7 to $9. How to serve and enjoy this wine: See CLOS DES MOUCHES.

BEERENAUSLESE One of the highest categories of German wines (white), very rich, luscious, and expensive. There is only one higher classification: Trockenbeerenauslese (see). Beerenauslese means "The late picking of the berries (grapes)." After the normal picking, the vineyards are gone over again, by hand, perhaps a half dozen more times, to pick each individual cluster at the fullness of maturity. Such wines can be made only in the most favorable of vintages. It would be manifestly criminal or insane, or both, to drink such nectar other than by itself in the company of dear, wine-loving friends. They'll have to be dear considering the price of Beerenauslesen (that's the plural in German): anywhere from $25 to $90. Such wines last virtually forever, but they are at their very best when they're between ten and forty years old.

BEREICH Simply ignore this word on a German wine label —it means "district," and the word that follows is the impor-

tant one: Nierstein, Bernkastel, etc. Look up your wine under that word.

BERINGER VINEYARDS (St. Helena, Calif.) This hundred-year-old winery has suffered a multitude of vicissitudes—lots of changes, in English—over the years. The latest was its acquisition in 1970 by the Nestlé Company, of chocolate fame. It's diabolically ironic that chocolate happens to be one of the very few items on God's green earth that is wholly inimical to wine. But the best evidence thus far makes it abundantly clear that Nestlé's is not allergic to California wine, nor vice versa. Beringer wines did suffer a decline in the 60s, but today they're once again mostly above average, despite their proximity to all that Nestlé chocolate. Beringer's jug "Mountain" wines are marketed under their Los Hermanos label (see).

Barenblut** There are several wines around called Bull's Blood, but this is the only Bear's Blood. Truth to tell, they sound equally unappealing, and this one, at least, is. The most unique thing about it is its name, for it's a very standard red wine, youngish and tartish. Well, it's better than no wine at all, but you'll do better with Beringer's Burgundy (see following wine)—and it's cheaper besides. Fair value at $2.75, but don't!

Burgundy*** A soft, simple red wine, above the cut of a host of California Burgundies. It tends to be a bit tart, but it's still a good value at $2.25. Good at your outdoor barbecue (hamburgers, steaks, spare ribs, whatever) or at any informal dinner. Serve at cool room temperature. Ready to drink when you buy it, it will keep for three or four years. Note that Beringer also makes a Mountain Red Burgundy under its Los Hermanos label; it's somewhat cheaper but lots inferior. Stick with this at only 50¢ more per fifth.

Cabernet Sauvignon Almost everybody agrees that Cabernet Sauvignon is California's finest red wine, and Beringer makes a rather good one. Of course it's more expensive than other California reds, but it is fit accompaniment for your finest cuts of beef, that roast leg of lamb, those grilled guinea hens. Serve at cool room temperature. Fair value, $5.

1969, 1970, 1971****—Most California Cabernet is drunk too young. These bottles, totally typical of the breed, should not be touched until at least 1977.

Chablis*** The name Chablis is one of the most abused words in the entire world of wine. Especially in California. Some pretty frightful stuff is sold under that name. But Beringer's product is a fine brew—all Chablis is a blend—and an excellent value at $2. Serve it as you would a true French Chablis: with fish, particularly seafood, or with fowl. It's ready to drink when you buy it, don't keep it more than a year or two. Be cautioned: There is also a Mountain White Chablis, no big deal at all. Even at about 40¢ less per fifth, this is still the better buy.

Chenin Blanc*** California makes Chenin Blanc in two flavors: sweet and dry. This one's smack in between: it has a touch of sweetness, but it's dry enough to be used as a table wine, with light foods, fish, seafood. It's best when young and fresh; drink it within

three years of purchase. Fair value, $2.75.

Club Sherry: See SHERRY.

Dry Sauterne** Forget we even mentioned this one . . . even the winery seems to be ashamed of it; it's scarcely to be found in their literature.

Fino Cocktail Sherry: See SHERRY.

Fumé Blanc The name means "White Smoke," which sounds ominously like the name of some vile, highly combustible brew of about 150-proof alcohol. Doesn't sound a bit like the name of a timid, dainty little white wine, which this is. It's on the dry side and will go well with fish, seafood, chicken, veal, pork. This is the kind of white wine that will improve with thirty minutes of air before serving it, chilled. Fair value, $3 to $3.50.

1970 and *1971****—Best drinking, 1975 through 1976.

Gamay Rosé*** Not just another pleasant pink tipple, this is a rosé with some substance. It's quite dry and has a good zingy tartness. It fits anywhere, almost, but will be especially appreciated at your outdoor barbecue or buffet luncheon. Serve chilled. Drink it young and fresh: within a year or two of purchase. Fair value, $2.

Grey Riesling*** Perhaps Beringer's best white wine. Use it exactly as you would the Fumé Blanc (above). They're quite similar, with the Fumé Blanc having a more earthy flavor; this, a more spicy one. Serve chilled. It's for youthful consumption—consumer or consumed, as you will—and should be drunk within two years or so of purchase. Fair value, $2.50.

Grignolino** An Italian-type red wine, not nearly as romantic as it might sound. As the man said when asked, "How's your wife?" "Humph, better than nothing . . ." It's for immediate drinking upon purchase, and will keep for several years. Serve at cool room temperature, with hamburgers, barbecued chicken, pasta, Italian dishes. Fair value, $3 to $3.50.

Johannisberg Riesling In California, though not in Germany, its native habitat, this white wine comes through as a dry, full-bodied table wine, not a delicate, flowery sipping wine. It's for table use, chilled. Serve it with light foods: fish, seafood, light casseroles, chicken dishes, Chinese food. Fair value, $3.90.

1970 and *1971****—Drink, 1975 through 1976.

*1972*****.

1973 Auslese****—This is a special bottling of a special wine touched with "noble rot," that greatly desired fungus that attacks the grapes. Rich, lovely wine. It will be in short supply and is worth searching out.

Malvasia Bianca**** This is a Beringer specialty, their most interesting wine, by their own saying. It's smooth, full-bodied, semisweet: perfect with fruit cake or other such rich desserts. Serve it well chilled. It's an excellent value, $3 to $3.25.

Pinot Chardonnay This dry white wine is not always one of Beringer's more notable successes, though Chardonnay is ordinarily California's tastiest and best white wine. Serve it chilled, especially with fish and seafood. It's the classic accompaniment for oysters. Fair value, $3.80 to $4.

1970**—At its best: 1975 through 1976.

1971*—Drink it now and through 1977.

1972***.

Pinot Noir This is a red table wine of no great distinction, though neither does it possess any serious flaws. In a Pinot Noir one looks for softness and richness, but Beringer's product is not overly long in those suits. It's best with roast beef, cheese (especially Cheddar), game. Air this wine about two hours and serve at cool room temperature. It's both Estate Bottled (made entirely on the premises) and vintaged (dated) and therefore more expensive, and it is certainly questionable whether it's worth its present asking price of $4.50.

1969 and *1970****—Both of these bottles will improve a bit with further aging. Try them first in 1975, and they'll be at the top of their bent through 1979 at least.

Port, Royal: See ROYAL PORT.

Royal Port** Considering that it doesn't have any of the real Portuguese grapes in its composition, this reasonably priced ($2) California Port comes off remarkably well. It might even improve if you lay it down in a secret cranny for a couple of years. Port may be served slightly chilled, in a wide-mouthed glass, so that the aromas may be appreciated. It's for after-dinner drinking.

Sherry Beringer's makes the standard California sherries, dry, medium, and sweet, and they're mostly standard. But the price is quite delightful: $2. The *Fino Cocktail*** is the driest of the three; it's a bit thin. *Club Sherry*** is medium-sweet, and you can serve it either before dinner or after. *Velvet Cream Sherry**** has a mite more flavor than the other two.

Zinfandel**** This "bramble-flavored" red wine—it really does have that kind of an "outdoor" wild-berry taste—is the only wine truly indigenous to California. It's produced nowhere else in the world. And, what's more, it's almost always a good buy. Beringer's "Z" is particularly recommended; it's one of their best wines. It's got some tartness, but it's a good tartness. Sip it, at cool room (or patio) temperature, before the meal with cheese—during the meal with hamburgers, steaks, barbecued chicken—after the meal with Camembert, Brie, fresh fruit. It's ready to drink when purchased, and will improve with an additional year or two in the bottle. It will keep for at least five years. Fair value, $3.

BERNKASTEL(ER) BAD-STUBE Excellent German Moselle wine—Bernkastel is the name of the town. Badstube, the name of the vineyard. How to serve this wine: See under MOSELLE.

BERNKASTEL(ER) or BERN-KASTEL(ER) RIESLING A regional Moselle (Germany) wine, not on a par with such as Bernkasteler Doktor and Bernkasteler Badstube, but can be a very good wine, and often a good value. Look for these:

Producer	Name of Wine
Anheuser	Bernkastel(er)
Deinhard	Bernkastel(er) Green Label
Guntrum	Bernkastel(er) Riesling
Kayser	Bernkastel(er) Urglueck
Kendermann	Bernkastel(er) Riesling
Kreusch	Bernkastel(er) Kurfurstlay
Langguth	Bernkastel(er) Riesling Landvogt
Madrigal	Bernkastel(er) Riesling
Sichel	Bernkastel(er) Riesling
Studert	Bernkastel(er) Riesling
Valckenberg	Bernkastel(er) Falkenkrone

These wines will range in price from $2.50 to $5, and you will get pretty much what you pay for. Avoid very cheap Bernkastelers: anything, surely, under $2. How to serve these wines: See under MOSELLE.

BERNKASTELER DOKTOR or DOKTOR UND GRABEN (or DOCTOR) A very famous and very good Moselle wine, so well known, in fact, that most experts believe it is usually overpriced. One eminent critic said that the '34 (Deinhard) was the best Moselle he ever drank. The '59 was another great year; a Trockenbeerenauslese (Dr. Thanisch) is a Classic. How to enjoy and serve this great wine: See under MOSELLE.

BERTOLLI, F. This is the name of an important producer of Italian wines, mainly inexpensive Chiantis. The wines are generally reliable. Some recent vintages:

1964 Chianti Classico: ***
1965 Chianti Classico: ****
1968 Chianti (in fiasco): ***
—Slightly *frizzante.* A good value at $2.50. There is also a 1968 in a "Bambino" bottle, something like a Burgundy bottle, with sloping shoulders—it's a lesser wine.

1970 Chianti Classico: **—A lot of people are unenthusiastic about this one.
Fair value for current vintages: Chianti in *fiaschi,* ca. $3.

BEST WINES: See FAVORITE WINES.

BEYCHEVELLE, CHÂTEAU

Excellent red Bordeaux wine (Claret), one of the most delightful and sprightly of them all. It's superb when the vintage is good, dismal when the vintage is poor. Officially Beychevelle has a low ranking, but everybody agrees that it deserves much better—and that's where it sells, among the very best. How to serve it: See under BORDEAUX.

1945—Near-Classic—Fair value, $30.

1947—Near-Classic—Fair value, $25.

1953—Near-Classic—It should be reasonably priced: $12 to $15. Now at its best.

1955—Not recommended at $15. Now at its best.

1957—*****—At its best now and to 1980.

1959—Near-Classic—Now at its peak but don't keep it too long—drink before 1980. Fair value, $14.

1960—Not recommended.

1961—Classic—Not quite ready—Will be at its best, 1978–1990. Fair value, $15.

*1962*****—Best drinking, 1975 through 1980. Fair value, $10.

1964—Already fine drinking but will be even better: 1976–1990. Elegant, aristocratic wine. Fair value, $15.

1966—Near-Classic—Will be at its best, 1977–1999.

1967—*****—Best drinking, 1975–1985. Fair value, $11.

1969—***—Not recommended at $15. Nor at $5.

1970—****—Will be at its best, 1978–1985. Fair value, $10.

1971—From here it looks like a great one.

BEYER, LEON—GEWÜRZTRAMINER

Leon Beyer of Eguisheim, Alsace, is a highly reputed shipper of Alsatian wines, and the "Gewürz" is one of their best wines. Their '66 and '67 were outstanding: ***** and ****, respectively.

BEYER, LEON: RIESLING

Fine Alsatian white wine made from the noble Riesling grape of Germany. Some recent vintages:

1964 Cuvée Exceptionnelle: It is! *****—Drink soon, at the latest.

1966 Cuvée Spéciale: ***. Spicy and good. Alsatians say it can a company sauerkraut!

1966 and 1967 Cuvée des Ecaillers. It means "The Wine of the Oyster Men," which is interpreted to mean a good wine to accompany oysters. Many Alsatian shippers are now using this kind of nomenclature. It's a good trend, for Alsatian wines, unlike their German counterparts, are spicy and dry enough to accompany food, especially shellfish and oysters. The 1966: ****, the 1967: ****.

1968 Cuvée des Ecaillers: ***. Good wine considering the vintage. Drink very soon!

1969 Cuvée des Ecaillers: ***. At its best through 1975.

1970 Cuvée des Ecaillers: **** Drink through 1976.

1971 Réserve: ****. Best drinking, 1975–1977.

1971 Cuvée des Ecaillers: *****. Best drinking, 1975–1978.

1972 Cuvée des Ecaillers: ***. Drink, 1975–1977.

BEZE, CLOS DE: See CHAMBERTIN CLOS DE BEZE.

BICHOT You may think this is the name of the wine when you see it on a label, for it is always in large bold type, the most prominent word on the label. But it's the name of the *Negociant-Eléveur*, the producer of the wine (*Eléveur:* the "Elevator," the one who elevates, improves the wine). A. Bichot & Cie. deals only in Burgundy and Bordeaux wines, usually the more economical ones, such as regionals. Wines vary, even wildly at times, but Bichot is usually a dependable name in its price range.

BIENVENUE-BÂTARD-MONTRACHET A white Burgundy (France) wine, one of the world's great dry whites. It's not often seen in the U.S., however—or anywhere else, for that matter, for it's in extremely short supply. It is also very expensive. For further details: See MONTRACHET.

BLANC DE BLANCS The name means simply "White from Whites," meaning white wine from white grapes. The name is not as dumb as it might at first sound, for much sparkling wine is made from black grapes (the color of the wine comes almost entirely from the skins, which are quickly removed). The name was used originally only of sparkling wines and even today it is used principally in this connection. A few American wineries, however, do make a still (nonsparkling) Blanc de Blancs, notably Fetzer and Wente (see both).

When a California vintner uses the name for a sparkling wine he usually means that this is the very finest Champagne he knows how to make. For a comparative listing of California's best sparkling Blanc de Blancs, see CHAMPAGNE, AMERICAN—PRIDE OF THE HOUSE.

Most of the great French Champagne houses also make a Blanc de Blancs, and it is sometimes their "Best of the House," sometimes not. It is always a supremely light and delicate wine. But truth to tell, it would often take an expert to distinguish between a Blanc de Blanc and a "straight" Champagne from the same house.

For a listing of France's best Blanc de Blancs: See under CHAMPAGNE.

BLANC FUMÉ: See SAUVIGNON BLANC.

BLANCHOTS: See CHABLIS, FRENCH.

BLUE NUN A popular and dependable brand name of German wine owned by the huge Sichel wine firm. Blue Nun Liebfraumilch (see, below) was so successful that Sichel now markets a Blue Nun Bernkasteler Riesling as well.

BLUE NUN BERNKASTELER RIESLING Dependable little German wine, regularly ***, but, sad to relate, it's selling today for around $4.50, which is sometimes more than it's really worth. The '71, however, is worth all of $4.50: ****.

BLUE NUN LIEBFRAUMILCH SUPERIOR As far as Liebfraumilch goes—really not very far—this is a mostly trustworthy name. The '70 was fine, ***, the '71 ditto, and the '72 likewise, all of them thoroughly enjoyable, and a fair value at $3.90.

BODEGAS BILBAINAS A huge and reputable shipper of Spanish wines in the town of Haro in the Rioja region of northern Spain, whence come Spain's best table wines. The following wines of the Bodegas Bilbainas are individually assessed in this book under their proper, "given" names: Brillante, Cepa de Oro, Viña Pomal, Viña Zaco.

BODEGAS RIOJANAS: A Spanish wine firm. See under

the names of the wines: BRIL-
LANTE, CEPA DE ORO, VINA
POMAL.

BÖCKELHEIM, SCHLOSS:
See SCHLOSS BÖCKELHEIM.

BOLLA VALPOLICELLA: See
VALPOLICELLA.

BOLLINGER One of France's
great Champagne houses, with
a specialty for high-quality
nonvintage wines. Their "Best
of the House" is their R.D.
($18), not *Reader's Digest,* but
"Recently Disgorged," meaning
that the wine has been well
aged and has only recently been
"disgorged," that is, recapped
and marketed. It's a great
Champagne, usually *****.
Their nonvintage Brut is called
Special Cuvée ($12); they make
no vintaged Brut. The Special
Cuvée is a marvelously dry,
lively wine, deeply flavorful,
regularly **** or better.

**BONET, JACQUES
CHAMPAGNE*** Don't let the
fancy French name fool you:
Jacques Bonet & Cie. is as American as MacDonald's. It's a label
owned by the huge Italian Swiss
Colony Winery of Asti, California, which in turn is a part of
United Vintners, which finally
is a part of vast Heublein, Inc.
Selling at a mere $2—of which
amount half goes to pay for the
tax and the bottle—perhaps it
can be said that Jacques Bonet
Champagnes constitute good
values—after all they do sparkle
and they *are* wine. But just
barely on both counts. They're
almost flavorless—but for $2,
wha'ja expect, Mumm's Cordon
Rouge?

(LES) BONNES MARES
Splendid red Burgundy wine,
often a good value, since, for
some inexplicable reason it's
not well known. (Do Americans suspect that it has something to do with female horses?)

Note the high percentage of exceptional ratings—seven Near-
Classics—in the vintages listed
below. For details on the enjoyment and serving of this
wine: See MOREY-SAINT-DENIS.
Some notable vintages:

1934 Splendid, luscious wines.
1945 Belorgey: *****
1959 Roux: Near-Classic—
Now at its best.
1961 Drouhin Laroze: Near-
Classic
    Comte de Vogue: Near-
      Classic—Will be at its
      best from 1975 on.
1962 Comte de Vogue: *****
1964 Moillard: *****
    Comte de Vogue: Near-
      Classic
1964 Drouhin Laroze: *****
1966 G. Roumier: *****
    Drouhin Laroze: ****
    Comte de Vogue: *****
These 1966 wines are at their
best, 1975 through 1978.
1967 Comte de Vogue: ***
1969 G. Roumier: *****—
Will be at its best, 1977 on.
    Comte de Vogue: *****
      —Will be at its best,
      1977 on.
1971 Remoissenet: Near-
Classic—Already delicious but
should be kept at least until
1978.
    G. Roumier: Near-Classic
      —Keep it until 1978.
    Ponnelle: Near-Classic—
      Ditto.
    Domaine Clair Dau: ****
      —Ditto.
    J. Drouhin: *****—Keep
      it until 1978.

BOONE'S FARM* It would
probably be safe to wager that
most Americans, given a choice,
would accept a bottle of Boone's
Farm wine in preference to a
bottle of Les Grands-Echézeaux.
In so doing they would be preferring one of the world's
worst wines to one of the

world's best. Speaking very precisely, Boone's Farm is not a wine at all—it's a "Pop" wine, a fruit wine, a wine punch. It is the classic epitome of a wine for people who don't like wine: Kool-Aid with alcohol. But in honesty, most people, especially the younger set, will find Boone's Farm exceedingly pleasant, at least in short doses. The true fruit flavors do come through. It comes in three *flavors*, and flavors is exactly the word: Apple, Strawberry Hill, Wild Mountain. But let that cardinal principle of all wine appreciation be emblazoned on the clouds hovering over the Boone's Farm Winery (Gallo's) in Modesto, California: If ye like it, drink it, bless ye! (But go up higher, friend!) Fair value, ca. $1.

BOORDY VINEYARD (Penn Yan, N. Y.) Here's a winemaking operation like no other in these United States. These folks grow their grapes at either end of the continent: French hybrids in New York State, and European grapes in Washington State's Yakima Valley. Philip and Jocelyn Wagner, names well known in the history of American winemaking, have produced and are producing some fine wine, and some of them even seem to be getting better. Understandably, some of the wines have a soupçon of that distinctive eastern foxiness which many people so dislike. Boordy also makes a Pinard (see) family of wines, also distinctive.

Boordy Blumchen (or: Boordyblümchen)* Surely this is the only wine by this name in all the world—praise God for small favors! The name is a takeoff on a German Moselle wine name which means

flowers. The wine's really not very flowery and it's nothing like a real Moselle, but it's a pleasant, light, dry white wine. The winery says it's perfect for a warm summer's day. Serve it chilled. Fair value, $2.25.

Boordy 5276: See FIVE-TWO-SEVEN-SIX.

Dry White: See WHITE WINE.

Five-Two-Seven-Six (or: Boordy 5276)* Boordy's nomenclature is nothing if not different! This happens to be the name of the French American hybrid grape, Seyve-Villard No. 5276, from which the wine is made. It's a light, dry white wine similar to Muscadet (see). Fair value, $3.70.

Red Wine and White Wine (Dry) Would that all American wineries would give their wines such honest, homely names. These wines sound like next to nothing, but they're actually pretty good little wines, tasty and dry. The red has some foxiness, and is very different from any other red you're likely to encounter on this earth. It has to be experienced to be described. Serve it at cool room temperature. Serve the white chilled, with any light food. Fair value, $2.25.

Rosé Wine* Quite dry, fresh, and crisp. Rosés are well known for their adaptability. Boordy says this goes well with everything from steaks to seafood. So be it. Or enjoy it, sippingly, of a summer's evening—always chilled. A good value at $2.25.

Sémillon Sec Kipling said that never the twain would meet, but East and West meet in this wine: it's grown and fermented in Washington State, but bottled in New York. And it's a good little dry wine, just right to accompany light foods. Serve it chilled. Fair value, $2.80.

White Wine: See RED WINE and WHITE WINE.

BORDEAUX In the entire world of wine the single most important name is undoubtedly Bordeaux. This 500-square-mile area of southern France produces more fine wine than any other area on God's good earth. From Bordeaux come some of the world's greatest white wine (especially sweet ones, from Sauternes), but its greatest contribution to the happiness of wine lovers the world over consists in its great red wines, dubbed Claret by the British.

Folks have argued for centuries over which is the greatest red wine on earth, Bordeaux or Burgundy, but true wine lovers don't expend precious energy—we're running short on that commodity, you know— in bootless speculation; they simply love and enjoy both of these splendid gifts of God—as one loves and enjoys one's two-year-old son and five-year-old daughter. In fact, wine people describe Burgundy as being "masculine," and Bordeaux, "feminine"—in case that does anything to you. One writer says that red Bordeaux is the most "fascinating" wine in the world—not necessarily the greatest; another, that it is "essentially an intellectual enjoyment." Tell that to your cerebral friends!

Almost all of Bordeaux's best wines have the word "Château" preceding their proper name. This is for the very good reason that there actually is (in almost all cases) a real French château or manor on the premises. It's often pictured on the label.

The very finest of Bordeaux's red wines, the *Grands Seigneurs* (the Great Lords), all extremely expensive, are listed here in a vaguely descending order of excellence based on their selling prices during this century: Château Lafite-Rothschild; Château Mouton-Rothschild; Château Latour; Château Margaux; Château Pétrus; Château Haut-Brion; Château Cheval Blanc; Château Ausone. Underscore "vaguely descending order of excellence," for these wines are all *crème de la crème*, and in any given year any one of them can surpass the others.

Don't look for the word "Bordeaux" on a wine label, it's seldom there. What is there is the name of the district from which the wine comes—that carries more prestige than the generic name "Bordeaux." However, if the wine is a blend from several different districts then it must call itself simply Bordeaux or Bordeaux Supérieur. This will not be very good wine and almost never a good value.

Red Bordeaux is the classic accompaniment not only for red meat (particularly beef and lamb) but also for poultry, especially when roasted. It is also a marvelous complement to cheese—as almost all good wine is—particularly these: Brie, Camembert, Cheddar, Munster, Pont l' Evêque, Port Salut, Roquefort, Stilton, and Valençay.

Few wines appreciate "breathing time" more than red Bordeaux. The older the wine, the less airing required. As a rule of thumb for the "average" Claret (the big classic first growths go by their own rules)

Young wines (1965 on): Air 2 hours.

Middle-aged Clarets (1955–1965): Air 1 hour

Old wines (older than '55): A half hour.

Check these older wines for sediment, and decant if necessary.

It is difficult to set down precise rules for the maturity of Clarets, for this varies from vintage to vintage and from château to château. Here are some rules of thumb: even the sorriest Claret needs at least four years to mature and will hold for one or two years. Better wines, "middle-class" Bordeaux, will be at their best when they are between eight and twelve years old. Fine wines will be at their peak when they are between ten and twenty years old. First growths take even longer to mature and longer to decline. (See the individual wines under their own names.) Serve red Bordeaux at cool room temperature: around 68°F.

The price of all French wines rose precipitously, to ridiculous heights, in the early 70s, none more so than those of Bordeaux. Something had to give, with single bottles of current wines tagged at $100 and $200 per 24 ounces. But it was only in mid-1974 that things began to right themselves, and prices finally began to level off, and even to decline in some areas. Prices are still exaggerated but some semblance of reason has finally begun to return to the Bordeaux wine scene. Expect the happy decline to continue over the next several years—happy day for wine consumers, bad day for the wine speculators. Divine justice!

The California equivalent of French Claret is not California Claret—often an execrable potion—but Cabernet Sauvignon (see), likewise a fine wine. The two wines have much in common, but perhaps just as much wherein they differ. Try them once, side by each—most enlightening.

The best wines of Bordeaux, both red and white, are individually assessed in this book. Find them under their proper names (disregard the word "Château"): Montrose, Yquem, etc.

BORDEAUX, WHITE Most people think of Bordeaux in terms of red wine (Claret) because it is so good and so famous, but a great deal of Bordeaux's wine is white. It comes in two very distinct styles: a dry and a sweet. The dry comes from the district of Graves (see) and the sweet from that of Sauternes (see). The best châteaux will be found, individually assessed, along with individual vintages, under their proper names (disregard the word "Château").

BOTTLE SHAPES There are some weirdly shaped bottles hoving about in winedom these days. The word: Give them wide berth, the wilder the bottle, the wider the berth. Note, however, that Chianti often comes in a squat flask, and Chilean and a few German and Portuguese wines in a similar flat-sided flagon—these are quite standard, not weird. The weird bottles—three-foot-long necks, fish-shaped—are invariably promotional gimmicks devised to peddle inferior or at best nondescript wine. More attention and expense go into the bottle than into the wine.

BOTTLE SIZES At first glance, virtually all wine, whether domestic or imported, seems to come in bottles of the same size. Not so. European wines come in 24-ounce bottles, and almost all American wine in 25.6-ounce bottles, a "fifth." A lot of Italian Chianti (see), however, comes in 32-ounce bottles, and there are also 23-ounce bottles, 22-ounces, even 24.3-ounces and 23.5-ounces. The moral: Read before you leap. The precise contents are on the bottle somewhere—on the bottom of the bottle if not on the label.

BOUCHARD There are several wine-shipping firms by this name in France's Burgundy region: Bouchard Aîné & Fils (that's Bouchard, Sr., and Sons) and Paul Bouchard & Cie. It's all in the family, and both are reputable and dependable. The name is one of Burgundy's most venerable, dating back to 1731. But, as with all wine producers, whether in Burgundy, France, or St. Helena, California, wines can vary widely, and Bouchard on a label is not an absolute guarantee of excellence. Look up your particular wine under the name of the wine: Bâtard-Montrachet, Mercurey, or whatever.

BOUGROS: See CHABLIS, FRENCH.

BOURGOGNE The word means simply "Burgundy," but you'll rarely find it on a Burgundy label. The reason is simple: plain Bourgogne is just about the lowest official grade of Burgundy wine. The more specific the label, naming the district, the township, and even a single vineyard, the better the wine. The few simple Bourgogne wines that do find their way to these shores are usually good wines, ***, and good values—if any French wine can

be a good value in the U.S. today. They will range in price from $3 to $5. If the label has the phrase "Passe-Tout-Grains," it is a step below Bourgogne and should sell for around $3.: ** only.

BRAUNEBERG(ER) JUFFER Marvelous German wine, one of the richest of all Moselles. Some recent vintages have been good values: *1967 Feine Auslese:* ***** ($6)—*1969 Feinste Auslese:* **** ($4.25)—*1970 Spätlese:* **** ($4.60). The '71s, however, are expensive ($7 for a Spätlese) but are tremendous wines. How to serve wines: See under MOSELLE.

BREATHING TIME OF WINE: See AIRING OF WINE.

BRILLANTE It's *Brilliant* only in name. This is a white Spanish wine from the Rioja region, made by the reputable Bodegas Bilbainas. The *Cosecha* (vintage) 1966, currently available, has no body, no depth, no nothing, only sweetness. Unless recent vintages have improved vastly, the verdict is *Nyet!* Not recommended.

BROLIO CHIANTI CLASSICO This is the Barone Ricasole's second-best Chianti—it's a reliable, tasty red wine, a good value at ca. $3.90 per quart or $3.25 per 24 ounces, but vintages and bottles vary. It is also labeled Castello di Brolio. Ricasole's best is Brolio Riserva (see). For details on vintages, serving, etc.: See under CHIANTI.

BROLIO RISERVA One of Italy's finest Chiantis, with a worldwide reputation. It's made by the huge Barone Ricasoli firm—Brolio is actually the name of the castle. This Riserva is Ricasoli's "Best of the

House," and when you buy it, it's already been aged at least five years, but it will continue to improve for at least another two or three years. It will sell for ca. $4.65, and it's a fine wine for that price. Some notable bottles:

1952: Gone, departed.

1962: Past its prime—it was nice.

1964: At its best, soft and delicious—drink it *now*.

1966: ****

1967: It recently took a British wine award: ****. Drink, 1975 through 1978.

1968: Full rich wine, excellent—drink now and through the 70s.

1969: Average.

BROOKSIDE VINEYARD (Guasti, Calif.) Even if this huge winemaking operation had never produced a drop of respectable wine, Brookside ought to receive some kind of an award for their wild, kaleidoscopic array of wine labels. Surely no other winery in all the world can boast of such a gaudy and extravagant assortment. Under their various brand names (Assumption Abbey, E. Vache, Vin de Biane Fres, Old Guasti), these folks produce an incredible number of wines—approximately one hundred of them, you count 'em! Their wines may sometimes leave something, or lots, to be desired, but their labels, never. The wines and near-wines range from the standard generics (Chablis, Burgundy) and varietals (Pinot Chardonnay, Chenin Blanc) to such things as Apricot, Mint, Hausmarke Rote, La Mancha, even Chocolate, the latter surely constituting some kind of an ultimate, for wine and chocolate are mortal enemies. Almost by definition these are wines for people who don't like wines. Or more exactly, near-wines, for, properly speaking, wine is the fruit of the grape alone—not of the apricot or the Mancha! Most of Brookside's wines are very inexpensive, many under the Brookside label selling for only $1 per fifth.

Claret** It may not bear much resemblance to true French Claret, but it's a good little red wine and will serve to accompany your grilled hamburgers, steaks, barbecued ribs, or chicken. It's pleasantly peasant-priced: $1. Serve at cool room temperature. Drink it within a year or two of purchase.

Mouvedre** This is the name of a little-known French grape; the wine is very dry, a light rosé, which will go well at your outdoor barbecue or buffet luncheon. It's a very youthful wine, and should be so consumed; within a year or so of purchase. Fair value, $2.50.

At a full $1 less there is *Vino Rosado*, which took a silver medal at the Los Angeles County Fair in 1973. And then there's *Rosé Suave*, at only $1.10; it received a gold medal at Los Angeles in '73. All rosés should be served chilled, and should not be kept more than a year or so after purchase.

Vino Rosso** but pennywise, *** It means simply "Red Wine," and that's exactly what it is: simple hearty *vin ordinaire* for your hamburgers, barbecued ribs, pasta. It even won a gold medal at the Los Angeles County Fair, 1973. An incredibly good value at $1. Consume within a year or two of purchase and serve at cool room temperature.

BROUILLY and CÔTE DE BROUILLY Regularly: **** This is a fine red Beaujolais— the label may read either "Brouilly" or "Côte de Brouilly," and the latter is judged somewhat superior. Brouilly is the lightest of all Beaujolais wines, fruity and flavorful. Mommessin makes an excellent one, and other reputable shippers are listed under BEAUJOLAIS. Château de la Chaize is one of the best, the '71 and '72 meriting *****. How to serve it: See under BEAUJOLAIS. These wines are at their best when they are between two and four years of age. Don't buy anything more than three years old.

BRUCE, DAVID (Los Gatos, Calif.) A small, ten-year-old, mostly one-man operation, producing a limited number of prestigious wines in limited quantities. David Bruce's approach to wine is strictly experimental, and every batch of wine is different from every other. Most of the wines are sold by mail. If you're looking for some rare wine adventure, search out some of Bruce's products. The wines tend to be on the rich side, flavor-wise and money-wise.

Black Muscat Fie, vile turpentine laced with alum! Bruce says people will either like it or they won't—those who don't may come to number in the millions, if they possess at least two taste buds. As for those who are going to like it, they're going to be extreeeeemely rare. Remember how Mother was forcing oatmeal down Billy's throat, lecturing him severely that there were millions of Chinese who would love to have such a bowl of oatmeal, and remember Billy's response: "Name one!"

Cabernet Sauvignon** Only a small amount of this is around, but it should be worth looking for.

Carignan** This is a grape usually used in blending, rarely made into a wine on its own merits. But Bruce is proud of this wine—he says it's a sleeper and he'd be happy to put it up against any Zinfandel in the land. It's a good red wine, very dry, will go best with good red meat. Air two hours. Fair value, $4.50.

Chardonnay One of Bruce's specialties. Chardonnay is generally conceded to be California's best white wine, but it's often (as here) a connoisseur's wine because of its dryness and austerity. It's an excellent complement to fish, seafood, chicken in white or cream sauce, pork, or ham. Serve it chilled.

1967***—Drink soon.

1968****—Many say this is one of the finest Chardonnays ever made; others say it's already begun to deteriorate. Majority vote says **** or more. Decant before serving. It originally sold for $5.

1969—Near-Classic—Here's one of the most controversial wines in all the history of winemaking. Some have called it the finest Chardonnay ever made—others call it, literally "Château Old Tennis Shoe." In one wine-tasting it outclassed some of the finest white wines in the world. In another tasting, out of 29 similar California and French wines, it placed —you guessed it—29th. But perhaps both are correct. The simple truth is that this is quintessentially a connoisseur's wine: only he will find its intensity attractive. For the connoisseur it's a huge, powerful **wine—for the uninitiated it's** too much of everything: too powerful, too concentrated, too much wine. Anyhow, only connoisseurs and millionaires are likely to be tasting it, at $22. Bruce put that price tag on it, saying simply that it's better than Le Montrachet, and that's what it sells for!

*1970****—Fine wine but overpriced at $12. The '71, at the same price, is a clear cut above it.

*1971*****—Huge and rich, big-bodied and complex, almost a masterpiece. Bruce recommends that you decant this wine, then air it one to two hours, and serve it at cool room temperature. It'll be worth the trouble. It's at its best right now and will hold there at least until 1980. Fair value—and it is worth it, $12.

1972—Big rich wine, too woody, perhaps, for some tastes, but great wine. **** to start with.

Grenache This is one of the biggest rosés you're going to come across. It's dry and flavorful and will appeal mainly to seasoned wine drinkers. At the price, $6.50, you will want to sip it on its own.

*1969***—1970 and 1971 **** Unlike most rosés, these wines will keep well, until 1977, at least.

Petit Syrah

1970—Bruce's wines are different, all right—he even spells the names differently. Most folks call this "Petite Sirah." And Bruce is nothing if not candid about his wines. He says that this wine, selling for a tidy $6.50 at the winery, may never be drinkable! It's too everything. Bruce says it's also the blackest wine he's ever seen, and it may live forever. Today, nary a *—tomorrow,

who knows? You remember the cartoon of the husband pouring himself a glass of wine, having already poured one for his wife, and he is asking her, "How is it, dear?" while she lies prostrate, out cold, on the floor behind him. It was this wine that he was pouring! This will probably be a great wine, *** or ****, someday, but that day is a "fur piece" down the road. . . . Check it again around the year 2000.

1971—Much tamer, already rates ****. Fair value, $5.50.

Pinot Chardonnay: See CHARDONNAY.

White Riesling Strictly experimental—even Bruce doesn't venture to guess how the two vintages, 1970 and 1971, will turn out. Price at the winery, $4. Strictly for gamblin' men . . .

White Zinfandel (Zinfandel Blanc de Noir)*—Mostly a curiosity, it was originally made by mistake. It's actually more orange than white, and it's definitely a connoisseur's wine. The '68 needs to be drunk soon. The '71 is still developing but, says Bruce, may turn out to be more drinkable than any of his other Zinfandels.

Zinfandel One of Bruce's specialties. "Z" is California's own red wine, made nowhere else. It's almost always a good wine and often a good value. Bruce's "Z" is sometimes one, sometimes both, sometimes neither. But it's always expensive. Zinfandel goes well with good red meats, hearty dishes, but at the price of Bruce's bottles, you'll want to savor it for all it's worth, on its own. It's a connoisseur's wine—wine novices may find it just too big.

1965 and *1966***—Now at their best and will hold thus

until 1980. Sold originally for $4.

1967****—Best drinking: 1975–1985.

1968****—Big-bodied, rich. Good drinking now and will live long, at least until the mid-80s. Sold originally, at the winery, for $4.

1969 Late Harvest****—This wine is a deep purple-black in color, has intense, concentrated flavor, is high in alcohol. It has a tinge of sweetness, giving it a Port-like quality. It would be instructive to compare this with one of Ridge's Zinfandels from the Lodi area—if your pocketbook is expansive. It's good drinking now and will last for decades. It sells for $7.50 at the winery.

1970 Late Harvest*****—This is even more of everything the '69 is. Bruce says it's an ultimate in its class. It will last for decades. Price at the winery, sorry, $8.50.

1971—It comes in three flavors: a "plain" ($5.50), a Late Harvest Dry ($7.50), and a Late Harvest Sweet ($7.50). Released only in late 1974, a preliminary report indicates three fine wines, safely ****.

BUENA VISTA VINEYARDS (Sonoma, Calif.) Buena Vista is a name steeped in California history—the winery itself is an official historical monument. It was founded in 1857 by Agoston Haraszthy, known as the father of California viniculture. You'll notice his name on the labels. A flamboyant character, he died in Nicaragua, apparently devoured by alligators. The winery was entirely abandoned for some forty years, reopened in 1943. Today Buena Vista is resolutely regaining its early glory.

Barbera, 1969**** Hearty red wine in limited production. It's always cask-bottled, which means it received special attention—and love. The price reflects it: $5, expensive for a Barbera. It's excellent accompaniment for red meats, Italian or Mexican food (if not too incendiary). May be consumed now, but it will be softer and better, 1976 through 1980. Air one to two hours. Serve at cool room temperature. Fair value, $5.

Burgundy*** The winery boasts that the formula for this wine is their particular secret. And, in truth, this is a reliable steady-as-you-go (if imbibed judiciously) red wine, fit accompaniment for your roast (beef, lamb, even pork), steaks, hamburgers. It's soft, with good flavor. It's usually advisable to give this wine a couple more years of bottle age after you buy it. It's at its best from six to twelve years after its vintage date. Serve at cool room temperature. Fair value, $2.75 to $3.

Cabernet Rosé (Rose Brook) This is Buena Vista's most popular wine, and in sooth, it's one of the best rosés in the land. One big reason for the popularity of rosés with Americans is the simple fact that they "go with anything." Which they do, by and large. A fine rosé, however, deserves more discrimination. Its best service is as an aperitif wine—then you can serve a heartier wine (white or red) with the dinner itself. But if you insist on serving your rosé with the meal, the food should be light: poultry, fish, pork, veal.

The excellence of this wine is largely due to the fact that it is made almost wholly from the

great French grape, the Cabernet Sauvignon, one of the most
expensive grapes in the world.
This explains why the wine is
perhaps the most expensive
rosé in all of California: $4.25
to $5.50.

Rosés are not for keeping.
They surely should not be kept
more than five years beyond
their vintage date. Serve chilled.

1970 and *1971*****—Drink
immediately.

1972***—Drink now and
through 1976.

Cabernet Sauvignon Buena
Vista makes two grades of this
classic red wine, a "plain" and
a "Cask." Both are vintage-
dated, both are excellent wines.
The "Cask," however, may not
always be worth the additional
$1. Good Cabernet such as
Buena Vista's deserves to be enjoyed on its own, with cheeses
and fruit. It's also the classic
accompaniment for grilled
steaks or lamb chops, barbecued chicken, roast leg of lamb.
Air one to two hours, serve at
cool room temperature. The
"plain" sells for ca. $4, the
"Cask" for $5.

1964***—Now at its best,
there to remain until 1980.

1965 and *1967*****—Drink
now and until 1982.

1968****—Drink now and
through 1985. A good value at
around $4.

Cardinal Port* Not very exciting. Fair value, ca. $3.

Chablis** This is a dry
white wine, the driest Buena
Vista makes. It's the proper accompaniment for fish, seafood
(especially oysters), and other
light foods. Drink it young;
don't keep it more than a year
or two. Serve it chilled. Fair
value, $2.50.

Gewürz Traminer Buena
Vista makes this white Alsatian

wine in two grades: a "plain"
and a "Haraszthy Cabinet," the
latter costing a dollar more, $4
vs. $5. It should be a better
wine, made, says the winery, by
a "new and unique procedure,"
but the truth is almost nobody
has had a good word to say for
it. One thing is certain, it has
not been worth the extra peso.
Things may be on the up-beat,
though—see the '72 Cabinet,
below. The "plain," everybody
agrees, has usually been a fine
wine; recent vintages, however,
have been extremely erratic.
Proceed with caution. "Gewürz"
means "spicy," and Buena
Vista's is, and is an excellent
complement for sausages (as
in Alsace), chicken, pork, ham.
Serve Gewürz chilled.

1967****—This is mostly a
historical note, for this wine is
probably gone physically and
spiritually: that is, no longer
physically available, and even
if so, past its peak, deceased.

1968***—Likewise—see
1967.

1969 and *1970**—Some even
rate these vintages as below
average. Eschew!

1971****—This is in the
true Buena Vista tradition:
marvelous flavor and spice.

1972 Regular: *

1972 and *1973 Haraszthy
Cabinet*****—Very flavorful,
both have a touch of sweetness.

Golden Cream Sherry** Fair
value, ca. $3.

Green Hungarian** to ***
Rather surprisingly, this is one
of Buena Vista's most popular
wines, though it's been quite
variable. Many vintages have
been solidly ***, but some recent ones (notably '71) have
merited ** or less. Green
Hungarian is a small white
wine, usually appreciated by

wine novices; it's crisp, light, on the dry side. Serve it, chilled, with pork, veal, fish. Drink it young: within two years of purchase. Fair value, $2.75 to $3.

Grenache Rosé** and **Zinfandel Rosé**** Buena Vista's strong on rosés: they make three different ones, each from a different grape: the Cabernet Rosé (see), and these two. The Grenache Rosé is the lowest priced (ca. $2.50) of the three; it has a slightly bitter edge. Beginning wine drinkers will not be wild about it. The Zinfandel Rosé is a new wine, softer than the Grenache, and sells for about $3. Both these wines should be consumed within two years of purchase. Serve them chilled, wherever, whenever.

Grey Riesling** A light white wine, with a bit of spiciness to the taste. Grey Riesling is particularly popular in California and one writer suggests it—in all seriousness—for breakfast drinking if you're tired of all those old Champagne breakfasts! But as we were saying, it will go well with any light food, especially fish and seafood—even Post Toasties? Serve it chilled, and drink it young: within two years of purchase. Fair value, $2.75 to $3.

Johannisberg Riesling (formerly called **White Riesling**)******* Recent vintages have been in Buena Vista's best tradition: fragrant, tasty, dry white wine, with good, lingering aftertaste. Serve it chilled, with pork, ham, veal, fish (especially salmon). Fair value, $4 to $4.50.

Lachryma Montis*** It means "Tears of the Mountain," if that's any help. It's a blended red wine, a Claret type—the

formula is the winery's secret. Only two batches have been made: 1967, now sold out, and 1973, which won't be released until 1978. It sold for about $5 the first time around. If you happen to own the '67, it should be at the top of its form about now, but don't keep it much longer. Use it, enjoy it as you would their Cabernet Sauvignon (above).

Pinot Chardonnay Buena Vista has steadily improved this wine over the past decade—if this continues, by 1985 it's going to be in the heavenly heights, with **** stars ***** all over the place. Like most of Buena Vista's better wines, this one is 100 percent of the named grape, in this case, Pinot Chardonnay. This is the exception rather than the rule in California, as the law requires only that the wine be at least 51 percent of the named grape variety. Pinot Chardonnay is one of the world's great "noble" grapes, and it is always an expensive wine. It is the classic accompaniment for fish, shellfish, poultry, fondue. Serve chilled. There is also a Haraszthy Cabinet (in red on the front label) special bottling in the best years, when "conditions are perfect," says the winery. It costs $1 more and is usually worth the difference.

1966 and *1967*—Not recommended. Both of these wines placed dead last in several tastings. One critic said the '67 had a "skunky off-nose" caused by "funky redwood." Offhand, that sounds a bit ominous.

1968*** An improvement over '66 and '67. Drink now, soon!

1969*** Drink through 1975.

1971**** Best drinking, 1975 through 1977.

1972**** At its best, 1975 through 1978.

Pinot Noir Pinot Noir is the best "Burgundy" California produces—it is always better (and more expensive) than those wines labeled simply "Burgundy." But hardly any California winery is ever wholly consistent with its Pinot Noir, for it is a difficult grape. Buena Vista's recent vintages have, however, been remarkably consistent, the 1967, 1968, and 1969 all meriting at least ***, and some would confer **** upon the '67. All three wines are good drinking right now and will remain at their best at least through 1977. Pinot Noir may be sipped on its own with cheeses and fruit, or it may accompany poultry, veal, egg dishes, or that great Burgundian classic, Boeuf Bourguignon.

Rose Brook: See CABERNET ROSÉ.

Sherry: See GOLDEN CREAM SHERRY; ULTRA DRY SHERRY.

Ultra Dry Sherry** It's not all that dry. Fair value, $2.50 to $2.75.

White Riesling: See JOHANNISBERG RIESLING.

Zinfandel Buena Vista made the first Zinfandel in history more than one hundred years ago, and they're not about to relinquish their headstart. They've always made exceptional Zinfandel, as a long series of gold medals will attest. Many years it's made in two grades, a "regular," a good value at about $3, and a "Cask" bottling at $5. Zinfandel can accompany almost any food, but it seems to show off to its best with poultry, pasta, veal, pork. Serve at cool room temperature.

1966* Below Buena Vista's standards; drink immediately.

1967 (Regular)***—Cask 140: **** Drink soon.

1968 (Regular)**—Cask 160: **** Best drinking, 1975 through 1978.

1969*** At its best, 1975 through 1979.

1970 and *1971**** Best drinking, 1975–1980.

Zinfandel Rosé: See GRENACHE ROSÉ.

BULLY HILL WINE CO. (Hammondsport, N.Y.) The word for Bully Hill is unique— unique wines from unique grapes in a unique area, by a unique man. The wines have strange-sounding names: Seyval Blanc, Chelois Noir: they're mainly from French-American hybrid vines, 1,000 feet above Keuka Lake in central New York State, grown in rocky, infertile soil, in the most inhospitable of climates. And the man who makes these wines is Walter S. Taylor, a rebel from the giant Taylor Wine Company, founded by and named for his own grandfather.

Taylor boasts that he adds no water and no California wine to his wines. Further, they're all estate-bottled and vintage-dated. Taylor is particularly proud of the fact that he has virtually eliminated the well-known musky or foxy taste from these New York wines. Wine, says Taylor, is an art form, and "a product is an extension of a person's soul." Breathes there a man who would not drink a glass of wine to that?

Bully Hill wine is not cheap, however; you won't find a single bottle under $3. But if you're looking for inexpensive eastern wines, look to Taylor— if you're seeking higher quality, or vinous adventures, look to Taylor's grandson's wines at Bully Hill.

Aurora Blanc*** The name is that of the hybrid grape from which the wine is made—and it's 100 percent of that grape, not a mere 51 percent as required by law. This tasty white wine has no trace of foxiness; it's on the dry side, with just a touch of sweetness. It's flavorful enough for idle sipping of an evening, or to accompany light foods. Drink it young, within five years of its vintage date. Serve chilled.

Baco Noir The Baco Noir is a hybrid grape, half French and half-native American. So with this red wine made therefrom: it's somewhat like a French Claret and still has the slightest hint of native muskiness.

It may have some natural sediment crystals; no harm—just decant (which see). Serve this wine as you would a good Claret: with fine cuts of beef or lamb, or savor it by itself, or with bread and cheese. Serve at cool room temperature. Fair value, $3.60.

1970, 1971*** Will be at their best, 1975 through 1980.

Bully Hill Red: See RED WINE.

Bully Hill Rosé: See ROSÉ WINE.

Bully Hill White: See WHITE WINE.

Chancellor Noir*** The name comes from the grapes from which this red table wine is made. The winery boasts that it is European in style and flavor—rather like a light Burgundy. It will go well with grilled meats, pasta. It will keep well for at least eight years beyond its vintage date. Serve at cool room temperature, after one hour's breathing time. Fair value, $3.70.

Chelois Noir*** This dry red table wine is a blend of a number of different grapes, the Chelois Noir grape comprising only 55 percent of the *cuvée*. It's vaguely European in taste and is recommended to accompany red meats, hearty casseroles, stews, pasta. If there's any sediment present, don't panic, it's quite natural—stand it upright for twenty-four hours, then decant. Serve at cool room temperature. Fair value, $3.40.

Delaware*** The Delaware is a small red grape which comprises 92 percent of this good little white wine. The label boasts that it has a "fine *Native* taste." It has a vinous taste all its own. Check for sediment crystals—they're quite all right—and if present, stand the bottle upright for twenty-four hours and then decant. Serve chilled. Fair value, $4.30.

Diamond*** Another white wine from one of America's native grapes, the Diamond. The winery says proudly that the wine has a "fine *Native* taste." It's a clean, fresh little wine, fine to accompany fish, seafood, pork, ham, veal. Drink it young: within four or five years of its vintage date. Serve chilled. Fair value, $4.30.

Red Wine It takes an honest winemaker to call his wine by such an unpretentious name as this. Bully Hill also makes a rosé and a white. The winery says this wine can compare with the best French Château wines—well, now . . . But it is a soft, well-made wine, with a Bordeaux-kind of flavor. There's no foxiness at all. Air it one to two hours. It's ready to drink when purchased and will improve with two or three years of added bottle age.

1967*** Drink now and through the decade.

1968* At its best, present to 1978.

1969*** Best drinking, 1975 through 1980.

1970** Will be at its best, 1975–1980. Fair or not, it sells for ca. $6.70—per fifth, not gallon.

1971*** Best drinking, 1975 through the decade.

Rosé Wine, 1971** Only this one vintage has been made so far; it's light and fresh, with just a hint of muskiness—some will find that a plus, not a minus. It's quite inaccurate to say, as the winery does, that it's "far superior to the best European rosé." Drink soon. Fair value, $3.25.

Seyval Blanc*** The name is that of the French-American hybrid grape from which this tasty white wine is produced. The winery says that its flavor is similar to that of the Chardonnay, the noble grape of France's white Burgundies. The taste is definitely European, not native American; it's light and fruity. It's especially suited to accompany fish and seafood. It will be at its best from three to six years after its vintage date. If there is any sediment, it's okay, a sign of a good wine; stand it upright for twenty-four hours, then decant. Fair value, $3.50.

White Wine*** A very slightly sweet dinner wine, a happy combination of native American grapes with French-American hybrid grapes. It's soft, quite fragrant, will go well with all light foods, especially poultry, fish, seafood, pork, and ham. Bully Hill is not going to be 1 aking any more of this

wine, however—at least under this name. '71 was the last vintage. Serve it chilled. Fair value, $3.25.

BURGUNDY The name "Burgundy" is the widest and often the most meaningless name in all the world of wine. It can mean anything from a heavenly, very expensive red wine from Burgundy, France, which many consider the finest red wine in the world, to a flat, phony, sugared red American jug wine. (Australia and South Africa also make "Burgundy.") Strictly speaking, Burgundy can refer to either white or red wine, but when used alone, it almost always means red Burgundy.

Red Burgundy is the classic accompaniment for roasts (especially beef) and game (feathered or furred). It also goes well with braised meats, stews, beef casseroles, steaks, venison, goose. And, of course, fine Burgundy can be appreciated most of all if sipped slowly and gratefully with cheeses, fruits, nuts. It seems to be best suited to accompany Bel Paese, Cheddar, Port-Salut, Roquefort.

Burgundies six years old and over should be checked for sediment and decanted if necessary. Almost all Burgundy (except the very cheapest) will improve if allowed to breathe an hour before serving. Serve your Burgundy, French or American, at cool room temperature (65 to 72°F).

Burgundy (Red), American One of the most outrageous desecrations in all the world of wine is certainly to apply the revered name of Burgundy to some of the abominations that pass by that name in the U.S.A. These vinous horrors come in two very different styles: (1)

From California: flat, insipid, heavily filtered, sweetish "Burgundy." (2) From the eastern United States: odd-tasting red wine, near-vile "Burgundy" with distinctively musky under-, over-, and middle-tones. These are very inexpensive wines—as they ought to be. They should be free.

But the U.S. does make some respectable Burgundy—not the likes of those magnificent French aristocrats (not uncommonly $30 to $50 per bottle), but excellent wine in its own right. Remember the famous Thurber cartoon, the host proclaiming proudly as he pours for his guests: "It's a naïve domestic Burgundy without breeding, but I think you'll be amused by its presumption."

American wine that answers to the name of Pinot Noir is really America's best "Burgundy," though the name Burgundy almost never appears on the label. Many American wineries call their inexpensive red table wine, not "Burgundy," but simply "Red" or "Mountain Red," or some invented name incorporating red into the title. To all intents and purposes, these are the selfsame wines that other wineries choose to call "Burgundy," and they are included in the following list. Eastern wineries produce a number of Burgundy-type wines made from various hybrid grapes, and these are also included.

American Burgundies—
Comparative Standings
****
Very Good
  Beaulieu Burgundy, 1970, 1971 ($2.75)
  Souverain Burgundy ($3.75)
  Sebastiani Burgundy, 1967 ($3.85)

Beaulieu Burgundy, 1968 Special Bottling ($6)
***
Good
  Winemaster's Guild Burgundy ($1.40)
  Pedroncelli Sonoma Red ($1.60)
  Sebastiani Mountain Burgundy ($1.80)
  Concannon Red Dinner Wine ($1.90)
  Pedroncelli Burgundy ($2)
  Great Western Baco Noir Burgundy ($2.05)
  Simi North Coast Burgundy ($2.10)
  Martini Mountain Red ($2.15)
  Christian Brothers Burgundy ($2.25)
  Kenwood Burgundy, 1971 ($2.25)
  Novitiate Burgundy ($2.25)
  Inglenook Vintage Burgundy ($2.30)
  Masson Baroque ($2.30)
  Sonoma (or Windsor) Burgundy ($2.30)
  Charles Krug Burgundy ($2.35)
  Beringer Burgundy ($2.40)
  Martini Mountain Burgundy ($2.40)
  Oakville Our House Red ($2.40)
  Sebastiani Burgundy ($2.40)
  Sutter Home Burgundy ($2.40)
  Assumption Abbey Dido Noir ($2.50)
  Beaulieu Burgundy, 1969 ($2.75)
  Buena Vista Burgundy ($2.75)
  Mirassou Burgundy ($2.85)
  Bynum Nouveau Burgundy ($3)
  Heitz Burgundy ($3.35)
  Bully Hill Chelois Noir ($3.40)
  Bully Hill Chancellor Noir ($3.70)

Bully Hill Red Wine, 1967, 1969, 1971 ($4.75 at least)

**

Fair

Royal Host Burgundy ($1.05)

Cribari Burgundy ($1.20)

Valle de Oro Red ($1.30)

Gallo Burgundy ($1.35)

Roma Burgundy ($1.35)

Italian Swiss Colony Burgundy ($1.40)

Gallo Hearty Burgundy ($1.45)

Sonoma (or Windsor) Red ($1.50)

Los Hermanos Mountain Red ($1.60)

San Martin Mountain Burgundy ($1.60)

C. K. Mondavi Burgundy ($1.65)

Weibel Classic Burgundy ($1.65)

Napa-Sonoma-Mendocino Burgundy ($1.70)

Almadén Mountain Red Burgundy ($1.75)

Bynum Barefoot Burgundy ($1.90)

Inglenook Navalle Burgundy ($1.90)

Korbel Mountain Burgundy ($1.90)

Eleven Cellars Burgundy ($2)

Pinard Red ($2)

San Martin Burgundy ($2)

Almadén Burgundy ($2.10)

Cresta Blanca Mountain Burgundy ($2.10)

Taylor Lake Country Red ($2.10)

Widmer Naples Valley Red ($2.10)

Kenwood Burgundy, 1970 ($2.25)

Korbel Burgundy ($2.40)

Bargetto Burgundy ($2.50)

Concannon Burgundy ($2.50)

Beringer Barenblut ($2.75)

Bully Hill Red Wine, 1970 ($6.65)

*

Passable

Franzia Burgundy ($1.20)

Franzia Robust Burgundy ($1.25)

Parducci Burgundy ($2.75)

Not recommended

J. Pierrot Burgundy

Gold Seal Burgundy

Taylor Burgundy

Burgundy, French Alec Waugh, the English novelist and wine buff, once wrote: "At the age of twenty I believed that the first duty of a wine was to be red, the second that it should be Burgundy. During forty years I have lost faith in much, but not in that."

Most experts would agree at least in this, that over all, the world's greatest wines are red, not white. Red wines have more breadth and depth, more complexity of flavor, nuances, and subtleties of bouquet and aroma. And it is for this reason, incidentally, that beginners in wine invariably come to appreciate white wines first, but inevitably end up preferring the more complex reds.

If the further question is asked, as it inevitably is: Who makes the world's best red wines, one would have to answer, for fear of being struck dead on the spot: France. It would be much more difficult, however, to specify whether the world's best red comes from France's Burgundy or Bordeaux region. Both have their champions among experts and consumers alike.

Those who would vote for Burgundy point to its silky softness, its breed and distinction, its complexity of flavors. And all would agree that red Burgundy is easier to appreciate than red Bordeaux. Suffice it to say that red Burgundy is among the world's very finest red wines.

Here are some of the best, listed in vaguely descending order of excellence, but note that even those wines at the very bottom of this listing are still fine wines and relatively expensive. Note also that this list is necessarily an overview, an oversimplification if you will, but designed solely for wine novices, as a starting point: (Le) Chambertin; Romanée-Conti; Chambertin Clos de Beze; (Les) Richebourg; (La) Tache; (Le) Musigny; Clos de Vougeot; (Le) Corton; (La) Romanée; (Les) Grands-Echézeaux; Bonnes Mares; Romanée-Saint-Vivant; (Les) Echézeaux; Corton Clos du Roi; Clos de Tart; Charmes-Chambertin; Corton Grancey; (Les) Caillerets; (Le) Clos des Mouches; Pommard; Gevrey-Chambertin; Vosne-Romanée; Chambolle-Musigny; Morey-Saint-Denis; Aloxe-Corton; Nuits-Saint-Georges; Savigny-les-Beaune; Santenay; Volnay; Mercurey; Rully; Givry; Beaune; Côte de Beaune-Villages.

Note that all of these wines are individually assessed in this book under their proper names.

Burgundy, White When you see the name "Burgundy" alone, it always means red Burgundy. But, strictly speaking, "Burgundy" means simply a wine from Burgundy, France—and that can be red or white.

White Burgundy is a very elegant wine, clean, dry, exquisitely balanced. Most experts say simply that it is the greatest dry white wine in the world. And very expensive, at least the best of it is, for it is in exceedingly short supply. These are some of the best, in roughly descending order of excellence: (Le) Montrachet; Chevalier-Montrachet; Bâtard-Montrachet; Bienvenu-Bâtard-Montrachet; Corton-Charlemagne; Le Cailleret (Les Demoiselles); Chassagne-Montrachet; Puligny-Montrachet; Mâcon Supérieur; Mâcon Blanc.

Only one American winery bottles a "white Burgundy"—Mirassou (see). The closest thing in the U.S. to France's white Burgundy is Pinot Chardonnay (see), with Pinot Blanc in second place.

White Burgundy should be served chilled. It is the classic vinous complement to fish (especially the blander varieties: bass, flounder, halibut) and shellfish; it is also well suited to accompany sweetbreads, veal, pâté, fowl, pork, and ham, as well as pasta with a fish sauce.

BYASS, GONZALEZ: See GONZALEZ BYASS.

BYNUM WINERY (Albany, Calif.) Here's a homely little winery virtually in downtown Oakland, a most unlikely place for a winery. Yet the wines are likely and likable. The grapes come from some of California's choicest locations, the Napa and Sonoma valleys. L. Davis Bynum, owner and winemaker, says his goal is to produce the best possible line of everyday drinking wine. He's well on his way. Production, however, is somewhat erratic, wines coming and going. There's no guarantee that you'll be able to find all—or any—of the wines listed below—but stay with it, they'll show up sometime, somewhere. All Bynum wines, unless otherwise noted, are for "now" consumption, and don't keep them more than a year or two.

Amber Dry Sherry***

Barbera*** Lovely, young, soft red wine, with definite sweetness. Fine with hamburgers, steaks, stews, Italian food, even Mexican dishes, if not overly incendiary. Serve at cool room temperature. Fair value, $3.25. Air one hour.

Barefoot Burgundy** and *** (see text) Bynum makes a series of Barefoot wines—the name tells you they're designed for the peasantry, the *descamisados* (shirtless) and barefoot ones. And they're good wines for the money. Per se they would merit only **, but penny-wise, they deserve at least ***. Ideal hamburger wine for everyday consumption. Serve at cool room temperature. A good value at $1.90.

Barefoot Chablis** Light and fresh—no big deal but a good everyday white—serve chilled, with fish, seafood, light dishes. Fair value, $1.90.

Barefoot Zinfandel*** The best of Bynum's Barefoots . . . Barefeet? Reminiscent of the man ordering a pair of mongooses . . . not knowing the plural form, he wired: "Send one mongoose. P.S. Send another mongoose." Apart from that, this wine will go marvelously well with your grilled hamburgers, barbecued fowl, spareribs, pasta, stew. A very good value at $1.90.

Burgundy, Nouveau*** Light, young, fresh. The name Nouveau tells you it's new wine, to be drunk very young: within six months of purchase. Serve at cool room tempera-

ture, or slightly chilled. Fair value $3.

Cabernet Sauvignon*** Bynum's most expensive wine ($5 at the winery), Cabernet Sauvignon is always costly, the grapes being among the world's most expensive. Save this for your best steaks or that roast leg of lamb. Serve at cool room temperature.

Charbono*** A rarely-made Italian-type red wine, rich, rather heavy-bodied, flavorful. Perfect with spaghetti or lasagna. Serve at cool room temperature.

Port: See TAWNY PORT.

Rosé** Bynum makes a half dozen different rosés, all very acceptable, particularly the Cabernet Rosé, the Petite Sirah Rosé, and the Zinfandel Rosé. Rosés are eminently adaptable: they can function as aperitif wines, as with-dinner wine, or postprandially, even with a not-too-sweet dessert. Serve chilled.

Sauvignon Blanc, 1973—*** It won a silver medal at the 1974 Los Angeles County Fair.

Sherry, Amber Dry: See AMBER DRY SHERRY.

Tawny Port**

Zinfandel and Zinfandel Reserve**** This may be the best of Bynum's current wines. It's soft, with good varietal character. It goes with most good food; some say its happiest setting is with chicken and pasta. Fair value for the "straight" Zinfandel, $2.25; for the Reserve, $3.50.

C

CABERNET You will rarely be finding this name by itself on a bottle of American wine—it will almost always be either Cabernet Sauvignon or Ruby Cabernet. But if you do find it alone, be cautioned that it means Ruby Cabernet, a lesser wine, not the noble Cabernet Sauvignon.

Some countries, such as Chile and Australia, export a plain Cabernet to the U.S., and it will usually have both Cabernet Sauvignon and Cabernet Franc (a lesser French grape) in its bloodstream, though the latter will usually predominate.

CABERNET ROSÉ A California rosé wine made primarily from Cabernet grapes. It ranks as one of California's finest rosés; it is usually on the dry side. Simi and Buena Vista make two of the best. For a complete listing—there are only a half dozen—see the "Comparative Standings" under ROSÉ.

CABERNET SAUVIGNON Twenty years ago not one American in fifty knew the name Cabernet Sauvignon. Today, whatever the exact statistic, a mighty horde, counted in the many millions, knows that it stands for America's finest red wine. It's easy to see the reason for today's acclaim: this is the noble grape that accounts for the lordly red wines of Bordeaux: Château Lafite, Château Latour, Château Mou-

ton, and the rest of those towering giants.

The Cabernet Sauvignon grape behaves variously in the two different climes, California and Bordeaux, producing two different and distinct wines, similar, indeed, but each great in its own right. Also, the Cabernet grape is always blended with other "softer" grapes in Bordeaux—sometimes up to 50 percent—in the U.S. this is much less often the case, and, in fact, many of America's finest Cabernet Sauvignons are entirely composed of that grape. The Cabernet Sauvignon grape produces hard, very tannic wines, extremely long-lived—it takes decades for them to soften and realize their full potential. This makes California Cabernet one of the world's most durable wines. It is almost always drunk too young—and that's a cryin' shame—for only when it is full of years does it reach its full stature of grace and perfection. This makes Cabernet Sauvignon the wine par excellence for laying down. Buy a case or two (or twenty or thirty, wheee!) every year, and simply forget, for the next five or ten years, that you own them. You'll be magnificently rewarded and bless the name of this book forevermore!

Cabernet Sauvignon is usually drinkable after four or five years, but only the softer blended versions (such as Chris-

46

tian Brothers' and Sebastiani's) should be consumed before they are ten years old. Many Cabernets should not be opened until they are fifteen to twenty years old, some even longer. (Note that maturing dates are invariably given for individual bottles in this book.)

Cabernet Sauvignon is in short supply in the U.S. today, especially the very best of it. Hopefully the situation will soon improve, as there have been extensive plantings of the grape in the West over the past several years. In the meantime, however, you'll often have to search it out.

California's Cabernet Sauvignon at its best has a very distinctive and complex taste—as all great wines do. Some liken it to the taste of tea, others compare it to herbs, many say it tastes of the forest or of eucalyptus, or of cedar wood, reminding one of the aroma of a cigar box. Take your pick. All agree on one thing: Cabernet Sauvignon tastes good—like a great wine should.

This is precisely the kind of wine you will want to reserve for some special occasion—somebody said it's for first-class meat and first-class guests. Like its French counterpart, Claret, it is the classic accompaniment for the finer cuts of beef, turkey, lamb, and mutton; it also shows nobly in concert with stews, pâté, innards. But the finest bottles of Cabernet Sauvignon may clamor not to be consumed amid the myriad distractions of the dining room, but to be savored, drop by precious drop, lovingly, pensively, gratefully, with fruit, or nuts, or cheeses. These cheeses in particular: Brie, Cheddar, Munster, Pont l'Eveque, Port-

Salut, Roquefort, Stilton, Valençay.

Serve Cabernet at cool room temperature, 65 to 72°F.

All of California's finest Cabernet Sauvignons are listed in this book, vintage by vintage, bottle by bottle, under the name of the winery.

Listed below are America's foremost Cabernet Sauvignons, in descending order of excellence. Where wines have the same rating, the least expensive is listed first. Prices are approximate.

California Cabernet Sauvignons —Comparative Standings

Near-Classic
    Heitz Martha's Vineyard, 1968 ($27)
    Beaulieu Private Reserve, 1941 and 1951 ($50)

*****

Exceptional
    Souverain, 1968 ($7)
    Beaulieu Regular Bottling, 1969 ($7.50)
    Beaulieu Regular Bottling, 1970 ($7.50)
    Oakville Reserve (Unfiltered), 1970 ($7.50)
    Charles Krug Vintage Selection, 1966 ($8)
    Chappellet, 1970 ($9)
    Mayacamas Cabernet Sauvignon ($10)
    Heitz Napa Valley, 1968 ($11.75)
    Mirassou "Second Harvest," 1967 ($13)
    Beaulieu Private Reserve, 1966 ($14)
    Robert Mondavi, 1969 ($15)
    Beaulieu Private Reserve, 1968 ($15)
    Ridge, 1968 and 1969 ($15)
    Heitz Martha's Vineyard, 1966 ($17)
    Beaulieu Private Reserve, 1964 ($18)

*****

Exceptional

The following are "priceless" bottles—wines for which it is impossible to determine a specific price, as they are too old or too much in demand, and usually both. All are collectors' items. You will probably pay even more for these following than for those listed directly above, with exactly the same rating. They are listed in alphabetical order.

Beaulieu Private Reserve, 1947, 1958, 1960, 1962

Fetzer, Cask 19, 1968

Inglenook, 1959, 1968, Cask No. 12

Charles Krug, 1960, 1964, 1965, all Vintage Selection

Martini, 1947, and Special Selection, 1960

Souverain, 1961

Spring Mountain, 1968–69 Marriage

****

Very Good

Pedroncelli, 1970 ($3.50)

Christian Brothers—It occasionally rates **** (see text p. 74) ($3.55)

Sutter Home, 1971 ($4)

Beaulieu Regular Bottling, 1971 ($4)

Charles Krug, 1970 ($4.50)

Simi, 1970 ($4.50)

Sterling, 1969 ($4.50)

Parducci, 1970 ($4.60)

Ste Michelle, 1969 ($4.75)

Beringer, 1970 ($5)

Fetzer, 1968, 1970, 1971 ($5, current vintage)

Heitz, Lot 62-65 ($5)

Llords and Elwood, Casks 1-121, and Cuvée 4, Cuvée 7 ($5, current vintage)

Paul Masson, Pinnacles Selection, No. 943 ($5)

Parducci, 1969 ($5)

Buena Vista, 1965, 1967, 1968 ($6)

Robert Mondavi, 1971 ($6)

Oakville, 1970 ("Plain") ($6)

Pedroncelli, 1967 ($6)

Sebastiani, Bin 32 ($6)

Souverain, 1969 ($6)

Sonoma (or Windsor), 1970 ($6.25)

Inglenook, Cask Bottlings 1969, 1970 ($6.50)

Freemark Abbey, 1969 ($7)

Beaulieu Private Reserve, 1969 ($7)

Robert Mondavi, 1970 ($7)

Parducci, Talmage, 1969, and Philo, Cask 33 ($7)

Sebastiani, Bin 34 ($7)

Spring Mountain, 1970 ($7.25)

Beringer, 1969 ($7.50)

Concannon, Limited Bottling, 1964, 1965, 1967, 1968 ($7.50 for current vintage)

Souverain 1970 ($7.50)

Freemark Abbey, Bosche, 1968 ($8)

Inglenook, 1967 ($8)

Heitz Napa Valley, 1969 ($8.25)

Oakville, 1968 ($9)

Beaulieu Regular Bottling, 1968 ($9)

Beaulieu Regular Bottling, 1965 ($9.50)

Chappellet, 1969 ($10)

Heitz, Martha's Vineyard, 1967 ($10.50)

Beaulieu Private Reserve, 1967 ($11)

Heitz, Martha's Vineyard, 1969 ($12.60)

Chappellet, 1968 ($15)

Beaulieu Private Reserve, 1965 ($15)

Simi, 1935 ($37.50)

****

Very Good

It is impossible to set a specific price for the following wines. All are collectors' items. Note that they have exactly the same rating as those listed directly above, and these will probably be even more expensive than those above, as they are mainly older and scarcer.

Beaulieu Regular Bottling, 1966, 1967
Beaulieu Private Reserve, 1963
Heitz, 1965, 1966 (both Regular Bottlings)
Inglenook, Cask G-24, 1964
Louis Martini, 1951, 1952, 1968
Martin Ray, 1966 and 1968

***

Good

Martini, 1969, 1970 ($3.50)
Paul Masson ($3.50)
San Martin ($3.50)
Christian Brothers ($3.55)
Weibel ($3.60)
Korbel ($3.85)
Novitiate ($4)
Ste Michelle, 1968 ($4)
Sonoma (or Windsor) ($4)
Simi ($4.05)
Sebastiani ($4.25)
Davis Bynum ($5)
Freemark Abbey, 1967, 1968 ($5)
Kenwood ($5)
Mirassou, 1971 ($5)
Paul Masson, Pinnacles Selection ($5)
Llords and Elwood, Cuvée 5, Cuvée 6 ($5)
Pedroncelli, 1968, 1969 ($5)
Mayacamas, 1968 ($7.50)

**

Fair

Almadén ($3)
Eleven Cellars ($3.20)
Cresta Blanca ($3.65)
Parducci, 1968 ($4.50)
Mirassou, 1970 ($5.25)

*

Passable

Concannon, 1966 ($7.50)

Not Recommended:

Martin Ray, 1953, 1964

See also: CLARET, AMERICAN.

CABINET: See KABINETT.

CADET, MOUTON: See MOUTON CADET.

(LE) CAILLERET (or: CLOS au CAILLERET—or: LES DEMOISELLES) The great vineyards of Chevalier (the Gentleman) and Les Demoiselles (the Young Women) are adjacent, and there were so many bad jokes on the subject that the name now usually used is Le Cailleret. They said the bad jokes were turning the wine to vinegar. Under either name, here's a fine dry white wine, one of the best of all France. It's at its best when it's four to seven years old. It goes well with light foods (chicken, veal, fish, pork), but it's so good it deserves to be appreciated on its own, or with simple cheeses and bread.

1966 Joseph Drouhin: *****
Now at its best.

1969 Joseph Drouhin—Near-Classic.

1970 Bouchard (Les Demoiselles): *****

Current vintages sell for around $11.50. How to serve it: See under MONTRACHET.

(LES) CAILLERETS: See VOLNAY.

CAIRANNE: See CÔTES DU RHONE.

CALIFORNIA WINE ASSOCIATION: See ELEVEN CELLARS, GREYSTONE, VINO FINO.

CALON-SÉGUR, CHÂTEAU Officially this red Bordeaux wine (Claret) has a middle ranking, but most experts say it deserves better. It's a powerful wine, full-bodied yet soft, and above all, it's consistent, perhaps never rising to the very heights, but never descending to the depths either. Fine wine such as this deserves to be appreciated on its own merits, not in competition with a meal, though Calon-Ségur will go admirably with beef or lamb. But it goes even better with just cheese, bread, fruit, nuts. Serve it at cool room temperature.

1948, 1949—*****—Just now at their best—Fair value, $15.

1955—****—Fair value, $12 —Now at its best.

1959—*****—Best drinking, 1975–1985.

1961—*****—Best drinking, 1977 on.

1962—****—Now at its best—Fair value, if only your wine merchant will recognize it: $10.

1966—****—Best drinking, 1976–1980—Fair value, $15.

1968—Not recommended.

1970—*****—Don't touch it until at least 1980.

CALVET An important shipper of French wines, one of the largest, though their wines are not as widely seen in the U.S. as, say, those of Cruse and Sichel. Calvet was founded in 1823, and like all such large and established wine firms, it is a name that can be trusted, though Calvet's wines, like everybody else's, can vary widely. Calvet deals predominently in the more economical wines of Burgundy and Bordeaux. Look up your particular wine under its proper name.

CALWA CHAMPAGNES* Calwa stands for the California Wine Association, a giant cooperative with headquarters in San Francisco. They make four different bubblies under this label: White Champagne, Pink Champagne, Sparkling Burgundy, Cold Duck. They are neither better nor worse than other California sparklers in this lowly price range of around $2. If you want something that drinks easy, looks and sounds festive, but you hate wine, this may well be your special beverage.

CAMBAS RODITYS*** This is a rosé from, of all places, Greece. And, lo, it's a nice little wine—no superlatives, just nice. There's a touch of sweetness; it sells for the not unseemly price of $3. How to serve rosés: See under ROSÉ.

CAPPELLA RED TABLE WINE: See ITALIAN SWISS COLONY.

CAPPELLINI, LUIGI: See VERRAZZANO.

CARIGNANE (or: CARIGNAN) This is one of the most widely grown grapes in all of California, but you'll rarely find it on a wine label. The reason is because it's a lowly, prolific grape used almost wholly in blends, especially Burgundy (red). It's distinctly undistinctive, but a few California wineries have recently begun to bottle it on its own, and with some success. In general, Carignane should be served as you would a California Burgundy: with red meats, hearty casseroles, pasta, most everyday fare. Serve it at cool room temperature, 65 to 72°F.

Here are California's Carignanes in descending order of excellence: **** Bruce Carignan ($4.50); *** Oakville Grand Carignane ($3.25); *** Ridge Carignane, 1971 ($3.65); *** Fetzer Carmine Carignane ($2.50); ** Simi Carignane ($2.85).

CASAL GARCIA VINHO VERDE*** This is one of the most popular table wines in all of Portugal—and those Portuguese love their table wines—they have about one twentieth the population of the U.S. and drink three times as much wine! That's in toto, not per capita! How to serve Vinho Verde: See under VINHO VERDE.

CASAL MENDES VINHO VERDE* Fresh, young, frizzy white wine from Portugal—delightful summer refreshment. How to serve it: See under VINHO VERDE.

CASTILLO YGAY: See MARQUÉS DE MURRIETA.

CATAWBA A *New Yorker* cartoon some years ago showed a husband saying to his wife at a cocktail party: "You mean you *knew* they were going to serve sparkling catawba juice?" It never has gone over very well at cocktail parties—not even sparkling Catawba wine. But it was the first commercial sparkling wine produced in America, and it was one of the first American wines to win an international award, in Vienna, in 1873. But Catawba wine has lost considerable ground in the intervening decades. Only a handful of American wineries, all of them in the eastern U.S., make it today.

Catawba is an unabashedly "foxy" wine—and that will delight some, distress most. For the former, listed below are America's most prominent Catawbas, in descending order of excellence. The stars should probably be awarded *conditionally,* the condition being that you appreciate the native Catawba flavor: *** Gold Seal Catawba (pink, red, or white) ($1.75); *** Widmer Sweet Catawba ($2.25); ** Meier's Sweet Catawba ($2); ** Great Western Pink Catawba ($2).

CEPA DE ORO* A pale golden wine from Spain's Rioja region, as tasty as it is pretty. It's made by the Bodegas Bilbainas, a very reputable firm. This is a delightfully balanced wine— meaning just the right proportion of sweetness and acidity. Many of Spain's white wines are hard and dull—not this one. A good value at $3.25. How to serve it: See under RIOJA.

CHABLIS One of the world's great white wines—France makes the best and the only really authentic Chablis. America makes the most and the cheapest, but some of it is good. Australia and South Africa also make Chablis. Classically and historically, Chablis accompanies oysters, but it also goes well with other seafood, fish, ham, pork, or any light food such as fowl, sandwiches, chicken salad, mild Chinese food, or mild white cheeses, especially Feta. Serve Chablis, French or American, chilled, 45 to 50°F.

CHABLIS, AMERICAN Many a Frenchman will cringe—or explode—at this heading, American Chablis, but the fact remains that Americans make a lot of wine they choose to call Chablis. For good or ill. And a lot of it is for ill. *Some* of it is totally nondescript— *most* of it bears not the faintest resemblance to French Chablis —*none* of it is really like the French wine. None of this is to say that American Chablis is all poor wine—it is only to say that it is not French Chablis and it is rarely even like it.

But some American Chablis can be fine wine in its own right, and you'll enjoy it even more when you consider the price, for American Chablis is almost always inexpensive.

American Chablis is the white counterpart of American Burgundy, and when it is right, it is clean, dry, crisp, tasty. It usually has just a tinge of sweetness, except the very cheapest (mainly from California's hot Central Valley) which has more than just a tinge.

A number of American wineries make an unpretentious white wine which they market simply as "White" or "Mountain White" or some similar nomenclature. Such names are a lot more honest than "Chablis," "Sauterne," and "Rhine." These "whites" are very similar to what goes to market as Chablis—it would often take a lucky expert or an angel from heaven to distinguish between them. These "whites" are included in the "Standings" below.

American Chablis— Comparative Standings

Listed here, in descending order of excellence, are America's best Chablis. Where wines have the same rating, the least expensive is listed first. Prices are approximate.

****

Very good
  Heitz Chablis ($3)

***

Good
  Gallo Chablis Blanc ($1.50)
  Pedroncelli Sonoma White ($1.65)
  C. K. Mondavi Chablis ($1.70)
  Almadén Mountain White Chablis ($1.75)
  Gold Seal Catawba White ($1.75)
  Pedroncelli Chablis ($2)
  Sutter Home Chablis ($2)
  San Martin Petite Chablis ($2)
  Simi Chablis ($2.10)
  Beringer Chablis ($2.15)
  Martini Mountain White ($2.15)
  Wente Chablis ($2.15)
  Christian Brothers Chablis ($2.20)
  Boordy Blumchen (or: Boordyblümchen) ($2.25)
  Martini Mountain Chablis ($2.25)

Charles Krug Chablis ($2.35)
  Oakville Our House White ($2.40)
  Korbel Sonoma Blanc ($2.45)
  Concannon Chablis ($2.50)
  Beaulieu Chablis ($2.70)
  Mirassou Chablis ($2.85)
  Bully Hill White Wine ($3)
  Bully Hill Aurora Blanc ($3.10)
  Bully Hill Seyval Blanc ($3.15)
  Boordy "Five-Two-Seven-Six" ($3.70)
  Bully Hill Diamond ($4.30)

**

Fair
  Franzia Chablis ($1.25)
  Valle de Oro White ($1.25)
  Franzia Chablis Blanc ($1.35)
  Italian Swiss Colony Chablis ($1.35)
  Winemaster's Gold Chablis ($1.35)
  Sonoma (or Windsor) White ($1.50)
  Los Hermanos Mountain White Chablis ($1.60)
  La Mont Chablis (French Colombard Blend) ($1.70)
  Napa-Sonoma-Mendocino Chablis ($1.70)
  Sebastiani Mountain Chablis ($1.80)
  Royal Host Gold ($1.85)
  Bynum Barefoot Chablis ($1.90)
  Korbel Mountain Chablis ($1.95)
  Eleven Cellars Chablis ($2)
  Great Western Chablis ($2)
  Masson Chablis ($2)
  Pinard Blanc ($2)
  Cresta Blanca Mountain Chablis ($2.10)
  Taylor Lake Country White ($2.10)
  Korbel Chablis ($2.25)
  Gold Seal Chablis Nature ($2.30)
  Inglenook Vintage Chablis ($2.30)
  Souverain Chablis ($2.30)

Widmer Delaware ($2.30)
Widmer Moore's Diamond ($2.30)
Widmer Naples Valley White ($2.30)
Widmer Vergennes ($2.30)
Sonoma (or Windsor) Chablis ($2.30)
Bargetto Chablis ($2.50)
*
Passable
Tavola White ($1.20)
Roma Vino Blanco ($1.25)
Weibel Classic Chablis ($1.65)
Concannon White Dinner Wine ($1.90)
Inglenook Navalle Chablis ($2)
Great Western Diamond Chablis ($2.35)
Buena Vista Chablis ($2.50)
Parducci Chablis ($2.75)
Not recommended:
Pierrot Chablis

CHABLIS, FRENCH This great white wine is famous for its "flinty" taste and its classic association with oysters. Strictly speaking, this is the only real Chablis, and it comes from a small (2,600 acres) and carefully specified area in central France. By French law it is made only from the noble Chardonnay grape.

True French Chablis is very dry, an exquisite wine with a unique stony flavor found in no other wine. It is never cheap —there's too little of it. The very best comes from one of seven *grand crû* (great growth) vineyards, and the label will proudly so declare—it will say Chablis Grand Crû with the name of the vineyard: Blanchots; Bougros; Les Clos; Grenouilles (frogs); Les Preuses; Valmur; Vaudesir.

All of these are imported to the U.S. and will cost you $6 to $8 for current vintages. One wine writer (Hugh Johnson) says that *grand crû* Chablis tastes "important, strong, and almost immortal."

Only a notch below these great French aristocrats are the *premiers crûs* (first growths). Often it would take an expert —with divine guidance—to distinguish between them. These wines won't always have the name of a specific vineyard on the label, but they'll always say "*premier crû*." The vineyards most frequently seen in the U.S. include: Chapelot; Fourchaume; Les Fôrets; Montee de Tonnerre; Montmains; Vaillons (or: Vaillon or Côte de Vaillon).

You can expect to pay between $4 and $7 for these bottles.

"Plain" Chablis will not have the words "*grand crû*" or "*premier crû*" on the label. It will just say "Chablis" and the name of the shipper. Over all, such plain Chablis is a fine wine, though it can vary noticeably from bottle to bottle. Your only guarantee here is the name of the shipper. To play it cautiously, don't buy any "plain" Chablis (French) unless it has the name of one of these shippers on the label: B & G (Barton & Guestier); Bichot, A.; Bouchard, Père & Fils; Chanson Père & Fils; Chauvenet, F.; Drouhin, Joseph; Jadot, Louis; Jouvet, T., & Cie.; Mommessin, J.; Patriarche, Père & Fils; Piat, Père & Fils; Prince de Merode.

"Plain" Chablis will cost between $4 and $6.

Finally, there is Petit Chablis (Small Chablis), lowest-priced of all French Chablis. You're best advised to avoid it—some of it may be quite good, but it's not worth the $4 to $5 gamble. You'll do better with one of California's better Chablis (p. 52). If you want to taste Petit Chablis at its best, drop in tomorrow—or later today—to one of those little bistros on the side-streets of Paris, where you can quaff it *en carafe.*

Recent Chablis Vintages:

1966 ***** (Exceptional)— Great wines, the "perfect" Chablis, but only the big ones (*grand crû* and *premier crû*) are still with us. Even these should be consumed, 1975 and 1976. "Plain" Chablis: departed this world.

1967 *** (Good)—*Grand crû* and *premier crû:* Drink, 1975 through 1977.

1968—Forget the whole thing—miserable!

1969 **** (Very good)— Small crop (therefore expensive) but fine wines. *Grand crû* and *premier crû:* best drinking, 1975 through 1979, at least. Plain Chablis: already at peak, drink immediately.

1970 ***** (Exceptional)— Big fruity wines; they're maturing quickly. *Grand crû* and *premier crû:* best drinking, 1975 through 1978. Plain Chablis: at peak, 1975.

1971 ***** (Exceptional)— *Grand crû* and *premier crû:* best drinking, 1975 through 1980. Plain Chablis: at best, 1975–1977.

1972—Dubious at best. The wines are excessively acidic. Proceed with caution. Be sure of your vineyard and/or shipper (see above). The *grand crû* and *premier crû:* not yet ready —try, beginning in '76. Plain Chablis: drink, 1975–1978.

1973—Huge crop, but prices are still high. Wines will be light but well balanced. Plain Chablis will be ready in early

'76. It's too early to assess the quality of the vintage.

Chablis, Gold: See under the name of the winery: ITALIAN SWISS COLONY.

Chablis Grand crû: See under CHABLIS, FRENCH.

Chablis, Pink: See under the name of the winery: FRANZIA, GALLO, or ITALIAN SWISS COLONY.

Chablis Premier crû: See under CHABLIS, FRENCH.

Chablis, Ruby: See under the name of the winery: ITALIAN SWISS COLONY.

CHAIZE, CHÂTEAU DE LA: See BROUILLY.

CHALONE VINEYARD (Soledad, Calif.) The Germans say that unless the vines suffer, no great wines can be produced. If this is true, Chalone is off to a good start in the production of great wines. The tiny, isolated winery is situated at 2,000-foot elevation in the rugged Gavilan Range, near the Pinnacles National Monument. The soil is rocky and infertile; the annual rainfall, a mere eleven inches; water is hauled by truck five days a week from down the mountain; the winery equipment is mostly primitive. Evidently the Germans are right: the vines suffer, the wines prosper. Understandably, they are both scarce and expensive, but worth searching for, waiting for, praying for. The front label of each bottle proudly declares exactly how many bottles of this wine were produced, of which your bottle is number *such.*

Chardonnay Chalone makes one of California's finest Chardonnays. Indeed, "one of the world's greatest white wines," according to one critic. Traditionally, Chardonnay accompanies the finest seafood: lobster, cracked crab, abalone. Chalone's Chardonnay deserves such elegant companionship—or better. Which is to say: to be savored wholly on its own, without distraction of any kind, except from the expressed wonderment of admiring guests. Serve chilled.

1967**—This is the exception (average wine) to prove the rule (that Chalone makes great Chardonnay). The must musta been bedeviled by sinister forces.

1969*****—Drink immediately; may already be on the decline. At the time of its release it sold for $7.50.

1971***** — Another huge wine, drink it, 1975 through 1978. Price at the winery, $9.

Chenin Blanc Chalone's Chenin Blanc is different in style from what is commonly sold in California by this name. This is a decidedly dry wine, with the delightful fragrance of the French oak in which it was aged. Most California Chenin Blancs are rather flowery, with a definite sweetness. This is a much more serious wine. All Chalone wines deserve to be enjoyed in solitude—the wine in solitude (no accompanying food), not you.

1969****—Drink, 1975–1976. It sold originally for $3.50.

1970 and 1971*****—Original winery price for the '70 was $4, for the '71, $6—but both wines are nearly priceless. These are huge, rich wines. Both will be at their best, 1975–1977.

Pinot Blanc This grape, a first cousin to the illustrious Chardonnay, is widely grown in California, but not very often bottled under its own name; it usually goes into Champagne and Chablis blends. On its own it's a clean, dry, tart wine, ideal to accompany fish, shellfish, chicken, veal, pork, or ham. Chalone's is among the best in the state. Serve it chilled.

1969*****—Now at its best but won't hold forever; consume, 1975 through 1976. It sold originally for $4.50.

1970**** at least—Best drinking, 1975 through 1977. Price at the winery when released was $5.

1971****—Has an engaging *goût de terroir* (earthiness); not yet at its best; drink, 1976 through 1978. It originally sold for $5.

Pinot Chardonnay: See CHARDONNAY.

Pinot Noir, 1969***** Just recently released, if you find a bottle lying about somewhere, apprehend it! This will be a great wine, starting in 1975 and through 1985 and probably beyond. Price at the winery when released was $9.

(LE) CHAMBERTIN Here's the apex of Burgundy's great red wines. Many experts say simply that Le Chambertin is the greatest red wine in the world. This is "Le Grand Seigneur," the favorite of Napoleon. It is, of course, very scarce and extremely expensive —presuming you can find it at all. The '71 (Louis Latour) is presently selling for around $35 —that's for 24 ounces, not per case. Some bottles, however, from other parcels of the vineyard sell for considerably less. Chambertin, though it is a mere thirty-two acres, is divided among numerous growers. As great, rare, and costly as this wine is, surely no sane and sober man, no matter how wealthy, would consider drinking it to the accompaniment of earthly food, no matter how gourmet-ish. Chambertin demands to be consumed on its own, pensively, gratefully, lovingly. Great red Burgundies such as this are at their very best when they are six to ten years old, though in fine years they can live on for decades. Air Chambertin about an hour, and serve at cool room temperature.

Some vintages:

1934—Now showing its age a bit but still in marvelous condition.

1945 Ponnelle: Near-Classic —It's still in excellent condition.

1947 Ponnelle: Near-Classic —Don't hold it any longer.

1957 Heritiers Latour: Near-Classic.

1959—Tremendously successful vintage.

1961—Fantastic year.

CHAMBERTIN-CLOS DE BÈZE This may be the very best red wine in the world—or then again, it may be only the second best. Most authorities consider it exactly the same wine as the illustrious Le Chambertin (above)—the vineyards are adjacent—and indeed it could go by exactly the same name if it so chose. It is a magnificent red wine—one writer says it is a "noble" wine in the true sense of the word. Treat it—"pamper" would be better —exactly as you would Chambertin.

Some vintages:

1947—Classic vintage.

1961 Ph. Duroche: Near-Classic.

1962 Drouhin Laroze—Not highly regarded.

1964 Ph. Duroche: ****

1966 Henri de Villamont: *****

1971 Bouchard: *****

1971 Le Baron: Near-Classic.

1971 Faiveley: *****

CHAMBOLLE-MUSIGNY This is a "village" wine, as distinct from a single vineyard wine, Romanée-Conti, for example, but it can be glorious—and inevitably with good Burgundy, expensive, though not completely beyond sight. It is one of the most charming and delicate of Burgundies, goes well with beef and lamb, and has a special affinity for good cheese, fruit, nuts. Chambolle-Musigny is at its best between its third and eighth birthdays (four to nine years old). Allow it to "breathe" about an hour before you serve it at cool room temperature. It can vary widely in price, depending on the shipper—anywhere from $6 to $12.

Some vintages:

1962 Drouhin: *****—At its best now and through 1976.

1966 Drouhin: ****—Now at its peak.

1967 Amiot: ****—Now at its peak.

1969 Alexis Lichine: ***** —Now at its peak.

1971 Schroeder-Constans: *****

   Bouchard: ****

   Ponnelle: ***

   Remoissenet (Amiral Vernon): ****

   Thorin: ***

   Hudelot: ****

   Faiveley: ***

These '71 wines will be at their best, 1975–1980. The very best wines of Chambolle-Musigny, in addition to having Chambolle-Musigny on the label, will also have the name of a specific vineyard; the most important are these: Les Charmes, Les Amoureuses (see both of these, below), and Le Musigny, to be found under its own name.

CHAMBOLLE-MUSIGNY, (LES) AMOUREUSES The name means "the Women in Love" and wine writers hasten to point out that the name is most apropos, for this red Burgundy is "warm," "tender," "caressing," "lyrical." It is indeed one of the finest of all the fine red wines of France's great Côte de Nuits. How to appreciate it: See Chambolle-Musigny. Some great ones: *1949 Leroy: *****—1961 Drouhin:* Near-Classic—*1962 Roumier: *****—1964 Berthau:* *****

CHAMBOLLE-MUSIGNY, LES CHARMES Great red Burgundy wine, eclipsed by its neighbor, the illustrious Le Musigny (see). How to serve and enjoy this splendid wine: See under CHAMBOLLE-MUSIGNY.

CHAMPAGNE The name sings of celebration, joyousness, gaiety—of ships' prows and babies' christenings, too. It's the happiest name in all the world of wine. And at its best, Champagne is one of the few truly great wines of this earth, the most exquisite and delicate wine given to man in this vale of tears.

Americans are not noted as Champagne lovers and are wont to say: (1) that they don't care for Champagne; (2) that it causes mammoth hangovers. Both contentions are old wives' tales and/or bilge. On the first point, if you don't care for Champagne, it's a fair assumption that you've never been exposed to the real thing, only to some ungainly American imitation. On the second, all other things being equal—though they rarely are—the amount of hangover is in direct proportion to the total amount of alcohol consumed in a given period of time . . . no more and no less. And that's as it should be, for remember that hangovers are the special creation of the Almighty to remind wayward, self-indulgent humankind that all of God's good things are to be enjoyed in moderation—from butterflies and sunsets to alcoholic beverages and soufflés Grand Marnier.

In the very strictest sense there is only one true Champagne, and it's of French extraction. It comes only from one particular delimited area of northern France. All other sparkling wines resemble—or do not resemble!—Champagne, but call them by some other name.

In fact, most European nations do honor this severe limitation and call their sparkling wines by some other name: in Germany it's *Sekt,* in Italy, *Spumante,* in Spain, *Xampan.* Even French sparkling wines, from areas other than the Champagne district, dare not put that revered name on their label but are content with *Vin Mousseux,* "Sparkling Wine."

America is the major nonconforming nation in this regard. In the U.S. virtually any sparkling wine can be called Champagne, including red wine. Even the French seem to be getting resigned to this as a fact of life. And now, irony of ironies, the prestigious French Champagne house of Moët et Chandon will be making a sparkling wine in California's Napa Valley in a few years—the vineyards are already planted—but what will they call their wine: Champagne (without quote marks) or sparkling wine?

America is producing some fine sparkling wines today, wines

that can proudly bear the name Champagne on their labels.

Somebody once said that there are two kinds of sparkling wines—Champagne and everything else. Or: all sparkling wine would be Champagne if it could. Unquestionably, the finest sparkling wine in the world is what the French label with that hallowed name.

The French put a vintage year on their Champagne only in the most favorable of years, and such Champagne is not necessarily better than nonvintage Champagne—only more distinctive and more expensive. In the ordinary course of human events, therefore, vintage Champagne is a superfluous extravagance reserved for the Gettys and Croesi (plural of Croesus), and nonvintage French Champagne is extravagance enough for the peasantry.

French Champagne houses usually produce several different Champagnes, each with its own "given" name and with widely varying price tags. Moët et Chandon, for example, makes a full dozen. One of these wines will usually be considered the producer's "Best of the House," often their Blanc de Blancs (see), just as in the U.S.

All Champagne made by the true *méthode champenoise,* involving some one hundred hand-operations, is necessarily expensive, and French Champagne is particularly so. In fact, the only proper word to describe the cost of some of it these days is outrageous.

Ordinarily the cheapest Champagne made by the great French houses will be their extra dry, which is less dry than their *Brut,* which, in turn, is less dry than their "Best of the House." But it is the Extra Dry that will

often be most appreciated by the uneducated palate, by the nonconnoisseurs, precisely because it is not totally, austerely dry.

It is paradoxical that Champagne, with all its delicacy and elegance, is one of the most durable of wines—the "best tempered" of wines, said one ancient writer. It can suffer all manner of abuse in transit and be none the worse for the joltings and ill treatment. It is said to be the only wine that can be consumed at the North Pole, the Sahara Desert, in the tropics, and at 45,000 feet.

Champagne, French, American, or of any other nationality, should be consumed young and fresh. Drink it as you buy it. It does not normally improve in the bottle. (There is such a thing as aged Champagne, but it is a rarity appreciated only by *aves rarae.*) Proverbially it is said that Champagne lasts seventeen years, but don't test it. A practical rule is to drink vintage Champagne before it is eight years old.

All Champagne should be served well chilled, around 40°F. Three hours in the refrigerator or a half hour in an ice bucket will do it. But don't store your Champagne in the refrigerator for endless ages— you'll mummify it. Serve Champagne in regular tulip-shaped glasses—those slender, elegant Baccarat crystal ones are ideal —never in shallow, sherbet-type glasses.

Reams have been written on Champagne and food. You will find people (with slightly or muchly addled brains) advocating Champagne to accompany, quite literally, everything from sauerkraut to sweet desserts. The sensible and sober consensus of mankind, however, says that: (1) Champagne, especially the drier types, is the ideal aperitif wine because of its lightness and delicacy. (2) It can accompany almost any kind of food—some say even curry—but this would be gross and sinful waste, as the Champagne will simply be obliterated in the midst of highly seasoned food. Ideal accompaniment for good Champagne: smoked ham or turkey, broiled lobster. (3) A sweet Champagne (*Sec*) or at least a non-ultra-dry one will bring a fine meal to a glorious finale, even to the accompaniment of a sweet dessert. (4) Champagne is the traditional wine for breakfast.

You remember how the Father Superior, when he sent the young monk to the wine cellar to fetch a pitcher of wine, said, "Brother, I want to hear you singing Plain Chant all the while you're down there." Dom Perignon, a French Benedictine monk and cellar-master (d. 1715), was given no such instructions. And mankind is the happier for it. And it is in consequence thereof that he is hailed as the inventor of Champagne, the man who put the bubbles in it. One day he emerged all aglow from the wine cellar and said to the Father Abbot: "I've been drinking stars!" History or fable, no better description of Champagne has ever been enunciated. Individual bottles of Champagne, both French and American, are assessed in the general index under their proper names. Vintage Champagne is not sold until it is about five years old, and is at its best for another five years or so. Nonvintage Champagne improves for a year after purchase and should be consumed within two. Some recent vintages for French champagnes:

1959—Great but past their peak.

1961—Great. Past their peak unless recently disgorged (it would so state on the label).

1962—Great. Some say better than '61. Past their peak unless recently disgorged.

1964—Excellent wines, now at their best but drink them soon.

1966—Great wines, even better than '64, now at their best, drink through 1976.

1967—Good vintage, wines at their best now and through 1977.

1969—Fine full-bodied wines. At their best, 1975–1980.

1970—A good year, wines rather light. Drink, 1975–1980.

1971—Excellent vintage— very small crop, will be expensive.

1972—Very good year. None are ready—not even marketed yet.

1973—Excellent. None are ready—not even marketed yet. Listed below in alphabetical order are France's greatest Champagne houses and finest Champagnes as generally available in the U.S. today. The principal wines of each house are listed in descending order of price. Needless to say, these are all superb wines, from the lowliest-priced to the most extravagantly (outrageously?) priced. Prices are approximate, usually a mean between the New York and California price. There are no finer sparkling wines this side of heaven. For many, alas, this will probably be the most unused listing in this book.

Ayala Blanc de Blancs— $14.50. Brut, N.V.—$12.

Bollinger R. D. (Meaning "Recently Disgorged": a happy note signifying that the wine was aged a long time)—$17.90. Brut, Special Cuvée, N.V.—$12. Extra Dry—$10.50.

Charles Heidsieck Cuvée Royale—$19. Blanc de Blancs —$15.25. Brut, British Cuvée (Vintage)—$14. Brut, N.V.— $10.25 to $13. Extra Dry— $10.75.

Heidsieck Dry Monopole Cuvée Diamant Bleu—Best of the House. Brut, Gold Top Special—$10.25. Brut, N.V.— $7.95. Extra Dry—$8.

Krug & Co. Blanc de Blancs —$23.50. Brut, Private Cuvée, N.V.—$20.

Lanson Red Label Brut, Vintage—$18.50. Black Label Brut, N.V.—$11.60. Extra Quality Dry—$9.90.

Moët et Chandon Dom Perignon—Best of the House, probably the most prestigious sparkling wine in the world today—$26.50. Brut Imperial, Vintage—$14.25. Brut Imperial, N.V.—$12. White Seal Extra Dry—$11.

G. H. Mumm René Lalou —$25—Best of the House. Cordon Rouge, Vintage—$15. Cordon Rouge, N.V.—$12.50. Extra Dry—$11.40.

Laurent Perrier Cuvée Grand Siècle, Brut—$22—Best of the House. Blanc de Blancs (Vintage)—$14. Brut, Special Cuvée, N.V.—$12. Extra Dry—$9.50.

Perrier-Jouet Blason de France ($29.50)—Best of the House. Special Reserve—$17. English Cuvée Brut, Vintage— $10.50. English Cuvée Brut, N.V.—$9.50. Cuvée Spéciale Extra Dry—$8.90.

Piper-Heidsieck Florens Louis—$17—Best of the House. Brut, Vintage—$14.50. Cuvée

des Ambassadeurs, Brut, N.V.— $13. Extra Dry—$12.

Pol-Roger Brut, Vintage— $11. Brut Reserve—$10. Dry Special—$9.50.

Pommery & Greno Avize, Blanc de Blancs, Vintage—$17 —Best of the House. Brut, N.V. —$11.60. Extra Dry—$10.75.

Louis Roederer Cristal— $23—Best of the House. Brut, Vintage—$16. Brut, N.V.— $13.50. Extra Dry—$12.50.

Ruinart, Père et Fils Blanc de Blancs—$15. Brut Tradition, N.V.—$8.

Taittinger Comtes de Champagne, Blanc de Blancs—$25.50 —Best of the House. La Française, Brut—$13.

Veuve Cliquot Ponsardin La Grande Dame—$23.50—Best of the House. Veuve Gold Label, Brut—$15.75. Yellow Label, Brut, N.V.—$13.75. White Label, Extra Dry— $12.50.

Individual bottles of Champagne, both French and American, are assessed under their proper names.

CHAMPAGNE, AMERICAN This term is getting to be less offensive these days to wine purists in particular and to Frenchmen in general, for the simple and good reason that America today is making some very good sparkling wine— Champagne, *s'il vous plâit*. An expert would sometimes be hard-pressed to distinguish between America's best Champagnes and some of the Gallic versions.

Yet the fact remains that America makes more poor Champagne than it does good. It's because we're too good at everything. We mass-produce everything from hot dogs to Cadillacs—and that includes Champagne. A horrendous amount of Champagne is produced in the U.S. by the "bulk" or "Charmat process"—by law this has to be noted on the label—and these "Champagnes" have precious little in common with the great French Champagnes—other than the name. These wines are unbelievably cheap—many as low as $2 per fifth—Vichy water costs that much!—but they can scarcely be called wine at all. After all, "Champagne" is sparkling *wine*, and if there is no wine to begin with, all the bubbles in the world will not produce "Champagne."

Good Champagne can never be cheap, for three reasons: (1) It is made from expensive grapes. (2) It is made by an extremely laborious process involving some 120 hand operations. (3) It is heavily taxed: federal tax is twenty times that of still wines: $3.40 per gallon compared to 17¢.

But with cheap American Champagne only (3) above is true. It is made from cheap grapes, including Thompson Seedless, which makes for good eating but lousy drinking. It is usually made by the "bulk process" method—or, at best, it is fermented "in *the* bottle," not "in *this* bottle." That might sound trifling, but it is not. The finest sparkling wines spend their entire life in a single bottle. But to bypass this tedious and costly process, some American wineries use a shortcut whereby the wine, in its later stages, spends some time in large tanks, and does not therefore spend its entire life in *this*, one and the same bottle. Most winemakers are convinced that such wines lose something in the bypass. They cannot legally be labeled "Fermented in *this* bottle," can

only say, "Fermented in *the* bottle."

American wineries make Champagnes of varying sweetness just as the French houses do. Usually the driest will be their "Best of the House" (see list, below) with *Brut* a close second; then comes Extra Dry, which, despite the name, has perceptible sweetness. Only a few American wineries make a truly sweet Champagne: *Sec*, which means dry! (Clearly, wine terminology can be mysterious! Witness also: an "average" vintage or bottle usually translates to "awful!")

America's Finest Champagnes
("*The Best of the House*")
Comparative Standings

Near-Classic
    Schramsberg Blanc de Blanc, 1966—Priceless
*****

Exceptional
    Korbel Natural Champagne ($6.55)
    Sonoma Chardonnay Blanc de Blancs and Blanc de Noir ($7.50)
    Hanns Kornell Sehr Trocken ($7.50)
****

Very Good
    Gold Seal Blanc de Blancs (Charles Fournier) ($6.25)
    Almadén Blanc de Blancs, 1972 ($6.50)
    Beaulieu Private Reserve ($7.10)
    Mirassou Au Naturel ($7.35)
    Weibel Chardonnay Brut Champagne ($7.50)
    Schramsberg Blanc de Blancs, 1967, 1968, 1969, 1970, 1971 ($8.50)

Champagne, American—Brut
Brut Champagne is every winemaker's baby—his pride and showpiece. This is because it's totally dry, the most delicate and elegant of all sparkling

wines, with no sweetness whatever to mask possible flaws. Except for special "Best of the House" wines (see p. 61), which themselves are extremely dry or bone-dry, even drier than *Brut, Brut* is always the most expensive of a particular winery's sparkling wines.

Here are America's finest, listed in descending order of excellence. When wines have the same rating, the least expensive is rated first.

America's Brut Champagnes— Comparative Standings

*****

Exceptional

  Windsor Brut Champagne ($7.50)

****

Very Good

  Great Western Brut Champagne ($5.10)

  Korbel Brut Champagne ($5.70)

  Hanns Kornell Brut Champagne ($5.70)

  Beaulieu Brut Champagne, 1968, 1969 ($6.10)

  Inglenook Brut Champagne, 1967 ($6.25)

  Mirassou Brut Champagne ($6.35)

  Weibel Chardonnay Brut Champagne ($7.50)

***

Good

  Le Domaine ($3.10)

  Masson Brut Champagne ($5.00)

  Great Western Special Reserve ($5.10)

  Taylor Brut Champagne ($5.30)

  Almadén Brut Champagne ($5.40) (Sometimes varies see text, pp. 2–3.)

  Cresta Blanca Brut Champagne ($5.50)

  Weibel Brut Champagne ($5.70)

  Beaulieu Brut Champagne, 1967 ($6.10)

  Inglenook Brut Champagne, 1968, 1969 ($6.25)

**

Fair

  Gallo Champagne ($3)

  Cook's Imperial Brut ($4.50)

  San Martin Brut Champagne ($4.75)

  Gold Seal Brut Champagne ($4.95)

  Christian Brothers Brut Champagne ($5.05)

  Heitz Brut Champagne ($5.35)

*

Passable

  Calwa White Champagne ($2)

  Jacques Bonet American Champagne ($2)

Champagne, American—Extra Dry A lot of wine terms are wholly relative—this is one: the wine is Extra Dry in comparison with what? Dr Pepper? Kool-Aid? Then it's precisely accurate. But in comparison to any given winery's *Brut* Champagne, then their Extra Dry could only be termed non-dry or slightly sweet. And since the winery's other sparkling wines are necessarily the norm, then Extra Dry will always be translated: Sweeter-than-*Brut*, or just-slightly-sweet.

And it is precisely for this reason that Extra Dry will often be more appreciated by the nonconnoisseur than will an austere *Brut* or Natural.

Extra Dry is an all-purpose Champagne: dry enough to serve as an aperitif wine, sweet enough to end a meal (except alongside a sweet dessert) or for simple refreshment.

Another thing in its favor: it's usually the lowest-priced Champagne a particular winery makes —other than such abominations as Cold Duck or Frozen Goose.

American Extra Dry Champagnes—Comparative Standings

****

Very Good

Masson Extra Dry ($5)

Llords and Elwood Extra Dry ($5.50)

Hanns Kornell Extra Dry ($5.70)

Korbell Extra Dry ($5.70)

Beaulieu Extra Dry ($6.10)

***

Good

Le Domaine Extra Dry ($3.10)

Christian Brothers Extra Dry ($5.05)

Great Western Extra Dry ($5.10)

Weibel Extra Dry ($5.25)

Taylor Dry Champagne ($5.30)

Almadén Extra Dry ($5.40)

Cresta Blanca Extra Dry ($5.50)

**

Fair

Franzia Extra Dry ($2)

Greystone Extra Dry ($2)

Lejon Extra Dry ($3.25)

Cooks Imperial Extra Dry ($4.50)

Gold Seal Extra Dry ($4.95)

Heitz Extra Dry ($5.35)

*

Passable

André Extra Dry ($2)

Jacques Bonet Extra Dry ($2)

Not Recommended:

San Martin Extra Dry

Champagne, American—Sec (or: Dry) Wine names can be confusing, and here's the ultimate instance. Champagne *Sec* literally means "Dry Champagne," and what this is is *sweet Champagne!* Champagne *Sec* is, in fact, the sweetest Champagne made by any American winery, and only a few still make it, as sweet Champagne has somehow fallen from favor over the past few decades.

It's strictly an after-dinner beverage, and can even accompany a sweet dessert. Be sure it's well chilled (ca. 40°F).

American Sec Champagnes

They are listed in descending order of excellence. Prices are approximate.

****: Schramsberg Cremant ($6.75)

***: Korbel Champagne Sec ($5.70)

**: Cook's Imperial Sec Champagne ($4.50)

Not recommended: Weibel Champagne Sec

Champagne, Pink and Rosé Even if it tasted awful—which it doesn't—everyone agrees that this, along with sparkling Burgundy, is one of the prettiest wines in all creation. That's one reason it's popular. Another is that it's usually relatively cheap, at least as sparkling wines go.

All Pink Champagne (or Rosé Champagne, as it's also labeled, French or American, tends to be sweet—it's almost always the sweetest Champagne a particular winery makes. And sweetness covers a multitude of vinous sins. Even if the base wine isn't particularly inspired, the sweetness will cloak the defects, making a salable wine.

This is not to say that all Pink Champagne is poor wine, but it is to say that a depressing amount of it is—most of it.

Pink Champagne, because of its sweetness, does not make a good aperitif wine but it does make a good refreshment or party wine—for mid-afternoon or late evening. The sweeter versions make good dessert wines. Be sure Pink Champagne is well chilled, around 40°F.

See also: COLD DUCK.

*American Pink and Rosé
Champagnes—
Comparative Standings*

Wines are listed in descending order of excellence. Where several wines have the same rating, the least expensive is listed first. Prices are approximate.

****

Very Good

Schramsberg Cuvée de Gamay ($6.75)

***

Good

Le Domaine Pink Champagne ($3.10)

Christian Brothers Pink Champagne ($5.05)

Great Western Pink Champagne ($5.10)

Weibel Pink Champagne ($5.25)

Taylor Pink Champagne ($5.30)

Hanns Kornell Pink-Rosé Champagne ($5.70)

Korbel Rosé (Pink) Champagne ($5.70)

**

Fair

Paul Masson Crackling Rosé ($3)

Gold Seal Pink Champagne ($3)

Gallo Pink Champagne ($3)

Lejon Pink Champagne ($3.25)

Weibel Crackling Rosé ($4.35)

Cook's Imperial Pink Champagne ($4.50)

Masson Pink Champagne ($5)

Almadén Pink Champagne ($5.40)

Almadén Rosé Champagne ($5.40)

Cresta Blanca Pink Champagne ($5.50)

*

Passable

Greystone Pink Champagne ($2)

Franzia Pink Champagne ($2)

Calwa Pink Champagne ($2)

Jacques Bonet Pink Champagne ($2)

André Pink Champagne ($2)

San Martin Pink Champagne ($4.75)

(LES) CHAMPANS: See VOL-NAY.

CHAPELOT: See CHABLIS, FRENCH.

CHAPOUTIER TAVEL VIN ROSÉ*** This is a typically dry French rosé from the Rhone Valley. It is a rather good one, if your taste runs to dry rosés. Chapoutier is the name of the shipper, a reliable one. It's a fair value at around $3.50. How to serve it: See under ROSÉ.

CHAPPELLET WINERY (St. Helena, Calif.) Another of those small, new, prestige California wineries. It was founded in 1969, and some are already tempted to call it "great." Time and wine will tell. Chappellet also has a secondary label, Pritchard Hill (see).

Cabernet Sauvignon Cabernet Sauvignon is the noble grape of Bordeaux (France), where it produces some of the greatest red wine in all the world. It also does nobly in California, especially in the hands of such small, patient, painstaking wineries as Chappellet. Such excellence really deserves to be appreciated on its own, with some cheese and/or fresh fruit. But this wine will also go beautifully with the finer cuts of beef or with a roast leg of lamb. It is unfined (not clarified) to preserve flavor; if there is sediment present, stand it upright for twenty-four hours, then decant. If there is no sediment, air at least one hour.

1968**** Will be at its best, 1975 to 1985.

1969***** Still very immature—stash it away and forget about it until about 1980. It will make for luxurious drinking to the turn of the century—if you intend to be around. *Skoal!*

1970 and 1971***** Will be at their best, 1976 through 1980, or beyond.

Chardonnay This is a noble white wine, a connoisseur's wine, of the same lineage as the great white Burgundies of France. It's elegant enough to be sipped on its own, though it will also demonstrate its nobility when it accompanies fish or seafood. Serve chilled.

1970, 1971, 1972**** Best drinking: 1975–1980.

Chenin Blanc Chappellet makes this tasty little white wine in a somewhat different style from that of most California wineries. It's dry and crisp, distinctive, full-flavored. It will go well with fish and seafood. Serve it chilled. Fair value, $4 to $4.50.

1968*** This was Chappellet's debut wine. It already augured well. Drink this soon, if not sooner.

1969**** Very dry. Drink, 1975 through 1976.

1970*** Drink, 1975 through 1976.

1971*** Very dry; best drinking, 1975 through 1976.

1972 and 1973***

Johannisberg Riesling This is the illustrious grape of the great German Rhine wines and Chappellet's version possesses some of the charms of its German forebears. It's usually light and flowery, like its German relatives, but it's much drier. It's a connoisseur's kind of wine. If you like a dry aperitif wine, this will fill the bill ad-

mirably. Otherwise, serve it chilled with fish, seafood, fowl, pork. Fair value, $5.

1969**** Best drinking, 1975–1976.

1970**** Drink, 1975–1976.

1971*** Best drinking, 1975 through 1976.

1972**** Best drinking, 1975 through 1977.

1973—Initial impression: ***.

Pinot Chardonnay: See CHAR-DONNAY.

CHARBONO This is the name of a good, sturdy red California wine, made from an Italian grape of the same name. It's similar to Barbera wine (see), but heavier and more tannic, which means that it will age better. Only two American wineries make it, but both do a good job with it. (In Italy it is never bottled under the name Charbono.)

Serve Charbono with red meats, pasta, hearty casseroles. The best of it deserves to be sipped carefully, on its own, with simple cheeses and plain bread. Serve it at cool room temperature.

The line-up:

    ****: Inglenook Charbono, 1959, 1967, 1970, 1972

    ***: Davis Bynum Charbono

    ***: Inglenook Charbono, 1965 through 1969

CHARDONNAY: See PINOT CHARDONNAY.

CHARLES FOURNIER: See GOLD SEAL.

CHARLES HEIDSIECK: See HEIDSIECK, CHARLES.

(LES) CHARMES: The French give names to their vineyards as we do to our children and "Les Charmes" (the Spells or Charms) is a favorite. Two important vineyards so named and covered in this book are located, one in Chambolle-Musigny and the other in Meursault (see both).

CHARMES-CHAMBERTIN

One of the world's greatest red wines—a path separates this vineyard from the illustrious Chambertin, the king of red wines. How to treat this wine (always reverently, of course): See under LE CHAMBERTIN. Some vintages:

1926—A magnificent vintage, the wine is still delicious.

1951—Drouhin: *****—Still in good condition.

1959—Avery: Near-Classic

1961—Ponnelle: Near-Classic—Will be at its best from 1975 or 1976 on.

1962—Leroy: *****

1964 — Rousseau: ***** — Fine drinking, now.

1966—Drouhin: *****

1966—Henri de Villamont: ****

1970—Rousseau: Near-Classic.

1971—Duroche: *****
Bouchard: *****
Ponnelle: *****

1972—Rousseau: *****

CHASSAGNE-MONTRACHET (RED)****

Because the white Chassagne-Montrachet is so well known and so good, this fine red wine tends to be overlooked and underpriced. It's worth searching out. It's at its best when it's four to seven years old. How to serve it: See under BURGUNDY. A good value if $4 to $5. Special vineyard wines (Château Maltroye, etc.) can be superb, *****, will cost, $6.50 to $7.50. Serve at cool room temperature, after airing about an hour.

CHASSAGNE-MONTRACHET (WHITE)

Excellent dry white wine from Burgundy (France), very similar to Puligny-Montrachet (see) wines, on the expensive side, but still less than half the price of the great Montrachets (see), to which it is kin. The wine is good enough to deserve savoring on its own, or with innocuous tidbits (mild cheeses, bland crackers). It also goes well with light foods: poultry, fish, seafood, veal, pork, ham. If the wine has the name of an individual vineyard on the label, it's even better—such as: Morgeot, Grandes Ruchottes (or Les Ruchottes), La Maltroye (or Château Maltroye, or de la Maltroye). Such wines will cost from $8 to $10. Even "plain" Chassagne-Montrachet from a reliable shipper—Picard, Leroy, Gagnard, Delagrange, Jaboulet-Vercherre, Bouchard, Deleger, Ramonet-Prudhon, Remoissenet—will be at least ****. It will range in price from around $6 (Bouchard's) to $7.50 (Remoissenet's).

CHÂTEAU:
See under name of.

CHÂTEAUNEUF-DU-PAPE

Perhaps it's because of its intriguing name—the New Castle of the Pope—that this wine has become so well known. It's a good wine, never a great one, from France's Rhone Valley. Because it's popular, it tends to be on the expensive side ($5 to $10), but often enough it's not worth the asking price. It's simply overpriced. On the other hand, avoid cheap Châteauneufs—anything under $4, as they can be execrable—go for a decent Côtes du Rhone instead. Châteauneuf-du-Pape is at its best when it's between four and nine years old. It goes well at the barbecue grill, with poultry (especially turkey, duck), game, pork richly prepared.

Some names to look for:

Château de la Gardine—The '66 and '67: *** The '69, fie, vile!

Domaine de Nalys

Château La Nerte (or: de la Nerthe)

La Bernardine—The '67 is ***

Domaine de Mont Redon

Domaine Jean Trintignant

Clos des Papes

Château des Fines Roches

La Marcelle, Chapoutier

Château Fortia—The '67 is ***

Alexandre Rochette—The '67: ***

Some vintages:

1968—Light wines—Avoid.

1969—Very good wines, solid and strong—Now at their best and through 1978.

1970—Excellent wines—At their best, 1975 through 1980.

1971—Very good year— Wines at their best, 1975 through 1979.

1972—The wines are irregular and generally poor—Best avoid.

1973 — Excellent vintage — Fine wines to lay down—Don't touch them until at least 1977.

CHENAS *** to **** Good red wine from the Beaujolais area of France, although Beaujolais will not always be on the label. It's similar to a Moulin-à-Vent (see), its next-door neighbor, though it's not quite as good a wine. Chenas is at its best when it's between three and six years of age. How to serve it: See under BEAUJOLAIS.

CHENES, CLOS DES: See VOLNAY.

CHENIN BLANC Here's a fresh, fragrant, totally delightful white wine, definitely in the ascendancy in America today. It was scarcely known—because it was scarcely grown—just ten years ago. Today it is one of California's most popular varietals.

It also goes occasionally by one of its French names, Pineau de la Loire. And rarely by the name of White Pinot, a total misnomer.

It's an ideal summertime wine —serve it as an aperitif or for refreshment on a hot afternoon. It varies considerably in sweetness from winery to winery. The listing below indicates the relative sweetness. The drier versions can be taken to the dinner table to accompany fish, shellfish, and even light meats: poultry (especially with a white or cream sauce), veal, pork. Serve chilled.

Peter Arno has a cartoon of two grizzled, woebegone, morning-aftered winos amid the alley debris and one is reading the back label of a wine bottle: "It's a pleasant accompaniment to fish, shellfish and the lighter meats but its delicate flavor is perhaps appreciated at the end of the meal with melon or dessert." Indubitably, a California Chenin Blanc!

Listed below are America's finest Chenin Blancs. Notice how many wines rank in the **** and *** categories, most of them at extremely reasonable prices. Chenin Blanc is clearly one of America's best buys in white wines.

In a given category, wines are listed in ascending order of price: the cheapest first. Prices are approximate.

American Chenin Blancs— Comparative Standings

*****

Exceptional

Chalone Chenin Blanc, 1970, 1971 (original winery prices, $4 and $6, respectively).

****
Very Good
  Simi Chenin Blanc ($2.60)
    —Touch of sweetness.
  Charles Krug Chenin Blanc
    ($2.80)—Some sweetness.
  Robert Mondavi Chenin
    Blanc, 1971, 1972, 1973
    ($3.30)—Touch of sweet-
    ness.
  Mirassou Chenin Blanc,
    1970, 1973 ($3.35)—
    Touch of sweetness.
  Sterling Chenin Blanc ($4)
    —Dry.
  Ste. Michelle Chenin Blanc,
    1972 ($4)—Semi-dry.
  Christian Brothers Pineau de
    la Loire ($4)—On sweet
    side.
  Cuvaison Chenin Blanc of
    the Napa Valley ($4.20)—
    Very dry.
  Pritchard Hill Chenin Blanc,
    1972 ($4.50)—Dry.
  Souverain Pineau Souverain,
    1971 ($4.80)—Medium
    dry.
  Chappellet Chenin Blanc,
    1969 ($5)—Very dry.
***
Good
  LaMont Chenin Blanc ($2)
    —Medium dry.
  San Martin Chenin Blanc
    ($2.10)—Medium dry.
  Almadén Chenin Blanc
    ($2.30)—Touch of sweet-
    ness.
  Pedroncelli Chenin Blanc
    ($2.35)—Touch of sweet-
    ness.
  Weibel Chenin Blanc ($2.40)
    —Touch of sweetness.
  Sonoma (or Windsor) Che-
    nin Blanc ($2.40)—Touch
    of sweetness.
  Masson Chenin Blanc ($2.55)
    —Touch of sweetness.
  Novitiate Chenin Blanc
    ($2.55)—Medium dry.
  Korbel Chenin Blanc ($2.65)
    —On the sweet side.

Beringer Chenin Blanc
    ($2.75)—Medium dry.
  Simi Chenin Blanc Sec
    ($2.75)—Dry.
  Inglenook Chenin Blanc,
    1968, 1969, 1971, 1972
    ($2.80)—Dry.
  Kenwood Dry Chenin Blanc,
    1970, 1972 ($2.80).
  Kenwood Chenin Blanc, 1973
    ($2.80)—Medium dry.
  Yverdon Chenin Blanc, 1971
    ($2.85)—Medium dry.
  Charles Krug White Pinot
    ($2.85)—Medium dry.
  Martini Dry Chenin Blanc
    ($2.85).
  Parducci Chenin Blanc
    ($2.85)—Dry.
  Bargetto Chenin Blanc
    ($2.95)—On the sweet
    side.
  Inglenook White Pinot ($3)
    —Dry.
  Christian Brothers Chenin
    Blanc ($3)—Dry.
  Oakville Chenin Blanc
    ($3.25)—Touch of sweet-
    ness.
  Robert Mondavi Chenin
    Blanc, 1970 ($3.30)—
    Touch of sweetness.
  Mirassou Chenin Blanc, 1969,
    1971, 1972 ($3.35)—
    Touch of sweetness.
  Ste. Michelle Chenin Blanc,
    1972 ($4).
  Pritchard Hill Chenin Blanc,
    1971 ($4.50)—Dry.
  Souverain Pineau Souverain,
    1970 ($4.80)—Medium
    dry.
  Chappellet Chenin Blanc,
    1968, 1970, 1971, 1972
    ($5)—Dry.
**
Fair
  Royal Host Chenin Blanc
    ($1.75)—Medium dry.
  Gallo Chenin Blanc ($1.85)
    —Touch of sweetness.
  Eleven Cellars Chenin Blanc
    ($2.50)—Medium dry.

Sebastiani Chenin Blanc ($2.55)—Medium dry.

Kenwood Dry Chenin Blanc, 1971 ($2.80).

Louis Martini Dry Chenin Blanc, 1967 through 1971 ($2.85).

Pritchard Hill Chenin Blanc, 1969, 1970 ($4.50)—Dry.

CHEVAL BLANC, CHÂTEAU

Offhand, one might be tempted to think this is a white wine—Blanc—but it's the château building, or outhouse, or something, that's white, not the wine. The wine is one of the great first-growth Clarets of France's Bordeaux region. Beyond question, this is one of the world's greatest red wines. One famous critic called it a "faultless" wine—another, one of the world's "most full-blooded wines." It's big, soft, rich, a wine that even beginners can appreciate. It's too good to be prostituted with common fare—with fine grilled beef, prime-rib roast, okay—rack, leg, saddle of lamb, okay—but otherwise appreciate this marvelous wine with bits of bread and cheese, or nuts and fresh fruit. Serve it at cool room temperature.

1895—Classic—A legendary wine—Don't look for it at the supermarket. Besides, it's just now beginning to fade.

1921—Classic—Some say this was the greatest wine ever ever!

1924, 1925, 1926, 1928, 1929 —All Near-Classic, but, alas, all now departed this world.

1934—Near-Classic—Fair value, $45.

1943—Outstanding wine even to this day. A great value at $25.

1945—Despite its fancy price tag ($50 to $75), most folks say this is a poor wine.

1947—Classic—Everybody agrees: one of the greatest ever, though some say it is fading fast in the stretch. Fair or not, it's selling for $50 to $60, and it was up to $100 in '73.

1948—Near-Classic—It's *almost* reasonably priced: ca. $25.

1949—Near-Classic—Just now reaching its prime. Fair value, $35.

1950—*****—Now at its best.

1953—Soft and delicate, *****—Fair value, $30.

1955—Round, soft, full—chewable! Near-Classic, but at $75?

1959—*****—Fair value, $35.

1961—Classic—Fair value, $50, but you probably won't be able to find it—it has evaporated.

1962—A letdown: ****— Not very enthusiastically recommended at ca. $20.

1964—*****—It's now at its best and will hold there until 1985. Fair value, $25.

1966—Near-Classic—It's nowhere near ready; will be at its best, 1980–1990. Fair value, if only you could buy it, for $25.

1967—Superb wine despite an indifferent vintage: Near-Classic—A *truly* fair value would be $25, but you'll be lucky to find it for $35.

1968—Forget the whole thing —miserable. Yet it's selling for $10 and more!

1969—Looks good, but final judgment is not in. A very tentative ****

1970—It's not there yet, but all the signs say this is going to make at least Near-Classic. Fair value is $25, but expect to pay $35.

CHEVALIER-MONTRACHET

Most experts agree that this glorious white Burgundy is second only to Le Montrachet itself, the queen of all the world's dry white wines. In fact, some people have always said that this wine (along with Bâtard-Montrachet) is more drinkable than Montrachet itself. It's very scarce and very expensive and may not always be worth its out-of-sight price: $20 to $30—per 24 ounces. It's regularly **** to *****, and in the best of years, in the best of hands, may well reach Near-Classic status. It's at its best when it's between five and ten years old. How to serve it: See under MONTRACHET.

CHIANTI Chianti is probably the single best-known wine in the world. This is not too surprising when one considers that Italians are the world's greatest wine drinkers and used to be the world's greatest travelers as well—Cristoforo Colombo started it. *Gli Italiani* simply spread the word about their favorite wine wherever they went.

Wines bearing the name Chianti, but often without the faintest resemblance to the Italian beverage, are made in many countries, notably the U.S. In fairness let it be said that these imitation Chiantis do resemble the Italian product in two ways: (1) the name's the same; (2) they're both red. (Actually there is also a white Chianti but it is infrequently seen in this country.)

Italian Chianti is made in three different styles. The first you can try on your next trip to Italy: it's a carafe wine, made to be consumed very young. It's got a little fizz to it—*frizzante*, the Italians call it. The second type is similar, actually kind of overlaps it: it's what most Americans think of as the only true Chianti: it's sold in the squat little straw-covered *fiaschi*. This can be a good wine, though it's never more than that.

The third type is Chianti Classico, the best, the one to look for. It doesn't come in the gimmicky straw-covered *fiaschi*, but in regular Claret-type bottles. Look for the seal of authenticity on the neck of the bottle: a black cockerel on a red and gold background: it guarantees authenticity, not necessarily quality; note that some fine Chiantis, produced outside the delimited "Classico" area, do not bear the *gallo nero*.

If you want even further assurance of quality, look for the word "Riserva" on the label; such a wine must be at least three years old and is the finest Chianti money can buy.

With the inflated price of French wines today, more and more Chianti, especially the cheaper kind in *fiaschi,* is seen on American retail shelves. Chianti in *fiaschi* can be a good value but one would be well advised to stay with established and trustworthy producers. Listed below (List A) are the best, in alphabetical order, followed by a second list (List B) of lesser producers. Don't buy Italian Chianti, especially in those straw-covered *fiaschi,* unless you find it in one of the lists.

With Chianti Classico (in Bordeaux-shaped bottles) one can buy with more confidence than in buying Chianti in *fiaschi,* but it would still be wise to stay with the well-established producers listed below. The "given" names of the wines are listed in the column to the right. These names will usually be the most prominent word on the label. "Chianti Classico" will often be in much smaller type, and in some cases it won't be on the label at all.

List A: Best Italian Chianti
Listed in alphabetical order by name of the firm.

Producer	Name of Wine
Marchesi L. & P. Antinori	Villa Antinori
	Santa Cristina
Conte G. Pasolini Dall'Onda Borghese	Barbarino
Luigi Cappellini	Verrazzano
Conti (Counts) Capponi	Calcinaia
Marchesi Corsini	Montepaldi
Marchesi De' Frescobaldi	Nipozzano
	Pomino
Letizia Rimediotti Mattioli	Nozzole
Melini	Stravecchio
Barone Ricasoli	Brolio Riserva
	Castello di Meleto
	Castello di Brolio
I. L. Ruffino	Riserva Ducale
Contessa Elena Sanmimatelli	Vignamaggio
Conti Serristori	Machiavelli

Most of these wines are treated individually in this book under their proper "given" names: Brolio Riserva, Villa Antinori, etc.

The above listing includes the very best and largest producers of Italian Chianti; these are wholly reputable firms and their wines will almost certainly be excellent. But their are at least a hundred brands of Italian Chianti presently being im-

ported into the U.S. These wines, especially those in *fiaschi*, vary greatly. Here is a listing of some of the more important and reputable firms, listed alphabetically. These names are not on a par with the giants of List A, but they are usually good and reliable wines; they give one a prima facie assurance of quality.

List B: Good Italian Chianti

Ancilli	Giannozzi
Barsottini	Mirafiore
Bersano	Orfevi
Bertolli	Pagni
Cantina del Papa	Soderi
Cappelli	Spaletti
Deifile Pescatori	Straccali
Ganzia	Suali

Chianti Classico (in the Bordeaux bottles), especially the Riservas, already has a few years on it when you but it, but it will improve in the bottle for four or five more years. Chianti has always been considered *the* wine to accompany Italian food, especially pasta. Nobody's going to argue against that alliance. Italian wine literature insists that Chianti goes with any food, but that's highly questionable—rather, incorrect. Like most good red wines, it is especially suited to accompany hearty casseroles, red meats, particularly roasts. It is demeaning to good Chianti to relegate it to accompanying only spicy Italian food; it deserves to be served alongside your finest steaks and chops and roasts—or even better, to be appreciated on its own, with cheeses and nuts.

Italian Chianti comes to this country in a mad jumble of bottle sizes. Be forewarned when you compare prices. The *fiaschi* are usually a full quart (32 ounces), but the regular straight-sided bottles are only 24 ounces, so the *fiaschi* contain one and a third times as much wine. But sometimes the very opposite is true. Sometimes Chianti is bottled in American "fifths," 25.6 ounces. There are even 23-ounce and 24.3-ounce bottles! It also comes in half gallons (64 ounces), in magnums (52 ounces), and now recently, in popular "Misura" bottles of 59 ounces. The neck label on these reads something like this: "Una misura Chiantigiana, 1971": "A measure of the 1971 Chianti." Remember that 59 ounces are the equivalent of almost two and a half of the regular 24-ounce bottles, and this can be an excellent value.

Italian Chianti, broadly speaking, is a good buy in the United States—it's almost always a healthy cut above *vin ordinaire*, and in these bloated (inflated) days, it can sell for as little as $2.50 for 24 ounces. Always be mindful, of course, that Italian Chianti is usually a good wine —never a great one.

"Plain" Chianti in *fiaschi* should be drunk young and fresh— within a year or so of purchase. And don't buy it—this is *important*—don't buy it if it is more than *four years old!*

Chianti Classici will usually be at least three or four years old when they appear on the American market. Riservas are often seven years old and more. Both will improve in the bottle up to at least ten years of age.

With Chianti Classico, vintages are never as big a deal as with, say, Bordeaux or German wines. There is rarely any great variation, vintage to vintage. Thus all vintages from 1964 through 1971 are rated excellent; 1962 was the same—1963,

however, was only fair, and 1972, the same.

CHIANTI, AMERICAN The name Chianti on a bottle of American wine was a much more common sight twenty years ago than it is today. Maybe it's just as well. What sells as Chianti in America has gotten worse and worse with the passing of the years. Speaking broadly, Chianti is the worst red wine made in the U.S. today. (Note quickly, however, that there are several good ones on the list below.)

The names of four red jug wines can be used almost interchangeably in the U.S. Burgundy, Claret, Mountain Red (or simply Red), and Chianti. At times it is impossible to distinguish between them. One is tempted to say that all four of these wines sometimes come from one and the same vat.

However, American Chiantis ordinarily do have one thing in common: besides being mostly dreadful wine, they are usually the sweetest—"mellow" is the word the wineries like to use— of all the American red jug wines. Which lowers them still further in the estimate of most wine lovers.

Listed below are most of America's Chiantis, in descending order of excellence. Included also are other red wines bearing Italian names, as well as some eastern wines of the same general nature. Where wines have the same rating, the least expensive is listed first. Prices are approximate.

American Chiantis—
Comparative Standings

***

Good

   Gold Seal Catawba Red ($1.75)

Sutter Home Chianti ($2)
Bargetto Chianti ($2.50)

**
Fair
Brookside Vino Rosso ($1)
Tavola Red ($1.20)
Gold Seal Concord Red ($1.50)
C.K. Mondavi Barberone ($1.55)
C.K. Mondavi Chianti ($1.65)
Almadén Chianti ($2)
Italian Swiss Colony Tipo Chianti (Red) ($2)
Louis Martini Chianti ($2.35)
Sebastiani Chianti ($2.40)

*
Passable
Gallo Paisano ($1.20)
Cribari Barberone ($1.20)
Gallo Chianti ($1.20)
Italian Swiss Colony Capella ($1.30)
Eleven Cellars Chianti ($1.90)
Great Western Red Concord ($2)

Not Recommended
Franzia Chianti
Italian Swiss Chianti
Franzia Vino Rosso

American Chianti, like its Italian namesake, goes well with red meats, pasta, and, in fact, with most everyday fare (other than seafood). Some of it may improve with a half hour or an hour's breathing time. It should be consumed within a year or so of purchase.

CHIROUBLES* Good red Beaujolais wine, usually one of the least expensive of them, and the lightest. It's also the fastest maturing of all Beaujolais. So drink it while it's very young, very fresh—before it becomes senile, at age two! Chiroubles can be a charmingly fresh and fruity wine, let it never be disparaged. How to serve it: See under BEAUJOLAIS.

CHRISTIAN BROTHERS In Europe, the close association of the Church with wine is rather taken for granted. Not so in the New World. Christian Brothers is the exception. A lot of Americans who don't know that the Christian Brothers is a French-founded teaching Order of the Roman Catholic Church, do know that Christian Brothers make some good wine.

That they do. For almost one hundred years, the Brothers have been making a lot of consistently good wine at very reasonable prices. Their wine is never great, but neither is it ever bad. None of the wines are vintage-dated, and they are almost always soft and mellow, immediately ready to drink when you buy them.

If you come across a particular bottle of wine that you especially like, you can make sure that you'll be buying exactly the same bottle of wine next time by referring to the code number stamped vertically on the back label. Further, some of the Brothers' wines will improve in the bottle, and if you want to know exactly how old your wine is, the code number tells you. There are five numbers: the first two are the month (05: May) the third number is the year (4: 1974) and the last two numbers are the day of the month when the wine was bottled. Thus: 05412: bottled May 12, 1974.

Christian Brothers also makes a complete line of altar wines sold under the brand name Mont La Salle (see).

Burgundy* Who says Americans have no couth when it comes to wine? They like this, don't they? This well-made red table wine has long been an American favorite. It has consistently placed high in tastings over the years. Serve it at cool room temperature, with any hearty, healthful food, especially red meats, pasta, casseroles, barbecued chicken. A good value at $2.

Cabernet Sauvignon* and occasionally **** Here's one of the world's best buys in premium red wines. Cabernet Sauvignon is the great and noble grape of Bordeaux (France) and everybody agrees that it's almost always California's finest red wine. Christian Brothers' version is extremely pleasant, soft, and mellow. It's always easy drinking. At times it ascends to **** status—use the numbering code (see above) to identify your superior batch.

Cabernet Sauvignon, Brother Timothy Selection (Bottled, 1967)**** This was a rare special bottling. Worth pursuing. Best drinking: 1975 through 1980.

Chablis* Refreshing, completely dry, inexpensive white wine to accompany fish, seafood (especially oysters), fowl. Serve it chilled. It's ready to drink when purchased, don't keep it more than two or three years. Fair value, $2.20.

Champagne The Brothers, overall, do a good job with their sparkling wines. But they're blatantly overpriced. All these wines are made by the "Charmat" or bulk process, which should keep the price down to where poor folks can afford them occasionally. Unfortunately, this is not the case. The Brothers' sparkling wines are almost as expensive as many of those made by the true *"méthode champenoise."* All of Almadén's sparkling wines, for example, are made by the true Champagne method. Yet their top-quality Champagnes sell for only $5.40 vs. Christian Brothers' $5.50. Almadén's cheaper line, sold under the Le Domaine label, and unbelievably, also made by the true Champagne method, sells for almost $2 less than the Brothers' bulk-fermented ones, $3 vs. $5.

Champagne, Brut The main label says only Champagne; the *Brut* is on the neck label. One critic says it tastes like Juicy Fruit gum! It's shown poorly in a number of "blind" tastings (labels were hidden). Look thou elsewhere.

Champagne, Extra Dry* The Extra Dry is on the neck label. Sweeter and better than the *Brut,* this will make a good "celebration" Champagne, though it's a questionable value at $5.50. Serve well chilled.

Champagne, Rosé* Medium-sweet, soft, pretty. Pretty expensive too: $5.50.

Château La Salle If you like sweet wines, you'll like this sweet white wine, and if you also like the taste of the Muscat grape, you'll love this wine. It has won an array of awards. Try it over vanilla ice cream. Serve chilled. Fair value, $2.35.

Chenin Blanc* Christian Brothers makes two wines from the Chenin Blanc grape: this one and one they call Pineau de la Loire (see.) This one is the drier of the two and less expensive, by about $1.25. Both are good wines, and this is the one you should select if you're looking for a nice little white wine to accompany fish, shellfish, or other light food. But if you want a charming medium-sweet white wine for graceful sipping, choose the Pineau. Serve chilled. A good value at $3.

Claret*** Just twenty years ago every winery in California and adjacent islands seemed to make a Claret—today they're as scarce as corkscrews at a Southern Baptist Convention—well, at a WCTU convention. It's refreshing to see a California red wine so labeled again. This is a soft light wine that will enhance grilled hamburgers, hot dogs, or chicken. Good value, $2.

Cocktail Sherry: See SHERRY.
Cream Sherry: See SHERRY.
Dry Sherry: See SHERRY.
Extra Cold Duck*** Though this fowl is as bonnie as most, even Cold Duck fanciers must give pause here to consider whether it's worth the $5 asking price. That's pretty high-flying for an American Duck —most ascend only to $2.50 or $3.

Gamay Noir**** Made from the grape that made the Beaujolais region of France famous, it should do the same for the Christian Brothers. This is a flavorful wine, soft, fresh, young, the kind of wine one could drink lots of quickly and happily. Few wines of this type will improve with bottle age— this one will if you can restrain yourself for a year or two. It's also a versatile wine: it will go well with any kind of meat, pasta, any kind of casserole. But it will be best appreciated by the true wine lover, supped lovingly on its own merits, with cheeses and fresh fruit. It deserves such consideration, it's that good. Serve it at cool room temperature. Fair value, $3.20.

Golden Sherry: See SHERRY.
Grey Riesling** A lesser light in the Brothers' firmament. Prefer one of the other whites: Chenin Blanc (see) to accompany light food—Pineau de la Loire (see), for leisurely sipping—Pinot Chardonnay (see) for either and for elegance.

Haut Sauterne** "Haut" means "High," and the French when they put it on a label want it to mean "Superior." When Californians put it on a label it means "Sweet." (In France, all Sauterne is sweet.) The Brothers' "High Sauterne" is medium-sweet, has some character, and at the price ($2.20) you can't go too far wrong. (Though there are better: Krug's Sweet Sauternes at a little more money, for example.) Serve it after dinner, chilled. It's ready to drink when you buy it and will keep well for at least three or four years.

Johannisberg Riesling*** This is not the best white wine made by Christian Brothers, but it's a standard example of this German grape in California. The wine lacks the light flowery charm of a good Rhine wine; it's drier, with a more assertive taste. It's a good choice to accompany fish, seafood, poultry, pork, ham. It's best when it's young: within two or three years of purchase. Serve it chilled. Fair value, $3.55.

Meloso Cream Sherry**** Christian Brothers makes an array of sherries (see: SHERRY) but this is the "top of the line." It's aged in oak for over eight years. It's mellow and rich, yet not cloying; ideal for after-dinner, with dessert. Serve cool or slightly chilled. Fair value, $4.

Napa Rosé*** This is a sweet-tinged rosé; Christian Brothers also makes a dry version of this, Vin Rosé. If you're looking for a wine to serve with food, you'll do better with the Vin Rosé. But if your heart yearns for a light, entrancing, romancing kind of wine, with a mite of sweetness, then this is your glass of rosé. Though it's decidedly on the sweet side, it does have substance. Serve it chilled, and drink it young and fresh, within a year or two of purchase. Fair value, $2.25.

Pineau de la Loire**** This is the rich, pampered cousin of the Brothers' Chenin Blanc. Both wines are made from the Chenin Blanc grape, which is called the Pineau (or Pinot) de la Loire in France. The difference is in the vinification —and the solicitude bestowed on the individual wines. This one gets more, and in consequence it's fuller and sweeter than the Chenin Blanc and quite a bit more expensive ($4 vs. $3). The Pineau is the wine you will choose if you are looking for a wine for entertaining guests. And for leisurely sipping in the cool cool cool of the evening. Serve chilled. It's best when it's young and fresh: within two or three years of purchase.

Pinot Chardonnay**** If you'll be dining with elegance and want a wine to do justice to your cracked crab, shrimp, lobster, red snapper—search no further. Here's a good value at $4—Chardonnays are expensive, as the grape is very shy-bearing. It's the noble grape responsible for the great white Burgundies of France. The Brothers' version is fragrant and clean, with just a wee touch of sweetness. Serve chilled. It's ready to drink when you buy it and it will improve with a year or so in the bottle.

Pinot Noir** Has sometimes been a bit irregular, varying from batch to batch. It's a dry red wine, smooth, especially recommended with red meats,

pasta, good casseroles. At the price, you could certainly do worse. You can drink it when you buy it—and it will improve with an additional year or so in the bottle. Serve at cool room temperature.

Pinot St. George*** Very few California wineries make this red wine, and lots of folks think that's as it should be, for the grape does not have much distinction. The Christian Brothers' product is "Estate Bottled," made wholly on their own premises from grapes grown on the Brothers' own property. It's soft and fruity, very drinkable, but not really superior. It's ready to drink when purchased, and will improve in the bottle for about two years. Serve at cool room temperature. Fair value, $4.

Rhine** Light, crisp, just off-dry. It's pleasant enough for a generic (a blend, grapes not specified), especially considering its plebeian price, $2.20. Serve it with light foods or for refreshment of a warm afternoon. Drink it within a year or two of purchase. Serve chilled.

Riesling** A German-type white wine with some flavor and small body, but really rather small all over. From a value standpoint one would do better with the Johannisberg Riesling at 50¢ more, or the Chablis at 50¢ less.

Sauterne** per se—*** price considered. "Sauterne" is another one of those grossly sinned-against wine names, like Chablis and Burgundy. In the U.S.A. it can mean almost anything the winemaker wants it to mean. The only thing you can know for certain is that it's a white wine. The Brothers' product is a trustworthy, medium-dry little wine, and is recommended for sipping on its own, with mild cheeses. It will also go well with light foods. Serve it chilled. Fair value, $2.20.

Note: Christian Brothers also makes a sweet Sauterne, called Haut Sauterne (see).

Sauvignon Blanc** A semi-sweet white wine, with a certain soft spiciness. It will be best enjoyed on its own, sipped in leisurely fashion, or after dinner, with a not too sweet dessert or with fresh fruit and mild cheeses. Serve it chilled. It's ready to drink when purchased and will keep well for at least three or four years. Fair value, $3.25.

Sherry The Brothers make above-average sherry, in four flavors, listed from driest to sweetest: *Cocktail****: It has a black "prestige" label—it's light, pale, mellow, $2.25—*Dry****: Just a touch of sweetness; it would still make a good cocktail wine and it's a bit cheaper: $2; some even rate it above the Cocktail, boosting it to ********—*Golden****: A medium sherry, can be used as an aperitif wine, or after-dinner—*Cream****: For after-dinner.

Sparkling Burgundy* Not very sparkling and not very Burgundy. Not recommended at $5.

Sweet Sauterne* You may still find some of this around, although it's been discontinued. And if you do, don't buy it. Not that it's *that* bad, but neither is it that good; besides, it may now be departed this world. Fair value, $2.20.

Tinta Cream Port*** Here's one of the closest things to real Port—or Porto, as it's now officially called—that you're going to find this side of Portugal. The "Tinta" comes from the fine Tinta-Madeira grape of true Porto wine. It's creamy-smooth. Serve it with immense pride and great verve after dinner— or as an 11:00 A.M. or P.M. wine. (*P.S.* Once opened, it will keep for weeks in the refrigerator, especially if you eliminate some of the air space by putting it in a smaller bottle.) Fair value, $4.

Vin Rosé*** Christian Brothers makes two rosés, this one and a Napa Rosé (see), the sweeter of the two. This Vin Rosé is light and dry, with good flavor. If you want an all-purpose rosé to be served before, during, and after the meal this should be your choice. It's ready to drink immediately upon purchase and should be consumed within a year or so. Serve chilled. Fair value, $2.20.

Zinfandel**** At $3 or so, this native California wine would have to qualify as one of the best premium red wine buys in the U.S.A.—and beyond. It's soft yet possesses good varietal character and a good soulful tanginess. Serve it (at cool room temperature) with any red meat, poultry, with pasta, stew, or any good casserole.

CHRISTMAS WINES Surprisingly there are some wines called Christmas something-or-other. Sure enough, the word's there on the label. It's occasionally on a German wine: rarely there will be a very late-picked German wine (a Trockenbeerenauslese or Eiswein) which is actually made on Christmas Day, and it will be called Christmas wine, *Weihnachten* in German. Even more frequently there will be a St. Nikolaus wine, the grapes having been picked on the feast of good Saint Nick, December 6. There is also a Christmas Carol Sherry made by Findlater (see). As for wines to grace your groaning festive Christmas board, see the recommendations under THANKSGIVING WINES. If goose instead of turkey constitutes your *pièce de résistance*, you might consider one of these wines to accompany your meal: Gewürztraminer (Alsatian or California); Hermitage; Beaujolais; Meursault.

Note also that on Christmas and during its Twelve Days, until the Feast of the Magi (Epiphany, January 6), the ban on noxious, intoxicating spirits is partially lifted in favor of genuine eggnog—homemade, of course, not the vomitous storeboughten brew—duly baptized with rum and/or brandy and/or whiskey. It's a drink for the elevenses, (A.M. or P.M.) and it does not go to the table or precede the meal.

CHUSCLAN: See CÔTES DU RHONE.

CK: See (C. K.) MONDAVI.

CLARET, AMERICAN Ten and twenty years ago this was a very popular name among American wines—today you have to search to find a bottle so labeled. No mortal really knows why.

Except, perhaps, that nobody knows what American Claret is. But nobody. Certainly not the wineries. What they label "Claret" today, they may call "Chianti" or "Burgundy" or "Mountain Red" tomorrow—if they think it will sell better. This is not fiction, not even hyperbole.

Factually, the wines listed below as Claret or Claret-types could almost as properly have been listed among the Red Burgundies, pp. 42–43. But the win-

eries call these wines Claret or Claret-types, so who's to argue? The only thing that can be said about "Claret" in distinction to "Burgundy"—and this will probably admit of as many exceptions as confirmations of the rule—is that a California Claret is ordinarily a bit lighter in body, softer, and drier than a California Burgundy. Theoretically at least. But as the waiter replied, when asked what his average tip was: "Well, it's about $3 average—but I hardly ever get up to the average."

Most American Claret is jug wine, everyday wine, economical and usually a pretty steady-as-you-go beverage. Don't look for anything more. But the best American Claret doesn't go by that name at all—it goes by the name of Cabernet Sauvignon (see), one of America's truly fine wines.

Listed below are American Clarets and Claret-types (as far as it is humanly possible to determine that), in descending order of excellence. Where wines have the same rating, the least expensive is listed first. Prices are approximate.

***

Good

Great Western Chelois ($2.05)

Christian Brothers Claret ($2.20)

Bully Hill Baco Noir ($3.50)

Buena Vista Lachryma Montis ($5)

**

Fair

Brookside Claret ($1)

Royal Host Claret ($1.05)

Italian Swiss Colony Claret ($1.40)

C.K. Mondavi Claret ($1.65)

Almadén Mountain Red Claret ($1.75)

Eleven Cellars Claret ($2)

Widmer Isabella ($2)
Charles Krug Claret ($2.35)
Martini Mountain Claret ($2.35)
Bargetto Claret ($2.50)
*
Passable
Inglenook Navalle Claret ($1.90)
Not Recommended:
Roma Claret

CLARET, FRENCH See: BORDEAUX. French Claret is synonymous with red Bordeaux.

CLERC–MILON–MONDON, CHÂTEAU (or simply: CHÂTEAU CLERC-MILON) Excellent red Bordeaux wine now owned by the illustrious Rothschild family. The vineyard directly adjoins the great Lafite vineyard—that's a pretty good neighborhood in which to grow wine grapes! And this wine is, indeed, of the same family and breed as the noble Lafite. The 1970 is *****, maybe just now reaching its peak, but it will be better drinking from '76 on. The '71 is also looking beautiful. Fair value, around $9.

CLIMENS, CHÂTEAU One of the greatest sweet white wines in the world, a genuine French Sauternes. Some rate Climens second only to the noble and illustrious Château d'Yquem. Every mortal should taste a real French Sauternes at least once during his earthly pilgrimage. Such luscious wine goes beautifully after dinner, with dessert, or after coffee, and it also makes a marvelous midmorning or mid-afternoon tête-à-tête wine. French Sauternes is one of the world's best bargains in fine wines today—it's out of fashion and hence reasonably priced, particularly so for a French wine. Serve Climens well chilled: 40 to 45°F.
1924, 1929, 1937, 1947, 1949

—All true Classics—Incredibly, all of these wines sold for less than $20 at auction in 1973—they were worth twice that. Many say they were greater than the respective Yquem vintages.
1959—***** Now at its best —Drink before 1980.
1961—At least Near-Classic, may well reach Classic—Sells, if you can find it, for around $10, a wondrous bargain!
1964—****—Now at its best.
1967—*****—Best drinking, 1975–1985.
1970, 1971—****—Already great drinking but will be even better, 1980–1990.

CLIQUOT, VEUVE PONSARDIN: See VEUVE CLIQUOT PONSARDIN.

(LES) CLOS: See CHABLIS, FRENCH.

CLOS AU CAILLERET: See (LE) CAILLERET.

CLOS DE BÈZE: See CHAMBERTIN, CLOS DE BÈZE.

CLOS DE LA PERRIER: See FIXIN.

CLOS DE LA ROCHE Full rich red Burgundy wine—one of the finest. It's noted for its resemblance to the king of red wines, the illustrious Le Chambertin. For details on how to serve and enjoy this wine: See under MOREY-SAINT-DENIS. Some notable vintages:
1959 Very fine, velvety wines, now at their best.
1961 Drouhin: *****—Just reaching its peak—it will live long.
1962 Beautiful, well-balanced wines—they will be long-lived.
1963 Lesser wines.
1964 Violland: *****
    Rousseau: *****
1966 Excellent wines.
1969 Big beautiful wines, will be at their best, 1976 on.
1970 Arlaud: *****—Will be ready, 1977 or 1978.

Clos de la Roche sells for $10 and upward.

(LE) CLOS DES CHENES: See VOLNAY.

CLOS DES MOUCHES Fine red Burgundy wine noted for its body, delicacy, and soft texture. This is not, perhaps, a great wine on a par with Le Corton and Le Chambertin, but it is the next thing to it. It will go well with fowl (roast turkey), lamb, beef. True wine lovers, however, will want to enjoy such a splendid wine to its utmost, on its own or with simple cheeses and bread. Clos des Mouches is at its best when it is between four and ten years of age. Air it one hour and serve at cool room temperature. This wine will cost anywhere from $7 to $12, depending on the shipper.
Some vintages:
1959 Great vintage, these wines are just now getting to their best.
1961 Coron: *****—Now at its best.
Chanson: *****—Now at its best.
1962 Coron: ****
1964 Drouhin: *****—Fine drinking today, but don't keep it too long.
1966 Coron: ****
Drouhin: ****
1969 Drouhin: *****
1970 Drouhin: *****

CLOS DES MYGLANDS: See MERCUREY.

CLOS DES PERRIÈRES: See MEURSAULT.

CLOS DES SANTENOTS: See VOLNAY.

CLOS DE TART Magnificent red Burgundy wine, as wine people say, a wine of "breed and distinction." It is noted for its delicacy. Clos de Tart is regularly **** and *****. How to appreciate and serve this

wine: See under MOREY-SAINT-DENIS.

CLOS DE VOUGEOT Here's one of the most famous single vineyards in all of France—indeed, in all the world. It comprises some 120 acres, but this is divided up among some seventy owners, and the wine can vary considerably from parcel to parcel. This magnificent red Burgundy is described as big, flowery, velvety, perfumed. It is noted for having the scent of violets. Clos de Vougeot deserves to be treated with reverence, which is to say, consumed and savored on its own, or with good cheeses (especially Brie, Bel Paese, Cheddar, Cantal) and bread. It's at its best when it's between six and ten years old.
1959 Lamarche: Near-Classic —Drink soon.
Noirat: Near-Classic— Drink soon.
1964 Lichine: *****
Ponnelle: *****
1966 Noellat: ****
Drouhin: *****
Roumier: ****
Grivot: Near-Classic
Hudelot (Lichine): *****
1969 Moillard: *****

CLOS DU CHAPITRE: See FIXIN.

CLOS GAENSBROENNEL (Gewürztraminer) WILLM "Clos Gaens-etc." is the name of a fine vineyard of the important Alsatian firm of A. Willm—say "film" with a "v" instead of an "f"—it's their best Gewürztraminer. A '64 was an exceptional wine, *****, and you may still find it around, but drink it soon. They're not exactly giving it away, though: ca. $8.75.

CLOS MARCEAU: See GIVRY.

CLOS ST. DENIS A fine red Burgundy wine (from the Com-

mune of Morey-Saint-Denis);
it's very similar to and often
compared with its neighbor Clos
de la Roche (see). It's a beautiful rich wine, slow to mature.
An outstanding bottle is the '61
by Ponnelle (the *Negociant,* or
producer) *****, just now at
its best. For how to serve and
fully enjoy this wine: See under MOREY-SAINT-DENIS.

CLOS ST. JACQUES: See
GEVREY-CHAMBERTIN.

**CLOS SAINTE HUNE, RIES-
LING** This is the name of an
Alsatian vineyard that produces
some of the finest white
Riesling wine of that nation.
And the Riesling grape, you recall, is the noble grape responsible for all those great white
wines of Germany. It is the
venerable firm of F. E. Trimbach that makes the wine—it's
in very small print on the label. Clos Sainte Hune is invariably an excellent wine, of
**** quality, retails around $6.

CLOS SAINT PAUL: See
GIVRY.

CLOS SAINT PIERRE: See
GIVRY.

**COCKBURN'S ALDOURO
TAWNY PORT** The proper
name of this Port firm is Cockburn Smithes & Co., Ltd., and
it's as British as it sounds, one
of the ancient and august British shippers of Portuguese Porto. Remember that Port is "the
Englishman's Wine": they have
appreciated it most, enjoyed it
most, promoted it most, and
drunk most of it. Cockburn is
one of the most reliable names
in the business. This particular
bottle is one of their least expensive Portos, a mere $5—
mere, he says—a good price for
a fine Porto: ****. How to
serve Port: See under PORT.

**COCKBURN'S SPECIAL RE-
SERVE PORTO** This is a
Ruby Porto, the humblest grade
of true Portuguese Porto, but
it's an elegant wine. This particular bottle will improve with
a year or two of further aging.
It rates *****. Fair value, $8.

**COCKBURN'S #25 DARK
RUBY PORTO** A good value
at $5. Immediately ready to
drink. Nice rich wine. A solid
****.

**COCKBURN'S VINTAGE
PORT** This is Cockburn's "top
of the line," and some of the
vintages have been tops, indeed.
Some of the greatest: 1896:
Classic—1912: Classic—1927:
Classic—1935 Coronation Bot-
tling: Near-Classic.

COLD DUCK, AMERICAN
To begin with, the name is probably a mistranslation: the German "Kalte Ende," "Cold Left-
overs," was mistaken for "Kalte
Ente," "Cold Duck." Well, the
whole enterprise has been mostly a mistake.

Not fiscally, of course. American Cold Ducks have netted
their producers (breeders?) millions of dollars. But vinously
they've been a mistake, for
they are mostly poor wine. And
after all, what can you expect
from a wine named after a
miserable, cold, soggy, splay-
footed fowl?

Cold Duck is a combination of
white Champagne and sparkling
Burgundy, both usually of inferior quality. The wine is giv-
en a liberal sweetening to make
it pleasant and easy-drinking.
And it's got a pretty "party"
color. It almost always has a
slight flavoring of Concord
grapes.

Cold Duck surely has had the
most meteoric rise of any wine
in the recorded history of man.
From zero sales just a few years
ago, it rose to spectacular sales
in the millions of gallons in

1971. Today, the flight of the Frigid Fowls has leveled off considerably. One might say that the high-flying Ducks have suffered from a *down*-draft.

Success breeds imitation—in this case, more fowls. Today you can find—hopefully you won't want to—Very Cold Duck, Very Very Cold Duck (to date no Very Very Very's), Cold Turkey, Hawk, and Eagle. Even Cold Bears, and, horrors, Cold Orange Duck. There is even—though you're not going to believe this—a Hot Goose. Scouts' honor!

In all fairness it should be added that Cold Duck is sometimes a victim of wine snobbery, and there are some good bottles of Cold Duck to be had. But they are the exception. However, that cardinal principle of all wine appreciation nowhere needs to be more clearly enunciated than in connection with this still-very-popular sparkling beverage: You are the ultimate connoisseur—if you like it, drink it—but watch out for the pinfeathers!

Serve Cold Duck (or Turkey, or Goose, or Buzzard, as the case may be) well chilled—for refreshment and parties. It is not well suited for before-meal consumption.

Listed below are America's best —and worst—Cold Ducks, in descending order of excellence. Where several wines have the some rating, the least expensive are listed first. Prices are approximate.

American Cold Duck— Comparative Standings

***

Good

Le Domaine Cold Duck ($3.10)

Masson Very Cold Duck ($5)

Christian Brothers Extra Cold Duck ($5.05)

Taylor Cold Duck ($5.30)

**

Fair

Franzia Cold Duck ($2)

Tres Grand Cold Duck ($2.50)

Lejon Cold Duck ($3.25)

Weibel Crackling Duck ($4.35)

Gold Seal Cold Duck ($4.95)

Great Western Pink Cold Duck ($5.10)

Korbel Cold Duck ($5.60)

*

Passable

André Cold Duck ($2)

Jacques Bonet Cold Duck ($2)

Calwa Cold Duck ($2)

Gallo Cold Duck ($3)

San Martin Cold Duck ($3.95)

Cresta Blanca Cold Duck ($5.50)

(LES) COMBETTES One of France's—if not the world's—best dry white wines. It ranks right after the great Montrachets (see), and sells at half the price, though it's still on the expensive side, $10 to $15. It's at its best when four to seven years old. How to serve it: See under MONTRACHET. A *1971 H. Clerc* is only *** (at $10.50 yet!)—a *1971 Leflaive* ($14), however, is Near-Classic—a *1970 Ampeau* ($10.50): *****.

COMTES DE CHAMPAGNE: See TAITTINGER.

CONCANNON VINEYARD (Livermore, Calif.) A winery with an Irish name is something like a Pope named Patrick O'Hoolihan. But it does happen occasionally—not with Popes so far, but with wineries. Here's one in California. (And there are others, even in Bordeaux— how about Château Lynch-

Bages, and believe it or not, Château MacCarthy?)

James Concannon came from Ireland in 1865, and by 1883 he was making wine in the Livermore Valley. His descendants have been doing a good job of it ever since. The Concannons first established their reputation by making outstanding white wines. Then in 1964 they did an about-face, concentrating on Petite Sirah, a red wine which nobody was making anywhere at the time. It's been one of their best wines and best sellers ever since. Today Concannon continues to expand and improve, and the third generation of Concannons is probably making the best wines of the winery's ninety-year history. Wine lovers can only say, over their glass of Concannon Petite Sirah or Prelude Dry Sherry, "Erin go bragh!"

Burgundy** Mellow, everyday red wine—even cremated hot dogs will taste better when washed down with a glass of this. It may even improve a whit with one or two years of added bottle age. Serve at cool room temperature. Fair value, ca. $2.50.

Cabernet Sauvignon, Limited Bottling Things were getting dull around the Concannon premises about ten years ago— they had already mastered the art of making fine white wines in the Livermore Valley. The Concannon boys began looking around for new worlds to conquer and they settled on an old established red wine and a new one. The new one was Petite Sirah (see). The old-timer was Cabernet Sauvignon. They were successful with both. Their Cabernet is made in the classic Bordeaux fashion: aged four years in small oak casks,

then given an additional year of bottle aging. It is an elegant wine, deserves to be drunk on its own or else accompanying the best cuts of beef and lamb. Serve at cool room temperature. The current vintages (1968, 1969) sell for ca. $7.50 . . . sorry.

1963*** Concannon's Cabernets are long-lived; this wine is now at its best; drink it within the next few years.

1964**** Just now reaching its best—will hold until 1979.

1965**** One critic awarded this wine 20 points out of a possible 20.

1966—* Something happened. Malevolent forces?

1967**** Ah, benevolent forces were at work. A good wine to lay down; it will do nothing but improve, and will be at its apex, 1976 through 1983.

1968**** Best drinking, 1976 through 1982.

Chablis*** Made in the classic Chablis style: dry, crisp, tart. Not about to displace true French Chablis, yet a nice everyday white wine to enhance those fish sticks, shrimp basket, oysters. Drink within two years of purchase. Serve chilled. Fair value, ca. $2.50.

Château Concannon*** This is a sweet white wine made in imitation of French Sauternes, which is always sweet. But right there most of the similarity ends. This wine tends to be sugary—true French Sauternes is simply luscious and rich. However, people who enjoy a sweet wine may like this one, for it does have a measure of fruitiness. Just don't drink it alongside an authentic Sauternes. Serve it after dinner. (If your taste or the occasion calls for a dry white wine, the following, Dry Sémillon, is what you need.) Château Concannon is a vintage-dated wine, and recent vintages (1968 through 1972) have been consistently good. Fair value, $3.

Dry Sauterne: See DRY SÉMILLON.

Dry Sémillon*** This is simply the dry counterpart of the preceding wine, Château Concannon. Until a few months ago it was called Dry Sauterne —the two names are used interchangeably in California. It's a good wine, with a distinctive taste of the Sémillon grape. It goes particularly well with chicken. Serve it chilled. It's at its best from two to six years after its vintage date. Recent vintages, 1968 through 1972, have been consistently good. Fair value, $2.50 to $2.75.

Dry Sherry, Prelude**** It's made in the traditional Spanish "flor" method, and is said to smack of apples and pears. As the name indicates, its best service is as a "prelude" to dinner. If you insist on chilling it, make it light—coldness inhibits the flavor. "On the rocks" is an abomination unto the Lord. A good value at ca. $3.

Johannisberg Riesling** Another good white wine by Concannon: big and fragrant, to go with light foods, especially poultry and seafoods. Serve chilled. Fair value, $4.25 to $4.50.

1968*** Drink immediately.

1969* Drink immediately, if at all.

1971*** Best drinking, 1975–1976.

1972** Best drinking, 1975 through 1976.

1973 Estate Bottled**** Worth looking for. Drink, 1975 through 1977. Fair value, $5.

Moselle** Moselle is an exquisite white German wine, named after the region in which it is produced. This is one of the few American wines so named. Ach, the only thing it shares with its German counterpart is its name. It has a slight floweriness, it's just off-dry, will go with light foods. Serve it chilled. Recent vintages, 1968 through 1971, have been consistently mediocre. The '72 is an exception: ***. Fair value, but not very enthusiastically, ca. $3.

Muscat de Frontignan*** A sweet white dessert wine with a pronounced Muscat flavor. Those who like such wines will be inclined to award it ****. There is also a Limited Bottling, at $1 more, which is richer and better. Save it for your richest desserts. Fair value, ca. $3.50.

Petite Sirah An historic wine for Concannon: they were one of the first to bottle it under its own name, some ten years ago, and it remains to this day one of their best wines, and their best seller. It's big, dark, rich, robust, ideal accompaniment for good hearty foods: steaks, stews, casseroles, roasts. Air all these bottles at least one hour. Serve at cool room temperature. A good value at $3.50.

1965**** Just now reaching its peak; drink now and through the decade.

1965 Limited Bottling**** It won't appeal to everybody—it's extra dry, yet soft and mature.

1966**** Now at its best and will so remain until 1980.

1967*** Drink, 1975–1980.

1968 and 1969**** Drink, 1975–1980.

1970, 1971*** Drink now and for a good decade to come.

Prelude Dry Sherry: See DRY SHERRY.

Red Dinner Wine Not recommended. Here's a fickle wine if there ever was one; at one moment—like right now—it's almost undrinkable, and the next moment, it's nothing but yummy. Only recently this honestly named wine was delicious: fruity, well balanced, an excellent value at $1.90, and clearly deserving ***. Today's offering —the bottom of the bottles are stamped '72—is a horrid brew, acrid, vile-tasting, not recommended at any price.

Sauterne, Dry: See DRY SÉMILLON.

Sauvignon Blanc Concannon's best white wine, and perhaps California's best of this breed. It's a dry wine, but does have a touch of sweetness; it's known for its earthy taste; it's clean and crisp. The winery says it's "born on the rocks," on the rocky soil of the Livermore Valley. (But, egad, don't serve it so; dilution is pollution, the profanation of the sacred.) It's usually good enough to merit solo consumption: drunk on its own, or with cheese and fruit. It's famous as an accompaniment for shellfish and will also go well with any light food. Serve chilled. Fair value, $3.50.

1968 and 1969*** Drink immediately.

1970** Drink soon.

1971*** — Limited Bottling **** Drink now and through 1977.

1972*** At its best, 1975 through 1978.

Sémillon, Dry: See DRY SÉMILLON.

Vin Rosé*** It deserves the *** at least price-wise. A mite sweeter and softer than the Zinfandel Rosé (see), the latter is the better wine, the tastier of the two. Good for casual evening-time enjoyment or to accompany light foods. Serve chilled. Fair value, $2.50.

White Dinner Wine* Water is cheaper.

Zinfandel Rosé*** An exceptional rosé, very fruity, clean, and tart, on the dry side. It can accompany any food with honor, but its best service will be on its own, chilled, or with cheeses and fruits. It's a vintage-dated wine, ready to drink when you buy it, and should not be kept more than four years beyond its vintage date. Fair value, $3 to $3.25.

COOK'S IMPERIAL AMERICAN CHAMPAGNE** This wine probably has the most bizarre history of any American wine. It was once owned by von Ribbentrop, Hitler's foreign minister, who was hung in 1946 for war crimes. It began as an Easterner, made in St. Louis, Missouri, at that time (midnineteenth-century), would you believe, the wine capital of America. Today it's made by the giant Guild Wine Company of San Francisco. It still proclaims its eastern origins in a small amount of Catawba in the blend. Cook's Champagnes have never been very spectacular, and they still aren't. They come in the standard flavors; Sec, Pink, Extra Dry, Brut, sparkling Burgundy. They are, to say the least, a dubious value at $4.50 or more.

CORDIER This name appears on a number of good red Bordeaux (French) wines but it's not the name of the wine, it's the name of the family who owns the vineyards. See the wines under their own names: Château Talbot, Gruaud-Larose, etc.

CORDON ROUGE: A Champagne made by G. H. Mumm

(Reims, France); See CHAM-
PAGNE and MUMM.

CORKS VS. METAL CAPS

The simplest rule in all the
wide world of wine is this: If
you want fine wine stay away
from any wine that doesn't
have a cork cork—as distinct
from a plastic or metal "cork."
The best wines are living things
and continue to "breathe" by
means of a cork cork. Cheaper
wines, which are often pasteur-
ized, are beyond changing and
need no real cork. Thus American jug wines ordinarily have
metal caps. They may be quite
satisfactory in their own category, but they are not, and
will never be, fine wines.

(LE) CORTON Illustrious red
Burgundy wine, the greatest red
of France's entire Côte de
Beaune. It is the most brilliant
in color of all Burgundies, a
perfect balance of fire and
light, someone has described it.
It's at its best when it is from
six to twelve years old, and in
great years it will live on for
decades. Such magnificent wine
deserves to be savored wholly
on its own or with fine cheeses
and bread. Air it one hour,
serve at cool room temperature.

Some vintages:
1923 Bouchard: Still tasty.
1959 and *1961 Leroy:* *****
1964 Brenot: *****
1966 Brenot: ****
   Maufoux: ****
   Doudet-Naudin: ****
1970 Remoissenet: *****—
Will be at its best, 1976–1985.
1971 Crispin: *****
Some very fine wines use the
famous name of Corton hyphenated with their own names:
Corton-Pougets,   Corton-Ren-
ards, Corton Clos du Roi, Corton-Bressandes. These are all
superb wines, should be enjoyed
and appreciated as you would
(Le) Corton.

CORTON-BRESSANDES: See
(LE) CORTON.

CORTON-CHARLEMAGNE

One of the most famous white
wines in the world, fully comparable to the magnificent Montrachets. It's a beautifully balanced wine, with a flinty taste
like Chablis, only much more
so. Burgundians say they can
detect the taste of cinammon.
Corton-Charlemagne may be
savored on its own, but it will
also go beautifully with light
meats, especially fowl (chicken
in a rich sauce), with shellfish,
or with cheeses, especially Brie
and Münster. Corton-Charlemagne is at its best when it is
between four and ten years old.
Serve it chilled.

Some notable vintages:
1964 Bonneau du Martray:
*****
1966 Chanson: ****
   Papet: *****
   Bonneau du Martray: ***
   —Past its prime.
1969 Drouhin: Not recom-
mended.
   Bouchard: ****
   Henri de Villamont: ***
   Bichot: ****
1970 Drouhin: Near-Classic
   Latour: *****
   De Luze: *****
   Jadot: *****

CORTON-CLOS DU ROI: See
(LE) CORTON.

(CHÂTEAU) CORTON-GRANCEY

Magnificent white
Burgundy wine made by the
prince of Burgundy shippers,
Louis Latour. Experts say it's
on a par with the greatest
Cortons, although it is not officially classified. How to appreciate and serve this wine:
See under (LE) CORTON.

Some vintages:
1953 Past its prime.

1955****
1957*****
1959*****
1961 Near-Classic
1962****
1963***
1964****
1966*****
1967 Near-Classic
1969 Near-Classic—Now at its best.
1970*****—Now at its best.
1971*****—Will be at its best, 1978 on.
1972****—Drink it, 1976–1980.

CORTON-POUGETS: See (LE) CORTON.

CORTON RENARDS: See (LE) CORTON.

COSSART NO. 26 DARK GOLDEN MADEIRA****
The British wine merchant, Cossart, Gordon and Co., produces some fine wines—this is one of them. Rich and full, velvety smooth. Try it, day or night, with food or without, room temperature or chilled. The importer, Munson Shaw Co., especially recommends it with canapés, cheeses, nuts. For more on the serving of Madeira: See under MADEIRA. A good value at $3.25.

COSSART VIVA MADEIRA**
As stated above, Cossart makes some fine wines—this is *not* one of them. Not recommended at around $3.25.

CÔTE DE BEAUNE: See BEAUNE.

CÔTE DE BEAUNE VILLAGES: See BEAUNE.

CÔTE DE BROUILLY: See BROUILLY.

CÔTE ROTIE The name means the Roasted Slope, and a lot of people think these are the best red wines of France's Rhone Valley. The wines mature for some years in wooden casks, but still are not ready to drink when first marketed. Some experts say that ideally these wines should not be consumed until they are at least ten years old—some say older. Surely no civilized *homo sapiens* will drink them before they are four or five years old. Infanticide! These are robust, heady, full-flavored wines, said to have a taste of raspberries. For details on how to serve them: See under CÔTES DU RHONE.

Some vintages:
1966 Jaboulet-Isnard: ****
    M. Chapoutier: ***
        The '66s are now at at their best.
1967 Jaboulet-Isnard: **
    M. Chapoutier: ****
    Paul Jaboulet: ****
1968 Domaine Gerin: ****
1969 Paul Jaboulet: ****
1970 Dervieux: ***
    Paul Jaboulet: ****—Will mature well.
1971 Paul Jaboulet: ****—Can be drunk comparatively young: from 1975 on.

CÔTES DU RHONE If you want to be a wise and frugal wine buyer, this is one of the names you'll look for when you want a substantial red wine, for whatever purpose. France's Rhone Valley still offers some of the best wine values in the world, and one of the few real values in French wines today. These are not delicate or subtle wines, but big, sturdy, heady ones, sometimes a bit rough, but age will usually cure that. Few wines, in fact, improve so much with bottle age as do these Rhone reds. Most of them are drunk far too young; they should be at least five years old before they're consumed, and ten years would be better still. Rhone wines, with their straightforwardness, are especially suited to accompany game, variety meats, beef, stews, even curry and other spicy foods. And, like any good red wine, they will be appreciated most fully when they're savored by themselves, or with cheeses. It is important to air a red Rhone (a little white wine is also made), especially if you're cheating and drinking it before it's five years old.

Some names to look for:

Delas Frères—The '70 and '71 were *** at least.

Thorin (Sumner Selection)— The '70 is now lovely: ****

Château Malijay—The '71 took an important British award: ****—The '72 is almost as good: at least ****

La Vieille Ferme—The '71 was excellent wine: ****, at $2.75, a marvelous value.

Alexandre Rochette—The '72 is ****, a big chewy wine, but it won't be ready until 1977.

Quien & Cie.—Usually an excellent value.

Domaine du Chevalet—The '69 is a fine value at $2.75, ***

Domaine de l'Enclos—The '71 is very good, dry and rich: ****

Chanson—The '70 is ****

Jaboulet Aîné—The '69 is especially fine: ****. It's at its peak.

Sometimes the word "Villages" is tacked onto the name; it's the same wine. If the label has the name Chusclan (or Villages de Chusclan) or Cairanne, it's almost certainly a dependable wine, *** to ****.

Avoid very cheap ($1.50 to $2) Côtes du Rhone. Respectable bottles will range from $2.50 to $4.

Vintages are not extremely important in the Rhone Valley, as the summers are uniformly long and hot, but there are differences. Some recent vintages:

1968—Poor wines; avoid this vintage.

1969—Rich wines, full-bodied and strong—Now at their best and will remain so through the 70s.

1970—Huge harvest and high quality—Fine wines, best drinking: 1975–1980.

1971—Not as successful as '70, but good wines, now ready to drink; they'll hold through 1978.

1972—Good, well-balanced, robust wines, will be good drinking, 1977 through the decade.

CRACKLING ROSÉ: See CHAMPAGNE, PINK.

CRESTA BLANCA This brand name has had as checkered a career as any in the history of American wine. Today it's owned by the immense Guild Wine Company of San Francisco, and the name Cresta Blanca on a wine label is looking more and more respectable with each passing year. But it had a long way to come. Vineyards have been acquired recently in northerly Mendocino County and that augurs well, for most of California's finest wines come from the northerly reaches.

Brut Champagne: See CHAMPAGNE.

Cabernet Sauvignon** Cabernet Sauvignon should be one of California's finest red wines, but Cresta Blanca's version doesn't come near. Some bottlings have deserved at least ***, but recent bottles have been uniformly disappointing. Cabernet goes well with beef and lamb; air one hour, serve at cool room temperature. It will improve if you keep it for a year or two. Fair value, $3.60.

Champagne Cresta Blanca makes five sparkling wines, mostly from good northern California grapes, mostly made by the classic Champagne method, mostly above-average. They are: Brut Champagne, ***: the best of the lot. It's crisp, lively, the driest of the five. Extra Dry Champagne, ***: took a gold medal in 1972, a bit sweeter than the Brut. Pink Champagne, ***: on the sweet side. Champagne Rouge, ***: most wineries call this "sparkling Burgundy"; it has some character and liveliness. Cold Duck, *: ho hum . . . All these wines sell for around $5.

Cold Duck: See CHAMPAGNE.

Dry Sémillon*** Here's a good choice to accompany your fish or seafood dinner or that pork roast. Serve chilled. It's ready to drink when you buy it and will keep for three or four years. Fair value, $2.50.

Dry Watch Sherry**** Cresta Blanca has always done a good job with its sherries, and this is the best of the three it now makes. A consistent medal winner, it's well aged in small oak cooperage (that makes it more flavorful). It's a bit sweeter than the Palomino Sherry, but still a cocktail type. Fair value, $2.75.

French Colombard*** This grape is not one of the "noble" varieties, but Cresta Blanca's wine comes off pretty nobly. It's mouth-filling and spicy. It's got a bit of sweetness too, and will make a good economical sipping wine, or it can accompany light foods. Drink it within two or three years of purchase. Serve chilled. A good value at $2.30 to $2.50.

Gamay Beaujolais*** This wine may not be as light and fruity as some California Gamays but it's got good body and flavor. Just right for that outdoor barbecue or picnic or buffet luncheon. Enjoy it while it's young, within two years of purchase. Serve at cool room temperature or slightly chilled. Fair value, ca. $3.

Green Hungarian* Ugh, blah . . . Water's cheaper and almost as tasty.

Grenache Rosé** Considering its price, ca. $2.20, there are a lot worse wine values around, though it's still a small wine. Rosés are best for refreshment, chilled, or to accompany light foods. Drink within two years of purchase.

Grey Riesling** Stick with the French Colombard—it's the same price and a lot more wine.

Grignolino*** "A light, happy red," says the winery, and that 'tis. Fine with grilled hamburgers, steaks, roasts, cheese dishes, pasta. Air one hour, serve at cool room temperature. It may even improve with a year or two in the bottle. A good value at ca. $3.

Mountain Burgundy** If you will age this wine at least six months, you'll probably award it ***, especially considering its modest price tag, ca. $2. Serve it and enjoy it exactly as you would the Grignolino (above). Don't keep it more than two or three years. Air one hour and serve at cool room temperature.

Mountain Chablis** Everyday white wine, economically priced, pronouncedly dry. It will go well with light foods, especially fish and seafood. Or take it on a picnic. Serve chilled. Don't keep it more than two years. A good value at ca. $2.

Palomino Sherry*** Cresta

Blanca's driest sherry. Fair value, $2.75—$3.

Petite Sirah* Robust red wine, flavorful, zesty. Good sipping for those who enjoy dry reds. It will enhance almost any hearty food: casseroles, pasta, red meats. Air one hour and serve at cool room temperature. Fair value, $3.

Pink Champagne: See CHAMPAGNE.

Pinot Chardonnay Not there yet. At $3.50, not recommended.

Pinot Noir* A substantial, well-balanced Burgundy-type red wine. If you like reds, you'll enjoy sipping this wine with cheese and stuff, but not overpowering garlicy or peppery stuff. Also good to accompany fowl, cheese dishes, soufflés, egg dishes. Air one hour and serve at cool room temperature. Fair value, ca. $3.

Port and Tawny Port Both: *** Two soft, mellow dessert wines, both selling for ca. $3. The Tawny is a bit fuller, richer; the plain Port is a trifle fruitier. One critic suggests laying down the Tawny for ten or twenty years; he's convinced it will improve immensely. Let 1 know!

Premier Sémillon Not made since 1966, this was an historic wine, a true collector's item; it was the first time a California wine was persuaded to develop some "noble rot," a fungus which has helped make German wines famous.

Rhine Sweeter than the Sauterne and not as good. Sip it, if you already possess some, casually, chilled. Don't keep it more than two years.

Sauterne* In the U.S. "Sauterne" is one of those vague wine names that can mean almost anything—and al-most nothing. With Cresta Blanca it means something: a distinctive little dry white wine, to accompany fish, seafood, fowl, pork. Serve chilled; drink within two years or so of purchase. A good value at ca. $2.10.

Sauvignon Blanc* Flowery young wine, very dry. It will ennoble any luncheon fare, fish or seafood dinner. Serve chilled. At its best within three years of purchase. Fair value, ca. $3.

Sherry: See DRY WATCH SHERRY, PALOMINO SHERRY, TRIPLE CREAM SHERRY.

Tawny Port: See PORT.

Triple Cream Sherry** It has won more than its share of awards and was Grand Prize Winner at the Los Angeles County Fair in 1963 and again in 1974. Fair value, $2.85.

Zinfandel* Tasty and berrylike in flavor, Cresta Blanca's "Zin" is a good value at $3 to $3.25. Red wine lovers will appreciate it on its own or with cheese and fruit. It also goes well with food, almost any food, other than ice cream or pickles. This wine seems to be getting better with each succeeding vintage, or rather, batch, as it's not vintage-dated; no Cresta Blanca wine is. Indeed, wine lovers have been watching for it as it's released each year, and it gets bought up as fast as it's put on the market.

CRIBARI, FAMIGLIA The winery's literature says that "Eighty years ago Beniamino Cribari made a mellow wine just for family and friends—and nothing's changed." That's about right—if ol' Beniamino's friends weren't too fussy. Cribari wines, a brand name owned by the huge Guild Wine Company (San Francisco), are simple, mellow (sweet, a wine critic would say), inexpensive wines. They're designed for two classes of people, the first of which encompasses about three fourths of the human race: novice wine drinkers, and the second of which encompasses about 99 percent of the mankind: the non-rich. And that's why Cribari wines are big sellers.

The most notable offerings:

Barberone: Innocuous, a wine for beginners, pleasant enough: *

Burgundy**: Light, soft sweet—non-wine lovers will love it . . . you won't have any trouble confusing it with Clos de Vougeot!

Mountain White Chablis: Very small wine, but preferable to water: *

Vino Bianco da Pranzo: The name means "White Dinner Wine." **

Vino Fiamma da Pranzo: The lengthy Italian name is loosely translated: Itsa rosé! ** And would you believe that these two Pranzo wines took gold medals, no less, at the 1974 Los Angeles County Fair?

Zinfandel**

CRIOTS-BÂTARD-MON-TRACHET One of the world's greatest dry white wines, but infrequently seen in the U.S. It's one of the great names of Burgundy (France), very rare and very expensive. Criots is similar to Bâtard-Montrachet (see). For further details: See also MONTRACHET.

CROEVER NACKTARSCH (or CRÖVER or KRÖVER NACKTARSCH) The name means a "bare behind" from the town of Cröv (Croev) and that's what you'll see on the label: a young lad of Cröv being spanked on his exposed posterior, in punishment for having pilfered some of father's fine Moselle wine. But the label, sad to relate, is usually better than the wine. (One humorless critic says the wine is better than the label.) But most Bare Bottoms are simply light, noticeably sweet blends of lesser Moselle wines. Over all: **. How to serve it: See under MOSELLE.

CROFT DISTINCTION FINEST TAWNY PORT Croft & Co. of London and Oporto, Portugal, is one of the most reputable of the Port-shipping firms. Its wines invariably command high prices. This particular wine is a rung below the "Vintage Character" Port listed below, but fine withal ****. It's already been properly aged—you don't have to lay it down for a century or two before you can drink it. Fair value, ca. $5.

CROFT FINE RUBY PORT This is the lowest-priced of the Croft Portos seen in this country, but it's one of the best of its class: ****. A fine value at $5, drink it within three years of purchase.

CROFT PARTICULAR PORTO***** This is the best Tawny Port Croft has to offer. Beautiful! Fair value, $6.

CROFT "VINTAGE CHARACTER" PORT This is not a true Vintage Port, but it's the next thing to it. It's fine wine, but they're not exactly giving the stuff away—it fetches $14 or $15. It has one tremendous advantage over true Vintage Porto, though—you can drink it today, you won't have to keep it until you're too old to enjoy it. Clearly *****.

CROFT VINTAGE PORT This is Croft's "top of the line"

their finest Port, rare and expensive. Some memorable bottles:

1924: Exceptional vintage, now at its very best—It sold at Christie's wine auction (London) in 1971 for a mere $9, compared with around $30 for the illustrious '27, but in at least one tasting this '24 rated higher. Near-Classic.

1950: Very good, though not oustanding vintage—But Croft's was exceptionally fine, perhaps best of the lot: *****

*1967 Quinta Da Roeda*** This is the name of a famous vineyard owned by Croft & Co., of London and Portugal. For some reason, however, this particular vintage is not up to standard. In one tasting it placed 26th of 26 entries.

CROZES-HERMITAGE A trustworthy, though never great wine of France's Rhone Valley, very similar to Hermitage (see), though not quite as good. Like Hermitage, there is both a red and a white. It is regularly: ***, and is apt to be a good value since it is not as well known as Hermitage. For some reputable shippers, see under CÔTES DU RHONE. How to serve it: See under HERMITAGE.

CRUSE This is a familiar name to a lot of American wine drinkers. Cruse et Fils Frères has been shipping French wines to the U.S. for decades, almost for centuries. Cruse is one of the largest and most reputable shippers of Bordeaux. Somebody recently wrote a hilarious novel entitled *Arigato* about the venerable firm. In October of 1974, the name of Cruse received some unwanted publicity when Lionel Cruse, the head of the firm, was haled into court along with some other wine merchants on charges of mis-

labeling some 8,000 barrels of wine. The fraudulent wine was confiscated by the government and will never be marketed, but the scandal, dubbed the *Winegate,* will probably affect the sale of Cruse wines. French wine laws are very strict and enforcement is excellent. This minor episode is only that, a minor aberration, for Cruse has been a reliable name for 150 years and will continue to be, perhaps even more so after this unsavory episode. But no name on a wine label is an absolute guarantee of quality. Continue to be judicious and sagacious in your selection of Cruse's—or anybody else's—wines.

Cruse Anjou Rosé The rosés of Anjou (France) are said to be below the quality of those from the Tavel region of France —not so in this case. This is an excellent little rosé, crisp, lively dry. A good value at $3.30. A Cruse Tavel Rosé, at around $5.25, is no better, only more expensive. How to serve this wine: See under ROSÉ.

Cruse Tavel Rosé—See preceding entry.

Other Cruse Wines—See under the names of the wines.

CUNE This strange name is an acronym for the long Spanish name of a wine firm of Spain's Rioja region. Never mind about the convoluted Spanish name, these folks know wine—Cune wines are among Rioja's finest. These are their best:

Rioja Clarete *** Good, soft, fruity red wine. Air it one to two hours. An excellent value at $2.50 to $2.75.

Imperial (or: Imperial Reserva) 1962 **** Fair value, $4.50.

Imperial Gran Reserva, 1956

and 1960: ***** Fair value, $6 to $7.

Vina Real **** A velvety-smooth wine that comes in a Burgundy-type bottle, and the wine is, indeed, Burgundy-like. The 1966 was particularly good. The current 1969 and 1970 will benefit from a few more years in the bottle. An excellent value at around $3.

How to serve these wines: See under RIOJA.

CUVAISON, INC. (Calistoga, Calif.) A small, new, prestigious California winery in the Napa Valley, begun in 1970. All Cuvaison wines are 100 percent varietals: made wholly from the specified grapes, no blending, and all are vintage-dated. Things are flexible at Cuvaison: they do not have a fixed "line" of wines but vary the wines made each year, and even their names, according to the way the wine develops. Their stated goal: to produce a limited number of dry table wines of highest quality. They're well begun. And the Germans say that's half done.

Cabernet Sauvignon, 1971 Now slumbering blissfully in Limousin oak barrels, it probably won't even be released until 1976, but it should be beautiful to behold when it emerges. There's not much of it and it's going to be in short supply. However, there's much more of:

Cabernet Sauvignon, 1973 It won't be released until 1978. Possess your soul in patience and you shall be amply rewarded.

Chardonnay of the Napa Valley, 1970 and 1971**** Chardonnay is often a connoisseur's wine and Cuvaison's is decidedly such: dry, rather austere, rather "oaky," assertive.

Much of this is to say that it's a good wine—but only provided you like it. Try it. Fair value, $5 to $5.50.

Chenin Blanc of the Napa Valley Most California Chenin Blanc is light, frolicsome, a little sweet, very fresh. Cuvaison's is more serious. Like most of their products, it's a connoisseur's type of wine: totally dry, zesty, elegant. The winery says it's to be drunk with bread and cheese. Fair value, $3.25 to $3.75.

1970****—Drink immediately.

1971, 1972** Drink now and through 1978.

Gamay Cuvaison changes the name of this wine according to its development. Gamay is America's version of France's Beaujolais: a light young red wine, very fresh and tasty. It goes almost anywhere: picnic, outdoor barbecue, buffet, informal dining. Drink your Gamay young: within four years of its vintage date. Serve at cool room temperature.

Gamay Nouveau, 1973*** This kind of very young red wine has become popular in the U.S. only in the past several years. The French have long enjoyed some of their Beaujolais when it is only a few months old. Sebastiani and Sterling, among others, make a wine of this type. (Sterling's is called Merlot Primeur.) It's a very very young-tasting wine, totally simple and sappy. You'll either like it or you won't—probably the former. This is one of the best specimens of an American "nouveau." Drink this wine immediately, without delay, as soon as possible, if not sooner. If it reaches its first birthday, it's already senile!

Wherefore you are counseled to look for:

Gamay Nouveau, 1974 Clairvoyantly: *** This wine exists today only *in potentia*, but presuming that Cuvaison will be making it—a likely presumption considering the success of the '73—the crystal ball says ***. Drink it as soon as you get your hands on it.

Gamay Rouge, 1970* This wine was made by a special process which gave it a deep red coloring: Rouge. It's full-bodied and hearty, and even fizzes a little when you pour it. This Gamay will even improve a bit with a few added years of bottle age. Drink, 1975 through 1976. Fair value, $3.

Gamay Vivace, 1971 and 1972* It's pronounced "veevahs," and it means "lively." Which it is. It's young and fresh, lighter than the red Gamay (preceding wine). Best drinking, 1975–1976. Fair value, $2.75 (in California).

Sauvignon Blanc, 1972** This is the only Sauvignon Blanc Cuvaison has made: a bright dry wine with excellent flavor and splendid aftertaste. Will go well with light, delicate foods, but it really deserves to be savored on its own, with mild cheeses, fresh fruit. Serve chilled. Fair value, $5.

D

DÃO Even if you don't know how to pronounce it, it's the best of all Portuguese table wines. It comes in two colors: red and white. The red is more readily available, but both are good little wines. (Dão is pronounceable only by a Portuguese—it's a nasal sound—say "down" and fade away on the "n.") Both wines are ready to drink when you buy them— don't keep the white more than a year or so—the best red Dãos will improve for an additional five or even ten years after purchase. You need not fuss over vintage dates on Dão labels, except that they tell you *approximately* how old the wine is.

The most reliable Dãos shipped to this country are assessed under their brand names (or producers' names): Grão Vasco; Real Vinicola; Magrico; Dom Bazilio; Santa Rey.

Red Dão (*Tinto*) resembles a red Rhone more than anything else: it's high in alcohol, very dark red in color, strong, smooth, mouth-filling. Serve red Dão at cool room temperature; white, chilled. The red goes well with red meats, stews, casseroles, pasta. The white, with fish, seafood, fowl, pork, veal. Dão wines are excellent values in these inflated days.

DÃO CABIDO: This is not the name of a wine; it's a grade of wine: "Finished Dão," the highest of three grades of red Dão (Portuguese) wine. See under the producer's name: REAL VINICOLA.

DECANTING The most important thing about decanting wine is this: Forget it! You will not decant one bottle in 500. Not in the ordinary course of human events. (Unless you're richer than almost anybody and can afford the kinds of wines that require decanting.)

The second thing is this: Decanting is a very simple process—it is as easy to decant a wine as it is to drink one—well, almost. . . .

Decanting has the sound and the aura of an elaborate ritual performed by candlelight, by an imperious sommelier flanked by a solemn, liveried butler while the awed bystanders observe in reverential silence.

But decanting means simply to pour a wine slowly from its original container into another vessel, leaving the sediment behind. And it is as simple as it sounds. Pour slowly and carefully, so that the wine proceeds and the sediment remains. Common sense tells one not to jiggle or shake the wine before decanting or there will be no sediment to leave behind.

Very few wines today require decanting. In this book these are individually noted; they are either very old wines (always expensive) or prestige wines (also expensive) specially produced, without fining or filtration.

Sediment does not harm a wine at all—nor will it harm you. In fact, sediment is usually the sign of a superior wine. It's misguided Americans who have this thing about sediment—in wine or almost anywhere else. Americans are convinced that it will clog their nasal, reproductive, and cerebral passages. But like everything else in wine, sediment is good for you—it'll make you strong and healthy and wise and wealthy.

When decanting is called for, stand the bottle upright for twenty-four hours—or at least a few hours if you're caught short—so that all the sediment will have settled to the bottom of the bottle. Do the decanting several hours before you will serve the wine. You'll do a better job of it if you use some kind of a light behind the bottle—a candle or flashlight, or at least do your pouring against a light background—so that you can see exactly when the sediment begins to flow.

Just proceed slowly and gently and you'll be one of the world's most elegant decanters, no matter what your shape.

(LES) DEMOISELLES: See LE CAILLERET.

DEL MAGNIFICO, RUFFINO *** This is an "invented" name of a red Italian wine, the property of the giant Ruffino firm of Florence, Italy. It's a popular wine, a soft, "mellow," and fruity one, sure to please wine novices. Fair value, $3.75.

DIEZ HERMANOS The name means "the Ten Brothers," a shipper of Spanish Sherries. Well, those ten brothers aren't always tending the *bodega*, for the wines are mostly average, **, and below. Though they're inexpensive for Spanish sherries, they are not recommended.

DOCTOR: See BERNKASTELLER DOKTOR.

DOKTOR: See BERNKASTELLER DOKTOR.

DOLCETTO The name means sweet, and sometimes it is very slightly so, but usually it's definitely on the dry side: a light, soft, youngish red wine, a kind of Italian Beaujolais. Occasionally it has the name of its village attached, as Dolcetto D'Alba. It can be a good value if it sells for $3 to $4. You can depend on it to be a steady ***.

DOM BAZILIO DÃO* An economical but sound Portuguese table wine, around $2, an excellent value. It comes in both red and white, and both are reliable and satisfying. How to serve: See under DAO.

DOM PERIGNON This is probably the world's most renowned and most revered single bottle of Champagne. Some say it is the world's most perfect Champagne. It is the "Best of the House" of the great French Champagne house of Moët et Chandon (see). It is horrendously expensive, around $27, and, truth to tell, it is too often purchased more for its snob appeal than for its inherent superiority. This is not to imply that this is not a superb wine—it certainly is—but there are many other French Champagnes surely equally fine; how good can a Champagne get?— at half the price. See the listing under CHAMPAGNE, pp. 59–60, for a starter. Some vintages:

1962—A grand wine, superior to the '61: *****

1964—Near-Classic—Vincent Price (a wine buff) calls it "super-marvelous."

1966—Near-Classic

DOM SCHARZHOFBERGER: See SCHARZHOFBERGER.

DOMECQ, PEDRO: See PEDRO DOMECQ.

DOPFF & IRION: Alsatian wine firm. See under the names of the individual wines: RIESLING, GEWÜRZTRAMINER, etc.

DOS CORTADOS: See WILLIAM & HUMBERT.

DOW'S BOARDROOM FINEST RARE TAWNY PORT Porto wines carry some of the most imaginative wine labels in the world—like this one, to be consumed in the corporation boardroom. It's not up to the quality of Dow's Vintage Porto (below), but it's excellent wine, *****, with "mellow majesty . . . satin smoothness," says one critic. It's not exactly free, however: ca. $10.

DOW'S VINTAGE PORT Dow is an illustrious name among Port wines, and Vintage Port is their finest.
Some memorable vintages:
1878: One famous critic said it was the best Porto he ever drank. If you have any lying about the house, best drink it soon—it won't last forever, only nearly so. Classic.
1963: It's expected to become one of Dow's finest ever, if you keep it another ten to twenty years. In '71 it sold at the Christie wine auction, London—you won't believe this—for a mere $3. Today it brings at least $12 and a good value at that. *****
1966: This wine was made by new methods of crushing and fermentation, and it seems destined for greatness. *****

(JOSEPH) DROUHIN This is the name of a prestigious and very dependable French wine firm dealing exclusively in Burgundy wines, including some of the very finest and most expensive. The name is all over the label—you might think it's the name of the wine. Look up your wine under its proper name: Meursault-Perrières, Volnay, Clos des Mouches, Beaujolais, etc.

DRY MONOPOLE: See HEIDSIECK DRY MONOPOLE.

DRY SACK: See WILLIAMS & HUMBERT, DRY SACK.

DUHART-MILON-ROTHSCHILD, CHÂTEAU (or simply: CHÂTEAU DUHART-MILON) Excellent red Bordeaux wine, owned by the Rothschild family since 1962. Only recently, however, has the wine been deemed worthy to bear the illustrious name of Rothschild. The wine actually has a rather lowly official rating, but most critics agree that it's underclassed.
*1964—****—*Now at its best and for five years.
*1966, 1967—****—*Best drinking, 1975–1980.
All the above are dubious values at $9 or more.
*1970—*****—*Not yet ready—Best drinking: 1978–1985.

D'YQUEM, CHÂTEAU: See YQUEM, CHÂTEAU D'.

E

EASTER SUNDAY WINES
Since Easter is historically the Jewish Festival of Passover, perhaps one ought to drink a Passover or kosher wine on this day. For a lot of people this would be easy enough, for they are already ardent devotees of such kosher wines as Manischewitz and Carmel (an imported Israeli wine) Concord Grape. These are sweet, pleasant wines, perhaps best enjoyed at midday or mid-evening.

"Kosher," with "Jewish" wines, means pretty much the same as "sacramental" does with "Christian" ones: namely, that the wines are natural and pure, unadulterated, made under the supervision of a rabbi for the kosher wines, of a bishop for the sacramental ones.

As for other wines for the Day of the Lord's Resurrection, one can abide by the recommendations to be found under THANKSGIVING DAY WINES. If the *pièce de résistance,* however, consists of smoked ham instead of roast turkey, one might consider one of these wines to accompany the meal: California Chenin Blanc; a light French red: Beaujolais, Volnay, Macon; a French white Burgundy (quite expensive).

(LE) ECHÉZEAUX Very fine red Burgundy wine, a first cousin to Grands Echézeaux (see), perhaps a trifle less good. Both wines can be fine values, at least relatively so, in this very expensive class of wines. It's rather like a Lear Jet being offered for a mere $750,000—it may well be a remarkable bargain. . . . How to serve and savor this wine: See under GRANDS ECHÉZEAUX.

ECU ROYAL This is the name of some French country wines—jug wines, we would call them—recently imported into the U.S. They are rather good wines but at around $4 per half-gallon they are dubious values at best. (When originally introduced, at $3, these were fair game.) American jugs, most of them selling for considerably less, and sometimes at half the price, $2 per half-gallon, are usually a smarter buy.

EGRI BIKAVER*** Literally it's Bull's Blood of Eger (the name of the town), a dark, heavy, quite dry red wine of Hungary. It regularly merits ***, fine to accompany red meats, stews, pasta, any hearty food. Fair value, $3.70.

EISWEIN It's pronounced, and is, in fact, Ice-Wine—in German: "Ice-Vine"—made in rare years when the water within the ripe grapes partially freezes, producing a richer and sweeter wine. Eisweins usually come only from the finest of vineyards; they are luscious and very expensive, magnificent after-dinner or very-special-occasion wines. A currently available 1970 Bernkasteler Doktor Eiswein retails for a cool $75

98

for 23.5 ounces, about $3.20 per ounce! Pour carefully.

ELEVEN CELLARS This is the top brand name of the California Wine Association, a huge cooperative of some 2,000 wine growers. Over the years, Eleven Cellars has won more than 300 awards at the Los Angeles County Fair, more than any other winery. This is not to say that Château Margaux, Clos Vougeot, or Schloss Johannisberger are about to be displaced, but it does say something. Mainly, that here's a winery producing some sound, top-of-their-class, inexpensive wines year after year.

Burgundy** Robust, mellow, no phony sweetness. Good hamburger wine. Fair value, $2 ($4 half-gallon).

Cabernet Sauvignon** Cabernet Sauvignon is conceded to be California's best red wine, and it's usually its most expensive. The Eleven Cellars' product, at $3 to $3.35, is one of the cheapest Cabernets you're going to find. It's sound, young, fruity, though it lacks the real depth of a fine Cabernet. Serve with grilled steaks or lamb chops, beef or lamb roast. Serve at cool room temperature, after airing about one hour.

Chablis** A pleasant dry white wine. Serve it chilled, with fish, seafood, poultry, cold cuts. Fair value, $2 ($4 half-gallon).

Chenin Blanc** This grape makes the lovely white wines of France's Loire Valley and it does in like manner in California, although this is not one of the state's best examples. It is, however, an adequate, fresh young wine, with just a faint edge of bitterness. Fair value, $2.50 to $2.75.

Chianti* Everybody knows how to drink Chianti—at room temperature, with Italian food or hamburgers. *Molto buono.*

Claret*** It's taken a number of awards. A clear dry wine, a bit lighter than the Burgundy. Serve it with poultry, lamb, beef, at cool room temperature. Fair value, $2.

Fumé Blanc and Sauvignon Blanc* Eleven Cellars may be the only winery in the world that makes both these wines, for they're generally considered synonymous. Truth to tell, it's quite impossible for a mere mortal to distinguish between them. They are (or it is) fresh, dry, youthful wines (or wine). For refreshment purposes of a summer's evening. Serve chilled; fair value, $2.60 to $2.90.

Gamay Beaujolais*** A zestful young red wine patterned after France's famed Beaujolais. Perfect for outdoor barbecue or picnic. Serve at cool room temperature or slightly chilled. Fair value, $2.70 to $3.

Haut Sauterne*** Unlike many, this is not a cloyingly sweet wine—it has a good sweetness and is a good wine. Sip it tenderly of a summer's evening—on the trellised veranda, or in the groaty kitchen. A good value at $2.

Johannisberg Riesling** $3 to $3.25 is not expensive as Johannisberg Rieslings go, but it is expensive for *this* one. Not recommended at the price.

Pinot Chardonnay** It's pretty far removed from California's *big* Chardonnays (Heitz, Stony Hill), though it's definitely not a poor wine. At its best accompanying light foods, especially seafood. Serve chilled. Fair value, $3 to $3.35.

Pinot Noir*** This is the

grape that produces France's great red Burgundies—you remember: Le Chambertin, La Tache, all that gang. Well, Eleven Cellars' offering does not quite supplant the likes of *them*, but considering today's generally horrendous wine prices, this is a sound and tasteful wine at a reasonable price, ca. $3. If you want to really appreciate it, sip it on its own, with cheeses and fruit. Air one hour, serve at cool room temperature.

Rhine* Drier than most California Rhine wines. Serve, chilled, with light foods. Fair value, $2.

Sauterne** Crisp and dry, well worth its lowly $2. To accompany fish, light foods. Serve chilled.

Sauvignon Blanc: See FUMÉ. BLANC.

Sherry The three standard sherries are produced, in ascending order of sweetness: Pale Dry Sherry, **: clean and dry. "Plain" Sherry, **: medium-dry, can be served either before meals or after. Cream Sherry, ***: a bit thin, but tasty; serve after dinner. Fair value, $1.90 to $2.10.

Vin Rosé* Humph, better than nothing . . .

Zinfandel*** "Z" is pretty cosmopolitan; it fits in anywhere. It especially belongs with barbecued chicken, pasta, omelettes. Air it one hour and serve at cool room temperature. A good value at $2.50 to $2.75.

ELTVILLE(R) SONNENBERG Elegant German Rhine wine— a label you can trust. The "straight," even without being a Cabinet or Spätlese wine, is regularly ****. It's at its best between three and eight years old, and is usually a good value.

EMERALD RIESLING A fresh, light, medium-dry white wine, invented and produced only in California. (The grape is a hybrid created by the University of California at Davis.) Not many wineries make this wine, for the grape is a fussy one, but it has yet to be poorly made—at least commercially —in California. (Note that there are no low ratings in the "standings" below.) Emerald Riesling is a big enough wine to be enjoyed wholly on its own—for refreshment, relaxation, rejuvenation. At the dining table it will go best with fish, seafood, poultry, anything made with a cream sauce. Serve it chilled, 45 to 50°F. It's ready to drink when you bring it home and should not be kept more than a year or so.

California's best—and only:

****

LaMont Emerald Riesling ($2)

Paul Masson Emerald Dry ($2.35)

***

San Martin Emerald Riesling ($2.50)

Assumption Abbey Emerald Riesling ($2.50)

ERBACHER MARKO-BRUNN: See MARCOBRUNNER.

ERDEN(ER) TREPPCHEN Some say that Bernkastelers are the best of all Moselle wines, and the Erdeners, second best. Treppchen is the best vineyard of the entire area. The '71s are marvelous wines: flowery, fresh, delightfully tart—Moselle raised to its highest power. If you can't find the '71s, the '70s from here are also good, but drink them soon.

ERMITAGE: See HERMITAGE.

ETIQUETTE, WINE If it's regarding the type of glasses: see GLASSES. If it's regarding the tasting of wine, see TASTING WINE. If it's about the order in which wines are served, see SERVING WINE. If it's about table placement, see here: (1) It is proper to serve only one wine per glass. (2) Wine glasses are kept to the upper right of the setting. (3) If water is served—*quod Deus avertat!*—it is to the left of the wine glasses.

TABLE SETTING OF WINE GLASSES

It is proper to serve only one wine per glass. Be sure to select the proper stemware.

If you are serving water, the water glass should be placed to the left and the wine glasses to the right. The example below is set for three (3) dinner wines and a champagne with dessert. As the individual courses are served, the china is removed.

The wine glasses should be removed at the same time, unless your guests wish to hold the glasses to compare the wine throughout the dinner. This is a lot of fun and is recommended.

Before serving a second glass of wine, ask the guest if he wishes it in order to keep from wasting any.

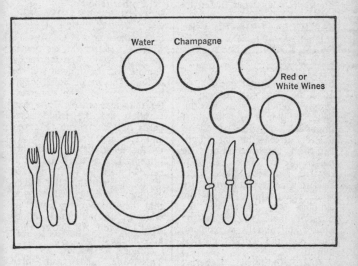

F

J. FAIVELEY A highly regarded, totally trustworthy shipper of Burgundy (French) wines. Faiveley handles some of Burgundy's very finest: Clos de Vougeot, Clos de Marechale, Gevrey-Chambertin, as well as some of the more economical Burgundies, such as Mercurey and plain Bourgogne (see all). Look up your wine under its proper name.

FAMIGLIA CRIBARI: See CRIBARI, FAMIGLIA.

FARM, BOONE'S: See BOONE'S FARM and GALLO.

FAVORITE WINES Perhaps the most persistent question of all in the great world of wine is simply: What is your favorite wine? And it is also the most impossible question of all to answer, at least in that simplified form. The question mus' be narrowed to: What is your favorite red wine, white wine, dessert wine, aperitif wine, dry wine, sweet wine? Perhaps the simplest way to answer the question, then, is to say that by almost unanimous agreement, these are the world's greatest wines:

Reds: California Cabernet Sauvignon; French Burgundies; French Bordeaux.

Whites: Germany's Rhines and Moselles; French Burgundy; French Graves; California Pinot Chardonnay.

Aperitif: French Champagnes; Spanish Dry Sherry.

Dessert (Sweet) Wines: Portuguese Porto; Spanish Cream Sherry; German Beerenauslesen; Trockenbeerenauslese; Eisweins; French Sauternes; Hungary's Tokay.

But to return to the original question: What is your favorite wine? Perhaps Diogenes had the best answer of all. When asked that question, he replied, "The other fellow's."

FETZER VINEYARDS (Redwood Valley, Calif.) One of the northernmost of California's wineries, Fetzer makes wines the hard way. The northerly climate and the difficult soil see to that. This means small yields but good wines. The vines suffer, the wines prosper. European parallels are the frigid vineyards of Champagne (France) and Germany. Fetzer's wines are unique, mostly good, reasonably priced. The Fetzers are dedicated winemakers—all thirteen of them, including the eleven children—and they will tell you that they know every barrel of wine as an individual. Wines need love too. All Fetzer wines are vintage-dated.

Blanc de Blancs, 1972*** This wine, made from three different white grapes, is usually called Sauvignon Blanc or Fumé Blanc; it's a medium-dry wine, with a good, earthy taste. It's perfect with shellfish; serve it chilled. Best drinking, 1975 through 1977. A good value at $2.50.

Cabernet Sauvignon Cabernet Sauvignon is almost always the best red wine an American winery makes—so with Fetzer, though their Zinfandel may be more famous. Cabernet, with its berrylike savoriness, goes especially well with beef, lamb, chicken. True enophiles—that's wine snobs' name for wine snobs —will want to enjoy this wine on its own, or with cheeses and fruits. Serve at cool room temperature. Fair value, ca. $5.

*1968***** This was the year of Fetzer's founding and they were off to a flying start, producing some of their finest wines to date in that first year of operation. This Cabernet has deep, complex flavors; it's now at its apogee and will remain there at least through 1979. The special Cask 19 merits *****.

*1969*** A letdown after the '68 but still a good bottle. Drink, 1975–1980.

*1970**** Best drinking, 1975–1982.

*1971**** Not yet mature. Best drinking, 1976–1983.

Carmine Carignane* The Carignane grape is widely grown in California but you rarely see the name on a label. The reason—it's used almost exclusively for blending purposes, especially in the production of California "Burgundy." It's prolific, but not very distinctive. So with Fetzer's Carignane (the "Carmine" is an invented name to denote the wine's deep red coloring): it's sound, economical, not very distinctive. It's vintage-dated and recent vintages (1970, 1971, 1972) are ready for present drinking and will keep for three or four more years. A good value at $2.50 to $2.75. Serve at cool room temperature.

Chardonnay** It's been in short supply, but is worth looking for. Fair value, ca. $5.

Dry Sauvignon Blanc* Dry white wine, fresh and flowery, to accompany light foods (poultry, fish, seafood, sandwiches); serve chilled. Sémillon (below) is similar; in fact, the grapes are often combined to make one wine. Fair value, ca. $5.

*1970**** Drink soon.

*1971*** Not recommended at $5.

Gamay Beaujolais* Nice fresh young red wine—enjoy it on a picnic, at your outdoor grill, or at lunchtime. Fair value, ca. $3.25.

Green Hungarian**

Mountain Sémillon: See SÉMILLON.

Petite Sirah, 1972*

Pinot Noir**

Sauvignon Blanc, Dry: See DRY SAUVIGNON BLANC (above).

Sémillon* A dry white wine similar to the Sauvignon Blanc (above), but softer, more earthy. The '69 was labeled Mountain Sémillon. Serve it as you would the Sauvignon Blanc. It's at its best when it's between three and six years old.

Zinfandel Some of Fetzer's good repute has been thanks to their "Z," a tasty, spirited, dry red dinner wine. It's a wine for all seasons: goes with red meats, fowl, Italian dishes, cheese dishes. Serve at cool room temperature. Fair value, $3.50.

*1968***** Fetzer's first vintage, an auspicious beginning, certes! Unhappily, Fetzer has never quite matched this initial offering. This wine is now at the top of its form and will hold there for another five years at least.

1969 and *1970*** Both these wines are enjoyable right now and will hold well until around 1977.

1971*** Best drinking, 1975 through 1979.

1972 It comes with four different labels from four different vineyards: Barra-Cinquini Vineyard ($3.50), ***—Mattern Vineyard ($3.50), ***—both are light, fruity wines—Lolonis-Stafford ($4.80), ****—Ricetti ($4.80) ****—these latter two are bigger, heavier-bodied wines.

FICKLIN VINEYARDS (Madera, Calif.) Here's one of the strangest wine operations in America: a California winery producing virtually only one wine, Port. And a remarkable job they've been doing of it for some twenty-five years, for everybody agrees that Ficklin makes the best port in the Americas. Indeed, they do it just as it's done in Portugal—except perhaps for treading it with their feet—same grapes, same vinification, same aging. And it's remarkably the same wine—not possessing the enormous richness and finesse of true Vintage Port, one of the world's finest and most expensive wines, but certainly on a par with some of the humbler Portuguese Portos, such as Ruby.

Ficklin even has some special bottlings of a vintage Port, sometimes available in small quantity at the winery.

Port is one of the great classic after-dinner wines, preferably served in the drawing room (the *what?*) following coffee. Perhaps with mild cheeses or with apple slices and walnuts. Serve Ficklin Port in large tulip glasses at cool room temperature, ca. 68°F. Fair value for the "straight" California Tinta: $4.25. It's a noble *****.

FINDLATER'S CHRISTMAS CAROL SHERRY**** Findlater, Machie, Todd & Co., Ltd., is an old London wine merchant specializing in Spanish sherries. They've been doing a good job of it for some 150 years now, and their prices are rather decent (as a Londoner might say). This Oloroso is elegant and mouth-filling, with deep, round nuttiness—it's a medium sherry leaning to the sweet side. As the name tells you, it's just the right wine for the Christmas holidays, and a good value at around $4.50.

FINDLATER'S CREAM SHERRY**** It's exactly what the label says: Full and rich—yet not overly sweet as some Creams are. It has a good, deep-down nutty flavor. A good value, around $4. How to serve it: See under SHERRY.

FINDLATER'S DRY FLY SHERRY**** Not bitingly dry, just right, with excellent body, yet light and delicate. A perfect aperitif wine, and a good value at $4.25. How to serve it: See under SHERRY.

FINDLATER'S LA LUNA VERY DRY MANZANILLA SHERRY*** The label says correctly: *Very dry,* probably too much so for many. Manzanilla is a special type of Fino (Dry) Sherry (from Spain), so delicate and light that it does not travel well. No Marco Polo here. Fair value, ca. $4.50.

FINO: A type of sherry. For general information, see under SHERRY. For evaluation of a particular bottle of Fino Sherry, see under the name of the producer.

FINO ELEVEN CELLARS: See ELEVEN CELLARS.

FIXIN There's no apostrophe after the "n" and it doesn't mean, as Texans might think, "getting ready to." It's pronounced "fee-sahn," and it's regrettable that it's so rarely seen in the U.S., for it's an excellent red Burgundy, often on a par with the great wines of Gevrey-Chambertin. Especially popular, and particularly outstanding are Clos de la Perrier and Clos du Chapitre, both regularly ***** wines. Fixin wines are long-lived and don't reach their peak until they are seven or eight years old. They are not inexpensive, but in their class they are actually good values, ranging all the way from $5 to $10. How to serve Fixin: See under BURGUNDY.

FLEURIE Almost always **** Excellent red Beaujolais wine, it's called the queen of Beaujolais—Moulin-à-Vent is the king. It's said to be the most typical of all Beaujolais, and to have the loveliest bouquet of all. Fleurie is a fragrant and fruity wine, silky smooth, understandably popular in the U.S., and usually a good value as far as French wines go these days. It's at its best when it's between two and five years old. How to serve it: See under BEAUJOLAIS.

FLOR SHERRY CREME and FLOR SHERRY SEC VIN DE BIANE FRES (Brookside Vineyard, Guasti, Calif.)** Hokey names, half Spanish, half French, for two honest and well-made sherries. But despite the weird, foreign-sounding nomenclature, these wines were produced almost in downtown Los Angeles! To be accurate, some thirty miles west of there: in Guasti, California, by Brookside Vineyards. The Creme is a sweet sherry (after-dinner use), the Sec, a dry cocktail type. Fair value, $3.25 to $3.50.

FLORA This is another of those California-invented wines (like Emerald Riesling and Ruby Cabernet, see both), developed by the University of California, Davis. And it's a fine little wine: fragrant, clean, spicy. It's also a versatile wine, good enough to be enjoyed on its own or as an aperitif wine, and yet with enough body and flavor to accompany a variety of foods: chicken, ham, pork, cheese fondue, seafood, even fishy fish. Serve it chilled (45-50°F). It's ready to drink when you buy it and it will keep for four or five years. California's best to date: **** Souverain Flora, 1971 ($3.50); *** Parducci Flora, 1970 ($2.50).

FLORENS-LOUIS: See PIPER HEIDSIECK.

FLORIO MARSALA ALMOND CREAM** A velvet-smooth Italian dessert wine with almond flavoring. Florio is the brand name, Marsala, the name of the wine. It's a very tasty, satisfying wine, and more Americans should know of it, especially with its inflation-beating price tag, $3.25. You can even enjoy it "on the rocks" or over vanilla ice cream.

FLORIO MARSALA, DRY (SUPERIOR EXTRA)** It's really not very dry—it's medium-sweet. Fine for between-meals resuscitation, after coffee, or even as an aperitif wine. Great to enliven soups. For more on this type of wine: See under MARSALA.

FOLLE BLANCHE A unique, if unspectacular dry white wine, made thus far by only one American winery: Louis M. Martini (see). And made as such, under its own name, by nobody else in the whole, old, cold world. And truth to tell, it makes better brandy than it does wine.

FONSECA VINTAGE PORT

Fonseca is the name of a fine, a *real* Portuguese Port—or Porto, as it's now called officially—made by the distinguished 150-year-old firm of Guimaraens & Co. It's a name you can trust. Here are some outstanding vintages:

1912: A huge success—Now somewhat past its prime but still good—Near-Classic.,

1927: An extraordinary wine of an extraordinary vintage: Classic—It sold for only—*only,* he says—$13 at Christie's wine auction, London, in 1971.

1966: Not one of the very greatest years, but this Fonseca is great wine: Near-Classic—Try it, 1982–1985, at the earliest.

How to serve Porto: See under PORT.

FOOD AND WINES

Whole books have been written on this subject* but the basic principles can be enunciated on one page. The most basic law, known to virtually every human being who has ever purchased a $1 bottle of wine, is: White wines with fish and white meats (fowl, pork, veal), and red wines with red meats (beef, lamb). When in doubt, let that simple rule of thumb be your guide. Of course the principle can be, and even should be superceded at times—it's flagrantly flaunted throughout this book. And the most fundamental law of all wine appreciation overreaches all: It's what *you* like. If you dig Chianti with your Baked Alaska, so be it!

Repeatedly throughout this book you are urged to appreciate a fine wine on its own,

without distracting, detracting, competing food accompaniment. Not everybody agrees wholly with that recommendation. Some will urge that wine, especially dry wine, is the natural accompaniment for food, destined by God for the table. Bob Travers of Mayacamas Vineyards (California) says: "Wine tastings are fine . . . but dry table wines are made to be drunk, not just sniffed, swirled, spat. And they are meant to be drunk with food. Final judgments on wines should be made in conjunction with meals . . . Look at it, smell it, taste it, polish your car with it, if you must, but please save a little to drink!"

Almost everybody would agree that at least the following wines should ordinarily be drunk on their own, without any food accompaniment: German Auslesen, Beerenauslesen, Trockenbeerenauslesen; French Sauternes and Barsacs; Madeira, especially Malmsey; Sherry, especially Cream; Tokay (or Tokaji—the real thing, from Hungary); Porto (the real thing, from Portugal).

Some would also include great dry whites such as Montrachet and California's best Pinot Chardonnays.

A few foods are wholly inimical to wine—the two simply clash. Serve these foods with beer, or Sneaky Pete or Sauerkraut juice, or something—even water, ugh, if there's no other way out. The anti-wine items are: vinegar, including salads with vinegar; citrus: oranges, lemons, grapefruit; pickled foods; anchovies, kippers; chocolate.

---

* E.g., William E. Masse, *Masse's Wine-Food Index* (New York, McGraw-Hill, 1962) and Guirne Van Zuylen, *Eating with Wine* (London, Faber & Faber, 1972).

(LA) FÔRET: Several vineyards have this name. See CHABLIS, FRENCH, and MACON BLANC.

FORSTER JESUITENGAR-TEN Marvelous German white wine—Forst is the name of the village, Forster is a wine from Forst, as we would say a man from Podunk is a Podunker. Jesuitengarten is the name of the vineyard; it means the Gardens of the Jesuits. German wines of this caliber are too delicate and refined to be consumed with food. Appreciate Jesuitengarten on its own, chilled, slowly, gratefully.

1953 Trockenbeerenauslese, Bassermann-Jordan: Classic— How to drink it (as though anyone would need lessons!): See under TROCKENBEERENAUS-LESE.

1966 Bassermann-Jordan: ****

1969 Bassermann-Jordan: Cabinet: *****

1971 Sichel: ****

Bassermann-Jordan: *****

FOURCHAUME: See CHABLIS, FRENCH.

FOURNIER, CHARLES: See GOLD SEAL.

(LA) FRANÇAISE: See TAIT-TINGER.

FRANCE—WINES During the darkling days of American Prohibition (see), a man who had come upon a bottle of fine French wine secreted it beneath his overcoat as he boarded a crowded streetcar. In the press of the crowd he felt something wet trickling down his side, and he muttered, "God, I hope it's blood."

Good French wine can be very precious and very expensive—today it is not uncommon for French wines to sit—lie, hopefully—on dealer's shelves with $100 and $200 price tags.

Which brings up the inevitable question: Who makes the best wines in the world? So broadly stated one would have to answer: France. More precisely: France makes more great wines than any other single country, Pre-Prohibition or Post-.

FRANK SCHOONMAKER: See SCHOONMAKER, FRANK.

FRANK, DR. KONSTANTIN Strange name for some strange wines. Dr. Konstantin Frank is a Russian-born enologist, still going strong, owner of and winemaker for Vinifera Wine Cellars, N.Y. Not strange wines, exactly—"unusual." Dr. Frank has had one goal in life: to prove that European vines can be successfully grown in New York's harsh climate. And prove it, he has, handily. It's necessarily been a small and painstaking operation, and the wines are rare and expensive.

Pinot Chardonnay* Fair (?) value, $6 to $6.50.

Riesling Spätlese, 1967**** A frank (no pun!) and successful imitation of Germany's late-picked Rhine wines. One California winemaker mistook this wine for a German Moselle. Frank once made the *ne plus ultra* of German wines from these very grapes: a Trockenbeerenauslese wine which sold for $45 (per bottle, not case!). One wine critic said of it: Try it before you say the price is too high.

Invite some wine-loving friends over for a "blind" (labels hidden) comparison of Riesling Spätlese with a good German Rhine wine and a superior California Johannisberg Riesling. They may rank this New York product ahead of both. Fair value, $6 to $6.50.

Riesling Spätlese, 1969** Some bad news and some good

news on this wine . . . The bad news: It's poor wine. The good news: It's hard to find. A poor value at $6.75.

FRANKEN RIESLING: See RIESLING.

FRANZIA BROS. WINERY (Ripon, Calif.) They must be doing something right down Ripon way, for they're bottling about 10,000 cases of wine per day. What they're doing right is producing standard, everyday wines at very reasonable prices. These are simple, uncomplicated wines, and nobody claims more. None of them is great, nor even approaching that.

Franzia was recently purchased by Coca-Cola—at times their several products are somewhat akin! Yet, while wine connoisseurs may peer down their noses and/or rend their garments, Franzia continues to sell millions of gallons of the kind of wine millions of Americans want: reliable, bland wines at economical prices. A single hope may be expressed: may all Franzia-devotees, as time, taste, and finances permit, look upward and go onward!

Franzia produces some forty different wines and only the more important are listed here. All of them are ready to drink when purchased and they will not improve in the bottle. Notice the metal screw caps on all except the sparkling wines; fine wines always have real corks through which they "breathe" and change. No Franzia wine should be kept more than two years.

Burgundy* Notice that there is also a Robust Burgundy (see), very similar, slightly more expensive, but some say, not as good as this "plain" one. This one has a little more sweetness. Fair value, $2.35 a

half-gallon. Serve at cool room temperature.

Chablis* Remarkably tasty —fine to accompany fish, seafood, all kinds of fowl. Serve chilled. Notice that there is also a Pink Chablis (see). Fair value at $1.25.

Chablis Blanc* A trifle more expensive ($2.75 half-gallon) than the plain Chablis, and of similar quality. Serve as you would the Chablis.

Champagne* Dollar for dollar—or rather, dime for dime, for these wines sell for less than $2, $1.99, to be exact —this is surely one of the best sparkling wine values in the world. At the price, don't look for Moët et Chandon Dom Perignon, but you can expect a light, fresh wine at an incredibly low price, a full dollar cheaper than the Gallo product, and $1.50 cheaper than Lejon Champagne. Its competition, at the self-same price, is André (see) and Jacques Bonet (see), made by Italian Swiss Colony. Serve well chilled. Don't keep these wines more than a year or so. The variations: *Cold Duck,* **: There are other Frigid Fowls at twice the price which are not as good as this one. *Extra Dry Champagne,* **: Says one critic: "A workmanlike wine for a festive occasion." A bit sweeter than the plain Champagne. *Pink Champagne,* *: Prefer the "straight" Champagne or the Cold Duck. *Sparkling Burgundy,* *. Franzia has a second line of sparkling wines, under their *Louis the Fifth* label, slightly more expensive ($2.50 vs. $2) and consistently a little better, a touch more flavorful: **.

Chianti Not recommended.

Dessert Wines There are a host of these: Cocktail Sherry,

Cream Sherry, Muscatel, Port, Straight Sherry, Tawny Port, Tokay, White Port, Very Dry Sherry. One word covers them all: Ugh.

Grenache Rosé** It's got some character. A good value at $2.45 a half-gallon.

Muscatel: See DESSERT WINES.

Pink Chablis* The winery's description is as good as any: "The lively one, for the now generation." Serve chilled. Fair value, $2.35 a half-gallon.

Port: See DESSERT WINES.

Rhinewein* A big seller, on the sweet side. Sip it, chilled, of a summer's afternoon. A little goes a long way. Fair value, $2.35 a half-gallon.

Robust Burgundy* See also the "plain" Burgundy, a little cheaper and perhaps a little better. The Robust is the drier of the two. Fair value, $2.45 a half-gallon.

Sauterne** Fresh and clean, nice little white wine to accompany fish, seafood, poultry. Serve chilled. Fair value, $2.35 a half-gallon.

Sherry: See DESSERT WINES.

Tokay: See DESSERT WINES.

Vin Rosé** Perhaps Franzia's best value of all, at only $2 a half-gallon, it is fragrant and fresh, not overly sweet. Serve chilled, for refreshment purposes.

Vino Rosso Not recommended. Franzia's commercial version of—excuse the ethnic slur, but there is no synonym— "Dago Red," and about as palatable.

Zinfandel** Most experts agree that this is Franzia's best wine, a very good value at $2.45 a half-gallon ($1.35 a fifth).

FRASCATI A light and youngish white Italian wine which tastes better in Rome than it does in the U.S. They say no two are ever quite alike. Frascati in the U.S. is usually on the dry side, with just a touch of sweetness. Frascati is as ancient as the town it's named after. Victorious Roman soldiers, it is said, attributed their success in battle to their good Frascati. Small wonder they conquered the world! If it has the word "Superiore" on the label, it's a bigger, somewhat better wine and can improve with a year or two in the bottle. Some trustworthy names: Cella; Marino; Orfevi; Valle Vermiglia.

FREEMARK ABBEY WINERY (St. Helena, Calif.) A small winery with a big reputation. That's Freemark since 1967. It's actually one hundred years old, but produced nothing memorable, indeed nothing very drinkable during those first ninety years. Today, Freemark Abbey is a name known and respected by wine lovers around the world. The winery is headed by some of the most competent and knowledgeable people in the California wine industry. Further, they limit production here to a few premium wines— would that other American wineries would get the message and cease from producing those hordes of mostly mediocre (and a few ghastly) wines. Nobody can excel at everything! The Romans knew that truth: Divide and conquer!

Cabernet Sauvignon "Strong and delicate, infinitely rich in nuance, yet completely balanced and harmonious," is the way one writer describes California Cabernet wines in general. What he means to say is that it tastes good. Freemark's, even more so. It's usually so good, in fact, that it should be enjoyed purely on its own merits, without benefit of distracting food accompaniment. Mild cheeses and fresh fruit only. Serve at cool room temperature and enjoy, enjoy!

1967*** This was their first offering, already an auspicious beginning. It's now at its best and will hold at least until 1980. Fair value, $5.

1968*** Best drinking, 1977–1985. Fair value, $4.50 to $5.

1968 Bosche**** Bosche is the name of a special vineyard, and the wine's a bit special too. Not quite mature—drink, 1977–1985.

1969****, hoping to reach ***** Each year, these Cabernets get a little better; this one is now the equal of the 1968 and it shows more promise, may even reach *****. It will be at its best, 1977 through 1985. Fair value, $6.

1970 "Regular"**** Reminiscent of the '68, though a bit lighter. It will be at its very best, 1977 through 1985. Fair value, $6.

1970 Bosche***** Already soft, beautifully balanced, brimming over with flavor . . . black currants? Cinnamon? It's going to be in short supply and will certainly become a collector's item. It's already fetching ca. $9. Will be at its very best, 1978–1988.

1971 "Regular"**** Great promise. Best drinking, 1977 onward . . .

1971 Bosche***** May well reach Near-Classic when mature. Stash it away in some dark, secret nook and don't even look at it for at least four years.

1973 Bosche Still in the wood, the winery says it will be great.

Johannisberg Riesling If you ever want to study, very painlessly, what one and the same grape can do in two different climes and soils, take a bottle of this wine and drink it carefully alongside a good bottle of German Rhine wine. The German wine will be light and flowery, delightful sipping—the California wine will be bigger, drier, to be taken, as the doctors prescribe, with meals. Freemark's is good enough to be consumed on its own but it will also serve as a most gracious accompaniment to seafood, pork, ham. Fair value, $4 to $4.50.

1969 Lot 92**** The grapes that went into this wine had a touch of "noble rot," but that's good, not bad. It makes the wine richer and fuller. It's ready for present drinking and will hold until 1977.

1969 Lot 91 and *Lot 93**** Sound, tasty wines but not up to Lot 92.

1970**** Grapes again suffered a touch of "noble rot." At its best, 1975 through 1978.

1971 and *1972*—At least *****. The '72 has a touch of "noble rot," giving it a tinge of honey. Both are for present drinking and will hold until 1980.

1973—Be on sharp lookout for this wine. It's still in the tank and unless demonic forces interfere, it's going to be beautiful. There will only be about 1,500 cases. It's got more of everything the '71 and '72 have and promises to be a totally unprecedented wine. The forecast: Near-Classic.

Petite Sirah Petite Sirah is a strong dark wine, one of California's best reds, commonly overlooked, and hence usually a good value. This is a specialty wine with Freemark, and they started making it only every second year. It's been so successful, however, that they're going to make it every year if they can get the grapes. Fair value, $4.75.

1969**** This is an intense, peppery wine, one that will appeal more to connoisseurs than to neophyte wine drinkers. Somebody said: You may not like this wine but you won't forget it. If you can find it— very little of it was made—you can drink it now or within the next decade or two.

1971***** Similar to the '69, just more of the same. This wine will last for a long time; it will be better in 1985 than it is today.

Pinot Chardonnay Wine experts generally agree that Chardonnay is California's best white wine, but beginning wine drinkers don't often agree, as it's a dry, strong wine, often with a distinct woodiness. It's a taste one has to work at—sheer drudgery, but don't lose heart! Freemark Abbey makes one of the best in the business. It's an ideal accompaniment for fish and seafoods, but it will be even more appreciated, sipped in leisurely fashion, on its own. Serve chilled.

1968**** Big, full-flavored, earthy—a connoisseur's wine, not for novices. Fair value, $7.

1969***** This wine caused something of a sensation in March, 1973, when it took an easy first place in a blind tasting (labels were hidden) of similar California and French dry white wines. (In fact, California wines took all the top honors; there were some embarrassed grins.) It was downright gauche, not to say rude, for this California upstart, selling for a mere $6, to outdistance some of the world's most illustrious white wines selling in the $25 vicinity. (It was providential that General de Gaulle had departed this world at the time —Franco-American relations were already in a depressed state.)

1970***** This wine is only a hair's breath behind the '69; it's similar in character: big and rich. Best drinking, 1975–1978.

1971 and *1972****** These are just now beginning to be ready, and final word may not yet be in on them, but from here they're looking very much like the '69 and '70. They will remain at their best at least through 1980. Fair value, $6.

Pinot Noir This is the great grape of France's illustrious red Burgundies. It does well in California, but not *that* well. It's the classic accompaniment for poultry, veal, cheese, eggs, soufflés, and it will enhance any red meat, though a Claret or California Cabernet are more suited to that.

1967*** Drink before 1977. *1968****** Best drinking, 1975 through 1978.

1969*** Best drinking, 1975 through 1978.

1970**** May be Freemark's best Pinot Noir yet. Good flavor, on the dry side. Best drinking, 1975 through 1979.

FRENCH COLOMBARD This grape probably makes better Cognac than it does wine—at least in France it does. Transported to California it's widely used in blending (Chablis, Champagne, etc.), but it's now being bottled on its own, under its own name. As such, it's a good little white wine, crisp and dry, slightly spicy. It comes in varying degrees of dryness— Cresta Blanca's and Oakville's lean toward the sweetish side. It goes well with all manner of light food: from sandwiches to poultry to seafood to ham and pork. The sweeter versions you may want to enjoy on their own or with fresh fruit, cheeses, nuts.

Drink French Colombard before it's four years old, chilled, of course (45–50°F).

Herewith, California's current crop of French Colombards. It can be safely said that every one of these wines is a good value —notice the respectable ratings and the low prices.

French Colombards—
Comparative Standings

***
Good
  Inglenook Navalle French Colombard ($1.90)
  LaMont French Colombard ($2)
  Cresta Blanca French Colombard ($2.45)
  Sonoma (or Windsor) French Colombard ($2.50)
  Oakville French Colombard ($2.75)
  Parducci French Colombard ($2.80)

**
Fair
  Gallo French Colombard ($1.85)

FRESCOBALDI CASTELLO DI NIPOZZANO This is not strictly a Chianti Classico—notice that the word "Classico" is not on the label—because it is made just outside the delimited Classical area, but it's almost always a fine wine. Nipozzano is a big wine, noted for its longevity. For recent Chianti vintages, as well as how to serve Chianti: See under CHIANTI.

FRITZ KOBUS GEWÜRZTRAMINER: See GEWÜRZTRAMINER.

FRONTIGAN, MUSCAT DE: See MUSCAT DE FRONTIGNAN.

FUMÉ BLANC This good white wine usually goes by the name of Sauvignon Blanc (see) in California. The principal California wineries using this name are Beringer, Eleven Cellars, and Robert Mondavi. See all of these for evaluations of individual bottles.

G

E. & J. GALLO WINERY
(Modesto, Calif.) In the entire
recorded history of wine, the
world over, the single most important name may well come to
be that of E. & J. Gallo. Millions of Americans who could
not cite the name of a single
other wine or winemaker know
the name of Gallo. Incredibly,
almost half of the wine California produces bears the name
Gallo—more than 100 million
gallons per year. This immense
quantity alone makes Gallo important and influential. The
winery has also led the way in
new trends—the introduction of
"Pop" wines, for example—
and new technology. The staff
comprises dozens of graduate
enologists. Even the wine
blends are computerized.

All of which makes Gallo
wines among the most con-
sistent and predictable of any
in the world. It also makes
them, in a sense, the dullest—
they are never any better, never
any worse. As Baron Philippe
de Rothschild, the French mil-
lionaire vintner and owner of
the celebrated Château Mouton,
said of California wine in general (not quite fairly): "The
wine all comes out industrially
uniform, like Coca-Cola."

Gallo doesn't make any bad
wine, certainly, but they make
millions of gallons of bland, undistinctive wine—emasculated,
it's so filtered and fined, some
would say—and they also make

a few meriting an honest ***,
objectively, not merely price-
wise.

For honest, everyday wine at
reasonable prices, one must
needs bless the name of E. & J.
Gallo. Along with Italian Swiss
Colony, Franzia, Bear Mountain, and Guild, there are probably no better wine values in
the entire world.

Gallo has been millions of
Americans' introduction to the
great, multifarious world of
wine. May they all proceed onward and upward, to the vinous
heights!

Barbera*** In October,
1974, the Ernest and Julio Gallo Company made history: they
did something wholly unprecedented in their forty-year history—they put a cork in a
bottle of Gallo wine. That is
the most literal truth. Up to
that point, not 'a single bottle
of the million upon millions of
bottles that have spewed from
the Gallo maw, lo, these many
years—not one of them—has
had a cork stuffed into its neck.
Corks are used only for the
better wines that need to
"breathe" and age while they're
in the bottle. An almost infallible rule says that lesser
wines have metal caps, better
wines have corks.

Barbera was one of eight superior wines introduced by
Gallo in late 1974, all of them
using real corks—cork corks
from Portugal. Gallo's initial

113

order for corks, incidentally, was fifty million—those Gallo brothers—Ernest and Julio—mean business. All those wines are to sell at the inflation-beating price of less than $2. That fact, along with that familiar old name of Gallo on the label, guarantees that these wines are going to sell well, as well they should.

This Barbera rates a confident ***, it has fine varietal character, does not have any phony sweetness. It will even improve with an added year or two in the bottle. Fair value, $1.75 to $2.

Boone's Farm—See under its own name.

Burgundy** Note that Gallo also makes a Hearty Burgundy (see), a more noted wine and a little more expensive, ca. $2.80 a half-gallon, vs. $2.25. (eastern U.S. add 50¢). It would take an expert to distinguish between them, blind. This is good "hamburger wine," no greatness, no complexity, but simple, adequate red table wine to enhance everyday fare. Serve at cool room temperature, don't keep it more than three years.

Burgundy, Hearty: See HEARTY BURGUNDY.

Burgundy, Sparkling: See SPARKLING BURGUNDY.

Chablis Blanc*** Here's one of the best white wine values in all the world: a light, clean, dry wine, with good flavor. This is good enough to be enjoyed on its own, before dinner, chilled and it will also do nobly in accompanying any light food, especially fish and seafood. Fair value, $2.80 to $3.10 per half-gallon.

Chablis, Pink: See PINK CHABLIS.

Champagne** It has some good grapes in its lineage, and it has some flavor—often a rather remarkable feat with these lesser California Champagnes. A good value at ca. $3. Gallo makes Champagne under another label, André (see), a cheaper and poorer wine.

Champagne, Pink: See PINK CHAMPAGNE.

Chenin Blanc*** Price-wise. Another of Gallo's new "varietals." A varietal is a wine named after a specific grape variety and it must contain at least 51 percent of that grape. It is a higher class wine than a generic, for a generic is a blended wine and can contain any kind of grape at all. Gallo's other new varietals: Barbera, French Colombard, Ruby Carbernet, Sauvignon Blanc, Zinfandel (see all); also introduced at this time were two nonvarietals: Rosé and Riesling.

This Chenin Blanc is a pleasant light wine, with a fair amount of varietal character, or flavor, just slightly sweet. It will serve handsomely for summertime refreshment—or wintertime relaxation. Objectively it rates only ** but price-wise it's ***: most California Chenin Blanc's are around $3. Serve chilled. Fair value, $1.75 to $2.

Chianti* Experts have consistently downgraded this wine, and it has fared ill in tastings. It's quite sweet. Prefer the Paisano if you like this style of slightly sweet, mellow red table wine. Fair value, $1.90 to $2.20.

Cocktail Pale Dry Sherry** Not altogether dry, but leaning toward a medium sherry. Use it as such: before meals, or after. Or at eleven A.M. or P.M. —or in between. A remarkable value at $1.10 to $1.30. See also VERY DRY SHERRY.

Cold Duck* There are tastier, fatter Ducks flying around, at the same price.

Cream Sherry: See LIVINGSTON CREAM SHERRY.

French Colombard** A little white wine, distinctly on the sweet side, pleasant enough, but it lacks character. Serve it chilled as an aperitif wine, or simply for refreshment, to pass the time of day. This is another of Gallo's new varietal wines. Fair value, $1.75 to $2.

Hearty Burgundy** This wine has been more highly touted than any other jug wine in the history of wine, worldwide. For the most part this acclaim has been richly deserved. Expert and novice alike have sung the praises of this good red wine, and more than one connoisseur has hailed it as the best value in red wine in the entire world. It may well be. But of late "Hearty" seems to have lost some of its heart. Recent batches have been softer, with less body and character. See also "plain" Burgundy, a very similar wine. Fair value, $2.80 to $3.30 a half-gallon.

Livingston Cream Sherry*** One wine writer says this bargain-basement wine is virtually the peer of Harveys renowned Bristol Cream, at approximately one sixth—repeat, one sixth—the price. A "majestic bargain," he calls it. It's an astounding wine for the price, but objectively it is simply not the equal of fine Spanish sherry such as Harveys. Serve it, with pride, after dinner. An unbelievable value at $1.20 to $1.50.

Old Decanter Sherry: See LIVINGSTON CREAM SHERRY and VERY DRY SHERRY.

Paisano* The name proclaims this to be an Italian-type red wine fashioned and priced for the *paisanos,* people of the land, the peasants, and so it is —if the tastes and standards of the *landsmänner* are not too high. It's a lighter wine, softer and sweeter than the two Burgundies (above). Fair value, $1.20.

Pink Chablis*** The name is an abomination unto the wine-knowledgeable, for Chablis, by definition, is *white!* But the beverage beneath this label is a frolicsome, slightly sweet, refreshing little wine, better than a mighty host of California rosés; it even has a tingling bit of effervescence. Freshness here is of the essence—don't buy this wine if the color shows any tinge of orange. Drink within one year of purchase. A good value at $1.40.

Pink Champagne** Fair value, $3.

Rhine Garten* Quite sweet, has a slight sparkle, and "soda pop" flavors. It has a certain fresh charm, but the charm is operative up to one glass only —one small glass. After that it tends to nauseate hurriedly. Fair value, $2.25 (eastern U.S., add 40¢). Serve chilled, don't keep it more than a year.

Riesling*** Another of Gallo's new wines, not strictly a "varietal," but a nice little white wine, fresh, crisp, tasty. For summertime refreshment, wintertime resuscitation. Fair value, $1.75 to $2.

Rosé*** Gallo also makes a Vin Rosé (see), but this is a much better wine; it's a new wine with Gallo, introduced in late 1974. Fair value, $1.75 to $2.

Ruby Cabernet*** Another of Gallo's new "varietal" wines (made from the grape specified, not a blend) introduced in October, 1974, and another success. This good red wine has lovely flavor, is well balanced: that is, it has just the right proportion of acidity vs. sweetness. Serve it with red meat or fowl —fine at the barbecue grill. It will even improve with a year or two of added bottle age. Fair value, $1.75 to $2.

Sauterne*** Pleasing, clean, dry white wine. It can be enjoyed, chilled, as an aperitif wine and can serve as honorable accompaniment to light foods, particularly fish and seafood. Don't keep it more than a year or so. A good value at $2.50 to $3 per half-gallon ($1.30 per fifth).

Sauvignon Blanc** This probably won't be as popular as the Chenin Blanc or Riesling (above), as it's decidedly dry on the tongue, but it has good depth of flavor and a lingering aftertaste. It will go well with fish, seafood, light foods in general. Serve it chilled.

Sherry: See LIVINGSTON CREAM SHERRY; VERY DRY SHERRY.

Spañada* The name presumably is meant to suggest Spain's delightful and popular Sangria, a wine punch, made with fresh fruit. But there all similarity ends. This is a very sweet potion, tasting wholly of fruit flavors, a "Pop" wine—nice if you like it!

Sparkling Burgundy** Well made, not offensive, but lacks body and depth. Fair value, ca. $3.

Very Dry Sherry** It's a long long way from Very Dry—it's closer to Very Sweet. This is really a medium sherry, semi-sweet and (would you believe?) semi-dry. It's extremely light in color, taste, and body. A good value, nonetheless, at $1.20 to $1.50.

Vin Rosé* Better than nothing—perhaps.

Zinfandel*** One of Gallo's new varietal wines—varietals are the best kind, as compared to generics or blends—introduced in late 1974. "Z" is one of California's favorite and best red wines—it's a California exclusive, made only there; it will go great with red meats, pasta, stews, poultry. Gallo's "Zin" is not a totally dry wine, has no "bite," in fact it has a touch of sweetness, which most people will appreciate. Wine connoisseurs—snobs?—may not be overly impressed. Serve it at cool room temperature. This wine will even improve with an extra year or two in the bottle. A good value at $1.75 to $2.

GAMAY and GAMAY BEAUJOLAIS

These two names are used interchangeably in California for a delightful young red wine, one of California's all-around best values. American vintners have done wonders with this wine of late years—it improves almost from vintage to vintage. As it's being made today, it's a fresh, fruity wine —not big, not great, but marvelously soft, youngish, ready-and-easy-to-drink. It's similar to France's ever-popular Beaujolais.

Gamay is a talented youngster, versatile enough to go almost anywhere, on any occasion, for whatever purpose. It does handsomely at the outdoor barbecue grill (steaks, chicken, hamburgers, shish kebab) or at a luncheon buffet (sandwiches, cold cuts, chicken salad), or even at a formal dinner (roast beef, turkey). It's equally at home on a picnic, to ennoble the lowly hot dog.

Gamay Beaujolais is a wholly youngish wine—to be consumed while it's young and fresh, the younger the better, surely within three years of purchase (or five years of its vintage date). Serve it at cool room temperature, or slightly chilled (55°F) if you prefer.

Below are the best of California's Gamays and Gamay Beaujolais, together with a sprinkling of other wines of a similar nature. Note well that the vast majority of the wines rate *** and ****, and that most carry pleasantly peasantish price tags. A lot of fine values here.

American Gamays and Gamay Beaujolais—
Comparative Standings

****

Very Good

Pedroncelli Gamay Beaujolais ($2.65)

Yverdon Gamay Beaujolais ($3)

Sebastiani Gamay Beaujolais, 1968, 1969, 1971, 1973 ($3)

Inglenook Gamay Beaujolais, 1971 ($3.10)

Christian Brothers Gamay Noir ($3.20)

Sterling Gamay Beaujolais, 1972 ($3.50)

Robert Mondavi Gamay, 1970 ($3.55)

Ridge Gamay, York Creek, 1971 ($4.25)

Inglenook Red Pinot, 1972 ($5)

***

Good

Almadén Grenoir Original ($2.30)

Weibel Royalty ($2.40)

Sonoma (or Windsor) Gamay ($2.70)—But some vintages are only **

Winemaster's Guild Gamay Beaujolais ($2.80)

Eleven Cellars Gamay Beaujolais ($2.85)

Simi Gamay Beaujolais ($2.90)

Wente Gamay Beaujolais, 1970, 1971 ($2.90)

Sebastiani Gamay Beaujolais, 1972 ($3)

Sebastiani Gamay Beaujolais, Nouveau ($3)

Almadén Gamay Beaujolais ($3)

Paul Masson Gamay Beaujolais ($3)

Cuvaison Gamay Vivace, 1971, 1972 ($3)

Beaulieu Gamay Beaujolais ($3.10)

Inglenook Gamay Beaujolais, 1970 ($3.10)

Inglenook Gamay and Gamay Beaujolais, 1969 ($3.10)

Cresta Blanca Gamay Beaujolais ($3.15)

Fetzer Gamay Beaujolais ($3.25)

Parducci Gamay Beaujolais ($3.30)

Mirassou Gamay Beaujolais ($3.35)

Weibel Gamay Beaujolais ($3.45)

Cuvaison Gamay Rouge, 1970 ($3.50)

Robert Mondavi Gamay, 1971 ($3.55)

Oakville Napa Gamay ($3.75)

Christian Brothers Pinot St. Georges ($4)

Sterling Merlot ($4)

Sterling Merlot Primeur, 1974 ($4)

Cuvaison Gamay Nouveau, 1973, 1974 ($4.50)

**

Fair

Charles Krug Gamay Beaujolais ($2.85)

Wente Gamay Beaujolais, 1969 ($2.90)

San Martin Gamay Beaujolais ($3)

GAMAY NOIR A young, fresh red wine not often made in California (nor anywhere else, as a matter of fact), at least not under its own name. In fact, Christian Brothers (see) is the only major winery to make a Gamay Noir. It's usually called Gamay or Gamay Beaujolais, but it's the identical wine. The Christian Brothers' product is listed in the "Comparative Standings" under GA-MAY.

GAMAY ROSÉ One of California's best rosé wines, but only a half dozen wineries make it; the prodominant grape is the Gamay. The wine is fresh, very slightly on the sweet side, with some fruitiness. At the moment Robert Mondavi (see) is making the best. All are listed in the "Comparative Standings" under ROSÉ.

GATÃO VINHO VERDE*** A light, fresh young white wine from Portugal, with a bit of fizz, and it comes in an odd-shaped bottle—but it's still a nice little wine. For refreshing summertime enjoyment. How to serve this wine: See under VINHO VERDE. A very good value at $2.50.

GATTINARA Excellent red Italian wine, similar to the illustrious Barolo (see), and said by some experts to excel it. Some say flatly that this is Italy's finest wine. It is distinctly dry, with a characteristically bitter aftertaste. Be sure to air it at least an hour. Like so many Italian reds, it goes especially well with roasts, and with all red meats. It is already aged a full four years before it goes to market, and it ages well in the bottle. Gattinara is at its best when it's between six and twelve years old. Serve it at cool room temperature. Gattinara is an extremely consistent wine: if it says Gattinara on the label, it's a virtual certainty that it will be at least ****.

GEMELLO SHERRY Gemello makes the three standard sherries of varying degrees of sweetness, all well-made wines: *Pale Dry Sherry,* ****, the driest of the three. *"Plain" Sherry,* ***: medium-sweet. *Cream Sherry,* ***: the sweetest; it's soft, nutty, full-flavored. All good values at $1.75 to $2.

(LES) GENEVRIÈRES: See MEURSAULT.

GEVREY-CHAMBERTIN If your wine just says "Gevrey-Chambertin" on the label, without "Clos" this-or-that, you are dealing with a "village" wine, not the very top rank, but still fine wine and selling at half the price of those big-time hyphenated-Chambertins (Charmes-Chambertin, Mazys-Chambertin, etc.). This is red Burgundy at its best, almost at its summit. It can vary, however, from grower to grower, so be wary. How to serve, drink, enjoy this wine: See under CHAMBERTIN. Gevrey-Chambertin is at its best when it's from four to seven years old.

1959—Past their peak.

1966—Jadot: ****—Now at its best.

1967—Chanson: ***
   Ph. Duroche: ****

1969—Remoissenet: *****
   Drouhin: *****
   Parisot: *****

1970—Drouhin: *****

1971—Ph. Duroche: ***—Not ready—Try it first in '76.
   Faiveley: ***
   Lebaron: ****

Bouchard: Not recommended.

Drouhin: Not recommended.

Ponnelle: Not recommended.

GEVREY-CHAMBERTIN CLOS ST. JACQUES One of the best of the great red Burgundies, and it commands a commensurate price. How to serve and enjoy this magnificent wine: See under CHAMBERTIN. Some vintages:

1961—Domaine Clair Dau: *****—Will be at its best, 1975 on.

1962—Disappointing.

1970—Louis Latour: ****— Not nearly ready—try it in '78.

1971—Pernot Fernand: Near-Classic.

GEWÜRZTRAMINER and TRAMINER Here's an unusual, unappreciated white wine you'll find in good wine shops from coast to coast. It comes from Alsace and California, primarily. It's the same tasty, spicy, German-type wine whether spelled as one word (as above) or as two (Gewürz Traminer), with an umlaut (Gewürztraminer) or mit-out, like so: Gewuerztraminer, or even if it goes by the name of Traminer. It's all one and the same.

"Gewürz"—the word means "Spicy"—comes in varying degrees of sweetness, and good examples of the wine are always perfumy, well balanced, very flavorful. Those with some sweetness make for marvelous hot-weather refreshment, by themselves or with fresh fruit. The drier examples can be used as aperitif wines or at the table, to accompany fish and shellfish in particular, but also ham and pork, poultry and sausage. In Alsace, it even competes with the likes of *pâte de foie gras* and sauerkraut. Serve it chilled, around 50°F, but be careful not to over-chill Gewürztraminer.

"Gewürz" is a wine for early consumption—not necessarily early in the day (though that might be fun too) but certainly early in its life—within a year or two of purchase. Or, if it's vintaged Gewürz, within four or five years of its vintage date. The original Traminer and Gewürztraminer come from Alsace, that buffeted little land between France and Germany, and they are two of the country's finest wines. Or rather, *it is* one of the country's finest wines, for as of 1973 it has all been labeled Gewürztraminer. Alsatian Gewürz is usually more intense in flavor than the American imitation, so much so, in fact, that people are sometimes put off by the taste . . . they usually end up as devotees, however, for this is an excellent wine, clean, crisp, deeply flavorful.

Listed below are California's best Gewürztraminers (and Traminers), listed in descending order of excellence. Where wines have the same rating, the least expensive is listed first. All of these wines, of course, will also be found elsewhere in this book, individually assessed, under the name of the winery.

California Gewürztraminers— Comparative Standings

*****

Exceptional

Simi Gewürztraminer, 1972 ($4.05)—On the dry side.

****

Very Good

Inglenook Gewürztraminer ($2.80)—On the dry side.

Almadén Gewürztraminer ($3)—Touch of sweetness.

Pedroncelli Gewürztraminer, 1973 ($3.30).

Mirassou Gewürztraminer, 1972 and 1973 ($4)—On the dry side.

Simi Gewürztraminer, Non-vintage ($4.05)—On the dry side.

Buena Vista Gewürz Traminer, 1971 ($4.50)—Some sweetness.

Wente Gewürztraminer, 1972 ($4.90)—On the dry side.

Buena Vista Gewürz Traminer Haraszthy Cabinet, 1972 ($5.50)—Some sweetness.

Stony Hill Gewürztraminer, 1969 and 1971 ($6)—On the dry side.

***
Good

Robert Mondavi Traminer, 1970 and 1971 ($3)—On the dry side.

Sebastiani Gewürz Traminer, 1969, 1970, 1972 ($3.05) —Some sweetness.

Louis M. Martini Gewürz Traminer, 1969, 1971, 1972 ($3.65)—On the dry side.

Charles Krug Gewürztraminer ($3.90)—On the dry side.

Oakville Gewürztraminer ($4)—On the dry side.

Sterling Gewürztraminer ($4).

Mirassou Gewürztraminer, Sixth Harvest, 1971 ($5.75)—On the dry side.

**
Fair

Charles Krug Traminer ($2.85).

Robert Mondavi Traminer, 1972 ($3)—On the dry side.

Sebastiani Gewürz Traminer, 1971 ($3.05)—Some sweetness.

Louis Martini Gewürz Tra-

miner, 1970 ($3.65)—On the dry side.

ZD Gewürztraminer ($4.50).
*
Passable

Buena Vista Gewürz Traminer, 1969, 1970, 1972 ($4.50)—Some sweetness.

GEWUERZTRAMINER CABINET WINE, SICHEL ET FILS FRÈRES Sichel is a huge international wine-shipping firm, probably best known in the U.S. for it's ever-popular Blue Nun Liebfraumilch. Their wines are almost infallibly reliable, but by no means are they always the best values in a particular category. This particular Gewürz deserves ****.

GEWÜRZTRAMINER, CHÂTEAU DE RIQUEWIHR This wine is produced by the 400-year-old firm of Dopff & Irion, of Riquewihr, Alsace, one of the most reliable of all Alsatian producers. The '69 was ***, the '70 Sélection Exceptionnelle, ****. Ditto for their "Les Sorcières" (the name of a special vineyard), 1967, still quite alive, but drink soon! It's expensive: around $6.50.

GEWÜRZTRAMINER, FRITZ KOBUS Kobus is a dependable shipper of Alsatian wines, and you can't say the firm suffers from egomania, for the name is almost invisible on the label, it's in such infinitesimal print. If it sells for around $4, it's a good value. The 1969 was especially good: ****.

GEWÜRZTRAMINER, GASCHY Antoine Gaschy is the Alsatian producer of this wine which is imported to the U.S. by Bercut-Vandervoort. It's dependable wine, and at ca. $3.50, a good value. A 1970 Spätlese was easily ****. The '71 "regular" as well as the Spätlese, ditto.

**GEWÜRZTRAMINER "HU-
GEL"** Hugel et Fils in the
Town of Riquewihr—it's on the
label—is the name of one of
the best shippers of "Gewürz" to
the U.S. Their Gewürz is totally
reliable, the "regular" a fair
value at around $4.75. They al-
so make a "super-Gewürz"
from late-picked grapes, called
"Reserve Exceptionelle," which
it is; it sells for $6.75. There's
also an in-between bottling,
"Sélection Premier," around
$5.75. One especially notable
bottle was Hugel's '69 "Regular" *****.

GIVRY Light red Burgundy
(France) wine, similar to Mercurey (see), its neighbor. It's
fresh and pleasant, usually a
good value, best served slightly
chilled (55°F). Drink it exactly as you would a Beaujolais
(see). It often has the name of
an individual vineyard on the
label, a further assurance of
quality: Clos Marceau, Clos
Saint-Pierre, Clos Saint-Paul.
(A wine under the tutelage of
both Saints Peter and Paul
can't help but be good!) It's at
its best when it's between three
and six years old. It's invariably **** and with the inter-
cession of Sts. Peter and Paul
may occasionally reach *****.
Fair value, $4 to $5.

GLASSES, WINE There are
hordes of wine glasses around,
a lot of them fit only to contain water or other such soul-
less liquid. Just about every nation under the sun has its own
traditional glass for its native
wines, and these may be fine—
if you like to collect glasses or
to spend money. But there is
one all-purpose wine glass you
can use for all wines, including dessert wines and Champagne. To wit: a clear, stemmed
tulip-shaped glass of at least 6-
ounce capacity (8 or 10 ounces
is even better). Such a glass
helps you extract everything
your wine has to offer: the
color can be fully appreciated
thanks to the clear glass—the
aroma and bouquet fill the
bowl and are funneled nose-
ward. The wine can breathe,
expand, stretch.

Always hold your glass by the
stem—not the base, not by the
bowl. Base-holding is affecta-
tion—bowl-holding is boorish,
and it changes the temperature
of the wine. But the most common sin in all the world of
wine-drinking is to fill a glass
too full. Under pain of excom-
munication and possible dam-
nation, never fill a wine glass
more than half full.

See also: TASTING WINE.

GLORIA, CHÂTEAU This
wine has the lowliest official
ranking of any Bordeaux wine,
crû bourgeois, but the wine,
even if it's not one of the
Grands Seigneurs, is clearly
above *bourgeois* status. It is
owned by a certain Henri Martin, who, it is said, "knows all
there is to be known about
wine." That's a lot! Gloria
wines are worth searching out,
as they will often be good values, although they're getting so
well known these days that inevitably their prices have begun
to rise, despite their lowly rating. How to serve Château Gloria: See BORDEAUX.

*1945, 1949, 1950, 1953, 1955,
1957, 1959*—All clearly ****,
and almost *****.

1961—*****—Now at its
peak and will hold until 1990.
Fair value, $8.

1962—****—Best drinking:
1975–1985. Fair value $7.

1964—****—Just now get-
ting to its best—Good drinking

from now through 1983. Fair value, $7 to $8.

1966 and 1967—*******—Will be at their best, 1976–1986. Fair value, $8.

1969—******—Best drinking, 1975–1980. Fair value, $6 to $7.

1970—Near-Classic—Has consistently placed well in blind tastings, even when pitted against top-ranked Clarets. It's not yet ready, however. Try it first around 1978.

1971—May reach Near-Classic, though it's too early for a final assessment.

GOLD SEAL VINEYARDS (Hammondsport, N.Y.) Gold Seal today is a wholly American operation. Almost disgustingly so: pushbutton automation, assembly-line efficiency. Big and successful. Yet Gold Seal's history was quite other—single-minded, dedicated men making good wines, against all odds, wholly on their own. Charles Fournier and Dr. Konstantin Frank finally succeeded in taming the foxy taste of native grapes and in growing European grapes in New York's harsh climate. Gold Seal's modern-day success was built upon the dedication and genius of these two men. They learned, at Gold Seal, how to make good wines before they learned how to make lots of wine.

Today they do both: lots of wine, something like 6,000 cases per day. But more importantly, a lot of it, good wine. Gold Seal's sparkling wines are their special pride.

Blanc de Blancs, Charles Fournier, New York State Champagne**** Charles Fournier was one of the talented pioneers at Gold Seal and the winery likes to put his name prominently on their best wines. And here they've put it in bold letters on the best of their best. This is clearly the best wine, still or sparkling, Gold Seal makes. The winery claims it as the finest Champagne in America, which it is not, but it is, indubitably, New York's finest. It does have a touch of foxiness but this is clearly a plus, not a minus. It's a *Brut*, very dry, though the word is not on the label. It was served to Queen Elizabeth on her visit to Chicago some years ago. Ironically it sells for less in California, ca. $6, than it does in New York, $6.50.

Burgundy Ugh.

Burgundy Natural A new wine from this well-known New York winery—and a good one. Notice that it's not labeled "New York State Burgundy," but "American"—that's because it's a blend of both New York and California grapes. It's a clean, tasty wine with just a touch of sweetness. Fine *vin ordinaire* at $2.40.

Catawba*** Gold Seal's history is inextricably bound up with native American grapes. The winery has learned, over the course of many years, to tame, not eliminate, the "foxiness," that distinctive wild taste of native grapes. Gold Seal does a good job with the Catawba, producing it in three flavors: Pink, Red, White. All three are lightly sweet and make for good summertime refreshment. Fair value, $1.80.

Chablis Nature, Charles Fournier** A unique wine, pure New York State. It's got a hint of native grape foxiness, which somehow enhances, doesn't detract. It's touted as a "still Champagne": made like a true French Champagne but skip the bubbles. It doesn't quite make that, but it's an interesting little white wine, crisp and dry. And a good value at $2.30. Serve chilled, don't keep it more than two years.

Champagne** Gold Seal's reputation has been built largely upon its Champagnes. Today they comprise a full half of the total production. Besides the Blanc de Blancs (see), they make the standard four "flavors": Brut (orange label): very light and dry; Extra Dry (white label): sweeter than the Brut, can even accompany desserts; also: Pink Champagne: the sweetest of the lot; Sparkling Burgundy; and, of course, the inevitable Cold Duck.

Charles Fournier Blanc de Blancs: See BLANC DE BLANCS.

Charles Fournier Chablis Nature: See CHABLIS NATURE.

Cold Duck: See CHAMPAGNE.

Concord Red** Quite sweet, rather fruity, but a bit heavy-handed. One of those rare wines that might go better "on the rocks." A good value at $1.50.

Pink Champagne: See CHAMPAGNE.

Pinot Chardonnay, 1971*** 100 percent from the noble Chardonnay grape, elegant, dry white wine, perfect with oysters and other seafood. Marketed for the first time in August, 1974, and presently available only in New York State. Serve chilled. Best drinking, 1975 through 1977. Fair value, $3.50.

Rhine Wine** Light white wine, no obtrusive foxiness, medium-dry. A good value at $2. Serve chilled, with light foods, seafood.

Rosé*** A good example of a light New York State wine: smooth, fresh, slightly sweet, a nice touch of foxiness. A good value at $2.

Sauternes** Sweeter than the Rhine, an economical, fresh little white wine for summertime sipping. Serve chilled.

Sparkling Burgundy: See CHAMPAGNE.

GONZALEZ BYASS NEKTAR CREAM SHERRY**** Gonzalez Byass is a Spanish sherry firm founded only in 1835, which makes it a mere upstart in the industry, as these things go in Spain. But this "newcomer" happens to be wholly dependable. This Cream is an excellent sweet sherry, probably as good as Harveys Bristol Cream, and selling for almost $3 less. How to serve: See under SHERRY.

GONZALEZ BYASS TIO PEPE SHERRY***** This is one of the most famous single wines in the world. It's clearly the most famous of all Fino (Dry) sherries. Incredibly Tio Pepe—roughly tranlated "Uncle Joe"—accounts for a full 70 percent of the international sherry market. It's dry, light, deeply flavored, an ideal aperitif wine. Serve it chilled. Fair value, $5.50. For further details on serving: See under SHERRY.

GRAACHER HIMMELREICH Jesus said at the Last Supper: "I shall not drink again of the fruit of the vine until that day when I drink it new in the kingdom of God." (Mark 14:25) But you can drink wine of the Kingdom of Heaven right here on earth if you buy some of this wine, for Himmelreich means just that, the Kingdom of Heaven. And truth to tell, this is a lovely Moselle (Germany) wine, fragrant and full-flavored. How to serve it:

See under MOSELLE. Some vintages:

1966—Auslese (J. J. Prüm): *****

1967—Spätlese (Prüm): ****
1969—(Kayser): **** Fine value.

    Spätlese (Weber): ****
    Spätlese (Prüm) ****
1971—Auslese (Prüm): ****
—One critic said it tastes like an armful of flowers.

    Kabinett (S. A. Prüm): ****

    Beerenauslese (Prüm): *****

    Eiswein (Prüm): Near-Classic.
    Spätlese (Prüm): *****— It's available at around $9.

(LES) GRANDES RUCH-OTTES: See CHASSAGNE-MON-TRACHET (WHITE).

GRAND VIN or GRAND VIN DE BOURGOGNE, BORDEAUX, etc. Simply disregard these words on a French label. They're pure propaganda, meaning "Great Wine," which the wine may well be, but these words don't establish the fact. Like American TV commercials, they're designed for the simpleminded.

(LES) GRANDS ECHÉZEAUX Magnificent wine, one of the best of all red Burgundies. It is soft and perfumed, definitely on the expensive side, though not as much so as some of like caliber. Grands Echézeaux is not as well known as it deserves to be—perhaps its ponderous name intimidates Americans. It is at its best when it is between six and twelve years of age. A wine as great as this one deserves to be savored, not at the dinner table competing with pizzas and sauerkraut, but on its own, slowly, appreciatively, or with cheese and bread,

or perhaps apple and pear slices, with nuts. A single exception is allowed: Grands Echézeaux may accompany duck done in the classic manner: Canard Montmorency or Caneton à l'Orange. Note that there is also a "plain" Echézeaux (see). Some vintages:

1933 Leroy: *****—Still in excellent condition—Drink soon.

1943 Romanée-Conti: Near-Classic—Don't keep it.

1959 An exceptional vintage; round, balanced wines.

1961, 1962, and 1964 Leroy: All Near-Classics—Now at their peak.

1966 Drouhin: *****—Will remain at peak another five years.

    Engel: *****—Now at its best.
    Romanée-Conti: Near-Classic—Now at its best.
1969 Engel: ****—Hold until 1976.

1970 Remoissenet: ****— Hold until 1976.

1971 Engel: ****—Needs another three years.

    Drouhin: *****—Needs another three years.

GRAN RISERVA: See (FEDERICO) PATERNINA.

GRAN SANGRE DE TORO: See TORRES.

GRAND VIN D 'ALSACE: This means simply "a Great Wine of Alsace," but it's not a "commercial"—it's an official designation. For evaluation of an individual bottle so labeled, see under the name of the wine.

GRÃO VASCO DAO TINTO **** Don't let the strange name scare you: here's a reliable and well-made red table wine from Portugal—Grão Vasco is the name of a famous painter, the wine's "given" name —Dão (see) is the generic name of the wine (like Burgundy, Chablis)—and Tinto means red. It's made by the same people who make Mateus Rosé. Red Dão is to the Portuguese what Chianti is to the Italians. A good value at around $3. How to serve it: see under DAO.

GRAVES. There's nothing ghoulish about this name, it's the name of a district in Bordeaux (France) and the name refers to the *gravelly* soil, not to burial sites; it's one syllable, pronounced "grahv."

Graves produces both red and white wines—some very notable ones in both categories. Most people today associate the name Graves with its dry white wines, for no very good reason. Across the board, the reds are good buys because they're recently out of fashion—again, for no discernible reason.

The best wines from Graves, red or white, will have the name of a château as the most prominent part of the label. (For an evaluation of these individually, see under their specific names.) The name Graves is always on the label, but it's hard to find amid all the French verbiage. It's usually in small type between the words "Appellation" and "Contrôlée."

But when Graves is the most prominent word on the label, and there is no château named, you're dealing with the lowest grade of Graves wine, red or white, but usually a pretty good wine at a decent price, between $3 and $3.50.

Be discreetly skeptical if the label says "Graves Supérieur" —this is a technical term referring to the amount of alcohol in the wine, and has nothing to do with the wine being "superior" in any way.

For serving the red Graves: See under BORDEAUX.

White Graves is a distinctive dry white wine with an engaging taste of the soil. It is the perfect complement to fish, seafood, ham and pork, creamed fowl. Serve it chilled, 45 to 50°F.

Some of the best White Graves in descending order of excelence:

Château Haut-Brion Blanc— Expensive.

Domaine de Chevalier— "Domaine" here takes the place of Château—Some say this is even better than Haut-Brion.

Château Couhins

Château Carbonnieux

Château Bouscaut—One of the very few French Châteaux that is American-owned.

Château Olivier

GREAT WESTERN This well-known label is the property of the Pleasant Valley Wine Company, a 115-year-old New York (Hammondsport) winery. It was Great Western that made the first New York Champagne, more than a century ago. Its greatest accomplishment, however, was convincing federal authorities back in the ill-starred days of Prohibition to allow them to continue making "sacramental Champagne" for the clergy! Consumption, rest assured, was strictly extra-sacramental, outside the liturgical. Sparkling wines are expressly forbidden for use in the Eucharist. Today the clergy indubitably continue to enjoy Great Western Champagne, but at least its consumption is now admittedly nonsacramental!

Aurora Sauterne ** Soft and fragrant, medium-dry—it's also medium-sweet, amazing!—highlights fowl, light casseroles, pork and ham. A good value at $2.10. Serve chilled.

Baco Noir Burgundy* Baco Noir is the name of a grape, half French and half American (a hybrid), and this wine follows suit: it's half French like a Burgundy, half American, with a touch of the taste of native grapes. It will go well with beef or lamb, and you can even chill it slightly, says the winery, to accompany spicy dishes. "Baco" will keep well for at least three years after purchase. A good value at $2.15.

Brut Champagne: See CHAMPAGNE.

Burgundy, Baco Noir: See BACO NOIR BURGUNDY.

Chablis The label says it has a "stony flavor"—that's what true French Chablis is famous for—and so it has, but it's just a touch. This is a fresh, clean wine; it will go admirably with fish, seafood, light foods. Note that there is also a Diamond Chablis (see). Fair value, $2.15.

Chablis, Diamond: See DIAMOND CHABLIS.

Champagne Much of Great Western's fame has been built on its sparkling wines. This is not too surprising, as the distinctive "foxy" taste of native eastern grapes is somehow muted, even becomes an asset, in sparkling wines. Every label of every bottle of Great Western sparkling wine proudly proclaims that the winery was winning awards for its sparkling wines more than a century ago: "Vienna, 1873, First Prize" reads the label. It was actually a "sparkling Catawba," no longer made, that won that first gold medal. Great Western makes all the standard sparklers

plus a couple: *Brut Champagne* (yellow label), ****: their best, it's brisk and dry. *Extra Dry Champagne* (white label), ***: sweeter than the Brut. *Special Reserve Champagne* (white label), ***: Between the Brut and the Extra Dry in sweetness. *Pink Champagne*, ***: the sweetest of all. *Sparkling Burgundy*, ***: medium-sweet. *Cold Duck, Pink*, **: All Cold Ducks are more or less pink, but this one has it on the label, prominently, just to make sure: in case the Cold Duck name doesn't grab you, perhaps the "Pink" will. All these wines retail for $5.30 in the eastern U.S., and for some mysterious reason, for somewhat less, ca. $5, in the West.

Chelois* You can pronounce it in Frenchly fashion, "shell-wah," or Americanized, "shell-oy." Some say this red wine resembles a French Claret; others say it's mostly American, with at least a whisp of the Concord grape. All agree that it's a good little everyday wine and a very good value at $2.20. Serve at cool room temperature; it will keep for at least three years after purchase.

Cold Duck: See CHAMPAGNE.

Concord: See RED CONCORD.

Delaware Moselle* The Delaware is a native American grape, one of the best and most expensive, widely used to make eastern Champagne. The label also says "Moselle," as the wine is said to resemble that elegant German wine. Well . . . it's a soft white wine, dry enough; it will go well with any white meat or with ham. Serve chilled, don't keep it more than a year or so. Fair value, $2.35.

Diamond Chablis* The Diamond is a hybrid grape widely

planted in the eastern U.S. It makes a distinctly dry wine, fragrant and fresh. Serve it at luncheon or with any light food, well chilled, says the winery, and young—don't keep it beyond one year. Fair value, $2.35.

Dutchess Rhine Wine*** Dutchess is not a female Duke —that's Duchess—it's a native American grape. The wine is a medium-dry dinner wine, white of course, somewhat flowery, pleasant enough, but as somebody said, more Dutchess than Rhine. Complements fowl, fish, seafood. Serve chilled, don't keep it more than one year. Fair value, $2.10. See also the "plain" Rhine Wine, which is less sweet.

Extra Dry Champagne: See CHAMPAGNE.

Isabella Rosé*** A nice little eastern rosé, semisweet, purely American in flavor, says the label, but not aggressively so. Correct. For preprandial sipping or to accompany light foods. Serve chilled; don't keep it beyond one year. Fair value, $2.35.

Niagara: See WHITE NIAGARA.

Pink Catawba** Catawba, a native American grape, was once the most popular wine in America. For one hundred years Great Western has been doing as good a job with it as any. Catawba has the distinctive taste of its wild origin, "foxiness," it's called, and millions of Americans appreciate that taste. And they will enjoy this rosé, served chilled, before dinner. It's on the sweet side. Fair value, $2.10.

Pink Champagne: See CHAMPAGNE.

Red Concord* The Concord grape makes good jelly and good grape juice but not good wine. This is a highly flavored, not well-flavored, wine, too assertive and too foxy for most. Recommended only for lovers of Concord and the stout of heart. It used to be called Pleasant Valley Red—some so labeled may still be lurking about. Serve at cool room temperature. Fair value, $2.

Rhine Wine** There is also a Dutchess Rhine Wine (see) somewhat sweeter than this wine. This is light and fresh, "recognizably New York and pleasantly so," says one critic. Serve it as you would the Dutchess. Fair value, $2.10.

Rosé*** On the sweet side, fragrant, fresh, and pleasant. Serve it, chilled, for refreshment anytime, or before dinner, or with fruit. A good value at $2.10. See also Isabella Rosé.

Rosé, Isabella: See ISABELLA ROSÉ.

Sauterne: See AURORA SAUTERNE.

Sparkling Burgundy: See CHAMPAGNE.

White Niagara** A soft, light, semisweet wine made from the Niagara grape, a native American grape. It's somewhat foxy but not unpleasantly so. The winery says it goes best with traditional American foods. Serve chilled. Don't keep it more than a year or so. Fair value, $2.10.

GREEN HUNGARIAN This unlikely name may derive—for all we know—from a greenish hued person of the Hungarian race. Nobody seems to know where the name comes from, much less where the grape comes from. But everybody knows where it goes *to:* it goes into a lot of American Chablis. And a half dozen California wineries also make it as a varietal, that is, under its own name. And as such, and at its best, it's light, crisp, fruity, easy to drink, tasty. At its worst, it's like some of our less noble American Chablis. Serve Green Hungarian as you would Chablis: with fish, especially shellfish, light meats (particularly suited to pork and goose), Chinese food. Serve it chilled (45 to 50°F). Drink it young: within two years or so of purchase.

California's best:

****

Very Good
   Weibel ($2.55)

***

Good
   Sebastiani ($2.50)
   Souverain ($3.25)
   Buena Vista, 1972 ($3.40)

*

Passable
   Cresta Blanca ($2.45)

GRENACHE ROSÉ An American rosé wine made primarily from Grenache grapes—which means that all other things being equal (they rarely are) a wine so labeled will be a better bottle than one labeled simply Rosé or Vin Rosé. Grenache Rosés are perfumy, fragrant wines, lightly on the sweet side. To learn which are California's best Grenache Rosés, see the "Comparative Standings" under ROSÉ.

GRENOUILLES: See CHABLIS, FRENCH.

GREY RIESLING Aside from the fact that the wine isn't *gray* and the grape isn't a *Riesling*, the name is pretty accurate! Actually, this generally good white wine is rather like a German Riesling—more so, in fact, than some of our California white wines made from true Riesling grapes. It's a very popular wine, especially in California, and it's often in short supply. It tends to be on the dry side, and goes well with fish, seafood, chicken, veal, pork—and the best examples you will want to serve as an aperitif wine, or for simple enjoyment or refreshment, on their own. One California authority recommends Grey Riesling for your breakfast enjoyment—no jest!—if you're jaded from too many Champagne breakfasts. Sounds like an extremely rare malady! But jaded or not, you'll find it sure beats prune juice!

California's finest:

   Grey Rieslings—
   Comparative Standings

****

Very Good
   Kenwood ($2.80)
   Ridge, 1972 Zeni Vineyard ($4.50)

***

Good
   Almadén ($2.35)
   Weibel ($2.55)
   Beringer ($2.60)
   Wente ($2.65)
   Inglenook, 1972 ($2.80)
   Charles Krug ($2.85)
   Korbel ($2.85)

**

Fair
   Royal Host ($1.85)
   Cresta Blanca ($2.45)
   Sonoma (or Windsor) ($2.70)
   Buena Vista ($2.75)
   Christian Brothers ($3.20)

GREYSTONE

Champagnes The Greystone label is owned by the California Wine Association, a huge cooperative producing wines under a half dozen different labels. Greystone Champagnes have won a host of awards at the Los Angeles County Fair. They're not Taittinger's Comtes de Champagne, but they sell for $1.99, not $22.50. *Extra*

Dry Champagne, **; *Pink Champagne,* *. See also Calwa, another C.W.A. Champagne label.

GRIGNOLINO This is a good, light-bodied red wine, made first in Italy, and now also in California. The Italian version often reads: Grignolino D'Asti (Asti is the name of the town). It's lighter in color than most reds, sometimes so much so that it's simply bottled as a rosé! Some say they can detect strawberries in the aroma and oranges in the taste . . . beats Tutti-Fruiti. With its distinct flavor, Grignolino is ideal to accompany pasta, red meats, especially spicy stews, roast beef, beef casseroles. And to be appreciated most of all, drink it on its own or with simple cheeses. Drink Grignolino rather young—two or three years after purchase is ideal. Don't keep it more than four years. If it's vintage-dated (the Italian ones always are), drink it when it is from three to six years old.

These are California's present Grignolinos:

Comparative Standings
***
Good
    San Martin ($2.50)
    Cresta Blanca ($3.15)
    Heitz ($3.50)
**
Fair
    Beringer ($3.25)

Some notable recent Italian Grignolinos:

1968 Giri: ***—Drink immediately.

1969 Carnevale: ***—Already on the decline.

1969 Bersano: **—Drink soon.

1970 Marchesi di Barolo: ***—At its best, 1975.

1971 Bruno Giascosa: ***

—Will be at its best, 1975–1976.

GRUAUD-LAROSE, CHÂTEAU (or: CHÂTEAU GRUAUD-LAROSE SARGET, or GRUAUD-LAROSE FAURE) Excellent red Bordeaux (French) wine, first cousin to the popular Talbot, both owned by the Cordier family—the name is on the label. The wine is noted for its fruitiness and its consistency. When in doubt in a restaurant, this or Talbot is a safe bet. How to serve and enjoy this wine: See BORDEAUX.

1959—*****—Good drinking, 1975–1985.

1960—****—Good wine in poor year—Drink soon. Good value at $5.

1961—Near-Classic—It's just now reaching its best and will be there for a long time to come. Fair value $15.

1962—*****—Best drinking, 1975 through 1985. Fair value $8.

1964—****—Best drinking, 1975 through 1985. Fair value $8.

1966—*****—Will be at its best, 1978–1985. Fair value $8.

1967—****—Best drinking: 1976–1982.

1970—*****—Beautifully balanced and very fruity wine. It will be at its best, 1978 to 1990.

GUILD WINERIES (San Francisco, Calif.) This is an enormous cooperative of growers, more than a thousand of them, with vineyards stretching from one end of California to the other. Guild is the third largest winemaker in the nation, producing millions of gallons of standard, economical, mostly forgettable wines, under a host of different labels: Cresta Blanca (see), Roma (see), Cook's Imperial (see), Tavola (see), Wine Masters (see), Famiglia Cribari, (see Cribari, Famiglia). No wine at all is marketed under the simple name of Guild—in fact, the name Guild won't be found at all on most of these labels. This is mostly wine reduced to its lowest common denominator. But it's cheap, and it sure beats no wine at all!

GUNTRUM This name on a German wine label is a good guarantee of quality, though Guntrum wines, like everybody else's in this fickle, finite world, can vary from vintage to vintage, even from bottle to bottle, from great to merely passable. The full name (also on the label, smaller type) is Weingut Louis Guntrum, established in 1824. Look up your particular wine under its proper name, e.g., Liebfraumilch, Oppenheimer.

H

HANNS KORNELL: See KOR-NELL, HANNS.

HANZELL VINEYARDS (Sonoma, Calif.) Hanzell is the granddaddy of all those prestigious, exclusive little wineries that have been springing up out of the California landscape over the past decade. Hanzell, founded in the 1950s, was itself modeled after the illustrious Clos de Vougeot in Burgundy (France) and so became, unwittingly, the prototype of California's new breed of top-flight, small-production wineries.

In the European tradition, they make only two wines at Hanzell, a Chardonnay and a Pinot Noir. One European wine critic calls the wines "brilliantly rich and intense." These are strictly connoisseur's wines, and they sell at connoisseur's—or capitalist-industrialist's—prices: the cheapest are around $6. They're usually worth their premium prices—but it's like that Lear Jet being offered at a bargain price, just $900,000—it may be worth every penny of it, but . . .

Chardonnay Without question, one of California's greatest Chardonnays. Great Chardonnays are a happy blend of two very disparate taste-sensations: that of the grape (called fruitiness) and that of the wooden barrel in which the wine was aged. Hanzell's Chardonnay constitutes precisely such a delightful blend, without an overdose of woodiness, as in the case of some expensive Chardonnays. It's like the man said: "If I enjoyed the taste of wood, I'd chew on a shingle." This is California Chardonnay at its finest, a worthy rival of the great white Burgundies of France.

For the historical record only, bottles all long departed this world:

1959, 1960*****
1965, 1966, 1967****
1968**** Big, intense wine, will be at its best, 1975–1976.
1969***** Best drinking: 1975 through 1978.
1970**** It may reach *****, will be at its best, 1975 through 1978.

Pinot Noir Perhaps not quite on a par with Hanzell's Chardonnay, but fine wine still. A prestigious French wine periodical recently paid homage—probably grudgingly—to this wine. Both these Hanzell wines deserve to be consumed—because of price alone, if for no other reason—on their own, in lordly isolation, or with simple cheeses, walnuts, fruits.

1965**** Best drinking, present through the 70s.
1966**** Now at its best and will hold there through 1982.
1967***** Best drinking: 1975–1984.
1968**** Final word is not in on this wine—it's still maturing—but it's certainly going to merit at least its present

****. It will be at its best from 1975 or '76 onward.

1969 First reports say it's a disaster, but reserve judgment for the nonce. Hanzell has had very very few vinous disasters . . . maybe none.

HARASZTHY CELLARS: See BUENA VISTA.

HARVEYS BRISTOL CREAM SHERRY***** This is undoubtedly the most famous sherry in the world—and with pretty good reason, for it is a magnificent wine. Some experts say simply that it is the best sherry in the world. One cannot question the wine's excellence, velvety smooth and luscious, but one can certainly question the price tag, now hovering around $8. It is not that much superior to a host of Spanish cream sherries selling for $5 to $6. If it's an authentic after-dinner cream sherry you're looking for, you'll save a bunch of pesos if you will look for one of these: Palomino Cream —Wisdom Golden Cream— Sandeman Fine Rich Cream— Gonzalez Byass Nektar Cream —and especially, the very best: Williams and Humbert Canasta Cream and Pedro Domecq Celebration Cream. How to serve this wine: See under SHERRY.

HARVEYS BRISTOL FINO SHERRY***** Note that there is also a Bristol Dry (***), not nearly as good a wine. This Fino is bone-dry, a brilliant and luxurious wine, an ideal aperitif. It completes an illustrious trio of Harveys Bristols, sells for around $7.50. How to serve this wine: See under SHERRY.

HARVEYS BRISTOL MILK SHERRY***** This is a medium sherry, not as sweet and rich as the Bristol Cream, but equally great. One critic describes it as "languorously seductive." It should sell for about a dollar less than the Cream: around $7. How to serve this wine: See under SHERRY.

HARVEYS GOLD CAP RUBY PORT** This Harvey is John Harvey & Sons of Bristol, England, the makers of the famous Bristol Cream Sherry (see). This is a good, though not exceptional bottle of the lowliest type of real Portuguese Ruby Porto. Fair value, $5.

HARVEYS THE DIRECTORS' BIN TAWNY PORT This wine is designed—or at least named—to be enjoyed by the board of directors. That makes it expensive, which it is, ca. $10 —but that doesn't necessarily make it good—which it ain't— at least not $10 worth. Tag it: ***.

HARVEYS TICO COCKTAIL SHERRY***** One of Harveys finest: light, very dry, velvety smooth. Just right for the eleven o'clock (A.M. or P.M.) drop-in—if he (she—it) is a drop-out, serve him (her —it) water. A good value at around $5. How to serve this wine: See under SHERRY.

HATTENHEIM(ER) NUSS-BRUNNEN One of Germany's finest white wines, elegant and graceful. Hattenheimers, like most Rheingaus, are at their best when they are between three and six years old. Two great ones:

1949—Von Simmern: One wine critic said it is one of the most flawless wines he ever drank.

1953—Trockenbeerenauslese (*Von Simmern*): Classic.

HAUT-BRION, CHÂTEAU One of the very great red wines of Bordeaux, it has never been as popular—nor, therefore, as expensive, as the other great first growths (Lafite, Latour, etc.), perhaps because it is located in the Graves area, whose wines, for no good reason, have been out of favor, lo, these past decades. Haut-Brion is an ancient wine—its history goes back to the Middle Ages. It's a full, powerful wine, noted for its special flavor due to the gravelly soil of the vineyard, up to sixty feet deep in some places! It is also noteworthy in that it is the only one of the great Châteaux owned by an American: Clarence Dillon. Fine red Bordeaux goes beautifully with beef and lamb—especially the finer cuts —but a wine of such renown and excellence as Haut-Brion deserves its own private setting: savor it with bits of cheese and bread, in company with wine-appreciating souls who will sip and slurp (see TASTING WINE), not gulp and slobber.

1871, 1874, 1875—In case you find any lying around, they were all Classics.

1899, 1900—As above.

1906—Near-Classic.

1920—Near-Classic—Fair value $50.

1923—*****

1925, 1926, 1928, 1929—Avoid!

1945—Classic—Some have called this the wine of the century. It has just now reached its peak and will hold at the top of its form until the year 2000! Fair value, $50.

1949—*****—At its best, now and to 1980. Fair value, $35.

1953—*****, but has just begun to decline—drink soon. Fair value, $35 to $40, not $90 as on some price tags.

1955—Near-Classic—Fair value, $40 (not $100)—Don't

hold this too long. At its best now and through 1977.

1957—Good wine in poor year: **** Fair value, $15.

1959—Near-Classic—Best drinking: 1975–1985. Fair value. $45.

1961—Classic—Will be at its best from 1978 on. Fair value, $50, not the $100 on some price tags.

1962—Near-Classic—Just now reaching its peak and it will be marvelous drinking for at least a decade.

1964—Near-Classic—Now at its best, and will remain there until 1980. Fair value, $25.

1966—Classic—Just now reaching its peak and will hold at least until 1980. Fair value, $35.

1967—Near-Classic—Now at its best, will hold there through the 70s. Fair value, $25.

1968—A moderate success considering the vintage: **** Drink soon. Fair value, $7.50.

1969—It's not there yet, but it's going to be a Near-Classic. It's *almost* fairly priced, ca. $25. Try it first in 1976.

1970—Going to be a great one: Near-Classic at least. Try it first, 1978. Fair value, $35, and wonder of wonders you may find it at that price!

1971—The crystal ball says it's going to be a Classic.

HAUT-MÉDOC Haut means "High" in French, and it's often abused, or at least misunderstood or misread on wine labels, but here's one place where it means exactly what it says: High Médoc. This is the high part of the Médoc (see) both geographically and qualitatively. All the best red Bordeaux come from here. Of course the best wines from the Haut-Médoc go to market under the names of their châteaux, but a small proportion are marketed simply as Haut-Médoc, and these will be better wines than those labeled Médoc. How to serve these wines: See under BORDEAUX.

HAUT-SAUTERNES If you see this term on a Franch label, ignore the Haut (pronounced simply *Oh!*) and treat the wine exactly as you would a simple Sauternes, which it is.

HAWKER'S CREAM SHERRY**** It's sold only in the Boston area, but it's a good one and a good value at around $5.

HEARTY BURGUNDY: See GALLO HEARTY BURGUNDY.

(CHARLES) HEIDSIECK One of France's great Champagne houses. Their best is Cuvée Royale ($19) and the current vintage, 1966, is highly recommended: *****. The British Cuvée is a *Brut* Champagne, exceedingly dry, but the current 1964 is not recommended at $14.

HEIDSIECK DRY MONOPOLE Excellent French Champagne, more reasonably priced than most of its regal competitors. The nonvintage Brut, consistently **** or better, is *only* $8—that's bargain-basement in this high-flying company. There is also a Brut Gold Top Special at around $10.25.

HEIDSIECK, PIPER: See PIPER HEIDSIECK.

HEITZ WINE CELLARS (St. Helena, Calif.) Here's a one-man operation, perhaps not physically, but spiritually: Joe Heitz, one of the best winemakers in America, is the guiding, strong-minded man behind the Heitz label. The wines are the products of his labors and display his personality.

Heitz wines are not always for wine beginners—nor are they always for connoisseurs. Most of the time they're straight, middle-of-the-road wines for the average wine lover. Once in a while they're for nobody—well, except those birds.

This is not to say, however, that every bottle of Heitz wine is equally good, or even simply "good," period. Even the very greatest of vineyards do not always, under all circumstances, in all vintages, produce outstanding wines. There are too many variables, too many ungovernable factors, too many human judgments, too many sinister forces.

Nonetheless, the Heitz label today to the wine-knowledgeable is prima facie evidence that you're dealing with an above-average wine.

Alicia**** A once-only wine, made in '67 from special grapes touched with "noble rot." It's a delicious sweet white wine, still available at the winery, but you may lose interest about now—at $27.50. It's a luscious and memorable wine, but that's a bunch!

Angelica**** A unique dessert wine made in limited quantity. Unlike standard Angelica (see), what Heitz produces is very flavorful, luscious, almost a liqueur; it's made from the distinguished Black Monukka grape which somebody said should be made a natural resource. You won't be finding empty Heitz Angelica bottles along Skid Row—it sells for around $6 a fifth.

Barbera*** This is an Italian-type red wine, bold, very tasty, dry. It's ideal with spicy dishes, red meats, Italian food. Heitz's Barbera is a good example of the breed. It improves very little with age—it's ready to drink when you buy it, and will keep for at least seven or eight years. Air at least one hour, and serve at cool room temperature. Fair value, $3.50 to $4.

Brut Champagne: See CHAMPAGNE.

Burgundy*** This "country" red wine sometimes rises to **** status, but in the ordinary course of human events it's ***. For outdoor barbecue, roast fowl (rabbit? marvelous!), pasta. For immediately drinking—it will keep four or five years at least. Fair value, $3 to $3.40.

Burgundy, Sparkling: See CHAMPAGNE.

Cabernet Sauvignon Here, with this great and noble grape of France, Joe Heitz is at his best. His Cabernet is consistently one of the best California has to offer. Cabernet shows off to full advantage when it complements lamb, steaks, pâté, eggs. But to savor it wholly, fully, down to its uttermost depths, sip it and slurp it (as experts do, taking in much oxygen, to bring out the flavor) on its own, with cheeses, plain bread, fruit. Serve at cool room temperature. Air for one to two hours.

Lot 62-65**** There's no vintage date on this wine, as it's a blend of different vintages. It's well made and well balanced. Worth looking for, a good value at ca. $5. At its best now and will hold there through the decade.

1965**** It's harmonious and tasty, now at its best, and will so remain through this decade. The price, unhappily, has more than doubled since it was first released; today's asking price is in the vicinity of $11—it's worth it, presumably, if your blood is that rich. (But

hang on, the prices get worse as we proceed—don't look below!)

1966 "Regular"**** The winery insists that this wine is a good value, and, in fact, the best Heitz has to offer among their Cabernets. Could be, but clearly this is pretty fast company we're keeping here, if this is a good value at $14.75 . . . we'd just hate to see the price tag on a poor value! The wine's generally had excellent reviews, though in one recent blind tasting with other Heitz Cabernets, it ranked almost last, and the comment was "thin and cloudy." Air for one hour.

1966 Martha's Vineyard ***** This was the first year Heitz had this special bottling from this super vineyard, called Martha's. It's extraordinary wine, even bigger and heartier than the '66 Regular. It's very drinkable right now and will be even better ten years from now. Stick around. The price, however, may incline you to depart: $17. Heitz is fully consistent about one thing at least —marking the wines' prices upward, regularly!

1967 Martha's Vineyard**** A "huge swashbuckling" wine, says one critic—some would award it *****, but even the winery acknowledges that it may be too overpowering for some. Very much a connoisseur's wine. Price at the winery —for the moment—$10.50.

1968 Napa Valley (Regular) ***** This wine has everything (including a fancy price: $11.75 at the winery; latest quotation): body, depth, flavor, balance. Beautiful. It's already totally enjoyable, saith the winery, but it will be even better around 1978 and onward.

1968 Martha's Vineyard—
Near-Classic A great critic of
French wines says it's "almost
a masterpiece." In one "blind"
tasting (labels were hidden) it
outranked some of France's
most illustrious Clarets, including a Château Lafite (see) and
a Château Mouton (see). It's
already good drinking, but it
would border on the criminal
to consume this great wine before 1980, when it should reach
its superb peak. At last report
it was selling, rather outrageously, at the winery for $27.
1969 Napa Valley (*Lot C-
91*)**** Sorry, not yet ready
—will be at its best beginning
in 1980. Winery price, $9.80—
at the moment.
*1969 Martha's Vineyard****
Just released. The winery boasts
that this wine may even surpass the '68 Martha's Vineyard
—a bold assertion. Time and
wine will tell. It's a bit early to
assess this wine accurately, and
it's far too early to drink it.
Don't even look at it until the
early 80s. The winery price is
starting at $12.75, and one
thing is certain—it will ascend
and ascend.
Chablis**** "Chablis" is
one of the longest, broadest
names in the American wine
industry. It is applied to some
of the blandest, most emasculated vinous brews in all of creation and in turn to some truly
fine dry white wine—as it is
here, with Heitz. This is one of
the best American Chablis on
the market. It's not going to replace the true French item, but
at about one third the price,
it's a lot more than one third
as good. It's immediately ready
to drink and should be consumed within two or three
years. An excellent value at
$2.50 to $3.

Champagne** Heitz makes
three sparkling wines: Brut
Champagne, Extra Dry Champagne, and Sparkling Burgundy.
Though they're all made by the
true Champagne method (bot-
tle-fermented), they are quite
standard. The best of them
is the Sparkling Burgundy.
They're sold only at the winery
—which may be just as well.
Fair value, $5.25 to $5.50.
Dry Sherry***
Extra Dry Champagne: See
CHAMPAGNE.
Grignolino** This Italian-
type red wine is made by only
a handful of California wineries, and none does a better
job with it than Heitz. It's a
tart, fruity wine, ideal with
hearty foods, Italian dishes. Air
it two hours and serve at cool
room temperature. It will be at
its best if you will age it a year
or two after you buy it. You'll
be glad you did. Fair value, $3
to $3.50.
Grignolino Rosé** Some
say this is California's best
Grignolino rosé—it's almost its
only one. It does have character
and body—more than you can
say for most rosés. Some say it
has a distinct strawberry aroma.
Serve it chilled, with light
foods, at a luncheon or on a
picnic. Fair value, $4.
Johannisberg Riesling This
grape comes to us from Germany but Johannisberg Riesling
wine is a distinctively California product: a big-bodied wine
for a white, neither sweet nor
dry, well balanced and flavorful. It shows to best advantage
when complementing fish or
seafood, light meats, cheese
dishes. Californians say it's the
perfect accompaniment for cold
cracked crab. Serve it chilled.
Fair value, $4.50 to $5.

1967** Drink immediately—at the latest.

1968*** Drink soon.

1969**** It's a little on the oaky side—beginners may not appreciate it. Best drinking, 1975 through 1976.

1970**** Now at its best and there to remain through 1977.

1971*** Best drinking, 1975–1977.

1972**** Deserves to be enjoyed on its own—it suffered—no, enjoyed—a touch of "noble rot," giving it added depth and dimension.

1973**** Joe Heitz says this may be the best Johannisberg Riesling he's ever made. Hmmmm.

Pinot Blanc Pinot Blanc is the poor cousin of the lordly Chardonnay, the noble grape of France's great white Burgundies. But even the Pinot Blanc can rise to noble heights, as it does for Heitz, who makes one of the best in the land. Indeed, it strongly resembles Chardonnay itself. Beginners in matters vinous will probably prefer this Pinot Blanc to the more austere Chardonnay. It's especially suited to shellfish, but also goes well with fish, poultry, light meats. Serve chilled. Fair value, $4.75 to $5.

1967**** Drink now.

1968**** Drink soon.

1969**** Consume, 1975–1976.

1970*** Comes in two flavors: McCrea and Lyncrest, after the vineyards from which the grapes came; the wines are not appreciably different. Check these wines for sediment—they were not filtered; if present, you may (but need not) stand the bottle upright for twenty-four hours, then decant. The sediment is not harmful—it'll do you more good than half the food on your supermarket shelves.

1971*** Best drinking, 1975 through 1976.

Pinot Chardonnay Many say that this wine is Joe Heitz's greatest achievement. It is certainly true that Heitz has brought it to illustrious heights, but whether it's always been worth the fancy price tags thereunto attached might be another question. Chardonnay is often considered a connoisseur's type of wine—price alone can often make it that! But Heitz's Chardonnay is one that will be appreciated by novice and expert alike, as it's usually soft and fruity, with a touch of sweetness. At the price, you will want to sip your Heitz Chardonnay slowly and thoughtfully—chilled, of course, but not too chilled—you'll freeze all those delightful nuances! Fair or not, these wines will all cost $7 to $10 or more.

1966 and 1967***** Drink immediately—at the latest!

1968**** There was a UCV 81 and a Lot Z-82, equally good. Drink soon.

1969 Lot 2-92-Z***** This wine was the grand prize winner at the Los Angeles County Fair, 1972, a rare distinction. It is said to taste of fresh peaches or apricots or pears—or something. There is also a Lot UCV 91, equally excellent. Drink now and through 1976. Fair value, $9 to $9.50.

1970***** There were two versions (bottlings) of this vintage (grapes were from different vineyards): Lot Z-02 and UCV-01; they are equally fine wines. These wines have done consistently well in many tastings and in some cases have even placed ahead of such

French giants as Le Montrachet. They will be at their best, 1975 through 1978.

1971 UCV-01**** Fine, not spectacular. Not up to its $7 price tag.

1971 Lot Z-11**** Will be at its best, 1975–1980. Fair value, $7.50.

Pinot Noir The Pinot Noir grape is one of the world's noble varieties, but it can be difficult and uncooperative when planted in California. Even Joe Heitz has trouble with it. It's good enough, however, to merit drinking on its own, with cheeses and fruits. At the table, it shows off its best stuff accompanying poultry, steaks and roasts. The nonvintage (***) (not dated) sells for $4 to $4.50, the vintaged (dated) from $5 to $6 and upward, if you're gullible enough to pay it. Air one to two hours. Serve at cool room temperature.

1959, 1962*** Drink now and within next few years.

1963**** At its best: now and through the 70s.

1966*** A short-lived wine, drink immediately.

1968*** Best drinking, 1975 through 1978.

1969**** Already good drinking but it will be better from 1976 onward.

Ruby Cabernet*** This is the lesser cousin of the great Cabernet Sauvignon grape and the wine it produces is similar to the Cabernet, though not as notable. Joe Heitz's version is praiseworthy and one of the few Heitz wines that comes near to representing a good value, at ca. $3.50. Serve it at cool room temperature, as you would a Cabernet Sauvignon; with any good meat, especially lamb and beef. Air one hour.

Sparkling Burgundy: See CHAMPAGNE.

Tawny Port**

Zinfandel

"Plain": No lot number *** This is the current batch of "Zin," a good brew, light and fresh. Drink it young: now and through 1976. A good value at $2.80.

Lot 63-69** This was a blend of the '63 and '69 vintages. It is an austere wine, quite tart, not for beginners. Serve it at cool room temperature, on its own or with chicken, veal, pork, or ham. Fair value, $4.

HENRI MARCHANT Good New York State Champagne at a good price. It comes in Brut, Sparkling Burgundy, Extra Dry, Pink, Cold Duck: all a solid ***. The Extra Dry is probably the best of them, light and sprightly, with no eastern foxiness at all. The Sparkling Burgundy has just a touch of it but it definitely enhances, does not detract.

HENRI, MONSIEUR: See MONSIEUR HENRI.

HENRIQUES, JUSTINO, MADEIRA See JUSTINO'S MADEIRA.

HENRIQUES & HENRIQUES MEDIUM DRY MADEIRA This is a typical Portuguese Madeira, with some sweetness, akin to a medium sherry. It isn't always a wine for the uninitiated, however, with its slightly "cooked" and caramelized taste. But one can learn, rather readily, to appreciate such a tasteful wine. How to serve: See under MADEIRA. Fair value, $4.

HERMITAGE (or: L'HERMITAGE or L'ERMITAGE) An excellent wine, which comes in both red and white, from France's Rhone Valley. The name is pronounced a little differently in French, but it means exactly the same as in English; nobody knows how the wines got that name.

The Red Hermitage is a full-bodied, strong, robust wine (like all Rhones), rough when it's young, but it ages well. Saintsbury, perhaps the most famous wine critic of all times, calls it the "manliest" of all wines. It throws a heavy sediment, and older bottles should be decanted. Hermitage is at its best when it's between five and fifteen years old, but the very best bottles will live on for decades. Be sure to air Hermitage at least one hour—younger bottles, two.

White Hermitage (Hermitage Blanc) is a good white wine, often overlooked because the red is so well known. It's a dry, perfumed wine, remarkably long-lived for a white: at its best between three and ten years of age.

Some vintage notes for the red (Rouge):

1930—Recently tasted, still sound but beginning to fade.

1959—Still excellent.

1960—Better wines than the 59s, a rare exception.

1961—Soft, elegant wines
  Paul Jaboulet: ****
  Chapoutier & Cie.: ***

1962 La Chapelle: ****
  Paul Jaboulet: ****

1964 Jaboulet-Isnard: ***
  Paul Jaboulet: ***
  (Drink 64s soon.)

1966 An exceptional year
  M. de la Sizeranne (Chapoutier): ****
  Paul Jaboulet: ****
  (At their best, 1975–1980.)

1967 An excellent vintage
  Rochette: ****
  M. de la Sizeranne (Chapoutier): ***
  Jaboulet-Isnard: ***
  Farconnets: ****
  Jaboulet-Vercherre: ****

1969 Chapoutier: ****
  Paul Jaboulet: ****
  (Will be at their best, 1975–1985.)
  Jallade: Not recommended at $7.50

1970 An exceptional vintage
  Paul Jaboulet: ****
  Ozier: ****
  Jallade: ***
  Frank Schoonmaker: ****
  Chapoutier: ****
  (Best drinking, 1976–1985.)

1971 Paul Jaboulet: ****
  Chapoutier: ***
  (Don't you dare drink these until at least 1976!)

HOSPICES DE BEAUNE When you see this name on a bottle of French wine, know that you are dealing with a very famous and very fine wine. Literally and in the first instance the name refers to a Hospital (Hospice) in the Burgundian town of Beaune to which, through the centuries, some very choice vineyards have been donated. These wines are among Burgundy's very finest—and most expensive. In fact, most experts say they're almost always overpriced, because of their high prestige value and because the proceeds from their sale go to charity, namely to the Hospices.

HUGEL: The name of an important wine firm of Alsace. Their wines are listed, as on the label, by the name of the wine: RIESLING, GEWÜRTZTRAMINER, etc.

I

ICE WINE: See EISWEIN.

IMPERIAL: See CUNE.

IMPERIAL RISERVA: See CUNE.

INGLENOOK VINEYARDS (Rutherford, Calif.) The name of Inglenook has been a properly respected one on the American wine scene for a long time, like one hundred years now. And it still is. This does not mean, however, that Inglenook infallibly means superior wine. Not even Lafite-Rothschild on a bottle means that. Wines vary—praise God! The giant Heublein, Inc., bought Inglenook a few years ago, and such mergers always tend to frighten wine lovers. But thus far the fears seem unfounded. Nothing has changed. Inglenook continues to make good wines and to sell them at reasonable prices—and how can you improve on that?

Brut Champagne: See CHAMPAGNE.

Cabernet Sauvignon This is Inglenook's pride, their showpiece wine. It's famous for its longevity—some nineteenth-century bottles were recently opened and were in excellent condition. The winery points with pride to the fact that some of its Cabernet Sauvignon has brought perhaps the highest prices ever paid for American wines: a mixed case of their Cabernet recently sold for some $77 per bottle.

Cabernet is the classic companion for beef and lamb. Inglenook's best bottles deserve to be consumed in splendid isolation, on their own, or at most with cheeses and fruits. Air older bottles one hour, younger ones, two. When issued, the regular Cabernet Sauvignon sells for ca. $5, the Cask for ca. $6.50.

1959***** Gorgeous wine, deep-flavored. It's only recently reached its peak and it will remain there for another decade at least. You won't be finding this wine on your supermarket shelf, but it does show up at wine auctions.

1960, 1962, 1963**** At their best now and into the 80s.

1964*** Drink within next three or four years. A special Cask G-24 deserves ****.

1965**** Best drinking, 1975 through the decade. The special bottling, Cask G-25 has not developed as well as the "regular" **.

1966**** Now fully mature and will remain at its best at least through the 70s. The special Cask F-29 is also ****.

1967**** This wine is now nearing full maturity and will be at its very best, 1976 or 1977, and for at least a decade thereafter. A Cask bottling of this vintage, ****, is as good as but no better than the regular, and is a poor value at $8 or more.

1968 "Regular"**** Will be

140

at its best, 1975 and through the decade, at least.

1968 Cask No. 12***** Marvelous drinking, 1975–1982.

1969**** There were a number of special Cask bottlings and they're all looking beautiful, but none of this wine will be really mature until at least 1977.

1970 It's showing **** promise today, though it's really too early for a definitive judgment. The winery says the Cask Reserve F34 is "the most powerful and most concentrated Cabernet in the last decade."

Champagne, Brut This is the only sparkling wine Inglenook makes; that usually augurs well —effort and solicitude are concentrated. Here's a fine California Champagne, made in the classic *"méthode champenoise,"* involving more than 200 hand-operations, the winery proudly proclaims. It's very very dry, well balanced, tasty, delicate. Save it for some auspicious occasion, solemn festivity. It's too elegant and delicate for any raucous party—it deserves to be sipped slowly, appreciatively. Well chilled, of course. It's vintage-dated, and recent vintages ('68, '69) are at least ***, and the '67 clearly ****. Fair value, $5.25 to $6.

Charbono One wine critic says this is California's best Charbono—it also happens to be almost its only one. It is an Italian-type red wine, distinctive, robust, somewhat resembling Cabernet Sauvignon. It should be used, consumed, enjoyed, served, exactly like the Cabernet, above. Fair value, $4.50.

1959**** Enormous wine, now at its best and will hold for another ten years. Air one

hour and serve at cool room temperature.

1965, 1966*** Both these wines are now at their best and will remain so through the 70s. Air one to two hours and serve at cool room temperature.

1967****—At its best, 1975–1980.

1968 and 1969*** Good drinking now, if you air them a few hours, but these wines will be even smoother and better if you hold them until 1976 or so. They will keep through the mid 80s.

1970 and 1972**** Good drinking now and will be even better from 1978 onward, for as long as twenty years. Stick around.

Chenin Blanc Chenin Blanc is always one of California's most delightful white wines. It comes in varying degrees of sweetness. Inglenook's is betwixt: medium-sweet, which makes it dual-purpose: good to accompany light foods, or to serve as an aperitif or "entertainment" wine.

1968 and 1969*** Drink immediately if not sooner.

1970** Drink soon.

1971*** Good drinking, 1975 through 1976.

1972*** On the dry side. Best drinking, 1975 through 1977.

1973*** Soft, slightly sweet. Drink it 1975 through 1978.

Cream Sherry: See SHERRY.

Dry Sémillon California does well by the Sémillon grape, producing both a sweet and a dry version. This dry white wine goes well with light foods: fish, seafood, pork, poultry. Fair value, $2.75 to $3. Serve it chilled.

1969 and 1970*** Drink, 1975 through 1976.

1971** Drink, 1975 through 1977.

Gamay and Gamay Beaujolais You can hardly go wrong buying California Gamay or Gamay Beaujolais: young, fruity, economical red wines, perfect for that outdoor barbecue (steaks, hamburgers, chicken), buffet, picnic, or even formal dining. The two names, Gamay and Gamay Beaujolais, are used almost interchangeably in California, although these are two different grapes. But it would take an expert— or an angel from heaven—to tell the wines apart most of the time. Inglenook is probably the only winery in the world that makes both of them. Serve at cool room temperature; it's not necessary to air the wine. Fair value, ca. $3.

Gamay 1964, 1965, 1966*** If you happen to own any of these, consume immediately.

Gamay 1967** R.I.P.

Gamay and Gamay Beaujolais 1968** Drink now.

Gamay and Gamay Beaujolais 1969*** Best drinking, 1975 through 1976.

Gamay Beaujolais 1970*** Best drinking, 1975 through 1976.

Gamay Beaujolais 1971**** Drink now and through 1977.

Gamay Rosé*** Americans love their rosés—millions of gallons of this simple, refreshing wine are joyously imbibed every year, most of it quite adequate and satisfying. This rosé, made from the trusty Gamay grape, is a cut above most of those simple rosés that bear no grape name.

Everybody knows that rosés are adaptable to every menu, but the better ones deserve to be served chilled, before dinner, or on their own. Ready for immediate enjoyment when purchased; don't keep this wine more than a year or two.

Gewürz Traminer 1973**** This is a new wine for Inglenook and it's off to a galloping start: a big, spicy wine, good to sip or good to uplift sausage or salads (potato, macaroni, chicken) or cheese or seafood. Drink it while it's young: 1975 through 1977. Serve chilled.

Grey Riesling** Light dry white wine, mild-flavored, economical. Inglenook's version is par for the course, rather unnotable. The current vintages, 1972 and 1973, rate ***, though. Some recommend this wine for *breakfast*—seriously. Those scrambled eggs will never be the same! Serve chilled. Drink it within two or three years of purchase. Fair value, $2.75 to $3.

Johannisberg Riesling *** This German-type wine is almost always one of California's finest whites; Inglenook's is pretty standard, which is to say, good. Recent vintages (1970, '71, '72) all rate at least ***, are ready for present drinking, and will remain in top form for another two or three years. Excellent accompaniment for fish, seafood, ham, pork, veal, poultry. Serve chilled. Fair value, $4.50.

Navalle Burgundy** Although "Navalle" is a contraction of Napa Valley, illogically enough, the wines with this name don't come from the Napa Valley at all, but from neighboring Sonoma County. Navalle wines are new with Inglenook, they're competitively priced (ca. $3 per magnum). This Burgundy is perhaps the best of them, a good hamburger wine. It's ready to drink when you buy it, and it should not be kept more than two or three years. Serve it at cool room temperature.

Navalle Chablis* Drink it within a couple of years of purchase. Serve chilled with sandwiches, fowl, seafood. For a little more money, you're well advised to prefer the Vintage Chablis (see). Fair value, $1.90.

Navalle Claret* This is a lighter wine than the Navalle Burgundy and not as good. In this price range, stick with the Navalle Burgundy. Fair value, $1.90.

Navalle French Colombard *** Fresh crisp white wine. For luncheon serving: with sandwiches, chicken salad, cold cuts. Serve chilled. Drink it within two years of purchase. A tremendous value at $1.90.

Navalle Rhine* Similar to the Navalle Chablis, only sweeter. Best for sipping on a warm summer's evening— chilled, of course. Fair value, $1.90.

Navalle Rosé** For summer refreshment, chilled.

Navalle Ruby Cabernet** A good value at $3 per magnum (two regular bottles). Be sure to air this wine, preferably in an open carafe, for several hours. It will improve in the bottle also, if you will stash it away for two or three years. Fair value, $1.90.

Pale Dry Sherry: See VINTAGE SHERRY.

Pinot Chardonnay Pinot Chardonnay is California's most esteemed white wine, and on occasion it has even fooled European wine experts. Inglenook's Pinot Chardonnay recently received high marks from a prestigious French wine review. It's dry, savory, big. At its best it deserves to be drunk

on its own; it's also the classic companion for fish, particularly shellfish. Serve chilled. Fair value, $5.

1967, 1968**** Drink *now.*

1969*** Drink, through 1975 and 1976.

1970** If it once had something, it's since lost it; not recommended today.

1971*** At its best, 1975 through 1978.

1972*** Best drinking, 1975 through 1979.

Pinot Noir Pinot Noir is California's best Burgundy-type wine and generally costs about twice as much as "plain" Burgundy. It's not always worth the difference, but Inglenook's is; it's one of their best wines. Really fine bottles need to be consumed thoughtfully and slowly, with cheeses and fresh fruits. It is also a marvelous accompaniment for barbecued chicken, roast turkey, cheese dishes. Serve at cool room temperature. Fair value, $4.50.

1966** Drink soon.

1967**** Drink soon.

1968**** Drink, 1975 through 1976.

1969**** Best drinking, 1975 through 1980.

1970**** A special Cask bottling (K 150) may get to *****. Best drinking, 1975 and for at least a decade.

Red Pinot Very few wineries make this wine—it doesn't even sound authentic. Perhaps it's just as well. It's not very distinctive, and Inglenook has discontinued production with their '70 vintage. It retails around $5, but isn't always worth it. Serve at cool room temperature.

1968*** Drink soon.

1969** Drink sooner.

1970**** This will be Inglenook's last vintage; they're ending in a blaze of glory, for this is the best they've ever made.

Sherry: See VINTAGE SHERRY.

Sylvaner Riesling* Forget it!

Vintage Burgundy* These "Vintage" wines are pretty good jug wines, but they're also a bit more expensive than most: around $4 a half-gallon, compared to $3.25 and even less. Some are worth the difference, some not. (Inglenook has an even cheaper line: Navalle [see], ca. $3 a half-gallon.) This Burgundy is the best of all these "Vintage" wines; it's soft, quite fruity, ready to drink when you buy it; it won't improve in the bottle. It's vintage-dated; drink it within six or seven years of the date on the bottle. Good everyday drinking with ordinary fare.

Vintage Chablis** A good dry white wine; it improves with a little breathing time (thirty minutes or so). Serve it chilled with light foods, especially fish and seafood. Drink within four years or so of its vintage date. A good value at $4 a half-gallon.

Vintage Rhine* Stick with the Vintage Chablis if it's a dry white you're hankerin' after. If it's a white with a little sweetness, look elsewhere, such as to Paul Masson's Rhine Castle. Fair value, $2.25.

Vintage Sherry "Vintage" sherry is almost a contradiction in terms if you know anything about the making of sherry—but let that go, it's a technical matter. The important thing is that, despite their nomenclature, these are good California sherries, all three of them: Vintage Pale Dry Sherry, ****: the driest of the lot, makes a perfect aperitif wine, full-bodied, nutty, smooth. Vintage California Sherry, ****: a medium sherry, all-purpose: before meals, with meals, after meals, and even, praise the Lord, between meals. Vintage Cream Sherry, ****: a dessert wine, smooth, nutlike flavor. Good values, all, at ca. $2.40.

Vintage Vin Rosé*

Vintage Zinfandel** Light, fresh, young red wine, it's more expensive ($4.60 a half-gallon) than the rest of the Vintage line. Air it one hour, serve at cool room temperature with fowl, beef, stews, pasta. It's ready to drink when purchased; you can keep it six years beyond its vintage date.

White Pinot Almost all California wineries today call this wine Chenin Blanc—it seems to sell better with that name. But Inglenook does well by it: it's fresh, delicate, distinctly on the dry side. Ideal with shellfish or as an aperitif wine—chilled, of course. It's vintaged, and current vintages, 1971, 1972, 1973: ***. Fair value, $3.

Zinfandel Be careful: there's also a Vintage Zinfandel, not nearly as good. Over the long haul, "Zin" may well turn out to be California's greatest gift to wine lovers. They do great things with this grape in California—and Inglenook is among the "they." It's a zesty red wine, very adaptable: serve it with red meats or fowl, stews or pasta, cheese or eggs. Wine aficionados will want to savor the best bottles simply, alone, or with cheese and bread only. Inglenook's "Z" is noted for its longevity; some nineteenth-century bottles were opened recently and were in excellent condition. Fair value, ca. $3.

*1964, 1965, 1966, 1967**** All excellent drinking through the 70s.

*1968***** Beautiful drinking right now and will improve even further. Top form until the mid 80s.

1969**** For present drinking and will improve through 1975; will keep well into the 80s.

1970**** Best drinking, 1975–1985.

1971** Reserve final judgment on this one, but present evaluation is low.

Zinfandel, 1972 North Coast Counties*** Soft, fruity, nice wine.

ITALIAN SWISS COLONY (Asti, Calif.) This is one of the most familiar wine names in America, a huge operation, said to account for a full 25 percent of all the wine sold in the U.S. The wines are sound, reliable, cheap, decidedly non-great. Of the three California giant producers of economical wines, Gallo, Franzia, and ISC, Franzia wines are usually the cheapest, Gallo's the most expensive, and ISC wines somewhere in between. Broadly speaking it may also be said that ISC's wines are better than those of Franzia, and better values than the Gallo wines.

ISC makes a multitude of wines under a variety of labels. Often their own name doesn't even appear on the bottle. Some of the brands (all will be found in this book): Jacques Bonet; Lejon; Napa-Sonoma-Mendocino.

Annie Green Springs—See under its own name.

Bali Hai* Properly speaking, this is not wine at all, though you might call it a "fruit wine," or more exactly, a wine punch. It's included because of its wide popularity. It's very similar to Key Largo (see), also an ISC product.

Fair price—if you want to pay it!—ca. $1.20.

Burgundy** Be careful here; ISC also makes a Burgundy under its more expensive label, Napa-Sonoma-Mendocino (see). This one has the words "Gold Medal Reserve" on the label and sells for around $1.35, compared to around $1.75 for the Napa-Sonoma-Mendocino. This is a pretty good value, it has a bit of sweetness, and it doesn't bite. Admirable hamburger wine.

Cappella Red Table Wine* Very bland is the best way to describe this imitation-Italian type wine. The winery calls it "mellow," but "sweet" is more accurate. It's cheap, all right, around $1.25, but that's about the only good thing one can say for it. Prefer the Burgundy (see above) at only about a dime more, or the Tipo Chianti (see) at around $2.

Chablis** A long way from true French Chablis, but a fresh white wine with a touch of sweetness, though still drier, for example, than Gallo's Chablis. For summertime sipping (chilled) or to accompany all manner of light foods. But be wary here: ISC makes at least two other Chablis, one under a separate label, Napa-Sonoma-Mendocino (see), and a third under this same ISC label but with the words "Private Stock" in bold red letters across the label. This Private Stock Chablis is better than this "straight" Chablis, but it is also more expensive: around $1.75 vs. $1.35. It's drier and tastier than the "straight," with good fruitiness. Both wines are good values.

Chablis, Pink: See GOLD CHABLIS.

Chablis, Ruby: See GOLD CHABLIS.

Chianti—Not recommended.

Claret** Has fared well in various tastings—mellow red, somewhat lighter in body than the Burgundy (above). Air it about an hour and serve it at cool room temperature, with simple fare: grilled hamburgers, hot dogs, pasta. A good value.

Gold Chablis* ISC makes three special "invented" Chablis: Gold, Pink, Ruby. They have one thing in common: they're 57 million light-years removed from anything remotely resembling true Chablis. They are all very sweet, designed for beginning or non-wine drinkers. The Gold is prickly and frizzy, the best of the three. The Pink is the quintessence of a wine for people who don't like wine. Besides, it's not pink—it's salmon-colored. The Ruby has distinct, but not unpleasant, fruit flavors. They are all three wines for very limited consumption. Their greatest selling point: they're cheap, ca. $1.30.

Grenache Vin Rosé** Very light wine, not very flavorful, but for all that, refreshing and pleasant. Fair value, $1.35.

Key Largo* A "Pop" wine, similar to ISC's Bali Hai, redolent with fruit flavors. A different fruit, whatever it is—guava? passion fruit?—seems to predominate in each of the wines. These are wine punches, not wines, and for those who enjoy sugar-sweet wine punches, "*Skoal!*" or "*Oogy Wawa,*" as they say in Zulu.

Pink Chablis: See GOLD CHABLIS.

Rhine* Not as sweet as the Rhineskeller, but equally blaaaaah . . .

Rhineskeller* Note that there is also a "plain" Rhine wine, somewhat more expensive, but equally unmemorable.

Ruby Chablis: See GOLD CHABLIS.

Sangrole* Ugh . . .

Sauterne*

Tipo Chianti (Red)** Italian-type wine: "Tipo" means "Type" or "Imitation." It's quite savory, quite dry. Trustworthy hamburger and hot dog wine. Serve at cool room temperature, after one hour's airing. Fair value, $2.

Zinfandel** Without doubt this is the best real wine ISC is currently producing. It's a good red *vin ordinaire*, fashioned to appeal to the experienced wine drinker as well as the beginner. A very good value at $1.50 and even less in the western states.

J

JACQUES BONET: See BO-NET, JACQUES.

JESUIT WINES: See NOVI-TIATE.

JESUITENGARTEN: See FORSTER JESUITENGARTEN.

JOHANNISBERG RIESLING This thoroughly Germanic name is very rarely seen on a bottle of German wine, but it appears on millions of bottles of California wine. It's the name of the noble grape that produces the great German wines of the Rhine and Moselle. But in Germany the wines go by the names of their vineyards (Schloss Vollrads, for example) or their villages (Erbach, Bernkastel) or by brand names such as Liebfraumilch. But it's one and the same grape that makes these famous German wines and that makes California Johannisberg Riesling. But it's not one and the same wine. The Johannisberg Riesling grape (White Riesling is the correct name) produces two very distinct wines in the two different climes, in two different soils.

Johannisberg Riesling is one of California's finest white wines, giving place, perhaps, only to Pinot Chardonnay. It's a rather expensive wine, for the grapes are shy-bearing and costly. It has a distinctively fragrant bouquet, it's medium-bodied, tasty, with a touch of sweetness. It definitely does not have the highly prized delicate floweri-ness of its best German coun-terparts, but it's simply a dif-ferent wine, to be judged on its own merits.

California Johannisberg Ries-ling is almost always good enough and big enough to be appreciated on its own, as an aperitif wine, or for an eve-ning's enjoyment, perhaps with cheeses, such as Gouda and Liederkranz. An interesting comparative tasting would con-sist of one or the other Cali-fornia Johannisberg Riesling alongside a couple of good German whites: a good Lieb-fraumilch, a Niersteiner and a Moselle, for example. It also makes an excellent dinner com-panion (more so than its Ger-man counterpart) to fish, sea-food, but more especially to pork, poultry (particularly goose and turkey), salmon. It's to be served chilled, but not over-chilled: 45 to 50°F is fine —one hour in the refrigerator will do it. Enjoy Johannisberg Riesling on the youngish side: within three years of purchase, or if it's vintaged, before it's seven years old.

California also produces a wine called, for some unknowable reason, Rhine or Rhine-Some-thing-or-Other, always inexpen-sive and almost always bad, bad (see Rhine Wine). It has noth-ing whatsoever to do with German Rhine wine nor with California Johannisberg Ries-ling.

There is a California wine,

though, that resembles German Rhine wine—somewhat distantly perhaps, but the kinship is there. It's called simply Riesling (see).

Below are California's best Johannisberg Rieslings, listed in descending order of excellence. Wines with the same rating are listed the least expensive first. Prices are approximate.

*California Johannisberg
Rieslings—
Comparative Standings*

*****

Exceptional

Llords & Elwood Johannisberg Riesling, Cuvée 6 ($4.25)

Freemark Abbey Johannisberg Riesling, 1971 and 1972 ($4.50)

Sonoma (or Windsor) Riesling Spätlese, 1972 ($5)

Château Montelena Johannisberg Riesling Spätlese ($5.50)

Wente Riesling Spätlese ($6.50)

****

Excellent

Pedroncelli Johannisberg Riesling, 1971, 1973 ($3.35)

Sebastiani Johannisberg Riesling, 1967 ($3.40)

Martini Johannisberg Riesling, 1969 ($3.65)

Simi Johannisberg Riesling ($3.85)

Yverdon Johannisberg Riesling, ($4)

Beaulieu Beauclair Johannisberg Riesling, 1971, 1972 ($4.10)

Concannon Johannisberg Riesling, 1973 ($4.25)

Ste. Michelle Johannisberg Riesling, 1972 ($4.25)

Robert Mondavi Johannisberg Riesling ($4.50)

Mirassou Johannisberg Riesling, 1971, 1972, 1973 ($4.60)

Freemark Abbey Johannisberg Riesling, 1969 Lot 92, 1972 ($4.75)

Heitz Johannisberg Riesling, 1969, 1970, 1972 ($4.85)

Chappellet Johannisberg Riesling, 1969, 1970, 1972 ($5)

Beringer Johannisberg Riesling, 1973 Auslese ($5)

Ridge White Riesling ($5)

Souverain Johannisberg Riesling, 1968, 1969, 1970, 1973 ($5.50)

Frank, Dr. Konstantin, Riesling Spätlese 1967 ($6.50)

***

Good

Assumption Abbey Johannisberg Riesling ($2.90)

Almadén Johannisberg Riesling ($3)

Sebastiani Johannisberg Riesling, 1969 ($3.40)

Christian Brothers Johannisberg Riesling ($3.55)

Weibel Johannisberg Riesling ($3.60)

Martini Johannisberg Riesling, 1972 ($3.65)

Charles Krug Johannisberg Riesling ($3.90)

Beaulieu Beauclair Johannisberg Riesling, 1969 ($4.10)

Beringer Johannisberg Riesling, 1970, 1971 ($4)

Llords & Elwood, Cuvée 5 ($4.25)

Concannon Johannisberg Riesling, 1968, 1971 ($4.25)

Kenwood Johannisberg Riesling, 1973 ($4.50)

Buena Vista Johannisberg Riesling ($4.50)

Inglenook Johannisberg Riesling ($4.60)

Heitz Johannisberg Riesling, 1968, 1971 ($4.85)

Chappellet Johannisberg Riesling, 1971 ($5)

Freemark Abbey Johannis-

berg Riesling, 1969 Lot 91
and 93 ($5)
Souverain Johannisberg Ries-
ling, 1971, 1972, Napa
Valley ($5.50)
**
Fair
Eleven Cellars Johannisberg
Riesling ($3.15)
Masson Johannisberg Ries-
ling ($3.35)
Martini Johannisberg Ries-
ling, 1968, 1970, 1971
($3.65)
Sonoma (or Windsor) Johan-
nisberg Riesling ($3.95)
Beaulieu Beauclair Johannis-
berg Riesling, 1970 ($4.10)
Concannon Johannisberg
Riesling, 1972 ($4.25)
Mirassou Johannisberg Ries-
ling, 1970 ($4.60)
ZD White Riesling ($4.75)
Souverain Johannisberg Ries-
ling, 1972 Alexander Val-
ley ($5.50)
*
Passable
Concannon Johannisberg
Riesling, 1969 ($4.25)
A small amount of German
wines reaches the U.S. under
the name of Johannisberg Ries-
ling. It's usually good wine and
is especially reliable if it's got
one of these names on the
label: Havemeyer; Kender-
mann; Madrigal; Sichel.
Individual bottles of Madrigal
Johannisberger Riesling are as-
sessed under that name, p. 175.
JOHANNISBERG, SCHLOSS:
See SCHLOSS JOHANNISBERG.
JOHANNISBERGER Some
German Rhine wine comes to
the U.S. with this simple name
on the label. These are good
wines. Look for one made by
Anheuser & Fehrs, it's invariably reliable, should sell for ca.
$5.50.
**JOHANNISBERGER ERNTE-
BRINGER** Johannisberg is the

name of the village, and a wine
from there is a Johannisberger.
Erntebringer is the name of a
group of similar vineyards.
Note that it says "Qualitätswein"
on the label: a quality wine,
the middle category of German
wines. The 1970 was relatively
dry, merits ***, a fair value at
$3.50. A 1972 by Leonard
Kreusch, also quite dry, is well
balanced and tasty, ****, a
good value at $3.50.
JOHANNISBERGER KLAUS
The name of the village is
Johannisberg, and Klaus is the
name of an excellent vineyard
adjoining the illustrious Schloss
Johannisberger (see). Because
of the tremendous prestige of
the *Schloss,* these wines from
adjacent vineyards tend to be
undervalued and underpriced.
Besides Klaus, look for these
Johannisbergers: Goldatzel;
Hansenberg; Hoelle; Kochs-
berg; Mittelhoelle; Schwarzen-
stein.
All of these fine wines will
have Johannisberger preceding
their name, and they will ordinarily merit a substantial ****.
Some notable Klaus bottles:
*1967 Spätlese Cabinet (Land-
graf von Hessen):* ****—Drink
during 1975.
*1969 Cabinet (Landgraflich
Hessiches Weingut):* ****—At
its best, 1975 and 1976.
*1970 Spätlese (Landgraflich
Hessiches Weingut):* *****—
Drink, 1975–1979. Fair value,
$7.20.
*1970 Riesling (Landgraf von
Hessen):* ****—A good value
at ca. $5.
*1971 Auslese (Graf von
Schonborn):* *****—Will be at
its best, 1976–1980.
**JOSMEYER GEWÜRZTRA-
MINER** Thats the way the
label reads, but what they really
mean is Joseph Meyer, the

Alsatian wine-shipping firm in Wintzenheim, Alsace. This is a dependable name. Their 1967 "Cuvée de Centenaire" was a clear ****, but is now beyond its best. The '69 Gewürztraminer, ***, should be consumed now!

JULIENAS *** to **** One of the best red Beaujolais, elegant and fruity, but the word "Beaujolais" often will not be on the label at all. It's a soft, fresh wine, needs to be drunk young; ideally, during its second year. How to serve it: See under BEAUJOLAIS. It will range in price from $4 to $6; stick with shippers listed under BEAUJOLAIS.

JUSTINO'S BOAL** This is a Portuguese Madeira (see) on the sweet side, though the Malmsey (below) is sweeter. The firm's name—it's on the label—is Justino Henriques Filhos, Lda. Serve this wine as you would a medium sherry—in the afternoon, or after dinner, with the coffee or after it, at room temperature or slightly chilled. A good value, around $3.50. There is also a Boal Solera 1900 at around $11, fine wine, but it's not three times as good as this one.

JUSTINO'S MALMSEY** Not up to standard. Try Leacock's Malmsey (see).

JUSTINO'S RAINWATER MADEIRA** It's light and clear, like rainwater. But tastier. And better for you. An ideal aperitif wine, slightly chilled. A fine value at around $3.50.

JUSTINO'S SERCIAL MADEIRA** Sercial is the driest of all Madeiras, makes an elegant aperitif wine. Fair value, $3.50. For more information: See under MADEIRA.

K

KABINETT (or: CABINET)
On a German wine label this word designates a wine somewhat superior to the same wine without Kabinett. The precise significance of the word has varied in the past, from producer to producer and even from year to year. But it now holds pretty steady, signifying a wine just below Spätlese classification—in other words, the first grade above the "straight" wine.

(JULIUS) KAYSER This is an important German wine-shipping firm located in Germany's Moselle area. Look up your Kayser wine under its proper name: Bernkasteler, Liebfraumilch, etc.

KENWOOD VINEYARDS (Kenwood, Calif.) A bunch of Pagans used to run this winery —the Pagani family. They made mostly inexpensive jug wines. Today the winery's in better hands, owned by a group of San Francisco wine lovers, and the wines are much improved, and getting better all the time. Besides, they're still making those good jug wines. Kenwood's are not great wines, at least not yet, but they're uniformly good and usually good values. How to serve these wines: See under their respective names (Barbera, etc.).

Barbera*** Be sure to air this wine at least one hour. It's for drinking when purchased and can be kept for three or four years thereafter. It took a gold medal at the Los Angeles County Fair, 1974. Fair value, $3.60 to $3.75.

Burgundy, 1970**

Burgundy, 1971*** Young wine with good flavor. A good value at $2.25.

Cabernet Sauvignon
1970*** Lovely light wine, can be drunk now but will be even better, 1976–1980.

1971*** Light Cabernet with a fresh berry flavor. Best drinking, 1977–1982. Fair value, $5.

Chenin Blanc, 1973*** Kenwood also makes a Dry Chenin Blanc (see), even drier than this which is already on the dry side. It's very fresh and young, almost grapey. A good value at $3. Drink now and through 1977. Fair value, $2.80.

Dry Chenin Blanc See also plain Chenin Blanc (above).
1970*** Drink immediately.
1971** Drink soon.
1972*** Drink, 1975 through 1976.

Grey Riesling, 1973**** Drink now and through 1977. A good value at $3.

Johannisberg Riesling, 1973 *** Drink now and through 1977. Fair value, $4.50 to $4.75.

Petite Sirah, 1972*** Drink now and for another three years. Fair value, $3.

Zinfandel
1970**** Best drinking, 1976–1980.

1971**** Will be at its best, 1976–1980.

1972***

KEY LARGO: See ITALIAN SWISS COLONY.

KOBUS, FRITZ: An Alsatian wine firm. See under the names of the individual wines.

KORBEL & BROS. (Guerneville, Calif.) For a hundred years the name of Korbel has been associated with only one wine: Champagne. It's been only since 1965 that Korbel has been making any other kind of wine. Today, like most major California wineries, they run the gamut—for good or ill—producing everything from Chablis jug wine to Zinfandel. Make no mistake, Korbel makes some good wines, especially in the sparkly department, but some are less than great, and a few are less than good.

Don't confuse Korbel Champagne with Kornell, another fine California Champagne.

Brut Champagne**** Korbel has been making some of California's finest Champagnes for more than a century, and their Brut has always been among the very best. Some, however, say that this wine has slipped perceptibly in recent years, deserving *** at best. You be the judge, test your critical faculties. This wine is not as dry as the Natural (see); it can be served either as an aperitif or an after-dinner treat. Serve it well chilled. Fair value, $5.75.

Burgundy** Light, dry, youngish—it might even improve with a year or two of additional bottle age. It'll enhance those grilled hamburgers or steaks, stews, or casseroles. Serve at cool room temperature. Fair value, $2.25 to $2.50.

Note that there is also a Mountain Burgundy, a jug wine.

Cabernet Sauvignon*** A light, young type of Cabernet, meant to be drunk in its youth; don't hold it more than two or three years. Serve it with finer cuts of beef or lamb, or savor it on its own, with cheeses and fruits. Serve at cool room temperature. Fair value, $3.75 to $4.

Chablis** A few years ago this wine was consistently ***; today it's just not that flavorful. But it will do a better job than water or Kool-Aid at improving that seafood platter, chicken casserole, or cheese fondue. Fair value, $2.15 to $2.35; serve chilled. Note that there is also a Mountain Chablis (see), a cheaper wine.

Château Vin Rosé** Quite dry, quite average. Drink it while it's young. Serve chilled. Fair value, $2.15 to $2.35. See also Mountain Rosé.

Chenin Blanc*** It's on the sweet side, with some fruitiness, and considering the price, $2.50 to $2.90, it's not to be spurned. A good sipping wine, chilled. Drink it fresh—within two years of purchase.

Cocktail Sherry: See SHERRY.

Cold Duck** It's not as sickly sweet as some of the myriad Frigid Fowls filling (fouling?) our American skies, but it's still just one more Duck. And you'll pay as much for it—if you insist!—as you will for Korbel's *good* sparkling wines (except for Natural, which is a dollar more), ca. $5.65.

Cream Sherry: See SHERRY.

Dry Sauterne**** It's not a Sauterne—the real kind, from France, that is—but it's a tasty, tart white wine, perfect to accompany fish, seafood, poultry, pork, or ham. Serve it chilled. A very good value at $2.15 to $2.35.

Extra Dry Champagne**** Sweeter than the Brut and the Natural, it will suit many American palates more. Fine for after-dinner enjoyment, serve it well chilled. Fair value, $5.75.

Grey Riesling**** This has aways been a good wine with Korbel, but now, with the grapes coming from a new vineyard, it's even better. One critic calls it "stunning." It deserves isolated consumption—the wine isolated from competing foods, that is, not necessarily you isolated. Serve chilled. A good value, at $2.75 to $3.

Mountain Burgundy** Until recently this wine was called Mountain Red. It's a solid, unpretentious red wine for daily consumption. Serve it at cool room temperature. It's a good value at ca. $4 a half-gallon. Note that there is also a "plain" Burgundy.

Mountain Chablis** Most would rate this white jug wine *** considering its price, ca. $4 a half-gallon. It's crisp and dry, will go well with light foods. Serve it chilled. Note that there is aso a "plain" Chablis.

Mountain Red: See MOUN-TAIN BURGUNDY.

Mountain Rosé** It's a little different from most California rosés: it's got some character! It's assertive, at least for a rosé. That doesn't mean it is great, but mostly that it's different. Try it. Serve it with food, or on its own, as you will, chilled. Drink it young and fresh. Fair value, ca. $4 a half-gallon.

Natural Champagne***** The label says "Extremely Dry," and that it is—it's Korbel's "top of the line." Many experts

say that this and Schramberg's Natur Blanc de Blancs Reserve Cuvée are America's two finest sparkling wines. One critic utters the ultimate vinous heresy when he asserts that this California Champagne is better than the very best French Champagne! You won't be drinking this wine on an everyday basis, however, not at $6.50 to $6.75, but how about it as an aperitif wine for your Thanksgiving or Christmas dinner? Serve it well chilled, carefully, proudly.

Pinot Noir* It hasn't always been as good as it is now, with good fragrance and fruitiness. It's fit to accompany anything grilled: steaks, hamburgers, chicken, shish kebabs. Or simply, with cheeses and fruits. Fair value, $3.75.

Rosé (Pink Champagne)* It's marketed in a clear glass bottle, so's you can admire the pretty pink color—which it hath, forsooth. But a great deal more than that, it hath not. It's definitely on the sweet side, but for the same price (ca. $5.75) you'll do better with the Extra Dry (see), which is slightly sweet.

Rouge (Sparkling Burgundy)** This sparkling red Burgundy wine is drier than most, with good flavor. Some would award it only ***, as it has not shown well in tastings. This kind of wine fits in almost anywhere: before dinner, with dinner, even after dinner (but not with dessert). Serve it well chilled. Fair value, $5.75.

Sec Champagne* Korbel's sweetest, it can be enjoyed with dessert. Fair value, $5.75.

Sherry* Korbel makes the standard three flavors, and they're just about identical in quality: ***, Cocktail Sherry: Very dry, but mouth-filling and rounded. Sherry (plain, no adjectives): medium-sweet; best slightly chilled. Cream Sherry: Serve at cool room temperature. Fair value, all three, $2 to $2.25.

Sonoma Blanc, 1972*** A new white wine, with slight sweetness; it's soft and fresh. You can sip it on its own or enjoy it with light foods, especially with sandwiches, fowl, seafood. Serve chilled. A good value at ca. $2.50.

Zinfandel, 1972*** Korbel's first offering of "Z": a fresh light red wine, to be drunk young, not beyond 1976. It's adaptable: it can serve admirably at your outdoor grill or at luncheon or dinner, with almost any type of food, even seafood. Serve at cool room temperature or slightly chilled. Fair value, $2.75 to $3.

(HANNS) KORNELL CELLARS (St. Helena, Calif.) Kornell makes some of California's finest Champagnes. Don't confuse the name, though, with Korbel (see), another notable name among California Champagnes. Every bottle is processed in the laborious classic *méthode champenoise*, requiring the daily handling of each and every bottle. The wines seem to appreciate all the tender loving care, for they are among California's finest sparkling wines.

Brut Champagne: See CHAMPAGNE, BRUT.

Champagne, Brut**** Everybody agrees that this is one of California's very best, and it's got the medals to prove it. It's got everything: color, sparkle, sprightly flavor. Save it for some special occasion or holiday, and serve it, well chilled, in lordly fashion, with paternalistic condescension. Fair value, $5.75.

Champagne, Extra Dry**** Sweeter than the Brut, and just as good. It took a gold medal at the 1974 Los Angeles County Fair. Fair value, $5.75.

Champagne, Pink-Rosé*** Quite dry for a "pink" champagne—it's not really pink, it's orange-amber—lively yet soft in the mouth. Since all these sparkling wines sell at the same price, one would be well advised to stick with the Brut or Extra Dry, unless one simply prefers a sweet Champagne. Fair value, $5.75.

Champagne, Sec** Kornell's sweetest Champagne. A dubious value at $5.75.

Champagne, Sehr Trocken ***** The name means "Very Dry" in German, and it's that, all right; it's Kornell's special pride, their "Best of the House." But beginning wine drinkers will probably not appreciate this wine's stark austerity. It's made in the style of German sparkling wines, primarily from the great German grape, the White Riesling, to the horror of Champagne purists. (They believe Champagne must be made primarily from the Chardonnay grape.) It will make a most elegant aperitif wine on that very special occasion. Fair value, ouch, $7.

Extra Dry Champagne: See CHAMPAGNE, EXTRA DRY.

Muscadelle du Bordelais*** This is a white sparkling wine made from the Muscat grape; it's similar to Italy's Asti Spumante, rather on the sweet side. It's strictly for after-dinner consumption; serve it well chilled. A rather dubious value at $5.75 or more.

Red Champagne: See SPARKLING BURGUNDY.

Sec Champagne: See CHAMPAGNE, SEC.

Sehr Trocken: See CHAMPAGNE, SEHR TROCKEN.

Sparkling Burgundy (Red)*** Not sweet and frivolous, but substantial and fruity. It recently won a gold medal at an international competition in Milan, Italy—one of only three American wines among 800 entrants. Fair value, $5.75.

KOSHER WINES: See EASTER SUNDAY WINES.

KREUZNACHER BRUECKEN (or: BRUECKES) A great German wine from an exceptional vineyard, Bruecken. There was a famous Trockenbeerenauslese (see) produced here in 1959: Near-Classic.

KREUZNACHER NARRENKAPPE Fine German wine from a famous vineyard: Kreuznach is the name of the town, Narrenkappe, the vineyard. There was a famous Eiswein (see) produced in both '61 and '62, both Near-Classics. They're worth a small fortune today.

KROEVER (KROVER) NACKTARSCH: See CROEVER NACKTARSCH.

KRUG & CO. Don't confuse this name with that of Charles Krug, the California winery—the names are purely coincidental. This Krug is one of France's great Champagne houses; it is not among the larger houses, but it is among the most prestigious and the best; it possesses a worldwide reputation. Maurice Healy, the famous Irish connoisseur, said Krug was the best of all French Champagne, the king of them all. It comes in only two versions, both expensive: a Blanc de Blancs at $23.50, and a Private Cuvée Brut (nonvintage) at $20. (If the latter says English Market or Cuvée on the label it's even drier than the "straight" Brut.) The Blanc de Blancs is available in only one vintage to date, the 1966, and of this a mere 7,000 bottles were made. It is perfection: Classic. The Private Cuvée Brut isn't exactly rotgut either; check some vintages:

1928—Healy said it was the best wine of the century!

1929—Still in relatively good shape.

1955—Some say one of the best Champagnes ever made.

1959—English Market: Still fine in '73, if you dig old Champagnes.

1961—English Market: ****, a comedown for Krug!

"Straight": Near-Classic.

1962—Light and refined—Vincent Price, a knowledgeable wine buff, calls it "divine."

1964—*****—At its best through '75 and '76.

1966—Typical Krug elegance —Henri Krug says you can smell and taste the grapes: Near-Classic.

CHARLES KRUG WINERY (St. Helena, Calif.) In the world of wine a name on a label is never an absolute guarantee of quality—as it might be, say, in buying an appliance. But over the broad spectrum of quality American wines, the name of Charles Krug on a label comes as close as any to being such a guarantee. Krug has been working at this kind of thing for well over a century. It was Charles Krug who made the first commercial wine in the Napa Valley, in 1858. Krug wines are consistently above average, and always reasonably priced, and how are you going to beat that?

Burgundy The name "Burgundy" on a bottle of American wine doesn't mean much —the only thing you can be absolutely certain of is that it's a red wine. But if the label also says Charles Krug, you can be reasonably sure that it's a good little wine. Serve it at cool room temperature with grilled hamburgers or steaks, with pasta, stew, casseroles. The 1966 and 1967, both ***, are perfect now, but don't keep them much longer. The 1968 and 1969 rate ***, especially considering their modest price tag, ca. $2.25. They're excellent values.

Cabernet Sauvignon Krug says this is their most interesting wine, and they should know. It's certainly been consistently above average over the past several decades. Cabernet is the American equivalent of France's great Clarets (Bordeaux reds) and the historic accompaniment for the best cuts of beef and lamb. To appreciate the wine's deep-down berrylike flavor, sip it ever so slowly with cheeses and fruits. Serve at cool room temperature. Krug has both a "regular" bottling and a special Vintage Selection, also called a Cesare Mondavi Selection (the words are on an orange strip on the upper left-hand corner of the label), somewhat more expensive and usually a better wine. Fair value: "Regular" bottling, $4.50 to $4.75; Vintage Selection, $6.50.

For the historical record only: 1950s—Almost all vintages were exceptional but all long gone in every sense. More history: Early 1960s, Regular Bottlings—Uniformally **** but all now past their prime.

1960 Vintage Selection***** Great drinking today but don't keep it beyond the 70s.

1962 Vintage Selection*** Past its peak—eschew.

1963 Vintage Selection**** Drink within next two–three years.

1964 and 1965 Vintage Selection***** Now at their best, there to remain, through the 70s.

1966 Vintage Selection***** Marvelous drinking now and for another decade.

1966 "Regular"**** Drink before 1978.

1967 "Regular"*** Best drinking, 1975 through 1979.

1967 Vintage Selection Nonesuch—none made this year.

1968 "Regular"****Now at its best and will keep so through the decade.

1968 Vintage Selection**** Drink during the 70s.

1969 "Regular"** Sinister forces must have hexed the *cuvée*—it's shown poorly in every tasting, and the Vintage Selection isn't much of an improvement.

1970**** Will be at its best, 1976 to the mid-80s. Excellent value at $4.50.

Chablis*** This has to be one of the best wine values in white wine in the United States, or in the world. It's dry, as Chablis should be, exceptionally flavorful. Ideal to accompany fish, especially shellfish, poultry, cheese dishes, light soufflés. It's ready to drink when purchased, don't keep it more than a couple of years. Serve chilled. Fair value, $2.25 to $2.50.

Chenin Blanc**** It was Charles Krug that started this good little white wine on the California road to fame—that was back in 1955. It's had its ups and downs with Krug over the years, but today it rates a proud ****. It's a brisk, fresh, sipping kind of wine (chilled, of course) and it has a touch of sweetness. Drink it within two or three years of purchase. Air it at least a half hour. See also Krug's White Pinot, a very similar wine. An excellent value, $2.75 to $3.

Claret** Claret is a name not often seen these days—somehow it's fallen out of style —but Krug's version continues to be a sturdy little red wine, of the Bordeaux-type, fine to accompany barbecued chicken, grilled hamburgers, cheese dishes. Serve at cool room temperature, after a half hour to an hour's airing. Don't keep it more than five or six years beyond its vintage date. Fair value, $2.25 to $2.50.

Cream Sherry: See SHERRY.

Dry Sauterne*** Definitely dry, with good deep-down flavor, perfect to accompany any light food. Fair value, $2.25.

Dry Sémillon*** This earthy-tasting semi-dry white wine recently seems to have lost some of its erstwhile zip. Mark: it will rise again. When it does, serve it chilled, on its own or with light foods. Consume within two or three years of purchase. Fair value, $2.75 to $3.

Gamay Beaujolais** Formerly called simply Gamay—you may still find some of it on retail shelves under that name—this is a fruity young red wine, ideal for a picnic or luncheon or outdoor barbecue. It's a vintage-dated wine, at its best when young: within two or three years of the date on the bottle. Serve at cool room temperature. Fair value, $2.75 to $3.

Gewürztraminer*** Zesty, tasty, slightly effervescent white wine—neophyte and expert alike will appreciate this delightful beverage. It traditionally accompanies sausage and similar hearty food, but it will be even more appreciated, sipped in wholesome fellowship, on its own or with cheese and bread. It's ready to drink when you bring it home and it's at its best for about three years thereafter. Serve chilled. Fair value, $3.75 to $4.

Grey Riesling*** This lovely white wine has just enough sweetness to commend it for pensive, relaxed sipping; it's good enough to deserve such treatment. Chilled, of course. It has lots of flavor, and will also make a good luncheon wine, a perfect complement for sandwiches, chicken salad, etc. Drink it within three years of purchase. A good value, at ca. $2.75.

Johannisberg Riesling *** California makes a lot of good Johannisberger, and this is one of the best: full-bodied, spicy, with a very slight sweetness. It's an ideal accompaniment for fish, seafood, ham, cold cuts, Chinese food. It's ready to drink when you buy it, and is at its best for about three years thereafter. Serve chilled. Fair value, $3.75 to $4.

Moscato di Canelli*** Luscious dessert wine, has a faint sparkle, not always available. Splendid wine for the "elevenses," A.M. and P.M. Serve it well chilled, savor it tenderly. Fair value, $5 to $5.25. (Retailers are gouging if they ask more, as some of them do.) Once opened, this wine will keep several weeks in the refrigerator if you eliminate the air space in the bottle.

Pale Dry Sherry: See SHERRY.

Pinot Chardonnay Everyone

agrees that Chardonnay is almost always a fine wine—with Krug's you can drop the "almost." In recent years they've never made a poor one. Chardonnay is a big enough wine to deserve being drunk on its own, or with cheese and fruit. It is also the classic accompaniment for fish, particularly shellfish. Serve chilled. Fair value, $4.50.

1966, 1967, 1968** All now past their prime.

1969*** Best drinking, 1975 and 1976.

1970*** Drink, 1975 through 1976.

1971*** Drink, 1975 through 1977.

Pinot Noir At its best, Pinot Noir is one of California's finest red wines, fragrant and fruity. Krug's version is sometimes there, sometimes not. Check vintages carefully. It's fine to accompany fowl, stews, cheese dishes. You may want to enjoy the better bottles some early or late evening, simply with cheese, walnuts, fruit. Fair value, $4.50, but the * bottles are not worth that.

1965, 1966*** Drink soon.

1968*** Best drinking, 1975 through 1977.

1969* Drink 1975 through 1977.

Pouilly Fumé** You'll find this name on lots of French wine, but rarely on an American wine. It's a fruity, dry white wine, made from the Sauvignon Blanc grape. Serve it chilled, with fish or seafood, or at a luncheon. It's ready to drink when you buy it and will be past its prime three or four years after that. Fair value, ca. $3.75.

Sauvignon Blanc* Krug has stopped making this wine—it's just as well—but you still may

find some around. It's rather sweet—the word used to be on the label. Drink it, if you must, chilled, for refreshment. Fair value, $3.

Sherry Krug makes the three standard sherries, none of them especially notable: *Pale Dry Sherry*, *: very dry, a cocktail wine. *Cream Sherry*, *: for after meals. "Plain" *Sherry*, **: a medium, all-purpose beverage, which means you can drink it before meals, during (with soup), or after. Or between. These wines can be kept three or four years after purchase. Once opened they will keep (especially the Cream) for several weeks if you store them in the refrigerator with as little air space in the bottle as possible. Fair value, $2.25 to $2.50.

Sweet Sauterne** Fragrant and flavorful dessert wine, this —or you can simply sip it, always chilled, refreshingly of a late morning, mid-afternoon, or late evening. It's ready to drink when purchased and will be at its best for about four years thereafter. Fair value, $2.75 to $3.

Sylvaner Riesling*** This clean, fruity white wine is more like a German Rhine wine than almost any made in America. It will be best appreciated sipped slowly, meditatively, on its own, chilled. Or, if you insist, serve it with light foods such as fish or chicken. Ready to drink when purchased, it will be at its best for three or four years after that. A good value at $2.75 to $3.

Traminer** Krug may be the only winery in America that makes both a Traminer and a Gewürztraminer. They are very similar wines—some believe they are actually one and the same grape. Krug's Traminer is a fresh and zesty little white, but less flavorsome than their Gewürztraminer. It will admirably enhance light luncheon fare, or you can sip it, chilled, on its own, some carefree evening. It's ready for drinking when purchased and will be at its best about three years thereafter. Fair value, $2.75 to $3.

Vin Rosé** Gay little pink wine—drink it, chilled, for refreshment or entertainment. Or almost anyplace else other than a WCTU convention. Don't keep it more than a year or two. A good value at $2.25 to $2.50.

White Pinot*** Krug must be the only winery in the world that makes both a White Pinot and a Chenin Blanc; the names are usually synonymous. Krug's White Pinot, however, is only about three fourths Chenin Blanc; the other one

fourth is Pinot Blanc. It is drier than the Chenin Blanc. It makes a fine accompaniment for fish, seafood, simply prepared poultry. Serve chilled. It's ready to be drunk when purchased and will be at its best for at least two years after that. Fair value, $2.75 to $3.

Zinfandel Not one of Krug's more notable successes, but in its own realm reliable tasty red wine, to be consumed while it's young. "Zin" is versatile—you can serve it at your outdoor barbecue, buffet luncheon, or with your dinner roast, pasta, stew. Serve at cool room temperature. Drink it within two years of purchase. Fair value, $2.75 to $3.

1966, 1967, 1968** Past their prime.

1969** Drink soon.

1970*** Best drinking, 1975.

1971**** You can drink it now but it will be at its best from 1976 on.

L

LA: This is simply the definite article in French—"the." If the name of your wine begins with "La," go to the next word—e.g., "La Mission"—look under MISSION.

LACRIMA CHRISTI (or: LACHRYMA CHRISTI) A sparkling white wine of Italy, somewhat drier than their Asti Spumante (see). The name means "the Tears of Christ," and while that may be somewhat of an overstatement in describing this wine, it can be a pretty good substitute for out-of-sight Champagne. It's important here that your wine comes from a reliable shipper. Here are some: Bosca; Fontanafredda; Gancia; Martini & Rossi; Mirafiore; Opera Pia.

LAFITE-ROTHSCHILD (or simply: LAFITE), CHÂTEAU If asked to name a truly great wine, probably more Americans would name this than any other. And their estimate would be right on, for Château Lafite is, indeed, a great wine—many would say simply the world's greatest wine, bar none. Probably more bottles of Château Lafite have earned the ultimate accolade of Classic than any other single wine.

Lafite is one of this earth's most elegant wines; one writer calls it "a perfumed, polished, gentlemanly production." A wine of such high repute and outstanding excellence can only be appreciated and enjoyed on its own, never accompanying merely earthly food. Of course it may well have a place at that "heavenly banquet." The poet was wrong: Not pie in the sky when you die—Wine, Lafite, in the sky when you die.

Check older bottles for sediment, and decant if necessary. Good Claret such as this improves noticeably with "breathing"—air young bottles (1950 on) one to two hours, older ones, one half to one hour. Serve Lafite with a flourish—bells clanging, lights flashing, trumpets blaring—at cool room temperature. But only to those with cultivated palates and grateful hearts.

1803—Classic—Don't go look for this at Dirty Dick's Cut-Rate Booze—it's rather hard to come by. A bottle was consumed a few years ago and it was in great shape. After 170 years!

1811—Classic—One for the books. This was the famous "Year of the Comet," and some sincerely believed it was the comet that made the wine so great. And even modern critics say this may have been Lafite's greatest ever.

1846—Classic—A 24-ounce bottle went for a neat $5,000 at a London auction in 1971, a world's record for a standard size bottle of wine. It's encouraging to know that 1846 was a good year—at about $280 per ounce it had better

160

be! They sipped it carefully, prayerfully, one presumes.

1858—Classic—A cheapie, it sold for a mere $830 in 1972. But don't buy more than a case or two, as it's definitely begun to decline.

1864—Classic—Experts have called this the greatest wine of all time, and whether it is or is not, it sells like it is. A jeroboam of this wine sold for $9,000 at a Heublein auction in Chicago in 1974. That is the second highest price ever paid for a single bottle of wine. (Highest: Mouton-Rothschild, 1929—see) A jeroboam is 104-ounces, four regular-size bottles. But the owners were bitterly disappointed at the miserly price—they had hoped for $15,000 to $25,000! Hard times, things are tough all over.

1865—Classic—Maurice Healy, the great Irish critic, said this was the finest Claret he ever drank. And they're practically giving it away: a jeroboam sold for a piddling $1,220 in 1973.

1869—Classic—First Lafite under Rothschild ownership.

1870—Classic—It's still in excellent condition, sold in 1973 for $200 per magnum.

1899—*****—Sold in 1973 for $95—Beginning to fade.

1924—Near-Classic—Sold for $54 in 1973.

1928—Poor wine, though it has sold for as much as $75.

1934—A magnificent year but Lafite was not among the best: ****, not recommended at $50 and more.

1945—Classic—Sold for up to $80 in 1973.

1947—Classic—Some retailers have been asking $150 for it, but a fair value would be more like $50 or $60.

1948—Near-Classic—Fair value, $30.

1949—It's still improving! Fair value, $50.

1952—Was ***** but is past its prime—Not recommended at any price, and especially at $120, its current asking price!

1953—Though it's been selling for $50 to $150, most authorities agree that this wine is past its peak—In its heyday, it's true, it was a full Classic.

1955—*****—Still at the top of its form. Some retailers peg it at $150 but it sold at auction in 1973 for a high of $57.

1957—Soft, elegant wine despite a mediocre year: ****

1959—Near-Classic—Fair value: not the $175 on some price tags, but more like $50 to $60. Now at its best, and will remain so for many years to come.

1960—****—About at its peak.

1961—Classic—Not yet ready, however. Try it first, 1979 or 1980. It's been on retail shelves at $100 to $200: sheer outlawry! A fair value, even considering the tremendous prestige of the '61 vintage, would be ca. $75.

1962—Near-Classic—Leave it lie for a few more years, until 1977. Fair value, $30.

1964—****—Fair value, $20—Will be at its best, 1976-1985.

1966—*****—Not ready; try it starting in 1979. Fair value, despite its present $50 to $60 price tag, $30.

1967—*****—Tremendous bouquet, huge wine, but needs more time in the bottle. Try it first in '78 or '79. Fair value, $20 to $25.

1969—Early peekers say: Very good—tentative *****

1970—Even better than the '69, according to early reports. May well make Near-Classic rank, or even full Classic.

LAGOSTA ROSÉ The name means "lobster," presumably because the wine goes well with that charming crustacean. Perhaps so, but if you can afford the lobster, you can afford a better wine accompaniment. None of which is to say that this Portuguese rosé is poor wine. Not so—it's soft, pleasant, slightly sweet—fine for summer sipping. Fair value, ca. $2.50. It also comes in a 25-ounce raffia-covered bottle (like those Chianti *fiaschi*) at $2.70: less wine for more money—you can't drink the silly straw, can hardly even eat it.

How to serve it: See under ROSÉ.

LAMBERTI VALPOLI-CELLA: See VAPOLICELLA.

LAMBRUSCO Five years ago not two Americans in one hundred would have recognized this name—only wine experts knew that Lambrusco was the name of a little red Italian wine, not that of one of the branches of the Corleone family. Today millions of American wine drinkers, young and old, beginner and experienced, know that Lambrusco is a light, frizzy, slightly sweet wine, delightfully young and zingy. Its popularity has risen just at the time when that of "Pop" wines began to decline (*Post hoc, propter hoc?*). It's a wine that almost everybody enjoys— at least initially, for it is a fresh, lively, happy wine—and perhaps most important of all, an inexpensive one. Its slight effervescence is one of the reasons for its popularity and some have suspected that CO_2

is sometimes added, but if so, it's been strictly without sanction, for that is expressly forbidden by Italian law.

Lambrusco is so light and frolicsome that it can serve beautifully as an aperitif wine, but perhaps its best service is, as in Italy, with heavy, substantial food—it will offset the likes of zampone, pasta, lentil, bean and sausage dishes. Lambrusco is to be consumed very young —ideally when it's less than two years old. Serve it chilled: 45 to 55°F.

Sometimes the label will read: Lambrusco di Sorbara, Lambrusco di Modena, or the name of some other town, but it's all the same wine. Also, it may have the word "Amabile" (sweet) on the label—it's :ill the same wine. Vintages are of no importance here, except to tell you if your wine is still young.

Be wary of very cheap Lambrusco—under $2. Here are some generally dependable names in vaguely descending order of excellence: Alberini; Calissano; Giacobazzi; Beccaro; Riunite; Nicoli; Cella; Mazzoni.

LAMONT, M. This is the principal brand name for the wines of the Bear Mountain Winery, a large cooperative of growers in California's San Joaquin Valley. The Valley produces huge quantities of wines but almost no premium wines. The summers are simply too hot for the great classic grapes. LaMont doesn't attempt to grow the great noble grapes of Europe (Pinot Noir, Pinot Chardonnay, Cabernet Sauvignon, Johannisberg Riesling) but skillfully matches grapes to soil and climate, and the result is some very creditable table wines.

Note that many of the wines are Estate Bottled, which means that the entire winemaking process, from growing the grapes to aging the finished product, has been accomplished on the premises—a further assurance of high quality. LaMont wines are almost all excellent values.

Barbera*** A brand-new wine, first marketed in 1974. It's a good example of this Italian-type red wine: tangy and dry. Fine with grilled hamburgers, barbecued chicken, pasta, Italian dishes. Serve at cool room temperature. A good value at $2.

Burgundy Cabernet (a Ruby Cabernet blend)** Notice that the LaMont generics—Burgundy, Chablis, Vin Rosé—mention specific grapes on their labels. One rarely sees this. In this case the grape is Cabernet. The winery is saying that at least 51 percent of this wine is made from Cabernet grapes (Ruby Cabernet, not Cabernet Sauvignon). And that's nothing but good, for the Ruby Cabernet produces superior red wines in hot climates. The wine has already won at least one gold medal (Los Angeles County Fair, 1973). Excellent with hamburgers, steaks, roasts (beef, lamb, pork). A good value at $1.60 to $1.85, and an even better value in gallons: $5.

Cabernet*** This is the rich cousin of the preceding wine. (Note, however, that it is not Cabernet Sauvignon, the aristocrat of all red wines, but its lesser relative, the Ruby Cabernet.) It's a little more flavorful, a little drier than the preceding. Enjoy it exactly as you would the Burgundy. It's ready to drink when you buy it, and the winery assures you that it will even improve with a year

or two of added bottle age. A good value at $2.

Chablis (a French Colombard blend)** Here's another of La Mont's new "generics": Chablis is a generic name, no grapes being specified, but it's ungeneric in that the grape (French Colombard) is specified. See also French Colombard, a very similar wine.

Chenin Blanc*** Light and fruity—quite adequate but could use more varietal character (taste of the grapes, to you). Serve chilled, with light foods. A good value at $2.

Colombard, French: See FRENCH COLOMBARD.

Emerald Riesling*** This is one of those grapes "invented" by the University of California. It's a clean, crisp white wine, medium-dry, and it will go well, chilled, with light foods, especially fish, seafood, chicken. Drink it young and fresh: within two years of purchase. A good value at $2.

French Colombard*** LaMont's Chablis is the poor cousin of this wine; the Chablis is cheaper and not as good. This grape is usually used for blending and you'll find few French Colombards around. It's a nice soft white wine, basically dry, but with a smidgen of sweetness. It goes well with fish, chicken, or simply when one wants a refreshing glass of cool white wine. A good value at $2.

Grenache Rosé*** LaMont makes two rosés: this and a cheaper (by 40¢ per fifth) Vin Rosé; this one would seem to be worth the difference. The flavor is more intense and it is a trifle sweeter. It'll go fine with light foods: poultry, fish, ham. It will also make for good idle sipping. A good value, $2.

Sémillon*** Wines, like almost everything else in God's creation, are subject to fads and trends—Sémillon wine has suffered an eclipse in recent years —for no good reason. Sémillon wine is one of the things that California does best. It comes in both sweet and dry versions; this one is betwixt. Fine with light foods (including fish and seafood) or on its own. Serve chilled. A good value at $2.

Vin Rosé** LaMont makes two rosés, this and a more expensive Grenache Rosé. For 40¢ more per fifth, you'd be well advised to vote for the Grenache. It contains more of the good Grenache grape, and it shows. Fair value, $1.65.

Zinfandel** "Zin" is perhaps California's greatest native wine, but it is not among LaMont's more notable successes. At the price, however, (ca. $2) it constitutes rather plausible everyday red wine. It's ready to drink when purchased and will keep for two or three years. Fair value, $2.

LANCERS VIN ROSÉ*** Portugal makes some of the nicest, sprightliest rosés in the world —here's one of them. Lancers is extremely popular both in the United States and Britain. Mostly deservedly—it's fresh, pretty, prickly on the tongue, with a touch of sweetness, a summer's day's delight. Whether there's $4 worth of wine in that cute crock, however, is a horse of a different hue, a wine of another pigmentation.

There is also a Lancers Rubeo, ***, a red wine, and a Lancers Vinho Branco, also ***, both a bit frizzy, both pleasant with a kiss of sweetness, and both slightly overpriced at around. $4.

LANSON One of the largest and most renowned of France's great Champagne houses. Lanson's "top of the line" is a vintaged Red Label Brut, at around $18.50, a marvelous Champagne, but it would take an expert to distinguish it from their nonvintage Black Label Brut, at a *mere* $11.60, regularly *****: beautiful, aromatic, elegant wine.

LASCOMBES, CHÂTEAU A highly ranked, excellent red Bordeaux, one of the few French Châteaux that is American-owned (by Alexis Lichine, see). The wine is often compared to and even, at times, ranked with the great Château Margaux. And Lascombes is a fine wine, full flavored and flowery—and if you don't believe it, ask Lichine—he'd be the first to assure you of the wine's superiority! He devised his own ranking of French Bordeaux wines a few years ago, and Lascombes was up there at the very tip-top. But honesty is also a virtue and everybody agrees that Lascombes *is* a superior wine, particularly since Lichine took over in 1952. How to serve it: See under BORDEAUX.

1949—*****—Good buy at $35—Still in excellent condition.

1953—*****—Sold for $11 at auction a few years ago—At its peak but don't keep it beyond 1978. Good value at $12.

1955—*****—At its best now and until 1980 at least. Fair value, $14.

1959—*****—Good drinking, 1975–1985. Good value at $12.

1961—****—Not up to Lascombes standard for such a superb year—Not recommended at $20. Best drinking, 1977–1987.

1962—****—Best drinking, 1975–1980. Fair value $7.

1964—****—Now at its best —drink by 1980. Fair value $8.

1965—***—Nice little wine in a poor year, but it should be cheap: ca. $4. Drink before 1980.

1966—****—Don't drink it yet—it will be at its best, 1978–1990. Fair value, $8.

1967—****—Will be at its best, 1978–1985. Fair value, $7.

1970—Near-Classic—It's going to be a great bottle of wine. Try it first around 1980. Fair value, $9.

LATOUR, CHÂTEAU There is only one *real* Château Latour, but there are a host of French wines with Château Latour or La Tour something-or-other on the label. There is even one whose legitimate name is simply Château Latour, but remember that *the* Château Latour has its portrait on the label: a Tower, La Tour, get it? And the label reads "Grand Vin de Château Latour."

This is one of France's and indeed the world's greatest red wines—in the same league with Mouton, Lafite, and Co. It is the most powerful of the great first growths, due to the rocky, infertile soil of the vineyard. Latour is notoriously slow to develop, and in its youth can be rough and coarse, which also makes it extremely long-lived. It is also famous for being a good wine even in poor years.

Under pain of being hung, drawn, and quartered, you may partake of such vinous excellence only in company with wine-appreciative friends, slowly, carefully, lovingly, sippingly, with bread and fine cheeses. And especially with gratitude. Neither God nor man intended Château Latour to accompany Giussepe's pizza or Pancho's enchiladas. Older bottles should be checked for sediment and decanted if necessary. All red Bordeaux should be aired— anything prior to 1950, air one half to one hour (the older the wine, the less the need to air); younger wines, 1950 forward, air one to two hours. Serve at cool room temperature.

1863—Classic—Still good drinking.

1865—Classic—In 1968 in excellent condition.

1869—Classic—In 1933 was still perfect.

1870—Classic—In 1969 still had a good deal of vigor, sold for $166 (24 ounces) in 1973.

1874—Classic—In 1967 still big and rich.

1878—Classic—Hilaire Belloc said it was the finest Claret "he had ever drunk in his long and well-wined life"—Sold for $100 in 1973.

1893—Classic.

1899—Classic—In 1967 just faintly tired.

1920—Classic—One writer calls it "precocious" . . . yes? Fair value, $60.

1922—****—Good despite indifferent year.

1923—*****—Médoc's best in a so-so vintage—Fair value, $25.

1924—*****—Sold for $73 in 1973.

1928—Classic—The best of the great first growths this vintage—Fair value, $65.

1929—Classic—It took all the marbles in this great year— Fair value, $70.

1934—It's been selling (at auction) for around $50, but it is not one of Latour's best: ****

1937—*****—Fair value, $45.

1945—Classic—It's now a full thirty years old, but experts say it is only just beginning to reach its peak. It will be splendid for eons to come. Fair value, $60 to $75.

1947—*****—Fair value, $50.

1949—*****—Just now reaching its peak; a fair value would be $40 but it's been on the shelves for $105.

1950—Exceptional wine for the vintage: *****. Fair value, $30.

1952—*****—Still not ready, say the experts—Try it in 1980. Fair value, $35, but some have had it tagged at $85.

1954—****—Now at its best. Fair value, would you believe, $9?

1955—Near-Classic—But it needs more aging. Give it until 1980. It's selling for up to $90 but a fair price would be $40, at most.

1959—Classic—It's not quite ready. Give it until 1978 at least. Fair value, ca. $50, but it's price-tagged at twice that.

1960—Near-Classic—1960 was not a great year, but true to form, this Latour is magnificent wine and a great value, if you can find it; it's been retailing at $35 and selling at auction for a high of $22— Seek and ye may find! Best drinking, 1975 through 1982.

1961—Classic—All agree: it's going to be great, some say it's the greatest of all '61s. May just now be beginning to be ready. It's got a $100 price tag but a fair value would be more like $50.

1962—Near-Classic—Not quite ready. From 1978 on . . . *Mirabile dictu*, it's selling at a rational, fair value: around $40.

1963—Another of those Latours that comes through in a poor year. This is fine wine: *****, fully mature. Look for it, you may find it at $10 or even less!

1964—Classic—Some say the best wine of the Médoc in this excellent year. But Americans, all searching for the famous '61, don't appreciate this wine and the price remains almost in sight: $30 to $40.

1966—Near-Classic—Will be at its best, 1976 on. Fair value, $40 to $45, and that's what it's actually been selling for!

1967—Near-Classic—Still immature. Give it at least until 1978. Some think it may develop into a full-blown Classic. Its high at auction in '73 was $24.

1968—***—Good considering the vintage, but not a good value at $12. Best drinking, 1975–1980.

1969—*****—Still very tannic—Try it first, 1980. Fair value, $30.

1970—Will be Near-Classic. Would be a great bottle to lay down if it weren't selling for $50—a fair value at this stage would be half that.

1971—Preliminary reports say it will be excellent.

LATRICIÈRES-CHAMBERTIN Great red Burgundy (France) wine, one of the very best, after Chambertin and Clos de Bèze. How to serve—and coddle—this wine: See under (LE) CHAMBERTIN.

LAURENT-PERRIER One of France's great Champagne houses recently has greatly enlarged its capacity. Laurent-Perrier's wines range from their Grand Siècle at $22 to their Extra Dry at $9.50. In between are a Blanc de Blancs at $14 and a nonvintage Brut Special Cuvée at $12. The Grand Siècle —the "Great Century" in which

Champagne was invented by Dom Perignon—is a magnificent wine; some have found the '64 disappointing, but the '66 is clearly *****. The Brut Special Cuvée is a much better value, at $12; in competitive tastings it has consistently placed high.

LE: This is the French definite article—"the." If the name of your wine begins with "Le," go to the next word—e.g., "Le Montrachet"—look under MONTRACHET.

LEACOCK'S FINE DRY SERCIAL**** Leacock and Co., Lda., is a British shipper of Portuguese wines. This Sercial is smooth and lovely. Serve it slightly chilled, as an aperitif wine or on its own. For more on this kind of wine: See MADEIRA.

LEACOCK'S MALMSEY SOLERA 1863***** Look for it —magnificent sweet dessert Madeira. Serve it with coffee or nuts or fruit or even with a luscious dessert: torte, trifle, raspberries and cream. Fair value, $8.

LEACOCK'S SAINT JOHN DRY MADEIRA*** Americans are missing a good bet in their ignorance of one of the world's most unique wines, Portuguese Madeira. Rather incredibly, in Colonial days Madeira was America's most popular wine. Now *there's* a custom that needs reviving for the nation's bicentennial! How to serve this wine: See under MADEIRA.

LEACOCK'S VERDELHO SOLERA 1872**** Verdelho is a dry type of Madeira wine (see)—Solera 1872 means that the oldest wine in this blend (in minute quantity) is of that vintage. This is one of the few wines that connoisseurs will

allow you to drink "on the rocks," it's that big-bodied and tasteful. You can serve it as an aperitif wine or with soup (marvelous!) or as a nightcap. Madeira has a special flavor like no other wine of this earth. Fair value, $8.

LE BLANC DE BLANCS: See BLANC DE BLANCS.

LE DOMAINE CHAMPAGNE *** This is Almadén's marque for their less expensive line of sparkling wines, and these five wines—Brut, Extra Dry, Pink, Sparkling Burgundy, and Cold Duck—surely constitute some of the best values in sparkling wines in the U.S., and perhaps the world. Don't misinterpret: These are not great wines, but at the price, about $3, they're profoundly hard to beat. The Brut is the best of them. If you have something to celebrate— or if you don't—and if you aren't related to Messrs. Croesus or Getty, this may be your slender tulip-shaped glass of bubbly. Serve well chilled. Don't keep any of these sparklers more than a couple of years.

Le Domaine Cold Duck: See CHAMPAGNE.

Le Domaine Sparkling Burgundy: See CHAMPAGNE.

LE DUC Here's a Champagne that's not a Champagne—it's a French sparkling wine that may not carry the word "Champagne" on its label, for it does not come from France's Champagne area. (It comes from the Rhone Valley.) But anyone less than a professional wine taster will be hard-pressed to distinguish this fine "Champagne"— whoops, sparkling wine—from the real McCoy. A good value at $6: ****.

LEJON CHAMPAGNE** This is Italian Swiss Colony's "top

of the line" Champagne. It's still very economical, $3 to $3.50, but their Jacques Bonet (see) Champagnes are even cheaper, ca. $2. The Lejons are clearly better, more flavorful wincs, but they're still not giving Moët et Chandon (French) any competition, nor, for that matter, Kornell or Almadén (American). They're all made by the bulk-process method, and all have plastic corks. Caution: Be circumspect in opening these wines—those plastic corks can become deadly projectiles. Open peaceably.

Lejon Champagne comes in the standard flavors: Extra Dry (these words are only on the neck label), Pink, Sparkling Burgundy. The Extra Dry and the Cold Duck are the best of the lot.

LEONARDO VALPOLICEL-LA: See VALPOLICELLA.

LEON BEYER: See BEYER, LEON.

LÉOVILLE–BARTON, CHÂ-TEAU There are three Léoville wines (see following two entries)—they were originally just one vineyard—they are all superb red Bordeaux (Clarets), and depending on which of the three you happen to prefer, you can find expert opinion to agree with you. Léoville-Barton wines have been especially good since World War II. How to serve: See under BORDEAUX.

1924, 1928, 1934, 1945—*****

1948—Near-Classic—Undervalued because it was between two great vintages—It sold in '73 (at auction) for only $15.

1949—Classic—It's now at its best and will hold there until 1990, at least!

1953—Classic—The owner said it was the best wine he ever made.

1959—*****—At its best now and to 1985.

1961—Near-Classic—The owner hails it as one of his best ever—Will be at its peak, 1977–1990.

1962—****—Now at its best and until 1980.

1964—***—Thin, disappointing—Not recommended, at $9 or $10—or $5. Drink soon.

1966—*****—Served aboard the French supersonic *Concorde* as it toured the U.S. in '73. Will be its best 1976 through 1990. Fair value, $11.

1967—This may be a sleeper . . . it's already looking like a Near-Classic—Best drinking: 1976 on. Fair value $12 . . . if you can find it.

1970—Conflicting reports on this one: some say marvelous— some say yukk . . . Wait, see.

LÉOVILLE-LAS-CASES (or LASCASES), CHÂTEAU A lot of experts say that this is the best of the three Léoville wines, but the opinion's far from unanimous. In fact, you will find expert opinion on the side of all three of the Léoville wines. Which is to say that all three of these are superb red Bordeaux wines, and in one year one will be the best of the three, in another, another. Las-Cases wines were especially good through the 60s, and happily these are the ones that are most readily available today. Las-Cases is unique in the fact that there is no château (manor) on the property, though it's a "Château" wine. Look, ma, no château. How to serve this wine: See BORDEAUX.

1900—*****—Still in marvelous condition. It sold a few years ago for around $40.

1928—Classic—In '73 sold at auction, $45 to $50.

1929—Classic.

1945—*****—Just now reaching its best. Fair value, $30.

1959—Near-Classic—At its best now and at least until 1980. Fair value, $17 to $20.

1960—****—Drink it soon. Fair value, $6.

1961—Classic—Not yet at its best. Keep it until 1976 to 1986. A good value if you can find it, at $17 to $20.

1962—*****—Will be at its best, 1976 through 1985. Fair value, $10.

1964—*****—Now at its best. Drink anytime in the next decade. Fair value, $10.

1966—*****—Not yet ready. Drink from 1977 on. Fair value, $10 to $12.

1967—*****—Will be at its best, 1976 onward. Fair value, $9 to $10.

1969—****—Best drinking: 1975–1980. Fair value, $6 to $7.

1970—Near-Classic—It's a long way from ready. Try it first around 1980. Fair value, $12.

LÉOVILLE-POYFERRÉ The "last" of the three Léoville wines (see two preceding wines) both alphabetically and, according to some, qualitatively. But again, you'll find some experts who say this is the best of the three Léovilles. All agree, however, that Poyferré produced fine wines in the 20s. Poyferré is a typical Claret: soft and round, full of flavor. How to serve it: See under BORDEAUX.

1924—Near-Classic—Some say second only to Lafite for this vintage. Fair value, $45.

1928 and 1929—Classic—Great wines with great reputations—still in excellent condition. Fair value, $45 to $50.

1934—Near-Classic.

1943—Near-Classic—Still at the top of its form.

1959—*****—Now at its best. Fair value, $15.

1961—****—Disappointing for this vintage and this vineyard. Not recommended at $17.

1962—*****—Best drinking, 1975–1980. Fair value, $13.

1966—*****—Will be at its best 1978–1990. Fair value, $15.

1967—****—It's already good drinking and will hold at least through the 70s.

1970—***—Disappointing for this fine year and this vineyard—at this point, not recommended.

LES: This is the French definite article—"the." If the name of your wine begins with Les, e.g., "Les Hervelets," see under HERVELETS.

L'HERMITAGE: See HERMITAGE.

LICHINE, ALEXIS This name has been one of the most important on the international wine scene for many a year. Lichine is all over the wine business: author (the *Authoritative Encyclopedia of Wines and Spirits*), vineyard owner, shipper, importer, exporter. Wines with his name on them are generally good but by no means guaranteed. They can vary widely, just as everybody else's wines. Look up your wine under its proper name.

LICHINE, ALEXIS: PINOT CHARDONNAY This is a French Pinot Chardonnay—most of the Pinot Chardonnay you see in the U.S. is from California. Recent imports by Lichine have been consistently bad, bad news. A grudging ** at best, a poor value even at a lowly $3.

LIEBFRAUENSTIFT This is the name of a small vineyard surrounding the Liebfrauenkirche (Virgin Mary's Church) at Worms-am-Rhein. In all probability this is where Liebfraumilch got its name. The wines are not of the very highest caliber, but this is usually a **** wine—it gives one a good idea of what Liebfraumilchs should always taste like. The '70 Riesling Spätlese was particularly fine: *****.

LIEBFRAUMILCH Even non-wine drinking Americans know this wine—it's probably the most famous white wine—certainly the most famous German wine—in all the world. Even whiskey-oriented Americans buy Liebfraumilch. And go back to it again and again because they know the name and can pronounce it unerringly—Liebfraumilch is safe. Such American instincts are basically correct: Liebfraumilch is usually a tasty little white wine, with a bit of sweetness, decently priced, fresh and appealing, fine with fried shrimp or a seafood platter. It has a secure and deserved place on the American wine scene. But the trouble comes when it is not only all that Americans know of German wines, but all they *want* to know. This is like halting one's food appreciation with Gerber's strained spinach. But the famous name does get abused. Liebfraumilch can come from almost anywhere in Germany—and sometimes does. Too often the very poorest of Rhine wine gets a Liebfraumilch label slapped onto it—it's the only way they can sell the stuff. To appreciate what all Liebfraumilch should taste like all the time, try Niersteiner Rehbach or Niersteiner Kransberg.

The name means "the Milk of the Blessed Mother," but despite its halo, it's not a name to be trusted blindly: there are good Liebfraumilchs and there are poor Liebfraumilchs and there are ghastly Liebfraumilchs. One's only, repeat *only*, guide in buying this wine is the name of the shipper.

There are surely worthy Liebfraumilchs other than those listed here, but as a starter, until you know your way around, it is strongly urged that you stay strictly, severely with the following shippers and brand names . . . be not lured to right or to left, not even by those pretty crocks:

Brand Name	Shipper
Black Tower	Kendermann
Blue Nun	Sichel
Crown of Crowns	Langenbach
Glockenspiel	Julius Kayser
Hanns Christof	Deinhard
Madonna	Valckenberg
Madrigal	Kobrand (Importer)
Meister Kronne	Langenbach

Other reliable shippers: Anheuser; Arthur Hallgarten; Guntrum; Leonard Kreusch (economical wines but can vary); Tytell (wines are economical, but can vary); Von Plattenberg.

Liebfraumilch goes well with mild foods such as poultry, fish, seafood. But as light and flowery as this wine is, it will probably be most appreciated on its own. It's a wine to be drunk young, from two to five years of age.

Decent Liebfraumilch will cost between $2.50 and $4.50. Avoid very cheap bottles: anything below $2.

LIVINGSTON CREAM SHERRY: See GALLO.

LLORDS & ELWOOD (Beverly Hills, Calif.) A winery with a British name and a Hollywood address? Well, despite the British moniker, the winery is pure American, the Llords part is pure fantasy; it just sounds classier than plain Elwood. Mike Elwood is a 100 percent Los Angeles American; the Beverly Hills street number is only the business address. The wineries—there were four of them at latest count—are all in northern California, exactly where they should be.

Llords & Elwood wisely limit the number of wines they produce; they say their purpose is to produce a limited number of wines "in the classic style." They're getting the hang of it. They've been in business only since 1961 and their wines have gotten progressively better.

Ancient Proverb Port*** Soft, not overly sweet. Sip it, after dinner, with walnuts, apples, cheese. Fair value, $3.50. It won a gold medal at the Los Angeles County Fair, 1974.

Cabernet Sauvignon Llords & Elwood boasts that they treat this classic grape in a classic manner, and so they do. The results are usually pretty classic too. The wine is not vintagedated but one batch distinguished from another by cask and *cuvée* numbers. Cabernet Sauvignon is the historic complement to the finer cuts of beef and lamb; serve at cool room temperature. Air the older bottles about one hour, the younger (higher cask numbers) two hours. Fair value, ca. $5.

Casks 1–121**** This wine was bottled in March of '68, is now at its best and will hold there through the 70s.

Cuvée No. 4**** This was bottled in June of '69. Best drinking, now and through 1980 —or beyond.

Cuvée No. 5*** Bottled, June '71. It's as good as it's going to get and it will remain so through the 70s.

Cuvée No. 6*** Bottled, September '72. Some think this wine, given another four or five years, may deserve ****. Perhaps, but you still shouldn't drink it before 1977.

Cuvée No. 7**** Bottled, September '73. Looks like a winner, but don't even try it until 1978.

Champagne, Superb Extra Dry Cuvée**** Llords & Elwood makes only this one sparkling wine and it shows: all their solicitude goes here. This is one of the finest of California Champagnes: dry and elegant, perfect for the holidays or some special occasion. Fair value, ca. $5.

Chardonnay, The Rare A dry white wine, ideal with seafood, made from the same grape (the Chardonnay) that produces the great white wines of Burgundy. Beginners don't always appreciate Chardonnay, as it's quite austere. But with painful (sic!) practice you can acquire a taste for it. Llords & Elwood's Chardonnay has been uneven of recent years; check *cuvée* numbers carefully. Serve well chilled. Fair value, $4.50.

Cuvée 1–100** Bottled, February, 1968. Non-great to begin with, now departed this world.

Cuvée 3** This wine was bottled March, '69. Never very much, rather less than that now. Past its best.

Cuvée 5*** Bottled, June, '72. Has had very mixed reviews—the ** represents the mean. There was actual variation from bottle to bottle. You may have a good bottle—then again, you may not. If it has a fine, powdery sediment, return it to your merchant. If not, drink, 1975 through 1978.

Cuvée 6***

Dry Wit Sherry**** Sherries were the first wines Llord & Elwood made, and they're still among their best. The fanciful names are almost as good as the wines themselves: Dry Wit, Great Day D-R-Ry, the Judge's Secret Cream. This one is a medium, all-purpose sherry—like the cartoon of the barroom brawl, one bartender to the other: "Hand me the all-purpose sherry." All-purpose sherry really means that it can be used as an aperitif wine (slightly chilled, if you like), or a with-the-soup wine, or as an after-dinner beverage. Fair value, $3.50.

Great Day D-R-RY Sherry *** The name's almost better than the wine! Llords & Elwood is pure American, but the winery loves the elegant Brrrritish sound of its name and the royal Brrrritish lion is on every label. So also, this sherry is, indeed, verrrry d-r-ry and verrrry Brrrritish, Britons being probably the world's greatest sherry-lovers, not excluding the Spanish. Fair value, $3.50.

Johannisberg Riesling (Castle Magic)*** This is a German-type white wine, though less sweet and flowery. It goes well with light foods: fish, seafood, pork, cheese dishes, poultry. Llords & Elwood does commendably with their Johannisberg; it's more consistent than their Chardonnay. It is bottled by *cuvée* numbers, not vintage years. Avoid any *cuvées* below No. 4, which was bottled in February, 1970, and is now at its best, but don't keep it beyond 1975. *Cuvée 5,* bottled, March, 1972, will be at its best,

1975–1977. Fair value, $4.50. *Cuvée 6,* bottled in 1972, deserves *****.

The Judge's Secret Cream Sherry**** One expert claims that this wine rivals Harveys famed Bristol Cream. It's rich and sweet—for after-dinner. Fair value, $3.50.

Magic Castle: See JOHANNISBERG RIESLING.

Pinot Chardonnay: See CHARDONNAY, THE RARE.

Pinot Noir, Velvet Hill California makes millions of gallons of Burgundy every year, and the very best goes by this name, Pinot Noir, the name of the classic grape of Burgundy (France). It goes especially well with beef, lamb, casseroles, stews, but especially with game and "bold foods," says the winery. Serve at cool room temperature. Fair value, $4.50 to $4.75.

Casks 99–238**** Bottled in 1968, this wine is now at its best, but it should be consumed within the next several years.

Cuvée 5**** Bottled in June, 1969, this wine is now at its best, but it should not be held. Drink it soon, now! Air this bottle fifteen to thirty minutes.

Cuvée 6*** Bottled, October, '70; drink it now.

Cuvée 7**** It won a gold medal, Los Angeles County Fair, 1972. Bottled, 1971, it's now at its best and will remain in top condition through 1979.

Cuvée 8**** Bottled, September, 1972; drink now and through 1980.

Port: See ANCIENT PROVERB PORT.

Rare Chardonnay: See CHARDONNAY, THE RARE.

Rosé of Cabernet*** It is said, only half in jest, that rosé wines are properly drunk with one's breakfast cereal, they are

that bland and innocuous. Truth
to tell, many California rosés
qualify: they belong with the
Post Toasties. Here's a notable
exception; this rosé of Llords
& Elwood is 100 percent from
the noble Cabernet Sauvignon
grape, and it's a big wine, perhaps even great, some say. It's
got some sweetness, fruitiness
too. For either casual sipping
or to accompany light foods—
not Wheaties. Serve chilled.
Fair value, ca. $3.50.

Cuvée 6 The wine was bottled early in 1972 and will begin to deteriorate if you keep
it much longer. Drink now.

Cuvée 7 Bottled, February,
1973. Drink, 1975 through 1976.

Sherry: See DRY WIT SHERRY;
GREAT DAY D-R-RY SHERRY; THE
JUDGE'S SECRET CREAM SHERRY.

Velvet Hill: See PINOT NOIR,
VELVET HILL.

LOBEN, VAN, SELS: See
VAN LOBEN SELS.

**LONGUEVILLE, BARON,
CHÂTEAU:** See PICHON-
LONGUEVILLE, CHATEAU.

LOPEZ DE HEREDIA: See
TONDONIA.

LOS AMIGOS SHERRY

SACK**** One of the finest
dry sherries made in these
United States. The wine is actually made by Souverain Cellars (see), and the name comes
from a famous old California
vineyard no longer in operation. Serve cool or slightly
chilled as an aperitif wine. An
excellent value at $3.

LOS HERMANOS** This is a
secondary label of Beringer
Vineyards of California. It is
used only for their "Mountain
Wines": Mountain Burgundy,
Mountain Chablis, Mountain
Rosé. All three of these are
jug wines—they come in half-
gallon and gallon jugs and are
inexpensive—popular and quite
ordinary. The best of the three
is the Burgundy, but even here
one may be best advised to
prefer the "plain" Burgundy
under the Beringer label. Fair
value, $1.60.

LOUIS, FLORENS: See FLO-
RENS LOUIS.

LOUIS MARTINI: See MAR-
TINI, LOUIS.

**LOUIS THE FIFTH, SPAR-
KLING WINE:** See FRANZIA,
CHAMPAGNE.

M

MACHIAVELLI (CHIANTI):
See SERRISTORI.

MÂCON BLANC Search out this country white French wine if your wallet screeches in pain every time you enter a wine shop. Reasonably priced, on the dry side, made from the noble Chardonnay grape, pleasant and refreshing, to be served chilled. Ready to drink when you buy it, don't keep it more than a year. Foods to accompany: pork, poultry, veal, all types of fish and seafood, especially shrimp, scallops, lobster. Fair value: $2.50 to $4, depending on the reliability of the shipper. The wine is especially trustworthy if the bottle bears the name of one of these shippers: Barton & Guestier (B & G); Bichot; Paul Bocuse; Calvet; Cruse; Joseph Drouhin ("La Fôret"); Louis Jadot; Louis Latour; Sichel; André Simon Selection; Marcel Vincent.
If it has the word "Supérieur" in its title, it's even better. Fair value: $3 to $4.

MÂCON BLANC VILLAGES (or simply: MÂCON-VIL-LAGES) This is virtually the same wine as simple Mâcon Blanc (see). It is a substantial dry white wine, particularly recommended with poultry, pork, seafood, a good value at $2.50 to $4. Serve chilled; it is ready to drink when you buy it.

MÂCON ROUGE A reliable, tasty little red French country wine, worth looking for these days, to replace old favorite Beaujolais, growing more costly by the hour. This wine may lack some of the fresh fruitiness of Beaujolais, but at half the price, it is much more than half as good. Ready to drink upon purchase, don't keep it more than a year or two, serve at cool room temperature (65°F). Fine to accompany most ordinary fare: hamburgers, meat loaf, pasta dishes, cheese dishes, casseroles, chicken or turkey. Fair value: $2.75 to $3.75, depending on the reliability of the shipper. It is especially trustworthy if the bottle bears the name of one of these shippers: Calvet; Caves de Charnay Bellevue; Cruse; Jaboulet-Vercherre; Jouvet; Patriarche Père; Sichel; André Simon Selection; Thorin.

MADEIRA Nicotine addicts, arise and acclaim this wine, the only one in the world, other than sherry, which, say wine purists, one is allowed to drink while smoking. Madeira is an excellent, totally distinctive wine from the Portuguese island of Madeira off the west coast of Africa. Americans don't know what they're missing here in this smoky-tasting, mouth-filling, wide-ranging wine. It comes in varied form: very dry (Sercial), medium sweet (Bual), sweet (Malmsey). It ranges in color from pale straw to brown, and in price from moderate to very expensive. Gourmet cooks love Madeira: it has more culinary uses than any other wine, sherry included. It's a great additive to soups, sauces, stews. Ham and Madeira have a famous affinity. Bake your next ham in a cup or two, baste often, and eat hearty. Try to find the Verdelho (dry) type for your cooking: it's less expensive.

For evaluation of individual bottles, see under name of the shipper: Cossart and Gordon, Henriques and Henriques, etc. The only American Madeira worthy of the name is Paul Masson's (see) at a most reasonable $2.

MADERIZATION It's wine language for old age—or rather, senility. It happens only with white wines when they are past their prime. They turn rusty, musty, and flat. A brownish tinge is the telltale sign.

MADONNA A very reliable German brand name, owned by the Valckenberg family, which has owned some of the original Liebfraumilch vineyards for almost two centuries. Madonna is a guarantee of authenticity and quality, although individual bottles will vary in excellence.

Madonna Liebfraumilch, Auslese, 1967**** White Rhine wine, of special picking. Drink it now and until 1979. Serve chilled. Drink it alone (it's so good) or with innocuous tidbits. Fair value, $7.

Madonna Liebfraumilch, Auslese, 1969**** From especially selected grapes. At its best until 1978. Serve chilled. Drink it alone, it's that good. Fair value, $7.

Madonna Liebfraumilch, 1970*** This "plain" bottling —not made from specially selected grapes—is ready for immediate drinking and will keep until 1977. Fair value, $4.25.

Madonna Liebfraumilch, Auslese, 1970**** A luscious white Rhine wine, from a special picking. Drink until 1978. Serve chilled, drink it alone; it's too good to suffer from distractions. Fair value, $7.

MADRIGAL BERNKASTELER RIESLING, 1969* Fragrant white German wine, could use a little more character, but sound and enjoyable. Such delicate Moselle wines are best appreciated when drunk by themselves without interference, or with very innocent tidbits. Serve chilled. It's at the top of its form right now and will hold there until 1979. Fair value, $4.

MADRIGAL BERNKASTELER RIESLING, 1971* '71 was a very great year in the Moselle, and this wine is living testimony—wine is a living thing—to the fact. A fine bottle, especially at $4. Best to savor this wine on its own, it's so light and flowery, chilled, not icy-cold.

MADRIGAL BERNKASTELER RIESLING, 1972* '72 was not up to the '71 vintage in Germany's Moselle region, but this is a well-balanced wine for early, easy drinking. Consume within next several years. Fair value, $4.

MADRIGAL JOHANNISBERGER RIESLING, 1969* A white Rhine wine, a "regional," not from a particular vineyard, and therefore not of first quality, but good wine withal. This and all the following Madrigal wines should be served chilled; they are good enough to serve as aperitif wines, or they may accompany fish, pork, poultry, seafood. Drink soon. Fair value, $4.

MADRIGAL JOHANNIS-BERGER RIESLING, 1970 *** Drink soon—at least by 1976. Fair value, $4.

MADRIGAL JOHANNIS-BERGER RIESLING, 1972 **** Fair value, $4.

MADRIGAL NIERSTEINER DOMTAL, 1970**** A good example of a sound, fruity, well-balanced German regional wine. Fair value, $3.80.

MADRIGAL NIERSTEINER GUTES DOMTAL, 1972*** Not a super wine but a good one. At $4 or thereabouts, a fair value. At its best, 1975–1976.

MADRIGAL ZELLER SCHWARZE KATZ, 1972*** "Schwarze Katz" means "Black Cat," and he's usually on the label of this white German wine. He's nowhere to be found on this bottle, and maybe that's what makes this bottle better than the general breed of Black Cats from the village of Zell, in Germany's Moselle Valley. The wine has a nice, light floweriness, the hallmark of Moselle wines. It's still young; it will be better in a year. Serve chilled, as an aperitif wine; it's too delicate to stand up to all but the blandest —or most tasteless—of food. Fair value, $4.

MAGDELAINE, CHÂTEAU Excellent French red wine (Claret), full and soft, with great distinction and body. To accompany red meats, especially barbecued steaks, roast beef, roast turkey or chicken, lamb simply cooked. Serve at cool room temperature. How to serve it: See under BORDEAUX.

1945**** Drink now or before 1980. Air for a half hour.

1959**** Drink before 1977. Air for one hour.

1961***** Drink now—if you must—but better, lay it away for a few years; it will improve to 1980. Air for one hour, minimum.

1962**** Drink through 1976. Air for one hour.

1964**** Drink now and until 1978. Air for one to two hours.

1966**** Excellent bouquet, big in taste. Air for one to two hours; drink, 1975–1979.

1967**** You can drink it now but it will continue to improve to 1980. Air for two hours.

1968 Not recommended even as a gift.

1969**** Good wine but may be overpriced. Not ready; drink it, 1976 through 1980. Air for two or three hours.

1970***** Stash it away at least until 1978.

MAGIGAL AMONTILLADO FINO SHERRY**** Lovely medium sherry—soft but not sweet. It's the real thing—authentic Spanish sherry, a fine value at around $3.50. How to serve this wine: See under SHERRY.

MAGIGAL JEREZ CREAM SHERRY**** Rich and sweet, a luscious after-dinner wine. And a good value at $4.50.

MAGNIFICO, DEL: See DEL MAGNIFICO, RUFFINO.

MAGRICO, VINHO VERDE, BRANCO "Vinho Verde" means "Green Wine" in Portuguese, but happily this refers to the wine's age not its color. This spritzy little white (Branco) wine will tickle your fancy, tongue, and budget. Try it some hot summer evening and serve it well chilled. Fair value, $3.

MAGRICO, VINHO VERDE, TINTO** A good vivacious young red (Tinto) wine from Portugal. Its green (Verde) prickliness will go well with grilled hamburgers outdoors of a warm evening. In its light-hearted way it's good before meals, too. This is one of those exceptional red wines that should be slightly chilled. Fair value, $3.

MAISON MARTINEAU CHAMPAGNE Voilà, it might sound French, but it's pure American: Maison Martineau means "the House of Martin," San Martin, that is, the huge California winery. This is their "second line" of sparkling wines. (The first line is bottled directly under the name San Martin.) Dollar for dollar, these Maison Martineau wines may be the better buy. They're pretty average, but they are also $1.50 less than the San Martins. The standard "flavors" are made: Cold Duck **, Extra Dry ***, Pink **, Sparkling Burgundy ***. Fair value, $3.25.

MALARTIC-LAGRAVIÈRE, CHÂTEAU (or: CHÂTEAU LAGRAVIÈRE) This is a good big red French wine which should not be extravagantly priced, as this château is in the Graves region of Bordeaux, lately fallen out of favor with the public—for no good reason. Officially, Château Malartic is not highly rated, but it is a fine and powerful wine, well worth looking for. Serve it at cool room temperature. The best vintages deserve to be lovingly savored on their own, or with Cheddar or Camembert.

*1950***** Full-bodied with a touch of sweetness. At the top of its ambit right now, but don't keep it more than a year or two.

*1959***** At its peak and will hold there until 1979.

*1961****** A very interesting and complex wine. Serve it on some momentous occasion.

*1962**** Not quite mature and will hold for a decade.

*1964**** Nice touch of sweetness. Ready from 1975 on.

*1966***** Will be great if you can resist drinking it now. Lay it down, at least until 1976. Make your first tasting July 4, 1976, our national bicentennial.

*1967*** Despite a generally good year, this wine is not up to standard. Not recommended.

*1968*** A light wine, rather pleasant. It's ready when you buy it, don't hold it.

*1969*** Still young; will be ready starting in 1976.

*1970**** Will be an excellent bottle when ready—starting in 1980 until 1990. Wherefore, a good wine to lay down, if you can find it reasonably priced, say $5 or $6.

MALBEC, CHÂTEAU, 1966 *** A sound, round red wine from one of the lesser Châteaux of Bordeaux (France). It is priced accordingly. It's not a masterpiece, but it's an excellent value at $3. This wine, at cool room temperature (65°, F), will improve your grilled hamburgers or chicken. It's just now ready for drinking and will hold at least until 1978. How to serve it: See under BORDEAUX.

*1970*** Smooth, good flavor; just reaching its peak and will hold until 1978.

MALCONSORTS, LES (or: AUX MALCONSORTS, or simply: MALCONSORTS) A truly great red Burgundy (French) wine, as expensive as it is rare. The name Vosne-Romanée should appear in bold print on the label; this is the district, one of the finest in all of France, in the heart of Burgundy. Save this splendid wine for Thanksgiving, Christmas, or an important anniversary, or your most spectacular gourmet dinner. It would be a sacrilege to serve this wine with every-day provender. Air one hour, serve at cool room temper-ature.

1959**** Robust, rich, now at its splendid peak. Drink with-in next four years. Fair value, $18.

1966**** Fair value, $16.

1967**** A poor year gen-erally, but some good wines were made, and this is one of them. A big wine, you can al-most chew it. Good value at $8.

1968 Not recommended. Di-saster.

1969**** Not quite ready; hold for one or two years. Fair value, sorry, $16.

MALESCOT-SAINT-EXU-PÉRY, CHÂTEAU This is a delicate, elegant, reliable red wine from one of the relatively high-ranked châteaux of Bor-deaux (France). It usually lives up to its ranking and is often a good value, perhaps because its forbidding hyphenated name frightens Americans away. Serve it at cool room temperature, with the finer cuts of beef, with game, lamb (simply cooked), chicken, goose, quail, partridge, or with salmon. Air at least one hour (especially the younger bottles).

1959**** Now at its best, this wine will remain in excel-lent form until 1980.

1960**** Delicious wine, but drink it soon.

1961***** This won't be ready until at least 1977, but you'll have a beauty then. Save it for some grandiloquent occa-sion and savor it in isolation—it, not you, in isolation—*sans* food, or with simple cheeses.

Unfortunately, '61 has become such an illustrious vintage that prices are frightfully exagger-ated and you probably won't find this wine for less than $20.

1962***** As good as the '61 and you may find it at half the price. Ready to drink and will hold through 1976.

1964**** Ready now; be sure to drink it before '78. Fair value, $8.

1966**** Fruity, good bou-quet, but not yet ready. Delay drinking until 1976 to 1980. Fair value, $9.

1967**** Ready now. Fair value, $7.

1969*** Rather light, it's ready for immediate drinking and will hold until 1978.

1970****—It's going to be soft and flavorful. Drink it, 1978 on.

MALLERET, CHÂTEAU DE Be careful here: there is also a Château Malleret, without the "de"; it is not nearly as good.

1964, 1966, 1967 This is one of the lesser châteaux of Bor-deaux (France). It is classed as *bourgeois*, but it's a good, handy little red wine—and not always so little at that. All three vintages are good drink-ing now and will remain so through 1978. It is still reason-ably priced, a good value at $4 to $5. Serve this at cool room temperature with any red meat or with poultry.

MALMSEY The sweetest type of Portuguese Madeira wine (see). This is a dessert wine and a fine one. One expert has said, with some hyperbole, that this wine, in the glory of old age, can claim to be the very finest wine in the world. It has a deeply satisfying, nutty flavor. Serve your Malmsey Madeira after a substantial meal, with the dessert. Or with a between-the-meals snack; that's the way our Victorian forbears cherished it. On the label disregard such words as "fine" or "special," it's all Malmsey. For evaluation of individual bottles, see under the name of the shipper: Henriques & Henriques, Leacock, etc.

MALVASIA BIANCA This is a white dessert wine made by only two California wineries: Beringer Malvasia Bianca, ******** and Novitiate Dry Malvasia, ******* (see both). A vaguely similar wine is Paul Masson's Madeira (see). San Martin makes a sparkling Malvasia, ******* (see). See also Muscat de Frontignan, a similar wine.

MANZANILLA: A type of sherry. For general information, see SHERRY. For a particular bottle, see under the name of the producer.

MARBUZET, CHÂTEAU DE Officially this is a *bourgeois* red wine, but connoisseurs know better. This Bordeaux (France) château has everything going for it: choice location, exposure to sun, excellent gravelly soil, good grape stock. Look for it. Serve at cool room temperature, goes well with all red meats, or with poultry, veal, pork. Air one hour.

1962**** Now at its peak and will hold at least until 1976.

1966*** Strong wine, slow-maturing. Now ready.

1967*** Full-flavored, a good value at $5 and $6. Not ready—taste it first in '76.

"MARCELLE, LA": See CHAPOUTIER TAVEL VIN ROSÉ.

MARCHANT, HENRI: See HENRI MARCHANT.

MARCOBRUNNER (or: ERBACHER MARKOBRUNN) A distinguished white Rhine wine noted for its full flavor, spiciness, and perfect balance. It goes well with fish, pork, poultry, seafood, and especially with salmon and other full-flavored fish, particularly if prepared with a rich sauce. Also recommended, the experts say, with venison, wild boar (from the supermarket?), almost all kinds of vegetables. But best fun of all, drink it by itself, chilled.

1921 Trockenbeerenauslese, Staatsweinguter—Classic Beyond compare. This wine, like the preceding, was made from carefully selected "berries": the highest type of German wine, one of the greatest sweet wines in the world. Drink it alone—without distraction, well chilled. A priceless bottle of wine.

1964 Spätlese, Cabinet, Fr. Langwerth von Simmern*** Now at its peak and will hold there through 1976. Fair value, $7.

1964 Cabinet Beerenauslese, Fr. Langwerth von Simmern*** Wholly luscious wine, special late picking. Drink now or until 1980. Too fine a wine to drink with food of this earth. Don't know if it's *fair*, but this will cost you at least $50. Serve well chilled.

1966 Auslese Cabinet, Fr. Langwerth von Simmern*** Drink now and through 1976. Serve well chilled. Drink it by itself or with fresh fruit. Fair value, $8.

1967 Trockenbeerenauslese Cabinet, Fr. Langwerth von Simmern—Near-Classic Superb wine, can be drunk now, but will continue to improve or at least remain at its present glorious peak for another twenty years or more. May be drunk with fresh fruit or a sweet dessert, but it is so spectacular that it is best drunk alone. Fair value, $30.

1970 Feine Spätlese, Schloss

Schonborn*** Drink before 1977.

1971 Spätlese, State Domain *** Smooth, lovely; ready for present drinking and will keep at least until 1980. Fair value, $6 to $7.

MARGAUX A good reliable red Bordeaux (French) wine. It is noted for its bouquet and delicacy. There is also a very famous Château Margaux wine. This "plain" Margaux will not have the word "Château" on the label. It is, by a large measure, the lesser of the two wines, but can be very good. Ideal to accompany beef or poultry simply cooked; also light-flavored game and mild cheeses. Air at least one hour and serve at cool room temperature.

Margaux, Château One of the most famous and best red wines (Claret) in the world. This expensive Bordeaux (French) wine is noted for its delicacy, exquisite bouquet, and longevity. It may be savored alone, it is so gorgeous, or with Camembert, Brie, or Cheddar. It would also be an excellent accompaniment for finer cuts of beef, or game, lamb, or goose.

The price of famous Clarets such as this one has risen astronomically in recent years, in large measure because a few Americans with more money than wine appreciation have been willing to pay ridiculous sums, not for the contents of the bottle, but for the label on the bottle. Prices listed below are *fair* prices—what the wines are actually worth. Unhappily, you may not be able to buy them even at these inflated prices.

1887**** This was only an average year, yet this wine is still elegant. If it has lasted this long, then drink it anytime within the next century or two! If it contains sediment, stand it upright for twenty-four hours, then decant.

1888**** Though only a mediocre year, the wine is excellent. Drink it anytime before the Parousia! If it contains sediment, stand it upright for twenty-four hours, then decant.

1893—Classic Wine of great distinction, incredibly rich. Drink now or hold until whenever. Such excellence deserves a special ceremony! If sediment has formed, decant! Fair value (unfortunately), $100.

1900—Near-Classic Drink now or hold without fear of deterioration. If sediment is present, stand it upright for twenty-four hours, then decant. Fair value, $30.

1906—Near-Classic Some have considered this the best Margaux ever. It is in perfect condition and should last many more years. Drink now or unto eternity. If sediment is present, decant, then drink it by itself. Don't linger over this wine; it fades quickly. Consume it within a half hour or so—force yourself! Fair value, $50.

1918**** A great year; the wine has high distinction and breed. If sediment is present, stand it upright for twenty-four hours, then decant. Drink it now or within the decade. Fair value, $20.

1920 Originally ***** This wine may be gone or at least past its prime; today, a calculated risk. Drink immediately. If sediment is present, decant. Fair value, if you're a gambling man . . . well, it went at auction for $11 in 1971 and for $125 in 1973!

1924—Near-Classic Drink it now—or whenever. Enjoy it on

its own, or with some cheese tidbits. If sediment is present, decant. Fair value, $45.

1928—Near-Classic Perfect balance, great delicacy. Drink it now, preferably without accompaniment. If sediment is present, decant. Fair value, $40 to $50. A magnum sold at auction in 1973 for $900!

1929—Classic Mellow, long on palate. Some bottles, however, may be past prime; one takes this chance. Drink it now, preferably on its own. Air one hour. Fair value, $50.

1934—Near-Classic Beautiful, smooth, great elegance. Some have said, the greatest Claret ever. Drink it soon—it may be beginning to fade. Air for a half hour. Fair value, $40.

1937***** Drink now, as it may be beginning to fade. Deserves to be savored alone or with tidbits. Air one hour. Fair value, $40, though some dupe paid $500 for a bottle in 1972.

1943*** The best Margaux of the war years, but may already be past its prime; it will not keep. Air one hour. Fair value, $12.

1945*** A bit austere, lacks fruitiness. Air one hour. Not recommended at $35 or more.

1947—Near-Classic Universally acclaimed; may be just beginning to fade; consume soon. Air one hour. Savor it without accompaniment. Fair value, $30.

1949—Near-Classic Now at peak and may not hold there much longer. Enjoy it by itself with cheese or fresh fruit. Air one hour. A good value at $30.

1950—Near-Classic Drink now and it will keep another five or ten years. Air one hour. Enjoy it by itself, without accompaniment or distraction. Excellent value at $25.

1952**** This will be a great wine; it is still young. Try it beginning in 1980. Then air it one to two hours. Fair value, $25.

1953—Near-Classic It has everything. Now at its peak. Fair value, $35.

1954—Not recommended.

1955—Not recommended.

1956—Not recommended.

1957***** Soft and lovely wine, now at its peak and will hold until 1978. Fair value, $20.

1958*** Never great, this wine is now past its prime. If you find it for $5, you might try it. Air one hour.

1959—Classic A huge wine, very agreeable now and will improve at least until 1981. Air two to three hours. Shame to detract from this wine with accompanying food. Fair value, $35 to $50.

1960***** This vintage has been underrated. Drink it now, and air fifteen to thirty minutes. Fair value, $20.

1961—Classic Magnificent wine with an extremely high reputation. It's just now ready and will be at its best until 1985. Air two hours. At the price you'll want to fondle this wine, savor it on its own—carefully and lovingly. Fair value, $50.

1962***** Just now reaching its best, will hold until 1980. Air two hours. Fair value, to $25.

1963—Not recommended.

1964**** Violet-scented, with lingering taste. Just beginning to be ready. Drink, 1975 through 1978. Air two hours. Fair value, $20.

1966***** Elegant, aristocratic wine, not yet ready. Drink it 1976 to 1980. Air two hours. Fair value, $25.

1967***** Not quite ready; keep it until 1976. Air two hours. Fair value, $20.

1968*** A decent little wine despite a generally poor vintage. Drink through 1975. Air two hours. Fair value, $5.

1969***** Looking beautiful at this point, though not ready. Drink, 1976 through 1983. Fair value, $20.

1970 Temperamental and unpredictable at this point—it's somewhere between * and Classic status! It's presently fetching around $35, which is either a steal or a mammoth rip-off!

1971 It's already on the market and it augureth well, but lacking a functional crystal ball, be slow to purchase, especially at $40 per!

MARQUÉS DE MURRIETA **** Excellent red wine of Spain (some good whites are also made), the friendly rival of the Marques de Riscal (see). Incidentally, the bold Ygay on the label is the name of the town, in the Rioja district, where the *bodega* is located. The red is soft and fruity, a good value at around $4. Murrieta's "top of the line" is their Castillo Ygay, a very old red wine, one of the Rioja's finest. One authority said of the '42 that he ran out of superlatives on it. How to serve it: See under RIOJA.

MARQUÉS DE RISCAL One of Spain's finest red table wines, often referred to simply as Riscal, and frequently compared with another excellent Spanish wine, Marqués de Murrieta. Spaniards love to argue about the relative merits of the two "Marquis." Riscal is a soft, fruity, full-bodied wine, a bit more expensive than most Rioja wines, ca. $4 for current vintages. It is said to be more like a French Bordeaux than any other Spanish wine. How to serve it: See under RIOJA. Some vintages:

1922: They say it's impeccable—if findable, *****

1961: ****

1967: ****—At its best: 1975–1980.

1968: **—Drink now and through 1978.

1969: ****—At its best, late '75 on.

MARQUIS-D'ALESME-BECKER, CHÂTEAU (or simply: CHÂTEAU MARQUIS-D'ALESME) This château, smack in the middle of the great Margaux region of Bordeaux (France), has a very fine location, and the delicate red wines generally show it. Goes well with light meats (veal, pork) and all kinds of fowl. The best bottles deserve to be sipped gracefully on their own merits or with bits of bread and cheese. Serve at cool room temperature, to 68°F.

1955**** Drink it now; this wine will not hold.

1958*** Drink soon, this wine is about to begin declining. Air one hour.

1962**** Floral over- and under-tones here; air it one hour. Fair value, $8. Good drinking right now and will hold until 1977.

1967**** Beginning to be ready and will keep. Fair value, $6.

1970**** A good wine to lay down, it's already looking good and may well rise to *****. A good value at $6.50.

MARQUIS-DE-TERME, CHÂTEAU This is a very well-tended vineyard in the heart of the Margaux region of Bordeaux (France). Officially it has a middle rating, and produces consistently good red wines—at times, even great ones. Drink with beef, lamb, chicken, veal, pork. Serve at cool room temperature. Air two hours.

MARQUISAT BEAUJOLAIS BLANC Marquisat is a brand name owned by the French wine firm of Pasquier Desvignes—the Marquis is there on the label in his top hat—and it's a name you can trust in Beaujolais wines. What's more, these are excellent values in these days when there is rarely a good value to be had in French wines. This white Beaujolais is invariably excellent, vintage after vintage. The 1969, 1970, and 1971 are all ****. How to serve it: See under BEAUJOLAIS BLANC.

MARQUISAT BEAUJOLAIS-VILLAGES**** Marquisat is a trusted name in Beaujolais wines, and this wine, year after year, shows you why. From 1969 through 1972, there has not been a poor bottle among them. A good value at $3.50 to $4. How to serve it: See under BEAUJOLAIS.

MARSALA Italy's best-known fortified wine, imported, like Mafiosi, from the Island of Sicily. It vaguely resembles sherry, has an unusual smoky or burnt flavor, and is not everyone's cup of wine. It comes in various grades of sweetness; the label will tell you whether it's a sweet, medium, or dry wine. The driest is Marsala Vergine (Virgin Marsala). It goes great with soup. Or try it as an aperitif. Special Marsala comes with all sorts of added flavorings: egg yolks (zabaglione), almonds, even quinine. The sweet or Cream Marsala makes a marvelous after-dinner drink and you can even add chipped ice to it or slosh it over vanilla ice cream.

If you buy a bottle of Marsala and don't like the unusual flavor, nothing's lost—use it as an additive to your soups. It can transform your lowly broth to empyrean heights. Or use it to baste your fresh or smoked ham. It's also good accompaniment for any rich food.

For evaluation of individual bottles, see under the brand name: Florio, Sicilian Gold, etc.

MARTIN RAY: See RAY, MARTIN.

(LOUIS M.) MARTINI WINERY (St. Helena, Calif.) Louis Martini is one of the largest producers of fine wines in California. The wines are well made, moderately priced, very reliable. Some, indeed, are quite extraordinary. At the price of oversimplification, one may say that their reds are better than their whites. Martini's most famous vineyard is Monte Rosso, high up in the hills—hence the word "Mountain" on their labels.

Barbera A somewhat heavy, fairly tart red wine, made from the Barbera grape. Usually a good value, it is ideal with Italian food or foods with rich or spicy sauces; also goes well with game, beef, goose, duck. Serve at cool room temperature.

*1956 Private Reserve****** Drink this within the next several years. Air it one hour. Fair value, $10.

*1961 Private Reserve**** Not quite as flavorful as one might hope, but good. Drink it now or until 1980. Air one hour. Fair value, $7.

*1962, 1964****** Drink now or until 1980. Air one hour. Fair value, $7.

*1965*** Rather tart and

acidic, but if you must, drink it now and until 1980. Air one hour.

1966**** One of the best Barberas you're likely to find. Drink it now or until 1980. Air one hour.

1967*** Drink now and until 1980. Air one hour.

1968**** Hearty wine, mouth-filling; air it two hours. It's ready now and will hold well until 1980. Excellent value at $4 to $5.

1969*** Soft, engaging wine, goes down good. Air one hour; preprandial sipping or with dinner. Good value at $3.

1970****

Cabernet Sauvignon Cabernet Sauvignon, the "informing" grape of the great French Clarets, is California's finest red wine, and it is one of Martini's very best. The winery is particularly proud of this wine and considers it their most interesting one. It is very consistent, has good flavor and bouquet. Goes well with meats, roasts, game, cheese.

1947***** Drink soon—some say it's already begun to fade.

1951, 1952**** At their best but don't keep these much longer.

1955 Private Reserve**** Drink now and until 1990, or even beyond. Air one hour. So good it should only be drunk with mild cheeses, or by itself. Fair value, $25.

1957 Private Reserve*** Now at its peak; don't hold this one. Air one to two hours; enjoy it with cheese or simply prepared red meat. Fair value, $20.

1958 Private Reserve Not recommended. For some reason this wine is gone.

1959**** Mouth-filling, pow-

erful. Can be enjoyed now but will soften and improve until the year 2000. Air one hour. Fair value, $10.

1960 Special Selection***** Best drinking, now and until 1990.

1961**** Full of taste, mature. Drink now or until 1990. Air two to three hours. Fair value, $8.

1962**** Drink now and until 1990. Air two to three hours. Fair value, $8.

1963**** Fruity, flavorful. Now drinkable but will improve immensely with time. Try it beginning in 1980. Fair value, $7.

1964**** Big and robust, lots of flavor. Just beginning to be ready; drink it within next twenty years. Air two to three hours. Fair value, $6.50.

1964 Special Selection**** Not quite ready—give it a year or two, and then drink it anytime this century. Air two to three hours. Fair value, $8.

1965**** Not quite ready. Give it at least two more years and it will remain at its peak at least until 1980. Air two to three hours.

1966**** Best drinking, 1975 through 1985. The Private Reserve rates *****. Air three to four hours. A good value at $7.

1967*** Drink 1975 through 1985. Air three to four hours. Fair value, $6.

1968** to ***** (see text) A controversial wine. Some say it's an average Cabernet and should be consumed right now. Others say this is an exceptional wine and it won't be at its best until 1978. On balance: final (?), definitive (?), infallible (?) assessment: **** (?), with best drinking (?), 1976 (?) through 1985 (?).

1969*** Fruity and tasty, it
will be better if you hold it
until 1976. It may well make
**** by late 70s. Good value
at $3.50.

1970***

1971 Hesitantly: ***, no
more.

Chablis, Mountain: See
MOUNTAIN CHABLIS.

Chardonnay: See PINOT
CHARDONNAY.

Chenin Blanc: See DRY
CHENIN BLANC.

Chianti, Mountain: See
MOUNTAIN CHIANTI.

Claret, Mountain: See
MOUNTAIN CLARET.

Dry Chenin Blanc A delicate soft wine with an exceptional bouquet. Goes best with
seafood, fowl, or light meat
such as veal or pork. Serve
chilled. Current vintages sell
for around $2.85.

1967** Done gone and departed.

1968** Quite dry, fresh, and
fruity. Drink it now before it
leaves you.

1969, 1970, 1971** Drink
now.

1972, 1973***

Dry Sauterne** Fair wine,
rather undistinguished; not very
flavorful. Serve chilled. Ready
for immediate drinking when
purchased. It will falter badly
after four years or so. Fair value, $2.25.

Dry Sémillon** You may
still find this wine around
though it's been discontinued
for some time now. Dry, crisp
white wine, well made. Chill,
serve with light foods. Don't
hold it. Fair value, $2 to $2.25.

Dry Sherry*** Aperitif
wine, can be served slightly
chilled, a good value at $2.85.

Folle Blanche Martini is the
only winery making this wine.
It is light-bodied, delicate, a

trifle tart. It goes especially well
with fish, seafood, chicken, light
meats. It's ready to drink when
you buy it. Serve it chilled.
Fair value, $2.25.

1966** Probably gone by
now. Don't take a chance.

1967** Drink immediately,
chilled. Might improve with
thirty minutes' air.

1968, 1969, 1970, 1971, 1972
*** Air these good wines fif-
teen to thirty minutes.

Gamay Rosé*** For lovers
of rosé wines this is worth
searching out. An exceptionally
well-made wine: light-bodied,
relatively dry, pleasant, fruity.
It has more character than
most rosés and compares well
with the more expensive Portuguese rosés such as Mateus and
Lancers. An excellent value at
less than $3. Serve it chilled.
It is ready to drink when purchased, drink it within a year.
Rosés are "universal" wines,
going well with almost any
food, and this wine would be
especially welcome on a picnic,
at an outdoor luncheon, or
simply savored on a hot summer day. Recent vintages, 1970,
1971, 1972, 1973, have been
consistently good.

Gewürz Traminer Some say
that this is Martini's most consistently successful wine, and
their best. It is pleasantly spicy,
slightly aromatic, very reliable.
Splendid accompaniment for
lobster, frog legs, escargots,
small game, rabbit, curry dishes.
Also makes a beguiling aperitif.
Serve it chilled. A good value
at around $3.65.

1969*** Drink by the end
of 1975.

1970** On the dry side.
Drink by the end of 1975.

1971**** Perfumed, delightful. Before dinner or with dinner. Will hold until 1976.

1972*** Before dinner or with dinner. Will hold until 1977.

Johannisberg Riesling (White Riesling) A fine wine, one of the best of California's Rhine-type wines. Fruity, fresh, with a fragrant aroma. Splendid with fish, shellfish, turkey (roast, smoked), quail, veal, rabbit. Serve chilled. Ready to drink when you buy it, and for maximum freshness drink it within two years. Fair value, $3.50 to $3.80.

1966, 1967** Drink immediately.

1968** A touch of woodiness. Drink now.

1969**** This wine is big enough to stand by itself; sip it pensively and lovingly, in your trellised veranda (or grubby kitchen). An excellent value.

1970**

1971, 1972***

Moscato Amabile** Catch it if you can find it. This sweet dessert wine is Martini's only sparkling wine, and it's a good one. In limited production, it's usually available only at the winery, or in a few selected restaurants. It's worth looking for, especially if you dig the Muscat flavor. Keep it refrigerated, as it's very unstable, and don't hold it too long. Serve well chilled, after dinner with or without dessert. Fair value, $3.90.

Mountain Burgundy*** Martini considers this their finest generic red wine. It is dry, full-bodied, rather tart. Best to air this wine: try two to three hours. It is ready to be drunk immediately upon purchase, should be served at cool room temperature. It can accompany any red meat, and is especially suited to beef, game, ham-burger, cheese dishes. Fair value, $2.25.

Mountain Chablis*** An extraordinarily good wine considering its price. It has true Chablis flavor—something rather unusual with California Chablis! Serve chilled, not necessary to air. Very good with seafood, chicken, veal. Very good value at $2.25 to $2.50.

Mountain Chianti** Light, pleasant red table wine, but perhaps too light. For 25¢ more, prefer the Mountain Burgundy—or, at 25¢ less, the Mountain Red.

Mountain Claret** A rather light red wine, fairly flavorful, for everyday consumption. It is ready for drinking upon purchase, and remains so for up to four years. Serve it at room temperature, no airing necessary. It is a good value at ca. $2.25. It can be served with any red meat, but is especially suited for stews, meat loaf, casseroles of all kinds, cheese dishes.

Mountain Red*** At ca. $1.95 this may be one of the best wine buys in the world. It is strictly *vin ordinaire*, very dry, quite fruity. Drink it immediately upon purchase or within the following four years. Air the wine one to two hours, and enjoy it with beef, venison, elk, Italian dishes, hamburgers.

Mountain White*** At $1.95 or even less, this may well be one of the best wine buys in the world. A very dry wine, not ordinarily to be drunk by itself, but to accompany a meal. Can be drunk immediately upon purchase and for the next year or so. Do not hold it indefinitely; it will turn. Serve chilled. Especially good accompaniment for fish, shrimp, poultry, veal, pork, omelettes.

Pinot Chardonnay Chardonnay is the best white table wine made in the U.S., but Martini's product is in no way superior, though at its best it can be rich and full of flavor. Serve it well chilled, but not iced. Makes an admirable companion to poultry or delicate fish course. A good bottle can be enjoyed on its own merits, *sans* food accompaniment.

1967*** There were two bottlings of this wine, a "plain" and a Private Reserve, which will cost you an extra dollar. It's not that much better. Stick with the "plain," a good value at $3.50. Drink immediately.

1968**** Two bottlings of this wine, a "plain" and a Private Reserve. Prefer the "plain," at more than a dollar's saving. They're both good wines. Consume soon.

1969**

1970, 1971, 1972***

Pinot Noir Pinot Noir is the finest Burgundy-type red wine produced by California, and Martini makes one of the best: soft, smooth, almost velvety. Some claim that this is Martini's best wine. Air it about an hour and serve at cool room temperature. In especially good years it is available as Special Selection or Private Reserve. At its best when served with roasts, steaks, game, cheese.

Nonvintage Private Reserve **** Ready to drink when purchased and will keep for at least five years. Air thirty to sixty minutes. Fair value, $7.

1957**** Drink immediately; at its peak. Fair value, if you can find it, $12.

1958 Private Reserve**** Drink immediately. Fair value, $11.

1959**** Drink immediately. Fair value, $6.

1962 Special Selection**** Smooth, mouth-filling. Consume within next year or two.

1965 Private Reserve*** Not up to Private Reserve standards. If sediment is present, stand bottle upright for twenty-four hours, then decant. Now at its peak, will not improve.

1965 Special Selection**** Best drinking, 1975–1977. Fair value, $5.50.

1966*** The Private Reserve is not worth the extra $1.50 over the "regular." The Special Selection merits ****, will be at its best, 1976 through 1979. The "regular" is good drinking now and through 1976.

1967*** Can be drunk now, through 1978.

1968*** Good drinking now and will hold through the 70s. Current vintages sell for $3.50 to $3.80.

1969**** Big lovely wine, almost sweet. At its best, 1975–1980. Fair value, $3.50.

1970*** Best drinking, 1975 through 1977.

1971**** Will be at its best, 1976–1980.

Port, Tawny: See TAWNY PORT.

Rhine Wine** A light, fragrant, everyday white wine. It has no special distinction, but it is a fair value at ca. $2.25. Drink it when purchased and don't hold it more than a year or two. Try it with fish, chicken, clams, cheese dishes. Serve chilled.

Riesling (Sylvaner) An average white Rhine-type wine, light, dry, undistinguished. It does not have the character of Martini's Johannisberg Riesling, but it is also considerably less expensive. Goes well with prawns, clams, fish, chicken; serve chilled. Fair value, $2.25 to $2.50.

1968, 1969** Quite dry, pleasant. Drink now, don't keep.

1970, 1971, 1972** Drink soon, will keep through 1975.

Sweet Sherry*** Serve slightly chilled, with dessert. Fair value, $2.85 to $3.25.

Sylvaner: See RIESLING (SYL-VANER).

Tawny Port*** Port-sipping has become a lost art in the U.S. The more's the pity when one has inexpensive Ports such as this, at $2.85 to $3.25, a good value.

Zinfandel Many consider this dry medium-bodied red wine the best ever made from this grape. It is not as light and tart as some California Zinfandels and can be rough if not properly aged. At its best it will have the natural tangi-ness of the Zinfandel grape. Goes especially well with veal, lamb, game, hamburger, tongue, Italian dishes, especially pizza. In particularly fine years it is available in special bottling as Private Reserve, usually a very fine wine. Serve at cool room temperature.

1955 Private Reserve**** Probably still in good shape. Fair value, $8.

1956 Private Reserve and Special Selection**** Still in good condition. Fair value, $7.50.

1960 Private Reserve*** Mellow and pleasant. Drink immediately. Fair value, $6.

1962**** Mellow, smooth, now at its peak and will hold there for several years. Good value at $5.

1962 Private Reserve**** Delightful wine, now at its peak and will hold for at least another three years. Fair value, $6.50.

1963**** Now at its best but may not last. Drink it now.

1965*** At its peak; drink it now, don't hold it. Air one hour.

1966*** At its best and will hold for several years. Air one to two hours. Perfect with cheese. The Special Selection is disappointing, not worth $6.

1967*** Can drink it now but will improve through the 70s. Air it one hour.

1968**** Robust, complex. You can drink it now or lay it down; it will continue to im-prove during the 70s. Serve it with some savory lasagne, pizza, or with steaks, roast prime ribs, grilled hamburgers. Or savor it for its own sake, without food.

1969*** Drink any time be-fore 1982. Perfect for Italian food or spicy dishes.

1970**** Good drinking now and well into the 80s. Very good value at $2.50 to $3.

1971**** Will be at its best, 1976–1978.

MASSON, PAUL, VINE-YARDS (Saratoga and San Francisco, Calif.) Masson probably produces more pre-mium wines than anybody in the world—it is said the winery loses some 500 bottles of wine daily by evaporation. But mass production is not an unmiti-gated blessing, especially in winemaking. By definition, mass-produced goods are of standard, average quality—so with Masson wines. They don't make any *poor* wines, but neither do they make any *great* ones, nor even thus far many excellent ones. These are re-liable, average wines—if that's damning with faint praise, so be it. All Masson wines are ready to drink when you buy them, and will keep a year or two. Only a few (individually noted, below) improve with age.

Baroque*** A new wine, a new name: both invented by Masson. "Baroque" doesn't exactly describe the wine, though; "Contemporary American" would be more like it: simple, satisfying wine, made to American tastes. It should be everybody's favorite, with its softness and touch of sweetness. Ready to drink when you buy it, it won't improve in the bottle. To accompany beef, lamb, hamburger, cheese dishes, pasta. Good value at $2.25.

Burgundy*** A light, easy-drinking, very slightly sweet red wine, "classic" California jug Burgundy.

Cabernet Sauvignon*** It's generally agreed that Cabernet Sauvignon is California's best red wine. It's a little more expensive than most other reds and usually worth it. For the price, $3.50, Masson's is about as good as any, better than many. Recent bottlings have been particularly good, delightfully flavorful, touching ****. This wine is ready to drink when you buy it and will improve in the bottle for a year or two. Serve it at cool room temperature with one of your more ambitious culinary feats.

Cabernet Sauvignon, Pinnacles Selection, No. 843*** This wine was given more TLC than the preceding "plain" Cabernet, and it was aged longer. But one wonders if the wine really appreciated all that extra solicitude. It's a good wine, all right, but not that much better than the "straight," above, especially considering the additional $1.50 asked for it. It will improve with a few additional years of bottle age.

Cabernet Sauvignon, Pinnacles Selection, No. 943**** A blend of the '69 and '70 vintages, will be at its best, 1977–1985.

Chablis** No better and no worse than the vast bulk of California Chablis, none of which are Chablis, of course—that comes only from France. But this kind of light innocent white wine serves a purpose in providing a simple wine for casual sipping or to bolster a luncheon sandwich. Let it breathe a few minutes before serving. Fair value, $2.

Champagne, Brut*** In general Masson's Champagnes are better than their table wines. This is the driest they make, and it's quite good, sprightly, rather austere. For a quality Champagne it's reasonably priced at $5. California Champagnes taste a little different from their French counterparts, but the best are very valid in their own right. Here's proof patent.

Champagne, Extra Dry**** Another tasty Champagne by Masson, slightly sweeter than the Brut (above), and a better wine. There's a little earthiness in the taste, but that's not necessarily a fault: it's a tasty earthiness! At $5 this is a good value and better than most California Champagnes at the same price. Traditionally Champagne may accompany any food, at any time—but a light, delicate wine such as this is best appreciated when savored on its own, before dinner or after. *Sans aliments*.

Chardonnay: See PINOT CHARDONNAY.

Chenin Blanc*** You'll like this wine—it's a 99 percent certainty. Even novice wine drinkers find this sprightly little white wine a delight. Lots of California wineries make Chenin Blanc, and Masson's is as good as most, and cheaper than many. It's distinctive enough to be savored in leisurely fashion before dinner, or with fresh fruit and nuts, after dinner. Serve chilled. Fair value, $2.50.

Crackling Rosé** This pretty, very bubbly pink wine will appeal to most Americans, and it is a refreshing little beverage. Seasoned wine lovers may not be so impressed, as the wine lacks true character. On the sweet side, just right for a summer luncheon on the veranda for non-wine drinkers, and the price is appealing: ca. $3. Consume within a year or so of purchase.

Dry Sauterne** A rather ordinary jug wine, cheap (ca. $4 a half-gallon), but for a little more money, the Chenin Blanc (above) is a much better wine. Serve chilled, with light foods.

Emerald Dry**** The winery once said that this was their most interesting wine— not necessarily their best. Possibly it's both. It's interesting, for it is another one of Masson's inventions, made from a unique California grape: intriguing, piquant wine, with a touch of sweetness and a fragrant bouquet. Serve chilled, with light foods, especially poultry or seafood. It has enough character to make a good aperitif wine. An excellent value at $2.30.

Gamay Beaujolais*** Fresh young red wine, drink it lightly, freshly, young. Sip it as you nibble on cheese or serve it with your grilled hamburgers. Fair value, $3.

Johannisberg Riesling** This is one of Masson's newest efforts but it is not one of their most successful. A white German-type wine, average at best.

It sells around $3.25 but you'd be better advised investing in a $3.50 bottle of German Rhine. A special bottling labeled Pinnacles Estate, Cuvée 972 is a little better but unworth the $4.50 asking price.

Madeira*** Masson is one of the very few California wineries that makes this before-dinner Portuguese-style wine. Masson's product really isn't very good, but at $2, one mustn't be too fussy. Back in Revolutionary days the genteel art of sipping Madeira was an honored American custom—one that sorely needs resuscitating. Madeira is also a great adjunct to good cooking—it improves all manner of foods: soups, sauces, gravies, meat dishes, hearty casseroles.

Old Rare Sherry: See SHERRY.

Pink*** Simply named and simply good. Especially considering the price, ca. $2. Has a sweet edge. Air it one hour and serve chilled. As with all rosés, it can be served with any food. But if you prefer your rosé on the dry side, try Vin Rosé Sec.

Pink Champagne*** Americans drink more pink wine than anybody in the world— some of it pretty execrable stuff. This is one of the better of the pinkish brews; it's rather on the sweet side, but it has some body and is most pleasant. Serve well chilled, before or after dinner. Fair value, $5.

Pinot Blanc*** This grape usually produces a better-than-average, crisp, dry white wine in California, and Masson's version is a good example. Fair value, $3.

Pinot Chardonnay** This dry white wine has not fared well in recent blind tastings. It lacks depth and character. Not a good value at $3.50 or more. A special Pinnacles Selection, Cuvée 951, at $4 is higher in price, not in quality.

Pinot Noir** This red wine can be, and often is, one of California's finest. But Masson's version lacks depth of flavor; it's light and soft, but so is water. Hyperbole of the year may be the winery's claim that this wine has "unabashed gusto." Like water. Fair value, $3.10.

Pinot Noir, Pinnacles Selection, Cuvée 824**** Quite an improvement over the preceding, from grapes grown in Masson's Pinnacles Vineyards, Monterey County. This wine has a rich and heady aroma, a "sophisticated medley of flavors," says one expert. Serve at cool room temperature with any good hearty meal. Fair value, $3. Regrettable, long since sold out at the winery.

Port*** Masson makes good Port in a half dozen varieties. The best of them is their Rare Souzao Port, mellow and heartwarming, selling for ca. $3: a Port you can serve proudly with dessert or over cigars, or on its own at 11.00 A.M., or whenever. Also commendable: Tawny Port and Rich Ruby Port.

Rare Cream Sherry: See SHERRY.

Rare Flor Sherry: See SHERRY.

Rhine*** California "Rhine Wines" generally merit careful avoidance. Masson's is a happy exception.

Rhine Castle*** If you like Liebfraumilch, you'll probably like this little white wine with its definite touch of sweetness. Masson says proudly that this wine is an imitation of the German wine. It's for summer sip-

ping, well chilled, on the trellised veranda—or in front of the kitchen sink. A good value at $2.25.

Riesling** Not much. You'll do better with the Rhine Castle (above).

Rubion*** Another of Masson's inventions and another simple success. It's made to American tastes; soft, mellow, with a slightly sweet edge. This wine wasn't always this good; Masson has been improving the formula in recent years. It can be served with almost any food, including the soup course, or with fruits and nuts after dinner. Good value at $2.25.

Sherry*** Masson makes an array of sherries, and they're quite good, trustworthy, reasonably priced. If you like sweet sherry, the Rare Cream ($2) is a good wine. If dry sherry is more to your taste, Masson has a good one: Rare Flor ($3), extremely dry. Old Rare ($3) is their best medium sherry.

Souzao Port: See PORT.

Sparkling Burgundy** This bubbly red wine is not quite up to the standard of most of Masson's sparkling wines. It's rather sweet but lacks fruitiness. Fair value, $5.

Very Cold Duck*** As though it wasn't bad enough with all those merely Cold Ducks all over the skies, now we have to contend with Very Cold ones . . . But as these cold winged fowls go—hopefully they'll go ever farther and farther—this Masson wine is as good as most and a little better than some. Serve well chilled, as an aperitif or after dinner. Fair value, $5.

Vin Rosé Sec** If you prefer your rosé on the dry side, you should like this wine and its price, ca. $2. Serve it chilled (it doesn't need airing) with any food, or without food.

Zinfandel* The winery's newest red and one of their best. It has zest, as Zinfandels ought. It's already been somewhat aged by the winery, but it will improve with another six months or a year in the bottle, though it's quite ready to drink upon purchase. Zinfandel goes particularly well with zesty foods: Italian dishes, even Mexican food if not too incendiary. Serve at cool room temperature. Fair value, $2.50.

MATEUS ROSÉ* Portugal makes some of the best rosé wine on earth, and this is a good example. It is said to be the largest-selling single wine in the world. It's properly pronounced "Ma-tay-oosh," but people will think you're drunk if you say it. Wine connoisseurs can be somewhat condescending toward rosés, but they have their charm and their place. Particularly with non-millionaires, in hot climes, and with novice wine drinkers. Mateus is especially appreciated by those who like their rosé with a touch of sweetness. The label calls Mateus a "still" wine, but it has the tiniest frizziness. It is ready to drink when purchased, don't keep it more than a year. Serve Mateus chilled, any time, any place, with any food, in any circumstances, under any pretext, to anybody. Fair value, $3.

MATTIOLI, LETIZIA RIME-DIOTTI: See NOZZOLE.

MAUCAILLOU, CHÂTEAU Officially classed as a lowly *bourgeois* wine, this substantial French (Bordeaux) red wine deserves a higher rating. Connoisseurs have long appreciated its merits—and its lowly price

tag. Serve this good wine with light meats, with beef or lamb, or with fowl. Or to be even more appreciative of its qualities, sip it in leisurely fashion before dinner, with light hors d'oeuvres. Air one hour, serve at cool room temperature: 65° F.

*1966*** Well-balanced wine, now ready; it will not improve. Fair value, $5.

*1968** Good flavor, slightly tart. Drink soon; it will not hold. Air two hours. Fair value, $3.50.

*1969*** This wine will be at its best 1975 to 1982. Air at least two hours.

*1970**** This is going to develop beautifully—so don't you dare drink it before 1980! Air two hours. Unhappily, it's selling for $10.

MAXIMIN GRÜNHAUSER HERRENBERG Don't let the formidable name frighten you away—this is a marvelous wine from Germany's Ruwer area. Like all Saar and Ruwer wines, it needs lots of sunshine and is a poor wine in off-years. For a general appraisal of some recent vintages, see SCHARZHOF-BERGER. Somebody said—with a bit of hyperbole—that the '71s of the Saar and Ruwer are the greatest white wines of the century. No one doubts but that they're excellent, but they are not that good! How to serve and enjoy this wine: See under MOSELLE.

MAYACAMAS VINEYARDS (Napa, Calif.) Today this name stands for good wine—it was not always thus. Since the 60s the wines have steadily improved. A lot of California wineries stick the word "Mountain" on their labels to help sell their wines. Some of these "Mountain" wines come straight from the sweltering floor of the San Joaquin Valley. Mayacamas doesn't use the word on their labels, though they have every right to, as their vineyards are 2,400 feet high, in the Mayacamas Range. These are high-class wines, but unfortunately most of them also have a rather high-class price tag.

Cabernet Sauvignon Vintages prior to '66 were weak to start with, and if you happen to possess any, consume immediately; they are already on the decline.

1966*** Mayacamas is nothing if not patient—they released this wine only in November, 1974. It's now at its best and will remain so at least until 1982.

1967**** Now at its best, should be enjoyed during the 70s.

1968*** This wine may deserve **** by 1980: powerful and straightforward, it is aging very slowly and shows fine potential. Try it first in 1979. It's selling for $7 or $8 and you'll have to decide whether or not that's a "fair" price.

1969***** A fine wine to lay down for your most elegant dining in the 80s—if your pocketbook (or buried fortune) can cut it. This wine, selling today at around $10, will be much more than a $10 value when it reaches its peak, around 1980. Air it two hours, and serve with pride and élan, with your finest meat course.

1970**** Released in November, 1974; all indications say this is going to be one very fine, very big wine. Lay some down for marvelous drinking, 1980 to 1985.

Chardonnay This dry white wine is one of the noblest of wines; in the hands of Maya-

camas it becomes even more so. It's their special pride. It shows to its best advantage when used at the table: with seafood or other light dishes (sliced cold beef, potato salad). The winery says that vintages before the 70s are already beyond their peak.

1970**** Just now at its prime and will hold there for another year or two. Fair value, $5 to $5.50.

1971 and *1972***** Both of these wines are almost at their best—try the '71 in '75, the '72 in '76. Either or both of them may yet deserve *****, they're very intense, full-of-flavor wines. Fair value, $6.50 to $7.

1973 Still "in the wood" (barrel), the winery says this may be their finest Chardonnay in five years. That would mean ***** or better. Hmmmmmmm . . .

Chenin Blanc A good Chenin Blanc is a light fresh wine, but it's not the kind of wine Mayacamas does well with. They seem to appreciate the fact also, and are discontinuing this wine. It's still on the retail shelves, however. Use to accompany light foods, especially sandwiches.

1970*** If you have some, drink it immediately; it won't keep much longer.

1971** Consume by the end of '75. This is the last Chenin Blanc the winery will produce. Amen.

Zinfandel A good full-bodied red table wine, California's own. Over the long haul "Z" is just about your best buy in California reds. Mayacamas makes some fine ones. Serve with any good hearty meal, especially if it contains red meat.

1966, 1967** Throwbacks. Consume at once.

1968 Late Harvest—Near-Classic. Already an almost legendary wine, one of the "biggest" wines California has ever produced. It's almost black in color, is drinkable now, a huge mouthful, but it would be downright sinful to drink it before the 1980s have dawned. And it will probably outlive all of us. It's hard to find and speculators are asking ridiculous prices for it, but a fair price would be $15 to $20. It's so intense that you will certainly want to drink it slowly, lovingly, simply, with Cheddar cheese, apple and pear slices.

1972 Late Harvest—Today: ***** — 1980: Near-Classic — 1990: ??? Whee, here we go again—this is just an updated version of Mayacamas's fabled '68 Late Harvest Zinfandel, and it may well surpass it by the year 2000—seriously. This tremendous wine won't even reach its peak until 1985 or '90, and it will live for decades thereafter. It's already delicious but will get better and better. Bob Travers, talented and gracious boss-man at Mayacamas, says this wine will go best after meals, with cheese. Hearty concurrence. It's fetching $12 today, but recall that the '68 reportedly sold for as high as $80 per bottle toward the end of its availability.

Zinfandel Rosé 1972** This is the last rosé the winery will be producing. They're ending on a low-key note. Drink in 1975.

MAZIS (or: MAZYS)-CHAMBERTIN Great red Burgundy (France) wine. How to serve it: See under CHAMBERTIN. The '69 Gelin was fine wine: *****
—the '70 Remoissenet, *****
—the '71 Rebourseau, ****.

MAZZONI LAMBRUSCO: See LAMBRUSCO.

MÉDOC It's one of the most famous of all wine names, but you will rarely find the name on a bottle of French wine, except in small print. It's pronounced May-dawk. Médoc is a rather large area north of the city of Bordeaux, comprising all the best of the Bordeaux wine districts (Margaux, Saint-Julien, etc.). Wines rarely go to market under the name Médoc, however, as it's too generic. They go either under the name of a particular Château (Lafite, Léoville, etc.) or under the name of their respective districts (e.g., Pomerol). The rule is: The more specific the label, the better the wine. Those wines sold simply as Médoc are good red wines, not great, but certainly not bad either. How to serve them: See under BORDEAUX. They should be economically priced: between $4 and $5, and will usually rate a solid ***, and occasionally ****. See also HAUT MÉDOC. Some trustworthy names: Bichot; Chauvenet; Cruse; De Luze; Dreyfus-Ashby; Ginestet; Johnston; Jouvet; Leme Frères; Marson & Natier; Armand Roux; Sichel "Ruban Rouge."

MEIER'S This name appears on a wild assortment of labels: Meier's Isle St. George, Meier's No. 44, Meier's Original Wild Mountain, Meier's Château Reiem . . . These gloriously diversified wines and non-wines —some are nonalcoholic—are all produced by Ohio's largest winery, Meier's Wine Cellars of Cincinnati. All are very standard wines, economically priced. None are outstanding. The only one acclaimed at all is the Sweet Catawba **, and better Catawba is not to be found in this land—if Catawba's your glass of wine. Experts tend to demean Catawba, but it has its own individual charm. And regarding all of Meier's wines, recall the most fundamental principle of all wine appreciation: *You* are the ultimate connoisseur. If you like it, it's good wine.

Sparkling Wines Meier's also makes an array of sparkling wines, from a Spumonte (the word should be "Spumante," Italian for "Sparkling") to those inevitable Cold Ducks. The Catawba grape seems to show at its best in bubbly wines and this is what Meier's does best. These are all bulk-processed wines and lack the delicacy and finesse of true Champagne (and of some of California's best), and they're not especially good values at $3.50 to $4.75. But they're deservedly popular.

MELINI This is the name of a large and reputable producer of Italian wines, of Florence, Italy. Melini's straw-covered Chianti, selling for around $3.50 per quart, is a familiar sight across the land. It's usually a good wine and a fair value. It is, however, the lowest grade of Melini's Chiantis. Their very best is called Stravecchio—the name will be in bold print across the label—an excellent wine. Just below it is Melini's Riserva Classico, also fine wine, selling for ca. $4.30 per fifth. Notice that no Melini wine has the black cockerel seal of authentic Chianti Classico on the neck of the bottle—that's because the wine is bottled just outside the "Classico" area, although the grapes are actually from within the area. How to serve Chianti: See under CHIAN-TI.

Some of Melini's notable recent bottles:

1964 Chianti Classico Riserva: ****—Now at its best and should remain there for at least another five years—Air it one hour before serving.

1966 Chianti Classico: ***— Has begun to fade; if you possess some, bottoms up, now!

1966 Chianti Classico Riserva: ****—Drink soon, at the latest.

Melini Lacrima D'Arno Riserva, 1966* This name means "the Tears of the Arno (River)," a rather fancy name for a rather plain dry white wine. This particular bottle may be past its peak. Don't chance it.

Melini Lacrima D'Arno, 1968 * "The Tears of the Arno": A small white wine, probably already on the decline. Not recommended at the going price of $3.25.

MENDOCINO VINEYARDS A new brand name owned by the Guild Wine Company (San Francisco, Calif.) under which this huge cooperative markets its best wines. Thus far only one has received any real acclaim: a Pinot Noir which was the grand sweepstakes winner at the Los Angeles County Fair, 1971. Should be worth a try and should be a good value.

MERCIER A famous French Champagne—and an excellent one. Their finest is Reserve l' Empereur, a magnificent wine, but it is their Extra Dry that will probably be appreciated by most non-experts; it has consistently placed high in blind tastings the world around. For general notes on Champagne vintages: See under CHAMPAGNE.

MERCUREY**** Good red Burgundy (France) wine, one of the few not outrageously priced these days. It isn't a Pommard or Chambertin but it's sound, light red, often of excellent bouquet and finesse. "Plain" Mercurey should be drunk young: two to five years of age. How to serve it: See under BEAUJOLAIS (though it is not a Beaujolais). A Clos des Myglands (Faiveley) is particularly commendable, the 1969 and 1970 both meriting *****. The '69 is now at its best, the '70 should be enjoyed, 1976–1978. Both of these are excellent values, at $5. Serve at cool room temperature.

MERLOT An important red grape—but a demure one. It's rarely heard of—or from—for it's used almost exclusively for blending, especially in France, Italy, California. Only very recently has the Merlot grape spoken out at all; now it's begun to appear on labels all on its own—there it is Merlot. In California Sterling Winery (see) is the only one, at the moment, who is making it, and they do rather well with it.

A French Merlot made by A. Delor & Cie. is now being imported to the U.S., it's ***, dry and tasty, sells for $3 to $3.50.

Some Italian Merlot is seen on these shores, good little wines, ***, some are nonvintaged, and these are fine values.

Merlot wine, especially the California version, is vaguely similar to California Gamay and should be similarly consumed: anytime, anyplace, under any pretense. Drink it young and fresh, within a couple of years of purchase. Serve it as you would a Beajolais, at cool room temperature.

MEURSAULT Excellent white Burgundy wine, extremely dry but nonetheless soft and mellow, medium-priced. Meursault goes well with fish (especially one in a rich sauce), seafood (especially lobster and scallops), poultry (especially goose). And of course, with cheeses, particularly Gruyère. Serve it chilled.

The best vineyards of Meursault are these: (Les) Perrières (or Clos des Perrières); (Les) Genevrières; (Les) Charmes.

The name of the vineyard is usually tacked on to Meursault with a hyphen: Meursault-Charmes, Meursault-Genevrières, etc. These wines will cost between $8 and $12, and they are regularly **** and above.

Wines that say simply "Meursault" on the label, without naming a specific vineyard, are among the most reliable of all such "village" wines. They are medium-priced, at least relatively so in today's stratosphere of French wines: from $5 to $8. "Plain" Meursault is never less than ***. Meursault is at its best when it is from two to six years old.

MIRAFIORE This is the name of a reputable producer of Italian wines, principally Chiantis. (Other wines, see under their individual names, e.g., Valpolicella.) It's a name you can trust on a bottle of Chianti—even on a straw-covered one, though this, selling for around $3.25 per quart, is understandably a small young wine, albeit a sound one. Fair value, Riserva del Conte: $4.25. How to serve this wine: See under CHIANTI.

Some notable recent bottles:

1959 Chianti Classico Riserva del Conte: *****—A reputed wine—It's alive and well, but drink it soon.

1962 Chianti Classico Riserva

del Conte: ***—Drink immediately.

1967 Chianti Classico Riserva del Conte: ***

1969 Chianti Classico Riserva del Conte: ***

MIRASSOU VINEYARDS (San Jose, Calif.) Here's a California winemaker whose name wine lovers hold in benediction, for Mirassou produces a full line of fine premium wines usually selling at reasonable prices. Not that all Mirassou's wines are equally good, not even that they are all good. But the batting average is excellent. Most of the wines are good, some are exceptional; few are poor.

Burgundy* Good red dinner wine, double the price of many of those half-gallon jugs of Burgundy, but still in the quasi-economy class at ca. $2.75 a fifth. This is a vintaged wine, and the 1969, 1970, and 1971 are all above average. They're ready for immediate drinking and will improve in the bottle if you keep them for a year or three or four. Allow the wine a half hour breathing time and enjoy it with your Sunday roast, or sip it with cheese and fruit after dinner.

Cabernet Sauvignon Cabernet is usually considered the finest of California's red wines, and Mirassou's version, in particular, is very well regarded, by expert and novice alike. But, like all fine wines, it can vary from vintage to vintage. Unfortunately, it's not exactly in the economy class, $5.

Cabernet Sauvignon, 1963 ***** Some say this was Mirassou's best Cabernet Sauvignon ever. It's now at its best and will there abide for at least a decade.

Cabernet Sauvignon, 1964 **** Some say *this*, not the '63, was Mirassou's best ever, deserving *****.

Cabernet Sauvignon, 1965 *** Mirassou rates their Cabernet Sauvignon every year against the best French Clarets. For this vintage, they judged their wine the winner. They were wrong. It's still a good Cabernet though—drink it within the next few years.

*Cabernet Sauvignon, 1966 (Plain)*** The winery rated this wine inferior to Bordeaux's Clarets for this year. They were right.

Cabernet Sauvignon, 1966 Limited Bottling (First Harvest)****

Cabernet Sauvignon, 1967 **** One of their best vintages ever. The winery is convinced that this wine was better than its counterpart '67 French Claret. It was aged twenty months in French oak (that's good) and released only in late '72. It is now ready to drink but will improve still further if you can restrain yourself and lay it down for a couple more years. It will be excellent, 1977 through 1980. If it says Second Harvest on the bottle, it's even better and will cost you an extra dollar, *****. You will want to save this wine for some festive occasion. Let it breathe at least one hour. Fair value for the "straight," $7 to $9.

*Cabernet Sauvignon, 1968*** May be drunk now but better to keep it until 1976 through 1979, it will improve markedly. Air at least one hour and serve at cool room temperature, with festive fare. If the label says Third Harvest, it's even better, ****, and worth at least a dollar more than the "plain," which latter should sell for about $6.50.

*Cabernet Sauvignon, 1969***

This wine has had very mixed reviews. Try it for yourself—it's probably an excellent wine but is taking its own sweet time to develop. Lay it down until at least 1979 and test it then; it will probably be at its best around 1981.

If it says Fourth Harvest on the label, it will cost you at least another dollar and should be well worth it, ****. Down the line there, in 1980-whatever, when you drink it, remember to air it about an hour and serve it with your finest beef entree. Fair value for the "plain," $6 to $7.

*Cabernet Sauvignon, 1970*** At its present stage of development, a disappointment. It may come around, for the present . . . No.

*Cabernet Sauvignon, 1971**** Still too young for an accurate assessment. Will be at its best, 1979–1981. Fair value, $5.

Cabernet Sauvignon, 1972 Too young to be evaluated accurately but already showing promise. Nowhere near ready to drink. Try it first in 1978. Fair value, $5 to $5.40.

Chablis*** Not up to the standards of a true French Chablis, of course, but a crisp dry white wine, usually quite good. 1970, 1971, 1972, and 1973: all good wines in their own little way. Ready for immediate drinking and will keep at least a year. Serve it chilled, preferably with shellfish. Fair value, $2.75 to $3.

Champagne au Naturel*** Mirassou makes good Champagne, all by hand operation, a rarity in our automated day. This is their driest sparkling wine, clean and crisp, will especially appreciated by connoisseurs; the uninitiated may find it a bit austere. The '68,

'69, '70: all excellent. Good Champagne fits anywhere—including breakfast. It'll sure improve those scrambled eggs. Ready to drink when you buy it, one ought not to keep it more than a year or two. Fair value, $7.

Champagne Brut*** *"Brut"* means "Natural": with Champagne, naturally fermented, unsweetened—it's usually the driest Champagne a firm makes. Mirassou makes one even drier, their "Au Naturel." But for most the Brut will be preferred to the Au Naturel, as not quite as austere and dry. Besides, it's a dollar cheaper. California Champagnes are ready to drink when purchased and should not be held for more than a year or so. Fair value, $6.

Chardonnay: See PINOT CHARDONNAY.

Chenin Blanc Chenin Blanc is one of California's best white wines, and certainly its gayest: young, fragrant, often a bit "spritzig," entirely a California creation; there is no European wine quite like it. Mirassou makes one of the best. This wine deserves to be savored, sipped slowly, chilled, of a summer's evening, as an aperitif or after-dinner wine.

*1969**** If you happen to possess a bottle or run across one, drink it soon, as it's fading fast in the stretch.

*1970***** A gem. If you find it, buy it; if you possess it, treasure it. This is an historic wine: the first commercial wine mechanically harvested and field-crushed (to preserve freshness, fruitiness). Drink this engaging wine soon, certainly within the next year.

*1971, 1972**** Wine people talk about a wine being "well balanced." These bottles demonstrate what the term means: perfectly balanced between acidity and sweetness; one would not want the wine either sweeter or drier. The '71 is ready for now-drinking and through 1976; the '72 will be at its best 1975–1977.

*1973***** It took a silver medal at the 1974 Los Angeles County Fair. Drink, 1975 through 1977.

Gamay Beaujolais*** A relatively economical young red wine—the name tells you it's an imitation of the famous French Beaujolais, which in France is often consumed within mere months of the harvest. This light and tasty wine is usually a good buy, and Mirassou makes a good one year after year. It's ready to drink when purchased, and will remain fresh for about four years after its vintage date. To accompany those grilled hamburgers—or T-bones. Fair value, $3.25 to $3.50.

Gamay Beaujolais, Sparkling: See SPARKLING GAMAY BEAUJOLAIS.

Gewürztraminer This is a wine copied from Germany and Alsace, but the California imitations are often better than the originals. Mirassou's is very distinctive wine, "spicy" is the best word to describe its unique flavor. It deserves to be better known in America; it suits our Yankee tastes. It has enough character and flavor to accompany spicy foods—some say even curry—and it's famous as an accompaniment for sausages. It's ready to drink when purchased and will keep for a year or two.

*Gewürztraminer, Sixth Harvest, 1971***** This *was* a fine wine and if you have some lying about the premises, don't just stand there; drink it soon,

before it dies. If you find it for sale, make the merchant promise a refund if it's already departed this world. Fair value, to $5.

*Gewürztraminer, 1972 ****
Spicy, fresh, racy. A good value at $3.25 to $3.50.

*Gewürztraminer, Seventh Harvest, 1972***** Released late 1974, sure winner. Fair value, $4.50.

*Gewürztraminer, 1973****
Excellent drinking, now and through 1976. Fair value, $4.

Johannisberg Riesling This is the grape that made German wines famous; it also makes good wine in California, though quite different from the German ones. It's ready to drink when you buy it and will keep at least four years from its vintage date. Don't use it as an aperitif wine unless it's an exceptional vintage; usually it will show to best advantage with food, especially seafood; also excellent with pork or veal. Serve it chilled. Unfortunately Mirassou's prices have risen steeply on this wine over the past few years—it was a mere $2.50 in 1971, and is double that today. Decide for yourself whether it's *that* good.

*1970**** Drink soon.

*1971***** Slightly sparkling, very fruity. Consume, 1975 and 1976.

*1972***** The winery is especially proud of this wine and with good reason: Johannisberg Riesling at its best: Rhine-like in style, clean, an edge of sweetness. It should keep until 1977. Tasty enough to serve as an aperitif wine.

*1973****

Monterey Riesling This is a new name for an improved wine. It used to be called Sylvaner Riesling, and its new title is to honor the fact that the grapes now come from Mirassou's vineyards in Monterey County. It's a good, tasty wine, appreciated by beginner and connoisseur alike. It has a delicate touch of sweetness which makes it ideal for summer evening sipping or preprandial consumption. It should be drunk within a year of purchase, else it stands in danger of losing that beguiling freshness. Fair value, $3.25 to $3.50. Serve well chilled, no airing necessary.

1970*** Drink immediately.

1971**** Charming, delicately sweet, too gentle to accompany a meal. Sip it carefully with crackers. Drink it soon.

1972*** Best drinking, 1975 through 1977.

Petite Rosé A unique name for a unique wine, first made by happy accident in 1968. The "Petite" doesn't mean dainty but refers to the fact that the predominant grape is Petite Sirah. Even connoisseurs, who are not overly enthusiastic about the vast majority of rosé wines, generally give this wine rather high marks. It also costs a little more than most. Rosé is a general-purpose wine, but it's appreciated most on a hot summer day, chilled, with hamburgers or at lunch with sandwiches and potato or macaroni salad. It's ready for immediate consumption, shouldn't be kept more than a year or so. Fair value, $2.75 to $3.

1969, 1970, 1971, 1972*** All have a little dryness, good fruitiness.

Petite Sirah Good red table wine, commonly overlooked and underrated. Serve it with any hearty food, especially stews, meat casseroles, grilled

meat of any kind. It's ready to drink when you buy it and will improve with a year or two in the bottle. It will be at its best four or five years after its vintage date. Air at least one hour. Fair value, $3.50 to $3.75.

1967*** Rich, complex wine, still good drinking, but don't keep it too much longer.

1968*** Good drinking until 1977.

1969** Some have faulted this wine for its "vegetable" aroma; that may disappear with age. It just could become great with two years in the bottle.

1970*** At its present stage of development it's only good, but it may well develop into something beautiful to consume. Lay it down lovingly (in cool dark cellar) and taste it first in '77. Betcha!

1971*** If you'll lay this down until the late 70s, it will merit at least ****.

Pinot Blanc*** This wine is now called white Burgundy. The last two vintages under this name, 1969 and 1970, were both good, and if you have either, consume them immediately, or you'll lose them.

Pinot Chardonnay Chardonnay dry white wine is considered California's best white. But be cautioned that it varies widely from winery to winery. Mirassou usually makes a good one. It's California's answer to the great white Burgundies of France, at a much, much more reasonable price. Serve chilled, as an aperitif wine or at your most elegant luncheon, or with any type of seafood or cheese dish. Chardonnay is ready to drink when you buy it and is at its best four or five years after the vintage date.

A special bottling, Harvest Selection, is often made and will cost an additional dollar or so. It's not always worth it.

Pinot Chardonnay, Fourth Harvest, 1969**** One of the best Chardonnays Mirassou has made: full of flavor, lots of authority. Save it for festive dining: Coquilles St. Jacques or broiled lobster. Drink by 1976. Fair value, ca. $7.

Pinot Chardonnay, Fifth Harvest, 1970*** A substantial wine with some good oakiness (from the barrel it was aged in). Drink through 1975. Fair value, up to $6.

1971*** Some experts have not liked this wine. Drink through 1975.

1971 Sixth Harvest**** Suggest you lay this bottle down for one year; should be at its best, 1976. Fair value, $5.50 to $6.

1972 "H" Seventh Harvest **** A limited amount was released in the fall of 1974. It's already excellent, but will be at its very best, 1976–1978.

Pinot Noir This grape is responsible for some of the greatest red wines in the world, but it does not do particularly well in California, though it can result in some fine soft red wine. At its best it can be a great sipping wine—with cheese, crackers, fresh fruit—or to accompany any good hearty fare, especially red meats; poultry also, especially if richly prepared. It's ready to drink when purchased (see below). Serve at cool room temperature.

Pinot Noir, 1966*** Drink soon.

Pinot Noir, 1966 Special Bottling (First Harvest)**** One authority believes that this may prove to be the best Pinot Noir California has yet produced. It's just reaching its peak and will hold for a good three or four more years.

Pinot Noir, Second Harvest, 1967*** Has improved with age and is just now at its peak. Fair value, $6.

Pinot Noir, Dedication Bottling, 1969***** This will be wonderful wine, but it's not yet there. It's dedicated to Max Huebner, Mirassou's skilled winemaker for more than thirty years—a fitting tribute to a great artisan. Lay down this wine and try your first bottle in 1976.

1971*** Too early to give this recently released wine final evaluation, but omens are auspicious. It's already spent more than two years in the barrel, one year in small cooperage—that's all to the good, ages the wine better. Probably a good gamble. Fair value, $4.50 to $5.

Sparkling Gamay Beaujolais If you like sparkling red wines you will like this one; it's one of the best. Whatever else may or may not be said about sparkling red wines, they're among the prettiest of the world's wines. This wine has a $5.50 or $6 price tag, and it's your decision whether it's *that* good. Fine before dinner or with the soup course, or with dinner itself, if not too spicy. Don't keep any California sparkling wine more than a couple of years. Chill well.

1969**** Hearty wine, serve pridefully with barbecued chicken, Cornish game hens.

1970**** Lots of flavor. For holiday dining.

White Burgundy Previously called Pinot Blanc. Mirassou is the only California winery using this name. The wine really has very little in common with the great white Burgundies of France, some of the greatest white wine in the world, but in its own right, doing its own thing, this is a good wine, and Mirassou is properly proud of it. They say it bridges the gap between those expensive Chardonnays and the cheap Chablis ... it does. It should be drunk young, within three years. The best can be used as an aperitif wine, and it always goes well with light food (poultry, veal, ham) and especially with fish. Serve chilled. Fair value, $3.50 to $3.75.

1971**** There are two versions of this wine, this "straight" version, aged in French Limousin oak; the other, labeled "American Oak," (below) was aged in precisely that. This "straight" version is the better of the two. It's spicy, very tasty, and it would be a shame to allow it to be overpowered by food of whatever kind; rather, savor it lovingly, on its own, or at most, with bland tidbits. It's excellent for present drinking and will keep another two years at least. Good value at $3.50 to $3.75.

1971 American Oak*** The oakiness is a little too forceful.

1972**** Similar to the '71, it would be interesting to compare with that vintage, glasses side by side. You can drink it now but it will probably be even better a year from now.

1973**** Winner of a silver medal at the Los Angeles County Fair, 1974. Best drinking, 1976–1978.

Zinfandel One of California's best red wines, and Mirassou makes a fine one, a consistent award-winner. Zestful and tasteful, almost always a good value, ideal for accompanying roasts, steaks, hamburgers, rich food. It's ready to drink when you bring it home. It lasts longer than most Zinfandels, and even improves with bottle age. Fair value, $4.50 to $5.

1966*** Both the "plain" bottlings and those that say First Harvest are just getting to their best. They will continue to improve in the bottle for the next several years.

1967**** Both the "plain" and the "H" Second Harvest are fine, flavorful wines and can be drunk now, but the Second Harvest in particular will be even better from 1976 on.

1968, 1969**** Both the "plain" and the 1968 Second Harvest are already enjoyable and will improve until 1979.

1970*** Already drinkable, but restrain yourself and hold at least until 1977.

1971***

1973 The crystal ball says watch for it—it's going to be extraordinary.

MISSION CELLARS SPARKLING BURGUNDY** This is a secondary brand name owned by Weibel Vineyards, an excellent California Champagne maker. Considering its price, ca. $2.70, this is a rather remarkable beverage, clean and quite delightful. It has a touch of sweetness. Sparkling Burgundy goes well before dinner, or with almost any food. Or, of course, as a party beverage.

(LA) MISSION HAUT-BRION, CHÂTEAU A very fine red Bordeaux wine, literally just across the street from the famous Château Haut-Brion. It is said, in fact, that the wines of La Mission sometimes surpass those of Haut-Brion in a particular year, and the wines do, in fact, bear a close resemblance to those of Haut-Brion, though they tend to be slightly lighter and quicker to mature.

How to serve La Mission: See under BORDEAUX.

1948—Near-Classic—Fair value, $25.

1949—*****—Some say to be preferred to Haut-Brion for this vintage. Fair value, $25.

1953—****—Not recommended at $40, current asking price.

1955—Near-Classic—Fair value, $25.

1958—Good despite the year: ****. Now at its best. Fair value, $6.

1959—*****—Best drinking, 1975–1985. Fair value, $20.

1960—*****—The price should be right: around $7. Now at its best.

1961—*****—At its best, now and through 1985. Fair value, $25.

1962—Near-Classic—Big and delicious, now at its best and will hold until 1980.

1964—*****—Some say it was better than Haut-Brion of this year. Fair value, $15.

1966—*****—At its best, 1975–1985. Fair value, $15.

1967—Classic—Everybody agrees: exceptional wine, particularly for this vintage. At its best, 1976–1985. Look for this one; the price has not been outrageous: $10 to $15.

1968—Good despite the year: ****—A good value at $5.

1969—*****—Will be at its best, 1977–1985. Fair value, $12.50.

1970—Near-Classic—Far from ready—will be 1981–1990. Fair value, $17.

MOËT ET CHANDON The largest, far and away, of all the great French Champagne houses, and probably also the most prestigious. Their Champagnes are unquestionably among France's very finest. Dom Perignon (see) is Moët's "Best of the House." The real basis of the firm's reputation, however, is their Brut Impérial. There is both a vintage and a nonvintage, both excellent wines, but nonconnoisseurs will probably appreciate the White Seal Extra Dry most of all, a great wine, and the most economical of Moët's sparkling wines.

(C. K.) MONDAVI Don't confuse this with Robert Mondavi. This is the name given to the cheaper, the jug wines of the Charles Krug Winery (California). They are pretty standard wines, for the most part neither better nor worse than those of their competitors. That's no condemnation, however, as California jug wines are among the best wine values in the world. These wines—there are some dozen of them—are ready for immediate drinking upon purchase—and shouldn't be kept more than a year or so. Serve the reds at cool room temperature (65°F), the white chilled (55°F). They should sell at around $1.65 a fifth, $3.25 a half-gallon; $5.50 a gallon.

The more notable wines, for good or ill:

Barberone** One of the best of the CK line (perhaps the only wine in the world by this name), it's a hearty red, a good hamburger wine.

Bravissimo* Sounds like a red wine, but it's a cloyingly sweet white . . . no way.

Burgundy** Good hamburger wine.

Chablis*** Good white table wine—to accompany fish, shellfish, chicken, light foods.

Chianti**

Claret**

Rhine—Not recommended.

Zinfandel*** Above average

for Zinfandel at this price, $1.75.

MONDAVI, ROBERT (Oakville, Calif.) This is a respected name among California wine makers. Be careful, though: there is also a C. K. Mondavi brand of wine (see), not nearly as praiseworthy as the Robert Mondavi label. The Mondavi winery is a happy blend of the old and the new: small old-world oak barrels, for example, stand beside huge, glistening, double-walled (for temperature control) stainless-steel fermentation tanks. It is said that Mondavi wines are so distinctive they can be picked out in blind tasting. They make some great ones. One reason Mondavi has come so far so quickly —they're less than ten years old—is because they dragoon a certain Father Edward from the nearby Carmelite monastery to come over at harvest time every year and bless the first carload of grapes. Small wonder, with God on their side . . .

Cabernet Sauvignon Cabernet Sauvignon is California's best red wine—this is perhaps Mondavi's best wine—it is certainly one of California's best Cabernets. It's rich and complex, and that's what makes a wine great. Air at least one hour. Serve at cool room temperature. The winery recommends a roast leg of lamb to accompany their Cabernet, and it would also go gloriously with roast chicken or roast beef —the best bottles should be sipped lazily with Cheddar or Camembert. Some of these bottles, especially the unfined and unfiltered ones, may develop sediment. If so, stand them upright for twenty-four hours, then decant.

1966**** Rejoice, the winery will now, at long last, allow you to drink this wine! They recommend that their Cabernets be at least eight years old before you dare savor them. They should know. This is unfined (unclarified) wine, giving it additional substance and flavor. Will be at its peak for another decade, at least. Fair value, $12.

1967*** Now at its best and will hold there at least until 1980. Fair (?) value, $10.

1968 Worth looking for. There are two versions: a "plain" **** and an "unfined" (it's on the label), probably deserving *****. In one blind tasting this wine outclassed the great Château Margaux ('64). Fair value, $13.50.

1969***** Though scarcely five years old, this is already a famous wine. But curb your enthusiasm, if you own a bottle —don't you dare drink it until at least 1979. And if you don't possess a bottle, start looking. A fair price would be around $20, but a bottle recently sold at auction for somewhere around $100.

1970**** It's much too young for present drinking: try it starting in 1979. By that time it may well merit *****. Fair value, $9.

1971**** It's worth **** right now and it's going to go nowhere but skyward. Today it brings $6 . . . tomorrow? As the mother duck said to her daughter, "Lay some down. . . ."

Chardonnay Most wineries label this Pinot Chardonnay, but Mondavi uses the more accurate nomenclature. It's the classic grape that produces almost all of the world's great dry white wines. Mondavi's Chardonnay is said to resemble some of those great wines—it's certainly a positive and assertive wine, especially recent vintages. It's a food-accompanying kind of wine, goes well with poultry (even well seasoned), and all kinds of seafood. Serve chilled, but not icy.

1968**** At its best but won't hold much longer; drink 1975–1976. Fair value, $9.

1969*** A trifle thin but a good wine. Drink during 1975. Fair value, $7.

1970**** Good for present drinking and will hold at least through 1976. Fair value, $6.50 to $7.

1971**** Has placed first in a number of "blind" competitions (judges saw no labels). You can drink it now and it will hold, may even improve a bit, at least through 1976. Fair value, $6.50 to $7.

1972 (Unfiltered)**** It may reach *****.

Chenin Blanc Good fresh young white wine with a touch of sweetness, perfect for summer refreshment. It's too delicate to go with anything but the lightest, blandest of foods.

1970*** Fruity and spicy. Fair value, $3.25 to $3.50.

1971**** Good drinking now and will keep at least through 1978. Good value, at $3.25 to $3.50.

1972 and 1973**** Drink, 1975 through 1978. Fine value at $3.25.

Fumé Blanc Mondavi invented this name—or borrowed it, backward, from the French. They call theirs Blanc Fumé. It means "White Smoke," and the wine's white, all right, but it's hardly smoky, by the longest stretch of the imagination. But it's a tasty little wine, crisp, fresh, clean. Slightly dry, consistently good, serve it with fish —perfect with fillet of sole. Chill it: 45 to 50°F.

1968**** Worth searching for. A European wine authority calls it "absolutely charming." Drink now and through 1976. Fair value, $4.50 to $5.

1969, 1970, 1971**** All above-average wines, and all ready for present drinking and will keep in top shape through 1977 or 1978. If you like your aperitif on the dry side, these bottles will fill and overfill the bill. Fair value, $4.50 to $5.

1972**** Richard Nixon is said to have served this wine, with striped bass, at a banquet in Moscow in 1974—he was better advised than he was regarding his hi-fi system in the oval office. Excellent wine. Look for the unfiltered. Fair value, $4.50.

Gamay If you like Beaujolais—and who doesn't?—you'll like this. It's a frank imitation of that famous young French red wine. Beaujolais is traditionally a poor man's wine but with the skyrocketing prices of all French wines today, even good ol' Beaujolais has become a near-luxury. Here's a worthy substitute, at half the price. Gamay goes with almost any food, and even makes for good preprandial sipping, it's so fresh and tasty. Serve at cool room temperature (65°F), or slightly chilled (55°F). Good value at $3.25. Airing not necessary, and don't let your Gamay linger too long in your glass—scant danger!

1969 This was good wine but is now past its peak.

1970**** Drink immediately, while it's still young and fresh. By '76 it will be past its best.

1971*** Lively and fresh— excellent value at $3 to $3.25. Drink during '75 and '76.

1972**** Only one word for it: "loverly." Fresh, light, soft.

It has one flaw: it goes down too easily. One could quaff huge quantities in very short order! A marvelous value at $2.60 to $2.75.

Gamay Rosé As rosés go—not toooo far—this goeth some-deal well. It's got more heart—not mere sugariness—than most, but it's also a bit more expensive than most. Rosés are well known as "universal" wines, accompanying any food, but in fact they show at their best alongside light foods: fish, sandwiches, chicken salad. A good value, at $2.75 to $3.

*1967, 1968, 1969*** All above-average, but now past their peak.

*1970**** Drink immediately; may already have departed this world.

*1971**** At its freshest and best, but drink up, lads and lassies, soon.

*1972**** Drink through 1975 and 1976.

Johannisberg Riesling Good German-type white wine. It's not up to the elegance of the fine German whites; few wines are. But it fills in well for some of those Rhine wines, and it goes well with food, especially with fish, shellfish, turkey (roast, smoked, whatever), veal, omelettes. Serve chilled (55°F) but not over-chilled; one hour in the refrigerator is enough. Ready to drink when you buy it, drink it within three years to enjoy its freshness. Fair value, $4.50 to $4.75.

*1969**** Drink it soon—no, immediately.

*1971–1972**** At their best through 1975.

Moscato D'Oro* Quite sweet yet not cloying dessert wine, deep-down Muscat flavor. Serve it well chilled (45–50°F) with any dessert. Or savor it

for 11:00 sipping—A.M. or P.M. —if you can catch it. Because of short supply, it's available only at the winery, at $5.

Petite Sirah** Only once has Mondavi made this red table wine: in 1970. They should try again. It's fine: deep, dark color, deep, dark flavor. Serve it with any hearty meal, especially one featuring some form of beef or red game. Will be at its best through 1975 and for many years thereafter. This wine will live as long as you will. Fair value, $4.50 to $5.

Pinot Noir The early vintages (1965–1967) were pretty awful, but Mondavi now has the cow by the tail, the vine by the branch . . . ? Anyhow, the 1968 and 1969 vintages rate ***. The '70 and '71 are solidly ****, and may go higher. Be sure to air these bottles one hour. Pinot Noir is California's true version of French Burgundy, a hundred times closer to the original than most of those California jug (half-gallon) "Burgundies." This is a good wine to lay down; it'll do nothing but improve, probably until the mid-80s. Sample starting in 1975. Best appreciated when served with roasts, steaks, game, cheese. Fair value, $5 to $5.25.

Riesling A light, flowery luncheon white wine, economical cousin of Johannisberg Riesling, the lowest priced of California's better Rhine-types. Mondavi's version is a good example of the type. Makes for good summer sipping, or with sandwiches or chicken salad. Serve chilled. Fair value, $3 to $3.25.

*1971, 1972**** Drink through 1975 and 1976.

Traminer A wine not often made in California, a white

Rhine-type, suited for a summer's day casual sipping or to accompany light foods. It's a little spicier and more distinctive than the Riesling. Serve chilled. Fair value, $3.

*1970, 1971*** Drink through 1975.

*1972** Drink, 1975 and 1976.

Zinfandel "Z" is a native Californian—it's produced nowhere else in the world. Good examples have the natural tanginess of the Zinfandel grape . . . Mondavi's does. Ideal to accompany spicy foods, hearty meals. Serve at room temperature. Fair value, $3.50 to $3.75.

*1966*** This was an experimental wine—spell it "successful." It's unfined (not clarified), which usually makes for a fuller, more complex wine. Which this is. Now at its peak and will hold there through 1976, at least. An excellent value, if you can find it, at $4.

*1967*** Good drinking 1975 through 1976.

1970 and *1971*** Drink 1975 through 1980. The '71 may reach ****.

MONSIEUR HENRI SELECTIONS These may or may not be good wines—some are, some aren't—but they weren't selected by Monsieur Henri. There's no such person. If you'll read carefully you'll see that Monsieur Henri Wines Ltd. is the name of the importing firm. Look up your wine under its proper name.

MONT LA SALLE This is the label for Christian Brothers' (see) altar wines. These are exactly the same wines as the regular commercial wines, some having the same names (Chablis, Sauterne), some with fanciful "religious" names ("St. Benedict," thus being interpreted

signifieth: Cream Sherry . . . but, ah, a cream sherry by any name . . .)

MONTEE DE TONNERRE: See CHABLIS, FRENCH.

MONTE REAL A first-class red wine from Spain, made by the Bodegas Riojanas, in the town of *Ashtray*—really!— *Cenicero*, in Spanish—look on the label. The wine is sturdy, yet soft and mellow. It's an excellent value. Some notable vintages, all ****: 1952, 1959, 1966. How to serve it: See under RIOJA.

(LE) MONTRACHET A lot of people say simply that this is the greatest dry white wine in the world, the queen of all French white wines—the king is necessarily a red wine. There are four other very great wines that have Montrachet as part of their names: Bâtard-Montrachet—Bienvenu-Bâtard-Montrachet—Chevalier-Montrachet —Criots-Bâtard-Montrachet (see all). These wines may press closely at the queen's heels, but she alone reigns. Rabelais called this wine divine, and Dumas said it should be drunk kneeling with head bared. If you want to know what wine writers are talking about when they rhapsodize about a wine being "well balanced," taste a fine Montrachet. One British critic, Hugh Johnson, calls Montrachet a completely balanced wine: "It is sweet in its nature, yet there is no spare sugar; it is not syrupy, but dry and lively. It is soft to drink, but firm and clear-cut" (Hugh Johnson, *Wine*, Simon and Schuster).

Montrachet can vary, however, vintage to vintage and even parcel to parcel—the twenty-acre vineyard is divided up among a dozen owners. Even more important is the question of value: at $20 to $35 per bottle one must always ask: Is it *that* good?

Less than 1,000 cases of Montrachet are produced each year, and only half of this ever reaches the market.

In general, Montrachet is at its best when it is between five and ten years of age, and the greatest vintages (e.g., 1961) will live even longer. But it tends to maderize (see) easily, so watch your wine closely. Montrachet goes well with light foods: fish, seafood, chicken, etc., just as any dry white wine does, but as expensive and regal as it is, it would be madness to do anything with it other than to sip it carefully, lovingly, on its own —if not on one's knees, at least reverently.

Some notable bottles:

1953, 1959, 1962—Exceptional vintages.

1963 Bouchard—****

1964 Comte Lafon—***** Drink it soon.

1965 Thenard: *****—Drink it soon.

1966 Marquis de Laguiche (Joseph Drouhin): *****

1966 Bouchard: *****

1966 Prieur: *****

1966 Thenard: ****

1966 Romanée-Conti: Near-Classic

These '66's are now at their best; don't keep them much longer.

1967 Marquis de Laguiche: **—Very unrecommended at $27.

1967 Romanée-Conti: ***** —At its best, 1975–1978.

1969 Thenard: *****

1969 Marquis de Laguiche: ****

1969 Bouchard: ****

These '69's now at their best, and so through 1979.

1970 Marquis de Laguiche: ****—Not much of a value at $29.

1971 Thenard: ***—At $25 to $30, no way!

MONTROSE, CHÂTEAU A fine Claret (red Bordeaux) wine, popular in England, due in part at least to its simple British-sounding name. But it's a name of French origin and is correctly pronounced in the French fashion: the "t" is silent. This is a consistent wine, well balanced (not too sweet, not too acidic), often a good value. Don't worry about the L. Charmolue on the label—it's the name of the owner. How to serve it: See under BORDEAUX.

1869—Classic—It was still available in '73—at a tidy $50 or so . . . per 24 ounces, not case. If it's lasted this long, it may live on forever!

1955—*****—Astoundingly good in this indifferent year. Now at its best, don't keep it. Fair value, $12.

1957—****—Drink soon. Fair value, $8.

1958—****—Excellent wine in a poor year, and it's a fine value at $4 or $5, if you can find it.

1959—*****—Not yet mature—try it starting in '78. Fair value, $15.

1961—Near-Classic—Will be at its best, 1977–1990. Fair value, $12 to $14.

1962—*****—Now at its best and will hold at least until 1985.

1964—****—Not nearly ready: try it starting in '79 or '80. Fair value, $8.

1966—Classic—Marvelous big wine, but far from ready—will be at its best, 1982–2000. Fair value, $10 to $12.

1967—Near-Classic—Another huge wine, but stash it away until well into the 80s. Fair value, $10.

1969—*****—Best drinking, 1978–1988.

1970—*****—Lay it away for ten years, and you'll have a beauty. Fair value, $13.

1971—Looking beautiful.

MOREY-SAINT-DENIS This name is not seen very often on wine labels, and when it is, it's frequently in the tiniest print on the label. It's not that they're ashamed of their wine down Morey-Saint-Denis way, it's just that the name of particular vineyards are more famous than the name of the village, and so the wine often goes to market under that name: Clos de Tart, Clos de la Roche, etc. These are big sturdy red Burgundies, long-lived, usually good values, for they are the "forgotten wines of the Côte de Nuits." These wines go especially well with beef and lamb (particularly the finer cuts), game, venison. The finest bottles deserve to be savored on their own, or at most, with nuts, fruit, and cheeses, especially mild Cheddar, Port-Salut, Roquefort, Brie. Serve this wine at cool room temperature after allowing it to breathe for an hour or so. Morey wines are generally at their best when they are from five to ten years old.

Some wine does reach the U.S. under the name of Morey-Saint-Denis, and it will be somewhat cheaper than those single vineyard wines: $7 to $9, compared to $10 to $15. It is excellent wine and often a good value. Some recent beauties, all *****: 1969 Lupe Cholet; 1970 Joseph Arlaud (already good drinking); 1971

Sigaut (will be even better from 1976 on).

MORGEOT: See CHASSAGNE-MONTRACHET (WHITE).

MORGON *** to **** Fine red Beaujolais (the name Beaujolais may not be on the label), less fruity perhaps than some, but full bodied and full of flavor. It's at its best when it's from three to five years old. How to serve it: See under BEAUJOLAIS. Château de Pizay is one of the finest. You can also trust the Morgon of Paul Bocuse, Marcel Vincent, Jonchier, Jadot, and Pierre Olivier.

MOSCATO AMABILE: See MUSCAT DE FRONTIGNAN.

MOSCATO D'ORO: See MUSCAT DE FRONTIGNAN.

MOSCATO DI CANELLI: See MUSCAT DE FRONTIGNAN.

MOSEL SAAR-RUWER: See MOSELLE.

MOSELBLÜMCHEN (occasionally: MOSELLE BLÜMCHEN) The name is far and away the prettiest thing about this wine—it means "Little Moselle Flower." Too often the wine does not match. Moselblümchen is a regional blend, often of cheap wines, frequently sugared ones. One authority (Alexis Lichine) says simply, "It is totally bad." Things have improved some in recent years, however, and today there are some good Little Flowers blooming ever and anon. Note, however, that the wine is officially classified as *Tafelwein*, it's on the label, "Table Wine," the lowest grade of German wine in the new classification. But in truth this is demeaning to some of today's Moselblümchen.

The best: Anheuser; Beameister; Export Union; Guntrum; Hallgarten; Sichel; Steigenberger.

Good values: Deinhard; Havemeyer; Kreusch; Teitel.

Avoid very cheap Moselblümchen, anything under $2.50. How to serve and enjoy this wine: See under MOSELLE.

MOSELLE One of the most hallowed names in all of winedom, marvelous white German wines, like no others of this earth. What's more, this can be said even of the poorer examples—they have an indescribable perfume, elegance, and especially delicacy—that's the key word. Moselles are the world's most delicate wines.

What makes them so distinctive, experts tell us, is the slatey soil. The word in German is *lay*, and you will note how many vineyards have this word as a suffix.

Moselles can accompany light foods: sandwiches, smoked turkey, salmon, ham. But their singular delicacy and gentle spiciness will largely be lost when so consumed. To be truly appreciated, Moselles should be consumed on their own. They make marvelous aperitif wines. Moselles need to be drunk young (except special pickings: Auslesen, Beerenauslesen, etc.): between two and five years old. They are served chilled.

The label usually reads "Mosel–Saar–Ruwer," sometimes in bolder type than the name of the wine itself. Look up individual wines under their proper names: Bernkasteler, Zeller Schwarze Katz, etc.

Some recent Moselle vintages—remember that vintages are very important in Germany:

1969—Excellent wines, an especially fine year in the Moselle. Drink soon.

1970—Good year—Huge crop, but wines are on the light side, will not last. Drink immediately.

1971—A great year, comparable to the "classic" '34, '45, '53. The wines are expensive but worth it—if you can still find any. Will be at their best, 1976–1978.

1972—Good vintage, wines are light and pleasant—At their best, 1975–1977.

1973—Very good year—Wines will be at their best, 1976 to 1980 or so.

MOSELLE, AMERICAN: See RHINE WINE.

MOSELLE BLÜMCHEN: See MOSELBLÜMCHEN.

MOUCHES, CLOS DES: See CLOS DES MOUCHES.

MOULIN-À-VENT This is probably the best of all red Beaujolais wine—it's called the king of Beaujolais. It's a bigger, sturdier, longer-lived wine than any other Beaujolais. Incredibly it's been known to keep twenty and even fifty years. Moulin-à-Vent (it means "the Windmill") is normally at its best when it is from four to six years of age. How to serve it: See under BEAUJOLAIS.

Some notable bottles currently available—hopefully—somewhere:

1969 Louis Jadot: ****
   Mommessin: ****
1970 Louis Jadot: *****
1971 Paul Bocuse: ****
   Domaine de Pizay: ****
   Louis Jadot: *****
1972 Domaine de la Rochelle: **** Will be at its best, 1976–1979.
   Domaine de Pizay: **** Will be at its best, 1976–1979.
   Paul Bocuse: **** Will be at its best, 1976–1979.

MOUNT EDEN This is the new name for the wines that used to be labeled Martin Ray.

To date, only one wine has been produced under this name, 1972 Chardonnay, released in late 1974: *****. It's after the fashion of the late, departed Martin Ray wines: intense, controversial, expensive ($20). It won a gold medal at the 1974 Los Angeles County Fair and has generally received good marks from the experts, though some say it's overly oaky.

Their second wine will probably be a Pinot Noir, 1972, released in 1975. It augureth well.

MOUNTAIN RED WINE, AMERICAN: See BURGUNDY, AMERICAN.

MOURA BASTO VINHO VERDE*** Light, young, crisp, zestful white wine from Portugal. It's even got a tiny sparkle to it. How to serve it: See under VINHO VERDE.

MOUTON-BARON-PHILIPPE, CHÂTEAU First coussin, or perhaps second, of the illustrious Château Mouton-Rothschild, this red Bordeaux wine does not have a high official classification but many experts say it is underclassed. It is a fine, consistent, typical French Claret. How to serve it: See under BORDEAUX.

1962—*****—Drink it soon.
1966—*****—Best drinking, 1975–1982.
1967—****—At its best now and through 1978.
1970—***—Overpriced at $9 to $12.
1971—***—Overpriced at $8.50.

MOUTON CADET (CHÂTEAU) or: MOUTON CADET, BARON PHILIPPE ROTHSCHILD (or the reverse order of words) This red wine is probably the largest-selling Claret in the world. It has the lowest official rating of any Bordeaux wine, but it often outdoes itself.

It's a distant country cousin of the great Château Mouton-Rothschild—one writer says no blood relative—but in its own class, it is a good dependable wine, though at times overpriced. The '69 is ***, air it one to two hours. The '70 is just barely ****, a good value at $4.

MOUTON-ROTHSCHILD, CHÂTEAU This world-renowned Claret (red Bordeaux) is, beyond question, one of this earth's finest red wines. It is unique in two respects: (1) For more than a century Mouton did not have top official rating: it was classified only as a second, not first growth, though it has always sold with the firsts. (2) Since 1945 it has carried a different label each year. But as of June 21, 1973, Mouton lost its first uniqueness: after 118 years it was officially raised to *Premier crû* status. But may it never lose its second singularity, its unique labels. These are winedom's most striking and most artistic. They've been the work of such artists as Marc Chagall (1970), Joan Miró (1969), Henry Moore (1964), Georges Bracque (1955), Salvador Dali (1958). The artists are never paid for their work; they do the labels on the back of old envelopes over a bottle of Mouton. No wonder the labels are so inspired. They're an intriguing study, as each artist has tried to convey what the wine means to him.

Mouton is first cousin to Latour: stróng, dark, powerful wine, slow to mature, long to live, it uses a higher percentage of Cabernet Sauvignon (an intensely flavorful but tannic grape) than any other vineyard of the Médoc area (the heart of Bordeaux).

Mouton, like all other great wines, deserves to be consumed wholly on its own or with simple bread, cheeses, nuts. Never in competition with some gargantuan feast. Check older bottles for sediment and decant if necessary. The younger bottles, from 1950 on, should be aired one to two hours, and the older ones, one-half to one hour. Serve Mouton, well, perhaps not on bended knee, but with proper respect and due reverence, carefully, gratefully, slowly—at cool room temperature. You're allowed to speak—softly, reverentially, in hushed tones, as in a cathedral.

1929—Classic—It had better be classy and classic, for a jeroboam of this wine sold for more money than has any other single bottle of wine in the history of mankind. It sold for $9,600 at a Christie auction in Houston, Texas, in November, 1972. At this juncture it is legitimate to ask: Can any wine be *that* good? And the answer is NO! A wine can be only so fine, so perfect, so tasteful, complex, subtle. And that point is reached far, far this side of $9,600! Further, meditate on the fact that this wine was listed in the 40s on the wine list of Antoine's, the famous New Orleans restaurant, at exactly $9 for 24 ounces. Which means that it sold at the retail level for around $4.

1934—*****—It may be past its peak. Fair value, $40.

1945—Classic—One of the greatest Clarets of the twentieth century. Just now, at 30 years of age, reaching its peak. Fair value, $75, but it's been bringing around $150.

1947—Near-Classic—Fair value, $60—Alas, it's been fetching $150.

1948—Near-Classic—Largely overlooked, but a great wine. Fair value, $35.

1949—Classic—Big and rich, it's worth $70.

1950—Not recommended at anything more than $5.

1952—Classic—Sold at auction in '73 for a high of $33, but unfortunately people (not very bright) are paying $90 for it today. It's now at its best.

1953 and 1955—Both: Near-Classics—Both selling for an outrageous $105; a fair value would be something like $50. Both wines have just reached their peak and will hold there for a decade to come.

1959—Classic—Some call this the best of all '59s. It may just be beginning to fade. Don't hold it forever. It's been selling for $100 and more.

1960—Poor to start with and less than that today.

1961—Classic—Big and complex. Just now reaching its peak, and it will hold there for a decade at least. Fair value, $75, but expect to pay $100.

1962—Though some have downgraded this wine, it is a Classic, no less: strong, big, rich, round, one of the best of all '62s. It's now at its best, enjoy it anytime within the next decade. You should be able to find it fairly priced, $25 to $30, as the vintage, following the great '61, is overlooked and underpriced.

1964—****—Not up to Mouton standards. Surely not recommended at the likes of $50.

1965—Not recommended at almost any price—light, thin, harsh.

1966—Has not shown well in a single tasting, but Mouton

always shows poorly in its youth. It's now coming around, a big and beautiful wine: *****. At its best, 1975–1985.

1967—*****—Fair value, $25; at its best, 1975–1980.

1968—Eschew!

1969—Eschew again!

1970—It's going to reach Classic, starting in 1980 or thereabouts. Some say it's the best of all '70s. It's still relatively reasonably priced: $35 to $40.

1971—Tentatively: *****. Not ready; try it first in 1979. It's already bringing $22.

MUMM One of the largest and best known of France's great Champagne houses. Mumm's finest is their Rene Lalou (Lalu), very expensive ($25). The current vintage, 1966, is just now getting to its best: drink it, late '75 and through 1977. Mumm's big seller is their Cordon Rouge, a fine Champagne, which comes in both a vintage ($15) and a nonvintage version ($12.50). The vintaged Cordon Rouge, however, has not been showing well over recent vintages. The '61 was a complete throwback, not recommended at any price—the '62 and '64 and '66, all **** at best. The nonvintage Cordon Rouge is fine Champagne, regularly at least ****. Mumm's Extra Dry ($11.40) is most commendable, a "classic" Champagne in the best sense. To most palates it will probably be the most enjoyable of all Mumm Champagnes; it's got a touch of sweetness and can even go with a not-too-sweet dessert.

MURRIETA, MARQUES DE: See MARQUES DE MURRIETA.

MUSCADET Light, very dry white wine from France's Loire Valley. As other dry French white wines (Burgundies, Chablis, Pouilly-Fuissés) have zoomed out of sight in recent years, Muscadet has understandably gained in popularity, particularly in the U.S. It's no great wine, but it's a sound, fresh one, at a reasonable price, perfect with fish and shellfish. Drink it very young, the younger the better, and don't buy it if it's more than three years old. If it says De Sèvre et Maine on the label, so much the better. To be a good value, Muscadet should range between $3 and $4. Serve chilled.

MUSCAT DE FRONTIGNAN This is the name, borrowed from the French, of a sweet California dessert wine. It sometimes goes by its Italian name: Moscato Amabile, Moscato di Canelli, plus sundry variations. It's become quite popular and quite good over the past decade —particularly beloved of those who fancy the distinctive muskiness of the Muscat grape.

Listed below are California's Muscat wines, by whatever names they pass in society. They are listed in descending order of excellence, and when wines have the same rating, the least expensive is listed first. Prices are approximate.

California Muscat de Frontignan (and Associates)— Comparative Standings

****

Very Good

   Novitiate Muscat Frontignan ($2.85)

   Beringer Malvasia Bianca ($3.25)

   San Martin Muscato Canelli, 1973 ($4)

***

Good

   Beaulieu Muscat de Frontignan ($2.10)

Weibel Cream of Black Muscat ($2.60)

Novitiate Dry Malvasia ($2.75)

Bargetto Moscato Amabile ($2.95)

Novitiate Black Muscat ($3.10)

Concannon Muscat de Frontignan ($3.45)

Robert Mondavi Moscato d'Oro ($5)

Charles Krug Moscato di Canelli ($5.10)

**

Fair

Christian Brothers Château La Salle ($2.30)

*

Passable

CK Mondavi Bravissimo ($1.70)

Not Recommended

Franzia Muscatel ($1.05)

David Bruce Black Muscat ($4)

A few folks make this wine in a sparkling version, all rated *** (Good):

Weibel Moscato Spumante ($3.50)

Louis Martini Moscato Amabile ($3.90)

San Martin Malvasia Gran Spumante ($4)

Hanns Kornell Muscadelle de Bordelaise ($5.75)

MUSCATO CANELLI: See MUSCAT DE FRONTIGNAN.

(LE) MUSIGNY One of the world's great red wines, from Burgundy's illustrious Côte d'Or, the Golden Slope. The wine is famous for its silky texture and its femininity. One writer talks about its "lovely, haunting delicacy of perfume," its "uniquely sensuous savor"; another calls it a wine of "silk and lace." Because the vineyard, a mere twenty-five acres, is divided among many owners, Le Musigny can vary greatly parcel to parcel and shipper to shipper. Savor, appreciate, and enjoy your Musigny gratefully and slowly on its own or with cheeses, especially Cheddar, Brie, Bel Paese. Air it about one hour and serve at cool room temperature.

Some vintages:

1869 Classic vintage—Any lying 'round the kitchen?

1945 Outstanding year.

1947 Drouhin: Classic.

1955 Adrien: Near-Classic.

1961 Regnier: *****.

1962 Drouhin: Near-Classic.

1964 Drouhin: Near-Classic.

1966 George de Vogue: Near-Classic.

Drouhin: Near-Classic.

1969 Hudelot: ****

1971 Dufouleur: ****

Jadot: ****

Remossenet: *****

MYGLANDS, CLOS DES: See MERCUREY.

N

NAPA-SONOMA-MENDO-CINO This is a brand used by Italian Swiss Colony (see) for three of their premium table wines. The grapes come from the three named northerly California counties, which is a good start, for they produce superior grapes.

Burgundy** Good everyday drinking—dry, quite fruity. To accompany simple weekday fare. Note that there is another, a "plain" Burgundy, somewhat cheaper, marketed under the Italian Swiss Colony label: $1.35 vs. $1.75 for this one.

Chablis** Fresh, pleasant, medium-dry white wine. For refreshment or to accompany light foods and luncheon fare. ISC makes another Chablis, under its Italian Swiss Colony label, almost as good as this, and somewhat cheaper: $1.35 vs. $1.75 for this one.

Vin Rosé—Not recommended.

NEBBIOLO This is the name of Italy's noblest grape, the grape responsible for most of the great Italian red wines: Barolo, Barbaresco, Gattinara. But the name Nebbiolo is not on those labels at all. When a wine goes by the name of Nebbiolo it is a lesser wine, though a sound one, and often a good value as well, as Nebbiolo is not greatly in demand. Serve it with meat or Italian dishes. It is at its best when between three

and seven years of age. It is consistently ***.

NECTAROSÉ*** This is the name of a rosé wine, barely on the sweet side, from the Anjou region of France. Anjou rosés are widely available in the U.S., under a host of labels, and one would do well to stay on the trodden path and buy only those found in this book. Such as this one, a fair value at ca. $3. How to serve Nectarosé: See under ROSÉ.

NIERSTEIN (BEREICH) or NIERSTEINER or NIER-STEINER DOMTAL or DOMTHAL or GUTES DOMTAL Be not confused—neither dismayed: German wine labels are the most confusing in the world—at least to non-Germans. They also happen to be the most exact. A whole new set of laws was recently enacted (1971) to simplify and clarify the tangled jumble, and the above heading shows how simple things now are!

To all intents and purposes all the above names are just that, various names for virtually one and the same wine. There are others, but they were omitted from the above heading lest you become discouraged: Nierstein(er) Goldener Adler (Schmitt), Nierstein(er) Rote Erde (Schmitt), Nierstein(er) Kurfuerst (Sichel), Nierstein (er) Krone (Langenbach).

All these are simply regional wines from the Nierstein area.

They are actually very similar to the ever-popular Liebfraumilch, selling in about the same price range. The most popular of all the names is Domtal or Gutes Domtal, which means "the Valley of the Cathedral" and "the Good Valley of the Cathedral." None of these wines is as good a wine as for example, Niersteiner Kransberg or Niersteiner Hipping. Like Liebfraumilch they can be quite good, and they can also, if one is not careful, be pretty bad. As with Liebfraumilch, avoid very cheap Niersteiners—anything under $2.

Look for these names on your Niersteiner: Anheuser; Wilh. Christ; Guntrum; Hallgarten; Havemeyer; Kendermann; Kreusch; Langenbach; Langguth; Madrigal (see also under its own name); F. K. Schmitt; Sichel; Steigenberg.

Niersteiner is at its best when it's between two and five years of age. It will vary in price from about $2.50 to $5. Drink it just as you would Liebfraumilch, with mild foods (fish, poultry) or on its own, especially the sweeter versions. Serve it chilled: 45 to 50°F; two and a half hours in the refrigerator is just right.

NIERSTEINER HIPPING Fine German white wine, virtually on a par with Rehbach (see, below). A 1966 (Reinhold Senfter) deserves: *****—Drink it soon, sooner, soonest. A '69 (F. K. Schmitt) is a big wine, ***, now at its best.

NIERSTEINER KRANSBERG Good German Rhine (white) wine, particularly trustworthy if it has the name of Franz Karl Schmitt on it, as all these following do: 1967 Riesling Spätlese: beautiful, luscious wine, ****, but don't hold it.

The '70 is a glorious wine, has everything a Rhine wine should have and more: ****. 1971 was an outstanding year in Germany and the whole gauntlet of Schmitt's Kransbergs of that splendid vintage is available in the U.S., from the "straight" Qualitatswein ($4) to a Kabinett ($4.50) to a Spätlese ($5) to a Riesling Auslese ($7.50) to a Beerenauslese ($19), all of them worth their respective prices, demonstrating the validity of the saying that in German wines you get what you pay for.

NIERSTEINER ORBEL Good German white wine, not quite on a par with Rehbach (see, below) but reliable and sound. A '71 Riesling Auslese (Seip) is outstanding: **** and the same by F. K. Schmitt gets *****.

NIERSTEINER REHBACH Excellent German white wine from "Liebfraumilch" country, but better by 2,000 kilometers! There is a saying in Germany that all Liebfraumilchs would be Niersteiners if they could. "Straight" Rehbach (F. K. Schmitt) will usually rate **** and a '67 Hochfeine Auslese is a Near-Classic . . . alas, it fetches about $20. A '53 Rehbach-Mundelpfad, still available here and there, may God direct your steps, is perfect today: velvety soft, clean, heavenly: Near-Classic.

NIERSTEINER SCHMITT ROTE ERDE* Typical good German Rhine wine, very similar to a top Liebfraumilch: soft, very pleasant, easy drinking, a touch of sweetness.

NIERSTEINER SPIEGELBERG Good German Rhine wine, usually a cut above "plain" Niersteiners or Niersteiners Domtal. The '69 Spätlese took an impressive British wine award—they said it had a "suggestion of apples." Both the '70 Kabinett and Spätlese are fine wines, extremely fruity and flowery. All of these wines should be drunk during 1975 and 1976; all of them merit ****.

NIPOZZANO: See FRESCO-BALDI.

NOVITIATE (Los Gatos, Calif.) Wine and religion have always had a holy alliance. They still have: witness the many "religious" wine labels on European wines: Liebfraumilch (the Virgin's Milk), Châteauneuf-du-Pape (the Pope's New Château), Lacrima Christi (the Tears of Christ), and hundreds more. Even in the New World the alliance continues. Novitiate wines are made entirely by the Jesuit Fathers of California. Besides their commercial output, they also produce a complete line of altar wines available only to the clergy. Novitiate wines are ready to drink when purchased and will keep at least two years, but none of them will improve noticeably in the bottle. Novitiate's specialty: aperitif and dessert wines. Their more important offerings include:

Black Muscat*** An unusual sweet dessert wine; serve slightly chilled with a not-too-sweet dessert. Fair value, $3.25. It's the Fathers' most popular wine and the one that first won acclaim for their wines. It took a gold medal at the 1974 Los Angeles County Fair.

Burgundy*** Simple, attractive, a good value at $2.25 to $2.40. Serve at room temperature, with grilled hamburgers.

Cabernet Be careful here. If the label just has the one name,

"Cabernet," it's an older version of what Novitiate now calls Ruby Cabernet (see). It's not a real Cabernet Sauvignon.

Cabernet Sauvignon*** This grape produces California's best red wine; Novitiate's version has improved noticeably in recent years. Fair value, $4.

Charvet Rosé*** Drink it young, drink it cool.

Château Novitiate** Quite sweet, white dessert wine. Fair value, $2.25.

Chenin Blanc*** Aperitif wine, or with light foods. Fair value, $2.50.

Dry Malvasia*** A new wine, soft with a little sweetness. Try it with fresh fruit. Fair value, $2.75.

Dry Sauterne**

Dry Sherry*** Good aperitif wine. Fair value, $2.25.

Flor Sherry** The driest of Novitiate's sherries, they call it a "connoisseur's aperitif"—well, maybe someday, but not just yet . . . Fair value, $2.75.

Grenache Rosé*** Fresh and pleasant. Fair value, $2.50.

Muscat Frontignan**** Golden color, distinctive flavor and perfume, a tasty dessert wine. Try it with plum pudding or fresh fruit. It took a gold medal at the 1974 Los Angeles County Fair. Good value at $2.75 to $3.

Pinot Blanc**** Delicate sweet white wine. Serve as an aperitif or with fish, light foods. Fair value, $2.50.

Ruby Cabernet** Red table wine, good to accompany common fare. It has varied somewhat from year to year. Fair value, $2.50.

Sherry Novitiate makes many different sherries; this "plain" one is a medium sherry, semisweet, a good aperitif wine and a good value at $2.25 to $2.50.

NOZZOLE This is the name of a fine Italian Chianti, a "classic" one, the best kind. It's made by the firm of Letezia Rimediotti Mattioli of Florence. Notice that it comes in a "regular" straight-edged bottle, not in a straw-covered *fiaschi*.

How to serve this wine: See under the general heading CHIANTI.

Some notable recent bottles:

1957: Was great, now over the hill.

1962: ****—Drink soon or sooner.

1964: ****—At its peak—Drink, 1975–1977.

1967: ****—At its best, 1975–1980—Look for it . . . it may reach *****

1968: ****—Lay it down and drink it starting in '76 or '77.

NUITS-SAINT-GEORGES This is a rather middle-class red Burgundy wine—not one of the aristocracy, but not of the peasant class either. It's a slow-maturing, long-lived wine, big and strong like a Chambertin. Nuits-Saint-Georges is at its best when it is from three years old to about six. It can vary considerably from label to label, and in price from around $8 to $11. It's even better if it has the name of an individual vineyard on the label, such as Les (or Le) Saint-Georges, Les Porrets (or Porets), La (or Les) Richemone (or Richemonnes), Clos de la Maréchale. Like all good red Burgundies, it will be best appreciated if consumed slowly and appreciatively with cheeses, fruit, nuts. It can also accompany red meats: beef, lamb, veal. Air Nuits-Saint-Georges about an hour and serve at cool room temperature.

O

OAKVILLE VINEYARDS
(Oakville, Calif.) A name you
can trust on a California label.
Since the mid-60s this winery
has produced some remarkable
wines. Off to such a glorious
start, who knows what marvels
the future may hold?

Cabernet Sauvignon
1969**** Very dark in color,
a big wine, deep flavor. There's
also a Reserve bottling, very
similar, even a little better.
Neither wine should be touched
before 1979. Good though these
are, it's surely questionable
whether they're worth today's
asking price of ca. $9.

1970**** There's a "plain"
as well as a Reserve bottling of
this vintage—both rich, powerful wines—the Reserve (Unfiltered) rates *****

Chenin Blanc
1971, 1972, 1973*** California produces a lot of good
Chenin Blanc—here's one. It's
a slightly sweet white wine and
it makes a fine summer thirst-
quencher (served chilled) or a
charming luncheon wine. Ready
for immediate drinking and will
remain fresh and refreshing
through 1976. The '72 is reaching for ****. Fair value, $3.25.

French Colombard
1972 and 1973*** Some
sweetness—serve it after dinner
with fruit and cheeses. Fair value, $2.50 to $3.

Gamay Rosé*** One of the
best dry California rosés you're
going to find. One critic—they

don't dig rosés—rated the '71
near-perfect. Good summertime
sipping (chilled) or with light
foods. Don't keep this more
than a year or so. Fair value,
$2.25.

Gewürztraminer
1972*** A good wine despite
the fact it's not really a typical
"Gewürz," which has a definite
spicy flavor. This has a hint of
apricots (where'd they come
from?). Serve at luncheon,
chilled, or with light foods.
Good drinking now and it will
hold through '76. Fair value,
$4.

Grande Carignane
1973*** Carignane is the
name of the grape, but it's
rarely seen on a label, as it is
used almost exclusively in
blends, such as California Burgundy. Oakville felt that one
particular batch of the grapes
was so good that it deserved a
bottling all its own. The adjective Grande was tacked on to
give this lowly grape additional
prestige. And it's a good little
wine—the carignane grape by
itself simply cannot make a big
wine—fine to accompany grilled
hamburgers, barbecued spareribs. Fair value, $3.25.

Napa Gamay
*1969, 1970, and 1971/72
Marriage**** Gamay is a youthful, tasty red wine, usually a
good value in California. Oakville's version is a little more
expensive ($3.50 to $3.75) than
most, but may be worth it. An

interesting comparison would be to taste this wine against Robert Mondavi's excellent Gamay ($3). Ready for immediate consumption, don't hold beyond 1975.

Our House Wine (Red and White)* Luv those homespun honest names—and these wines are exactly what they sound like: honest everyday wines for the family dinner table. They're a little more expensive than most jug wines, but they're also a mite better. Don't keep either of these more than a year or two. They won't improve with age.

Sauvignon Blanc (N.V.)* You may still find some nonvintage on retail shelves. Be sure to drink it soon. Sauvignon Blanc is a dry white wine, perfect with seafood or creamed chicken.

*Sauvignon Blanc, 1971***** This wine has already achieved some fame. It's wholly different from Oakville's nonvintage version (above), a big rare wine with perfect balance. A special Reserve bottling is even better than the "plain." Both are worth looking for. As Sauvignon Blanc goes, this is rather expensive, ca. $5, but you can save it for some festive occasion. Now at its best and will hold there through 1977.

Sauvignon Blanc, 1972— None such: it was marketed under Van Loben Sels label (see).

*Sauvignon Blanc, 1973****

Sauvignon Fleur, 1972 and 1973* This is a sweet version of Oakville's Sauvignon Blanc. It may be the only wine so named in all of the U.S. Try it with dessert or fresh fruit.

Will keep at least through 1978.

Zinfandel
*1970, 1971, 1972**** "Z" is one of California's most distinctive and best reds. It differs considerably from producer to producer; Oakville's version is in the youngish style: light and fresh. Drink it now while it's so. Never hold a bottle more than four or five years. Serve at room temperature, with hamburgers, steaks, pasta.

OCKFEN(ER)   BOCKSTEIN
Ockfen is a town of Germany's Saar region; Bockstein is the name of the vineyard. It's a very fine wine—some say that Ockfeners are the best of all Saar wines. They need lots of sunshine and are hard in poor years. How to serve this wine: See under MOSELLE. Some vintages to look for:

1949—Exceptional year.

1953—Great vintage.

1959—Great wines.

1969—Magnificent year—Drink soon.

1971—Great year—Drink immediately.

1972—Good vintage—At their best, 1975–1977.

1973—Very good year—Wines will be at their best, 1976–1980.

OLOROSO: A type of sherry. For general information, see under SHERRY. For evaluation of a particular bottle, see under the name of the producer of the wine.

ORFEVI This is the name of an Italian wine firm, not the name of a wine, as it might appear. Find your wine under its proper name, e.g., Frascati.

P

PAISANO: See GALLO PAISANO.

PALMER, CHÂTEAU What a delight to have a real French Bordeaux wine with a nice, simple name that damned Yankees can pronounce, but wouldn't you know, it's not pronounced Palmer as in Arnold, but Palm-air. Well, it does make it sound more posh! And perhaps posh is the word for Palmer: it's a rich, fabulous wine, noted for its delicacy and finesse. It has a middle official ranking, but many say it is underclassified. Palmer is very popular in Britain—one would suspect because of the simple, British-sounding name.

1920, 1921—Near-Classic.

1928, 1929—Near-Classic.

1945—Classic—Now at its best and will remain so at least for a decade. Fair value, $25.

1947—Classic—Gorgeous wine, now at its best, and you may find it at half the price of the '45.

1948—*****—Fine wine in an indifferent year. Drink soon, will soon be fading. Fair value, $7.

1955—*****—It's begun to decline. Drink immediately.

1959—Near-Classic—It's already fine drinking, but it is not yet fully mature. Try it starting in '76 or '77. Fair value, $20.

1960—****—Light but delicious. Drink it before 1977 arrives.

1961—Near-Classic—Just about reaching its peak in '75 and '76 and will keep beautifully all through the 80s. All '61s are expensive, mostly because Americans know it was a good year; they are almost never good buys. This Palmer '61 is a case in point—it sells today for around $50 . . . yet the '59 and '62, equally good, sell at half and one third that price!

1962—Near-Classic—Will be at its best, 1977–1987. Good value, $14.

1964—****—Drink, 1975–1980. Fair value, $10.

1966—Near-Classic—Will be at its best 1978–1990. Fair value, $20.

1967—*****—In a tasting of 50 wines in 1970 this wine placed first. It's already at its best and will hold so through 1985. Fair value, $13.

1970—It's had rather mixed reviews, not as good as this vintage warrants, but on balance: ****. Fair value, $15.

1971—Contrary to the rules, this looks better than the '70: ***** or Near-Classic. Too early for a precise evaluation.

PALOMINO CREAM SHERRY**** This luscious Spanish sherry is not named after a golden-hued horse—Palomino & Vergara (it's on the label) is the name of the wine's producer. It's a good value at around $4.

PALOMINO & VERGARA DON JUAN SHERRY**
Beautiful cocktail sherry: clear amber color, full fruitiness, the perfect aperitif wine. A good value at $4.25. How to serve these Palomino wines: See under SHERRY.

PARDUCCI WINE CELLARS (Ukiah, Calif.) Here's a little ol' winemaker who's grown to be a great big winemaker. And what's more, a good winemaker. It's California's northernmost winery, and is now owned by—of all things—a gang of schoolteachers. (Any grade school courses in enology?) The Parduccis, however, continue to run the operation, praise God!
Be careful not to confuse these several American-Italian winemakers: there's Parducci, and there's Pedroncelli (see), and there's Pedrizetti, all separate, distinct, and autonomous.

Burgundy* Unfair price, ca. $2.50. You can find lots of better Burgundy for less money. See BURGUNDY in general index.

Cabernet Sauvignon
*1968**** Not recommended at $4.50 and more.
*1969***** This wine was made in a number of variations (see following wines), all commendable wines and all more expensive than this "straight" version. All these '69 Cabernets are big strong wines and deserve to be reserved for some special occasion, some grand feast. This is a good value, though still not cheap, at ca. $5. A robust, substantial wine, unfiltered and unfined. Will be at its peak 1976 through 1980. It will probably have thrown a sediment by then, so stand it upright for twenty-four hours, then decant.
*1969, Talmage**** Talmage

is a new Parducci vineyard where this wine originated. It's already been matured for three years in casks and it should lie peaceably in your cool dark cellar for another two or three years. Fair value, $7.
*1969, Philo Cask No. 33****
Philo is one of Parducci's ranches. Here's a rich hearty wine which will be at its best 1976 through 1980.
*1969, Kelseyville Cask No. 34*** This was the least successful of these glorious '69ers. Will be at its peak 1975 through 1978. Can't be recommended, however, at $6 or even $5.
*1970**** The winery says this is the best they've ever produced. A magnificent value at $4.25 to $4.50. Stash it away and open one bottle a year, starting in 1976. May need decanting—check for sediment.

Chablis* The winery seems to be the only one proud of this wine—why, we can't imagine. Fair value, $2.50.

Chenin Blanc* This grape, imported from France's Loire Valley, produces a fresh, flowery white wine in California. Parducci's recent offerings, 1971, '72, '73, all fill the description. They're ready to be consumed when you buy them, and don't keep any of them more than four years beyond their vintage date. Serve chilled; good as an aperitif or with light foods. Good value, $2.50 to $3.

Flora, 1970* This fruity, spicy white is a new wine, from a new grape; it shows promise. Very little of it is yet produced in California. Serve as you would Chenin Blanc (above). Good value, ca. $2.50.

French Colombard A fresh, tart little white wine, not often made in California. Bottled young, it should be consumed young (within three years). Serve chilled, for summertime refreshment or as an accompaniment for light foods. A good value at $2.50 to $2.75.

1970, 1971, 1972*** The '71 and '72 even have a slight sparkle—no extra charge.

Gamay Beaujolais*** Gamay, a sprightly young red wine, comes in different forms in California—this is one of the more sedate versions, which is to say that it needs a few years of aging. (Some are drunk within months of the harvest.) Wherefore it's also a little more expensive than most California Gamays: ca. $3.75 versus $2.50 to $3. Air the '69 or '70 for one hour; they'll remain at peak 1975 through 1977.

Petite Sirah This grape makes one of California's best red wines: full flavored, zesty, and relatively cheap. Parducci makes one of the best. Drink your Petite Sirah with roasts, steaks, any hearty food. If you're a true red-wine-lover (all connoisseurs are), you'll enjoy your Parducci P.S. on its own —or with Cheddar, Bleu, Port Salut. Air at least one hour; check for sediment and decant if necessary. Serve, cool room temperature.

1965*** Worth looking for. Just now reaching its peak, will hold through 1980. Good value, $5.50 to $6.

1967*** At its best 1975 through 1978. Good value at $5.

1968*** Huge almost pungent wine—it wasn't filtered or fined. Will be at its best, 1976 through 1981. Good value at $5.

1969 and *1971**** This wine spent four years "in wood" (oak casks) and it still isn't ready to drink. Give it another two or three years and it will keep until 1985 and beyond. Fair value, $5.

Pink Fumé** A new wine, but Gertrude Stein said it: a rose is a rose is a rose . . . This one is crisp and light, on the dry side. Summertime refreshment (if you're not too fussy). Fair value, $2.50 to $2.75.

Pinot Chardonnay
1971**** This regal white wine has a mite more sweetness than most California Chardonnays. Wherefore it'll make a glorious aperitif wine, yet it's worthy of your finest shellfish entree (Coquilles St. Jacques?). Good value, $4 to $4.50.

Pinot Noir
1969**** Serve it at cool room temperature, and it will go well with anything from hamburgers to coq au vin. Good value, $4.50 to $5.

1970 and *1971* It's a bit too early to give a final evaluation on these wines, but thus far, both are good-looking. Fair value, $4.25 to $4.50.

Sylvaner This good German-type wine is often under-appreciated by American wine drinkers. It can be a glorious beverage: big, mellow, full of flavor. And that's exactly what Parducci's is. It also has a bit of sweetness: ideal for summer (or any other season!) sipping, chilled. If you take it to the dinner table, be sure the food is light: fish, seafood, fowl simply prepared. Current vintages, 1971 and 1972: ****, good values at $3.50.

Zinfandel
1964****
1966, 1967, 1968**** "Z" is almost always one of California's best buys in red wines and this is doubly true with Parducci's version. Good hamburger wine, these, or with

more pretentious fare, especially red meat dishes. Now at their best and will hold through 1976. Air one hour, serve at cool room temperature.

1969*** Now at its best; drink through 1975 and 1976. Air one hour, serve at room temperature. Good value, $3 to $3.50.

1971 Allow this wine a tentative ***, though it's too early to give a final estimate. The winery thinks it will be good, and they should know. Fair value, $2.50 to $2.75.

(FEDERICO) PATERNINA This Spanish wine firm (in the town of Haro, in the Rioja region) is well known around the world; Paternina is one of Spain's largest exporters, and their wines are sometimes excellent values, though the price of some (especially the Gran Reservas) has been rising shamelessly over the past few years. Incidentally, the sweeping "Ollauri" that graces the label is the name of the town. The best buys:

Banda Azul It means "Blue Band" which it has, across the label. This was Ernest Hemingway's favorite wine—he surely could have afforded more expensive wine but he knew a good value when he saw one: today, $2.75 to $3.

Some vintages:

1952, 1955, 1959: ***** Seek and ye may find!

1961: ****—Good fruitiness, be sure to air it.

1964: ***—Give it a couple more years and it may rise to ****.

1967, 1969: ****—Already good drinking, and will probably improve even further.

1970: ****—It's even popular in Spain!

Gran Reserva Some have

been marvelous wines, the '61 and '64 for example, but the price varies widely. These are excellent values in the $2.80 to $3.80 range, but are certainly overpriced at $5.

How to serve these Paternina wines: See under RIOJA.

Viña Vial—Usually**** This wine is older than the Banda Azul when bottled, and sells for about a dollar more. It can also be a good value, but it's not quite as consistent as the Azul.

PAUL MASSON: See MASSON, PAUL.

PEDRO DOMECQ CELEBRATION CREAM SHERRY ***** Pedro Domecq is a very prominent Spanish wine firm producing an array of sherries, invariably dependable. This sweet sherry is a rich, smooth, heart-warming wine, a good value at $5 and a fair one at $6.25. How to serve this wine: See under SHERRY.

PEDRO DOMECQ DOUBLE CENTURY SHERRY*** This is a medium-sweet sherry—but only medium-good. It's one of Domecq's less successful endeavors. Selling today for around $4.75, it is not a very good value. How to serve: See under SHERRY.

PEDRO DOMECQ GUITAR SHERRY*** This is a Fino—dry—sherry, though not as dry as La Ina, below. It's usually the lowest-priced Domecq sherry available in the U.S., at around $4.25. How to serve this wine: See under SHERRY.

PEDRO DOMECQ LA INA *****Here's one of Domecq's best-known wines, and one of their best. La Ina is a fine Fino—if you'll excuse the uproarious pun—an excellent aperitif wine, very dry, clean, full flavored, with sprightly nuttiness. Fair value, $5 to $5.50. How to serve: See under SHERRY.

PEDRO DOMECQ PRIMERO SHERRY*** The label tells you it's an Amontillado, a medium sherry. Fair value, $4 to $4.50. How to serve: See under SHERRY.

PEDRO DOMECQ IDEAL PALE SHERRY*** A medium dry wine, somewhat sweeter than the Guitar, above, and selling for about the same. How to serve: See under SHERRY.

J. PEDRONCELLI WINERY (Geyserville, Calif.) Here's another of those little ol' California Italian winemakers who knows what he's about. For fifty years this has been a family operation, and still is. Some of Pedroncelli's whites leave something to be desired, but the reds represent some of the best wine values in the U. S. Say the Pedroncellis: "We treat our wines with delicacy and kindness." They usually show it.

Burgundy*** A tasty little red wine for your grilled hamburgers, stews, pasta. It's ready for immediate enjoyment when you buy it and will hold for five years. Serve at cool room temperature. Very good value at $2.

Cabernet Sauvignon This is one of the lowest-priced vintaged Cabernets in California—almost always a good value, especially if you buy the current vintage, at $3.25 or $3.50. Serve it (at cool room temperature) with pride with your best cuts of beef or lamb. Or enjoy it, sippingly, before meals or after —or any other time!

*1967***** Big wine, will be at its best, 1977 through 1983. Air 30 minutes. Good value at $6.

*1968**** Tasty and honest; drink, 1975 through 1980; air 30 minutes; good value, $5.

*1969**** Drink, 1975 through 1985. Air 30 minutes.

*1970***** Best drinking, 1976 through 1986. Excellent value, $3.25 to $3.50. Air one hour.

Chablis*** There is a lot of abominable "Chablis" made in the U.S.A. This, mercifully, is not some of it. This wine has improved noticeably in the past few years. Today it classifies as a good value, at $2 or even less. It's on the dry side. Serve it chilled, with shellfish, fish, poultry, mild casseroles. It took silver medals at the Los Angeles County Fair, both 1973 and 1974. Ready for immediate drinking—don't keep it more than a year or two.

Chenin Blanc

*1971 and 1972**** Refreshing white wine with an embroidery of sweetness. These will be best appreciated by themselves. At their best, 1975 through 1977. Fair value, $2.25 to $2.50.

*1973**** Fruity, on the dry side. Best drinking, 1975 through 1977.

Gamay Beaujolais   **** Fruity, youngish, light red wine; it was a gold medal winner at the Los Angeles County Fair in 1973 and again in 1974. Serve at cool room temperature, at your patio barbecue. Ready to drink when purchased, don't keep it more than two years. Fair value, $2.50 to $2.75.

Gewürztraminer, 1973****

Johannisberg Riesling Some recent vintages haven't been very exciting (1970, **), but the current 1971 and 1973, ****, in the dry style, has fine flavor and will do honor to your most elegant fish or seafood entree—or poultry in white sauce. Serve it chilled. A good value at $3.30 to $3.50.

Pinot Chardonnay This is the classic white Burgundy grape, but Pedroncelli's version has sometimes been rather unclassic. Recent vintages, however—1970, 1971, 1972, 1973 —have been uniformly ***. Its best use is to accompany fish, poultry, pork, ham. It will be at its best from two to six years after its vintage date. Fair value, $3.25 to $3.50.

Pinot Noir Pedroncelli does well by this illustrious grape of Burgundy (France). Here's a good value in fine red table wines: a wine fit to accompany your most impressive standing rib roast, your *boeuf bourguignon*, your best steaks. It will be at its best from five to ten years after the vintage date on the bottle. Air it about one hour and serve at cool room temperature. An unbelievable value at ca. $3.50.

1966***
1968****
1969****
1970***** Will be at its best from 1977 onward. A tremendous value—if you can find it!
1971**** at least. It took a gold medal at the 1974 Los Angeles County Fair.

Sonoma Red, Sonoma Rosé, Sonoma White*** Three first-rate California jug wines, made from grapes from northern California, not from the scorching interior valleys. Use these wines for your informal dining, employing the old basic rule of thumb: the whites with white meat, the reds with red, and the rosé with either or both or anything or nothing. Good values, all, at $3.50 per half-gallon.

Zinfandel*** Nobody's quite sure where this grape originated, but all agree that it makes a zesty, tasty red wine in California, and Pedroncelli's is about as good as any, and a good value. Recent vintages, 1969, '70, '71, have all been good. It goes well with Italian food, or with those grilled hamburgers (who can afford steak?), barbecued chicken, stew, casseroles. At its best from three to ten years after its vintage date. Serve at cool room temperature. An excellent value at $2.25 to $2.50.

Zinfandel Rosé*** Pedroncelli pioneered with this wine almost twenty years ago, and they've been doing a good job with it ever since. They say it's zingy—that's as good as any. It's on the dry side, which will please the initiated. It's a good value at $1.90 to $2.20. Serve it chilled with whatever—well, not with a banana split. Drink it while it's fresh: within two years of purchase.

PERIGNON, DOM: See DOM PERIGNON.

PERRIER, LAURENT: See LAURENT-PERRIER.

(LES) PERRIÈRES: See MEURSAULT.

PETITE CHABLIS: See CHABLIS, FRENCH.

PETITE SIRAH You can spell it just about any way you want: Petite or Petit—Sirah or Syrah —or any combination thereof, but it all comes out to the same thing: a lusty, spicy, big-bodied red wine of California. Nobody knows where the grape came from—the Rhone? Persia? Cucamonga?—but everybody knows where it's going *to:* upward and onward! It increases in popularity in America by the hour, as people learn about it.

Because of its relative obscurity plus the fact that Petite Sirah grapes are much less expensive than the likes of Cabernet Sauvignon and Pinot Noir, it is usually a good value. The wine does not, perhaps, attain to the complexity of those two premium California reds, but it can be an excellent wine, very dry, yet soft and tasty. It's famous for its peppery bouquet. Smell of it, even if you don't want to drink it!

Petite Sirah goes with a variety of foods: red meats, especially grilled hamburgers or steaks, roasts, hearty casseroles, pasta, even Mexican fare, if not too *picante*. Like all good red wine it can be appreciated most of all with cheese, especially Cheddar, Longhorn, Bleu, Port Salut, Bel Paese, Valençay.

Air all Petite Sirah at least one hour—young wine, two hours. Check older bottles for sediment and decant if necessary. Petite Sirah can be drunk relatively young—say within two or three years of vintage-date, but all except the poorest will improve with a year or two in the bottle. The very best shouldn't be drunk until they're about five years old, and they'll go on improving for another five years. Serve Petite Sirah at cool room temperature.

Below are California's best Petite Sirahs, listed in descending order of excellence. Where wines have the same rating, the least expensive is listed first. Prices are approximate.

Petite Sirah—
Comparative Standings

*****
Exceptional
Freemark Abbey Petite Sirah, 1971 ($4.75)
Ridge Petite Sirah, 1971 York Creek ($5)

****
Very Good

Sonoma (or Windsor) Petite Sirah, 1971, 1972 ($3)
Concannon Petite Sirah, 1965, 1966, 1968, 1969 ($3.50)
Parducci Petite Sirah, 1965, 1967, 1968 ($3.85)
Souverain Petite Sirah, 1969 ($4.75)
Robert Mondavi ($4.75)
Freemark Abbey Petite Sirah, 1969 ($4.75)

***
Good
San Martin Petite Sirah ($3)
Assumption Abbey Petite Sirah ($3)
Kenwood Petite Sirah, 1972 ($3)
Cresta Blanca Petite Sirah ($3.15)
Concannon Petite Sirah, 1967, 1970 ($3.50)
Mirassou Petite Sirah, 1967, 1968, 1970, 1971 ($3.65)
Parducci Petite Sirah, 1969 ($3.85)
Souverain Petite Sirah, 1968 ($4.25)
Ridge Petite Sirah, 1970 Mendocino ($4.25)

**
Fair
Wente Petite Sirah, 1969, 1970 ($2.65)
Sonoma (or Windsor), nonvintage ($2.70)
Mirassou Petite Sirah, 1969 ($3.65)
Souverain Petite Sirah, 1966, 1967 ($4.25)

PÉTRUS, CHÂTEAU The name is Latin for Peter, and sure enough, there is St. Peter himself on the label. Nobody seems to know exactly how Pete, if you'll excuse the familiarity, got on the label, or how the vineyard came to be named after the Prince of the Apostles, but it's a princely red Bordeaux wine, all right, a soft, well-rounded, velvety wine, said to taste of truffles—whatever they taste like! Though not officially ranked with the great first growth Clarets (Lafite, Mouton, etc.), in popular esteem, Château Pétrus has never been ranked anywhere else. A wine of such repute and excellence deserves to be appreciated on its own, not at a meal. For details on serving it: See BORDEAUX.

1947 Near-Classic At its best now and through the 70s and probably beyond.

1949 Classic Best drinking: now and until 1985, at least—Excellent value at $25.

1950***** Excellent wine in a lesser year.

1952***** Fine wine in a "mixed" year—Fair value $20, not the $100 at which some retailers list it!

1953 Near-Classic Just beginning to be ready, drink anytime before 1985. Fair value, $20 to $25.

1955**** It's been selling for beyond its worth, from $40 to $100. At its best now and to 1980.

1961 Classic Universally acclaimed. It's called a masterpiece. You are blest if you own it—or if you can find it. It's hard to come by. Fair value: What you're willing to pay—it sold at auction in '73 for a high of $83. Just now getting to its best and it will hold at its peak at least until 1985.

1962 Near-Classic At its best, 1975–1985. Fair value, $27.

1964 Near-Classic Fully mature and will hold at its peak until 1990. Fair value, $40 to $50.

1966 Near-Classic Perhaps it is not quite at classic status at this moment but as sure as the Lord God made little green apples, it's going to get there—say, around 1977. It's a good value—well, as these things go, relatively speaking—at $30 to $40.

1967 Classic Another great one, and again the price is relatively reasonable: $35 to $45. It's already very drinkable but it will be even better, 1977 onward.

1969 Not recommended at $30 to $40.

1970 Classic Some say the best of all 70s. It will be at its best from 1978 through 1990. Fair value, $45.

1971 Preliminary reports are glowing. Looks like another great one.

PICHON - LONGUEVILLE, CHÂTEAU (Also known as: BARON PICHON-LONGUEVILLE, or: PICHON, or: LONGUE-LONGUEVILLE AU BARON DE PICHON, or: PICHON-LONGUEVILLE, BARON DE PICHON) *Clear?* If you can get through the nomenclature, you'll like the wine! It's a superb Claret (red Bordeaux), some say similar to Lafite, though it actually adjoins Château Latour. Don't confuse this wine with its sister vineyard, Pichon-Longueville-Lalande (see). How to serve Pichon: See under BORDEAUX.

1928—Departed this world.

1929—Classic—Still with us, but don't keep it—drink it. Fair value, $30.

1943—Classic—Some say better than the Grands Seigneurs, this vintage. Fair value, if you can find it, $10.

1947, 1948, 1949, 1950, 1952, 1953—All *****, and all for present drinking. If you can find them, they should range between $10 and $20.

1955—*****—At its best. Fair value, $25.

1958—****—Surprisingly

good for this year. It should be cheap: ca. $5.

1959—*****—Now at its peak and will hold for a decade.

1960—****—Marvelous considering the vintage. Drink soon.

1961—*****—Best drinking: 1975 through 1985. Fair value, $15.

1962—Near-Classic, and it may even ascend higher—It's not ready, however—squirrel it away until at least 1977. A good value at $12 to $15.

1963—Near-Classic

1964—*****—Will be at its best, 1977 on. Fair value, $12.

1965—Eschew.

1966—*****—Best drinking 1976–1980. Fair value, $10.

1967—****—Needs time: try it starting 1980. Fair value, $10.

1970—Will probably come to *****, but it's going to take its own sweet time to mature. Lay it down until 1982—at the earliest! Fair value, $14.

PICHON-LONGUEVILLE-LALANDE, CHÂTEAU (or: PICHON-LONGUEVILLE COMTESSE DE LALANDE, or: PICHON-LONGUEVILLE-COMTESSE, or: PICHON-LALANDE) *Got it?* And don't you dare confuse it with Pichon-Longueville Baron or Baron Pichon-Longueville or Pichon-Baron or Longueville au Baron de Pichon or Pichon-Longueville, Baron de Pichon!
No wonder Americans flee to Mateus and Gallo Burgundy! But if you can cut your way through the nomenclature jungle you'll find a fine red Bordeaux (Claret) awaiting you. It's just across the street from its sister vineyard, Pichon-Baron, and the wines are equally superb. Lalande is somewhat faster-matur-

ing and not as long-lived. How to serve it: See under BORDEAUX.

1934—Classic.

1952—*****—Now at its best. Fair value, $12.

1959—****—Best drinking, 1975–1985. Fair value, $13.

1961—*****—At its best now and through the 80s. Fair value, $15.

1962—*****—Already good drinking but will be even better, 1976–1986. Fair value, $10.

1964—*****—Will be at its best, 1977–1985.

1965—***—Considering the year, it's not bad.

1966—Near-Classic—It will be at its best, 1978–1990. A good value at $10.

1967—*****—Just now reaching its peak and it will hold until mid-80s. Fair value, $11.

1969—Looks good.

1970—*****—Try it first in '78.

PIERROT, J. This is a brand name used by the giant wine cooperative, Guild Wine Co. At least one thing can be said for these jug wines (Burgundy, Chablis, Zinfandel): they're cheap, $2 per half-gallon, which is scarcely above the price of potable H_2O, which they're scarcely above, period. Even at their lowly price, not recommended.

PIESPORT(ER) (or: PIESPORT(ER) RIESLING) Piesport is a well-known village on Germany's Moselle River—a Piesporter is a wine from there. The name of the noble Riesling grape is often included in the title: Piesport(er) Riesling. Whatever it calls itself, it is one and the same wine, a "regional" from the Piesport area, not a top-flight Moselle such as Piesporter Goldtröpfchen. It can nevertheless be a fine wine, depending on the vintage and the shipper. How to serve and enjoy it: See MOSELLE. Sichel and Anheuser both make excellent Piesporter: ****. Leonard Kreusch's is the best value, however, at $2.35: ***. Ordinarily avoid cheap Piesporters, under $2.50.

PIESPORT(ER) GOLDTRÖPF-CHEN This is a more prestigious name than "plain" Piesporter or Piesporter Riesling. Goldtröpfchen is the name of the vineyard, a famous and popular name. These are Moselle wines at their best; they're rightly called the "queens of the Moselle," fragrant and flowery—"round and gently sweet," says one author. Some recent vintages:

1969 "Dom Klausenhoft" (Kessellstatt): *****

1970 A good year, but wines are not long-lasting—Drink up, now.

    (Hanover House): ***—A good value at $2.50.
    (Kreusch): ****—Excellent value at $4.
    (Lehnert): ***
    (Veit): ***—A good value at $2.50.
    Spätlese (Marienhof): ****
    Spätlese (Lehnert): ****
    Auslese (Lehnert): ****
    Kabinett (Veit): ****

1971 Great year—Wines are excellent drinking right now and will be at their very best, 1976–1978. Note that all the following bottles are of special pickings:

    Spätlese (Kessellstatt): *****
    Spätlese (Sichel): ****
    Spätlese, Fass 10 (Langguth): ****
    Spätlese (Weller-Lehnert): *****
    Spätlese (Dietzen): ****
    Spätlese (Kendermann): ***
    Spätlese and Auslese (Tobias): *****
    Kabinett (Lehnert-Matheus): ****
    Auslese (Kessellstatt): *****
    Auslese (Thomas): *****
    Auslese (N. Georg): ****
    Kabinett (Tobias): ****
    Auslese (Ludwig): ****
    Auslese (Kunsberg): ***

How to serve and enjoy these wines: See under MOSELLE.

PINARD RED, PINARD BLANC, PINARD ROSÉ** "Pinard" is a name borrowed from World War I by Boordy Vineyards, N. Y., for these three jug wines. "Monsieur Pinard" was the French front-line soldier's affectionate name for his daily portion of wine. "Monsieur Pinard" was even nominated for the Croix de Guerre! Boordy says the wines are "unpretentious but satisfying," and that's pretty accurate. Ready to drink when purchased, drink within a year or two. Good values at $3 per half-gallon.

PINOT BLANC This grape and this wine are the poor country cousins of the noble and lordly Pinot Chardonnay (see). Pinot Blanc wine doesn't attain to the lofty stature of a complex Chardonnay, but it can be a good, tasty white wine, crisp and dry, at half the price. In fact, it will often be preferred to Pinot Chardonnay by wine beginners, as it lacks Chardonnay's severe intensity.

California also makes a White Pinot, which, of course, is English for Pinot Blanc—but with our typical American brand of logic, White Pinot is not made from the Pinot Blanc grape at all, but from the Chenin Blanc! (One can only mutter parenthetically and disconsolately with the poet: "Logic, thou art fled to brutish beasts, and men have lost their reason . . .")

Pinot Blanc goes well with light foods: chicken, fish, shellfish, or for a special treat, with crab and San Francisco Sourdough bread. Serve it chilled: 45–50°F. Pinot Blanc is for young drinking—for consuming, certainly; for the consumer, as you will. Don't keep it more than a year or two after purchase; if it's vintaged, drink it before it's five years old.

Pinot Blanc—
Comparative Standings

*****

Exceptional
   Chalone Pinot Blanc, 1969 and 1970 ($5)

****

Very Good
   Wente Pinot Blanc, 1970 ($3.05)
   Novitiate Pinot Blanc ($3.55)
   Mirassou White Burgundy, 1971, 1972, 1973 ($3.60)
   Heitz Pinot Blanc, 1967, 1968, 1969 ($4.85)
   Chalone Pinot Blanc, 1971 ($5)

***

Good
   Almadén Pinot Blanc ($3)
   Wente Pinot Blanc, 1971 ($3.05)
   Paul Masson Pinot Blanc ($3.10)
   Mirassou White Burgundy, 1971 American Oak ($3.60)
   Heitz Pinot Blanc, 1970 ($4.85)

PINOT CHARDONNAY Everybody agrees that this is America's finest white wine: dry, very flavorful, aristocratic. And expensive. Some say you can detect the flavor of apples in California Chardonnay, and peaches in the French variety. (It's not called Pinot Chardonnay over there, however; it goes by a variety of names.)

The name, Pinot Chardonnay, is actually a misnomer—are there any American wines that aren't? The grape is not a Pinot at all—that's why you'll notice many of the newer California wineries are dropping the Pinot part, and calling the wine simply and correctly, Chardonnay. It's one of the world's noble grapes and is responsible for some of the world's greatest white wines, such as Chablis and France's great white Burgundies, including the illustrious Montrachets.

Chardonnay has skyrocketed in popularity in the U.S. in the past decade, until today it is California's most sought-after white wine. And with good reason: California vintners have done spectacular things with this wine over these past ten years. From an almost invisible 700 acres planted in California just ten years ago, there are more than ten times that number today, almost 8,000 acres. More California wineries are producing Chardonnay today than any other white wine.

Chardonnay is the white table wine par excellence, but as expensive as much of it is, you won't be serving it with fish sticks or tuna salad—you'll want to serve it with lobster or cracked crab or perhaps with that Christmas turkey. Chardonnay isn't a snob, however, and it goes well with humbler fare. Some of the lesser Chardonnays will be very much at home with fish, poultry, veal. But to savor every dollar's worth of your $5 or $10 Chardonnay you would be well advised to enjoy it, with some wine-loving friends, with only cheese, plain rolls, apple slices. Especially these cheeses: Emmenthaler, Liederkranz, Neufchatel.

Chardonnay is not a "weaning" wine, one on which to wean the Coca-Cola Generation from *plonk* (cheap sweet wine: Ripple, Thunderbird, and that ghastly ilk) to fine wine. It's too intense, too vinous, and often too oaky, from the casks in which it was aged. Try Chenin Blanc or Vouvray as weaning wines.

California offers a wide range of Chardonnays: from a few that are only Fair, to some of Near-Classic quality. Some of these latter have fooled experts and Burgundian growers alike, and in blind tastings were ranked above their $25 French counterparts.

Chardonnay is one of the few white wines that improves with age. It should never be drunk before it is at least three years of age, and it will usually be at its best when it is between three and six years of age. Some of the big big Chardonnays will hold at their peak until they are a good ten years old. Serve it slightly chilled: ca. 55°F.

American Pinot Chardonnays—
Comparative Standings

Near-Classic
  David Bruce Chardonnay, 1969 ($22)
  Stony Hill Pinot Chardonnay, 1970 (Priceless)

*****
Exceptional
  Heitz Pinot Chardonnay, 1969, 1970, 1971 ($6)
  Sterling Pinot Chardonnay ($6.50)
  Ridge Pinot Chardonnay, 1972 (Monte Bello) ($6.75)
  Freemark Abbey Pinot Chardonnay, 1969, 1970, 1971, 1972 ($7.50)

Stony Hill Pinot Chardonnay, 1968 ($8)
Spring Mountain Chard-nnay, 1971 ($10)
Hanzell Chardonnay, 1969 ($11.75)
Bruce Chardonnay, 1971 ($12)
Martin Ray Chardonnay ($32)
Chalone Chardonnay, 1969 and 1971 (unpriced)

****
Very Good
  Louis Martini Pinot Chardonnay, 1968 ($3.50)
  Wente Pinot Chardonnay ($3.90)
  Christian Brothers Pinot Chardonnay ($4)
  Parducci Pinot Chardonnay, 1971 ($4.50)
  Buena Vista Pinot Chardonnay, 1971 ($4)
  Simi Pinot Chardonnay ($4.60)
  Beaulieu Beaufort Pinot Chardonnay, 1970 ($4.60)
  Sutter Home Pinot Chardonnay, 1971 ($5)
  Fetzer Chardonnay ($5)
  Inglenook Pinot Chardonnay, 1967 and 1968 ($5.10)
  Mirassou Pinot Chardonnay, 1969 ($5.50)
  Cuvaison Chardonnay, 1970 and 1971 ($5.50)
  Chappellet Chardonnay ($6)
  Souverain Chardonnay, 1972 ($6)
  Stony Hill Pinot Chardonnay, 1969 and 1971 ($6)
  Sonoma (or Windsor) Pinot Chardonnay, 1971 ($6.25)
  Sterling Pinot Chardonnay, 1970 and 1972 ($6.50)
  Robert Mondavi Chardonnay, 1968, 1970, 1971, 1972 ($6.75)
  Mayacamas Chardonnay, 1970 ($7)
  Ridge Chardonnay, 1971 Monte Bello and Vine Hill ($7)

Souverain Chardonnay, 1970 ($7.35)

Freemark Abbey Pinot Chardonnay, 1968 ($7.50)

Heitz Pinot Chardonnay, 1971 UCV-01 ($7.50)

Spring Mountain Chardonnay, 1969, 1970, 1972 ($8)

Heitz Pinot Chardonnay, 1968 ($9.50)

Hanzell Chardonnay, 1968 and 1970 ($11.75)

Bruce Chardonnay, 1968 and 1970 ($12)

Martin Ray Chardonnay, 1966 ($30)

***
Good

Almadén Pinot Chardonnay ($3)

Martini Pinot Chardonnay, 1970 and 1971 ($3.50)

Gold Seal Pinot Chardonnay, 1971 ($3.50)

Pedroncelli Pinot Chardonnay ($3.50)

San Martin Pinot Chardonnay ($3.60)

Sebastiani Pinot Chardonnay, 1971 ($3.60)

Weibel Pinot Chardonnay ($3.60)

Wente Pinot Chardonnay, 1969, 1970, 1971 ($3.90)

Sonoma (or Windsor) Pinot Chardonnay, Nonvintage ($3.95)

Beaulieu Beaufort Pinot Chardonnay, 1972 ($4)

Buena Vista Pinot Chardonnay, 1968 and 1969 ($4)

Llords & Elwood, Cuvée 5 and Cuvée 6 ($4.35)

Beaulieu Beaufort, Pinot Chardonnay, 1971 ($4.60)

Charles Krug Pinot Chardonnay, 1971 ($4.75)

Bargetto Pinot Chardonnay ($4.95)

Beringer Pinot Chardonnay, 1972 ($5)

Inglenook Pinot Chardonnay, 1969 and 1972 ($5.10)

Charles Krug, 1969 and 1970 ($5.25)

Souverain Chardonnay, 1969, 1971 ($5.35)

Mirassou Pinot Chardonnay, 1970, 1971 ($5.50)

Ridge Chardonnay, 1972 ($6)

Sonoma (or Windsor) Pinot Chardonnay, 1970 ($6.25)

Frank, Dr. Konstantin Pinot Chardonnay ($6.25)

ZD Chardonnay, 1971 ($6.50)

Sterling Pinot Chardonnay, 1969 ($6.50)

Robert Mondavi Chardonnay, 1969 ($6.75)

Ridge Chardonnay, 1970 ($7)

**
Fair

Eleven Cellars Pinot Chardonnay ($3.15)

Cresta Blanca Pinot Chardonnay ($3.50)

Louis Martini Pinot Chardonnay, 1969 ($3.50)

Paul Masson Pinot Chardonnay ($3.55)

Sebastiani Pinot Chardonnay, 1972 ($3.60)

Wente Pinot Chardonnay, 1972 ($3.75)

Llords & Elwood Chardonnay, Cuvée 1-100 and Cuvée 3 ($4.35)

Sterling Pinot Chardonnay, 1969 ($4.60)

Inglenook Pinot Chardonnay ($5.10)

Ridge Chardonnay, 1969 ($10)

*
Passable

Assumption Abbey Pinot Chardonnay ($3.25)

Not Recommended

Martin Ray Chardonnay, 1970 ($50)

You will occasionally see a bottle of French Pinot Chardonnay on your wine merchant's shelves, or more likely, in some special "sale" display. It comes as plain Pinot Chardonnay or Pinot Chardonnay Mâcon—they're the same wine. And they can be good little wines—with the emphasis on *little*. And they vary widely, so don't buy unless you find your bottle listed in this book under the name of the producer or "Selector" ("Selected by . . ."): Lichine, Schoonmaker, etc.

A very similar, or identical wine goes by the name of Mâcon Blanc and Mâcon Blanc Villages (see both).

PINOT NOIR California makes three Burgundy-type red wines, and this is the grand-daddy, the best of them. They are, in ascending order of excellence: (1) Burgundy: mostly dreadful stuff, a parody on the noble name of Burgundy. (2) Gamay Beaujolais (or simply, Gamay): can be quite good; young, light wine, something and sometimes like a French Beaujolais. (3) Pinot Noir: at its best can be a big, rich wine, full-bodied and soft.

American winemakers generally agree that Pinot Noir is America's second-best red wine, after Cabernet Sauvignon. It can be a difficult grape, but California vintners, year by year, are producing better and better Pinot Noirs. And as good as some of them already are, experts agree that the Pinot Noir in California has not yet realized its full potential. Hallelujah, what vinous delights may lie ahead!

Many people, especially wine novices, will prefer Pinot Noir to Cabernet Sauvignon, as it is usually softer, less intense, less biting.

A glance at the "Comparative Standings," below, shows that Pinot Noir can vary greatly in quality—from merely Passable to Near-Classic. Avoid the wines with the lower ratings, even if they are economical—even if they're free! If it's an economical Burgundy-type red you're hankerin' after, look to a Gamay Beaujolais.

Pinot Noir is particularly versatile at the dining-room table—it's recommended, quite literally, for everything from soup to nuts. Its special affinity, however, is to meats, red or white: grilled hamburgers and steaks, barbecued chicken; also lamb or veal, even egg dishes and soufflés. The finest Pinot Noirs deserve to be savored on their own or with cheese, fruit, nuts. Pinot Noir goes especially well with these cheeses: Brie, Cheddar, Münster, Parmesan, Pont l'Eveque, Port-Salut.

Good vintage Pinot Noir will generally be at its best when it's between five and eight years of age. The very best bottles will go on improving until they're about ten years old. Serve Pinot Noir at cool room temperature: ca. 68°F.

*California Pinot Noir—
Comparative Standings*

*****

Exceptional

   Pedroncelli Pinot Noir, 1970 ($3.50)

   Mirassou Pinot Noir, 1969 Dedication Bottling ($4.50)

   Beaulieu Beaumont Pinot Noir, 1968 ($6)

   Freemark Abbey Pinot Noir, 1968 ($8)

   Hanzell Pinot Noir, 1967 ($11.75)

   Beaulieu Beaumont Pinot Noir, 1945, 1946, 1947 ($50 to $75)

Chalone Pinot Noir, 1969

****
Very Good
Wente Pinot Noir, 1966 and 1968 ($3.40)
Louis Martini Pinot Noir, 1969 ($3.50)
Pedroncelli Pinot Noir, 1968, 1969, 1971 ($3.50)
Weibel (Plain) Pinot Noir ($3.60)
Llords & Elwood Pinot Noir ($4.50)
Parducci Pinot Noir ($4.50)
Inglenook Pinot Noir, 1967, 1968, 1969, 1970 ($4.60)
Souverain Pinot Noir, 1964, 1972 ($5)
Paul Masson Pinnacles Selection, Cuvée 824 ($5)
Heitz Pinot Noir, 1963, 1969 ($5.50)
Weibel "Estate Bottled" Pinot Noir, 1968 ($5.50)
Robert Mondavi Pinot Noir, 1970, 1971 ($5.60)
Louis Martini Pinot Noir, 1962, 1965 Special Selection ($6)
Beaulieu Beaumont, 1962, 1969 ($6)
ZD Pinot Noir, 1970 ($7)
Louis Martini Pinot Noir, Nonvintage ($7)
Freemark Abbey Pinot Noir, 1970 ($8)
Louis Martini Pinot Noir, 1957, 1958 Private Reserve ($11.50)
Hanzell Pinot Noir, 1965, 1966, 1968 ($11.75)
***
Good
Almadén Pinot Noir ($3)
Eleven Cellars Pinot Noir ($3.15)
Cresta Blanca Pinot Noir ($3.15)
Wente Pinot Noir, 1964, 1965, 1969 ($3.40)
San Martin Pinot Noir ($3.50)
Pedroncelli Pinot Noir, 1966 ($3.50)

Louis Martini, 1965 Private Reserve, 1966, 1967, 1968, 1969, 1970 ($3.65)
Korbel Pinot Noir ($3.85)
Sonoma (or Windsor) Pinot Noir, ($3.95)
Simi Pinot Noir ($4.25)
Mirassou Pinot Noir, 1966, 1971 ($4.25)
Sterling Pinot Noir, 1971 ($4)
Ridge Pinot Noir, 1970 Coast Range ($4.50)
Beringer Pinot Noir, 1969, 1970 ($4.50)
Buena Vista Pinot Noir ($4.50)
Sebastiani Pinot Noir, Bin 121 ($4.65)
Weibel Estate Bottled Pinot Noir, 1966, 1967 ($5.50)
Robert Mondavi Pinot Noir, 1968, 1969 ($5.60)
Heitz Pinot Noir, 1959, 1962, 1966, 1968 ($6)
ZD Pinot Noir, 1969, 1971 ($7)
Beaulieu Beaumont Pinot Noir, 1964, 1966, 1970 ($7)
Freemark Abbey Pinot Noir, 1967, 1969 ($8)
**
Fair
Paul Masson Pinot Noir ($3.10)
Wente Pinot Noir, 1970 ($3.40)
Christian Brothers Pinot Noir ($3.55)
Sebastiani Pinot Noir ($3.55)
Ridge Pinot Noir, 1971 ($4.25)
Souverain Pinot Noir, 1971 ($5)
Beaulieu Beaumont Pinot Noir, 1965, 1967 ($6)
*
Passable
Charles Krug Pinot Noir, 1969 ($4.65)

Martin Ray Pinot Noir, 1962–1963 Marriage ($15)
Not Recommended

Martin Ray Pinot Noir, 1963 You may occasionally stumble across—okay, find—a bottle of non-American Pinot Noir: Chilean or French, mainly. Best advice: Avoid unless you find your bottle specifically listed in this book under the name of the producer.

PINOT ST. GEORGES A youngish, fruity red wine, rarely made in the U.S.—or anywhere else. But a rather upstanding wine for all that. It's similar to California Gamay and is listed in the "Comparative Standings" under that wine. Christian Brothers is the only important American winery to make a Pinot St. Georges (see).

PIPER HEIDSIECK One of France's great Champagne houses—the Heidsieck family has been important in the Champagne industry for centuries and there are three different houses: this, Charles Heidsieck, and Heidsieck Dry Monopole (see both). Florens Louis is their "Best of the House," and it's a gorgeous wine. The '37 and '55 are famous: Near-Classic—or, more accurately, were famous, for both are now long gone. The '61 is another gem: *****. The '64 was disappointing, not recommended at $17. Piper makes two Bruts, a vintaged, at $14.50 —the '64 rates ****—the '66 is beautiful: Near-Classic—and a nonvintage *Brut,* called Cuvée des Ambassadeurs, at $13, usually a fine value.

PIZAY, CHÂTEAU DE: See MORGON.

POGGIO REALE This is the "given" name of the best Chianti made by the Italian firm of Spaletti (Rufina, Florence).

It is invariably a good wine. The '67 was especially notable, ****, took a prestigious British wine award. At ca. $2.50 for a full quart, this is an excellent value—if you can find it.
How to serve this wine: See under general heading CHIANTI.

POL ROGER One of the more reasonably priced of fine French Champagnes, it is said to have been Winston Churchill's favorite bubbly. It comes in three styles: a vintaged Brut ($11), a nonvintage Brut ($10), and a Dry Special ($9.50). Both the '64 and the '66 Brut are solidly *****, and both are still "young."

POMEROL A wine district (reds only) of France's Bordeaux region. It's the smallest of the famous districts and its only outstanding wine is Château Pétrus (see). Very few of the wines go to market under the name of Pomerol—they mostly go under the name of their châteaux—but if you come across one, you'll be looking at a good, at least ***, Claret. How to serve it: See under BORDEAUX.

POMMARD Some experts tend to damn this wine with faint praise, saying it is not as good as its reputation, that it is popular (especially in England) mostly because it's easy to pronounce—the final "d" is silent. But it's a gorgeous red Burgundy, and not outrageously priced. It's not Romanée-Conti but neither is it $42 for 24 ounces. Pommard is a silky-soft wine, full of flavor, long-lasting. It can vary greatly, however, from shipper to shipper —proceed with caution.
It goes well with beef, lamb, and game, but you will want to enjoy your best Pommard on its own, or with cheeses and

bread. It's normally at its best when between four to ten years of age. Air it one hour and serve at cool room temperature. Some vintages:

1964 Boudry: *****—Soft and silky, excellent depth of flavor—Drink soon.

> *Parent:* *****—Drink soon.
> *Thorin:* ****—Drink soon.

1966 Drouhin: *****
> *A. de Luze:* ***
> *Cruse:* ***
> *Bouchard:* **
> *Mautoux:* ****

1966 wines now at their best.
1967 B & G: Not recommended.
> *Chanson:* Not recommended.
> *Calvet:* Not recommended.

1969 Chanson: ****
> *Parent:* ****
> *Bichot:* Not recommended.
> *Sichel:* Not recommended.
> *Chauvenet:* Not recommended.
> *Cruse:* Not recommended.

1970 Jouvet: ****
> *Mommessin:* Not recommended.
> *Jovet:* Not recommended.
> *Lichine:* Not recommended.

1971 Parent: ****
> *Jadot:* ****
> *Thorin:* ****
> *Drouhin:* *****

POMMERY & GRENO One of France's greatest Champagne houses. Their "Best of the House" is their Avize Blanc de Blancs ($17), one of James Bond's favorites. (That should convince you!) One critic said of the '61 that it was the finest Champagne he had ever drunk. Both their Brut and Extra Dry are also highly recommended, even noted as "good values"—relatively speaking, that is—in this rarefied price range! They're $12 and $11, respectively.

PONSARDIN, VEUVE CLIQUOT: See VEUVE CLIQUOT PONSARDIN.

PONTET-CANET, CHÂTEAU A consistent, excellent red Bordeaux (Claret) wine, particularly popular in Britain—and even popular in France! It has a lowly official classification, but almost everybody agrees that it deserves higher ranking. A great critic of a bygone day said that this wine is "always conscious of its duty to please and refresh" and never fails to do so. How to serve and enjoy it: See under BORDEAUX.

1928 and 1929—Near-Classic—They're both still in excellent condition. The '28 should be cheaper than the '29: Fair value, $25 and $30, respectively.

1955—*****—Now at its best, but don't hold it. Fair value, $7.

1961—*****—Best drinking, 1975–1985. Fair value, $13. Well, perhaps not wholly fair, but it's what you can expect to pay.

1962—****—For now drinking. Fair value, $6.

1966 and 1967—****—Drink now and until 1980.

1969—****—Will be ready, 1976.

"POP" WINES The wine industry hates the name "Pop wines" but it loves "Pop" wines. For the excellent reason that they've earned millions of dollars over the past decade. But "Pop" wine sounds faddish and condescending. "Mod" would be better. Yet specially flavored wines—"Pop," "Mod," Aromatic, whatever—have been around for a good long time: like centuries: Vermouth, Dubonnet, Byrrh, Campari, St. Raphael.

And wine punches—which is really what most "Pop" wines are, essentially—have been around even longer: at least since Homer wrote about that "wine-dark" sea.

Yet there are wine purists—wine snobs, some would call them—who would excise this entry entirely from a book such as this. They say simply that wine is the fruit of the grape alone, period, comma, but "Pop" wines are the fruit of fruit—or of berries or roots or bark.

The most creative thing about "Pop" wines is their imaginative names. For a starter, consider: Strawberry Hill, Swiss Up, Country Cherry, Zapple, Plum Hollow, Bali Hai, Silver Satin, Key Largo, Berry Frost, Mellow Days and Easy Nights, Wassail, Wild Mountain, Sangrole, Gran Pomo, Spañada, Arriba, Sum-Plum, Ripple, Mokka Lau, Twister. It's like American television: all the talent goes into the commercials.

The best thing that can be said about "Pop" wines is that they fill a need: the weaning of the Pepsi-Frito generation from soft drinks to good wine. The worst that can be said about them is that they are cloyingly sweet non-wines: wines for people who don't like wine.

PORT A few years ago wine people said that the only true Port comes from Portugal. Know what they're saying today? The very opposite: that the only true Port comes from America, South Africa, Australia. But don't panic—it's not that these countries are producing better Port than does its native land—it's simply that real Port from Portugal is now officially called Porto, precisely to distinguish it from its lesser imitations. If California now begins to label its product "Porto," somebody should declare a big fat war on somebody . . .

True Portuguese Porto, at its best, is one of the world's greatest wines, bar none—some experts say simply that it is the greatest wine of this earth. The finest is Vintage Port, always expensive, even when purchased young, made only in special years when conditions are perfect or very nearly so. It is the world's most famous after-dinner wine, so rich and full and fat (not to say precious and expensive, yet delicate withal) that it would be sinful—mortally so, sacrilegious no less—to drink it with anything except, perhaps, mild cheeses (Monterey Jack, mild Cheddar, Gruyère, Bel Paese) or walnuts (a famous combination) or apple slices. Some cognoscenti even frown upon mild cheeses with vintage Porto, and as expensive and rare as it is, one would be inclined to agree. Stick to the walnuts and apples—or Port alone! Lesser Portos—Tawny, Ruby, Late-Bottled Vintage—are allowed more leeway: they can accompany not-too-sweet desserts (fruit cake), melon, fresh pears or peaches, Roquefort, cream cheese, Stilton.

Vintage Porto takes an unconscionable length of time to mature—you can grow old or senile or impotent—or all three waiting for it. Twenty years is a minimum, and fifty years is not uncommon. It can live for a century. The wine-knowledgeable used to buy a bottle of Vintage Porto at the birth of a child and open it only on the occasion of the child's twenty-first birthday.

Porto labels are tricky: Vintage Port is only Vintage Port: it must say exactly that on the label. Not "Port of the Vintage," or "Vintage Character," or "Tipo Vintage" (Vintage type). Not even "Late-Bottled Vintage" with a year specified. This is fine wine, but it is not Vintage Porto.

But it's the next best thing to Vintage Port—at half or two thirds the price. It's a vintaged wine in that all of it comes from one particular vintage, but it ages in wood (barrels) much longer than does Vintage Porto, and thus matures at a younger age: it's ready to drink in a mere ten to fifteen years. Neither does it require decanting. "Late-Bottled Vintage" is a recent development, for our impatient generation.

Next, in descending order of excellence is Tawny Port, so called—logically enough—because of its tawny color. This comes with age, the best Tawny being aged (in wood) for fifteen to twenty years. But, praise the Lord, it's ready to drink when you buy it! It's expensive also, but not as out-of-sight as Vintage. It's lighter and usually drier than Vintage and can be used as an aperitif wine—slightly chilled, if you choose. Porto labels are sometimes entirely in Portuguese—in such cases the word to look for is "Alourado," "Tawny."

The lowliest grade of Porto is Ruby Port, so called because of its color—how refreshing this Portuguese wine logic! It's the youngest of the four types—two to five years old when it comes to the U.S.—and is ready to drink when you buy it. Ruby is lighter than the other types: fruity and appealing. It's ideal for the elevenses: A.M. or P.M.,

or for watching TV football of a crisp fall evening.

Vintage Port must be handled most gently and decanted most carefully (See DECANTING). All fine Port (especially Vintage) deserves its classic ritual—it demands respect, or rather, reverence. Such nectar is reserved for genteel after-dinner consumption—no smoking, of course, heaven forfend!—the women have been traditionally banned from the sacred area, but what with Ms. Steinem, bra-burning and all . . . The bottle (or decanter) starts with the host and moves clockwise, each man pouring for himself and passing the bottle to the man on his left, until it returns to the host who then serves himself. When the host offers a second glass—only after a seemly and goodly length of time—then the bottle is passed again from man to man, always clockwise and never across the table, until it reaches the man who has accepted the invitation to a second glass. It's all verrrry British, verrrry properrrr, and utterrrrrrrrly essential.

But if only one thing could be said, it should be this: Every mortal should taste at least one great Port on this earth before he comes to die—no matter what it may cost.

Serve Porto at cool room temperature (65 to 70°F) in large tulip-shaped glasses—that marvelous aroma needs breathing room. Keep Port stoppered, especially older bottles. If your bottle is not finished at one sitting, it can be kept for some days in the refrigerator if you eliminate extra air-space by putting it in a smaller container.

Only three or four times in a decade are conditions in the Oporto region ideal enough for

Vintage Port to be made. Even then not all shippers will consider their Porto up to Vintage standards, and some will not "declare" a vintage, will make no Vintage Porto that year. Below are some notable "declared" vintages:

1927: May now be gone, but was probably the greatest vintage of the century—A classic vintage.

1935: Very fine year—Near-Classic: May be past its peak —Taste before you buy.

1950: Delicate wines—Declared by thirteen shippers—Now at its best.

1955: Superb year—May just now be reaching maturity—Almost universally "declared"—*Near-Classic.*

1958: Good, not great—Declared by five shippers—Now at its best.

1960: Excellent wine—Declared by seventeen shippers—Try it around 1980.

1963: Superb wine—Many consider it the best of the decade—Declared by most shippers—It will be slow to mature, will probably be at its best, 1995 to 2000 . . . Don't leave! Classic.

1966: Excellent vintage—Declared by seventeen firms—Should be ready around 1982.

1967: Declared by seven firms—Fine wines, should mature, 1985–1990.

1970: Lay it down and just forget about it for a few decades—Excellent wine.

The following Portuguese Ports are individually considered in this book, under their proper names: Cockburn's; Croft, Dow's; Fonseca; Harveys; Sandeman.

The finest, the only *real* Porto comes from Portugal. But there are imitations around, principally from the U.S. And a few are quite plausible. They're not great wines by any means, but a Warre's Fine Old Ruby (real Porto, from Portugal) and a Ficklin California Port do have some things in common, and do taste similarly. This is wholly unlike such American abominations as "Rhine Wine"—vile, miserable bilge—with no resemblance whatever to the German original.

But there are millions of bottles of ghastly American Port wine on the shelves—at $1.09 per fifth, it's one of the cheapest forms of alcohol available in the world. In the "Competitive Standings" below only the better American Ports are listed, none of the horrors.

For evaluation of individual bottles of Port, whether Portuguese or American, see under the name of the producer: Christian Brothers, Cockburn, Masson, Fonseca, etc.

Below are listed the best American Ports in descending order of excellence. Where wines have the same rating, the least expensive is listed first. Prices are approximate.

*American Port—
Comparative Standings*

*****
Exceptional
  Ficklin California Tinta Port ($4.25)

****
Very Good
  York House Tawny Port ($3.75)

***
Good
  San Martin Rare Port ($1.90)
  Paul Masson Rich Ruby Port ($2)
  Paul Masson Tawny Port ($2)
  Weibel Rare Port (Solera Cask) ($2.60)
  Cresta Blanca Port ($2.85)

Cresta Blanca Tawny Port ($2.85)

Louis Martini Tawny Port ($3)

Paul Masson Rare Souzão Port ($3)

Llords & Elwood Ancient Proverb Port ($3.50)

Christian Brothers Tinta Cream Port ($4)

**
Fair

Beringer Royal Port ($2)

Heitz Tawny Port ($3.50)

*
Passable

Buena Vista Cardinal Port ($3)

POUILLY-FUISSÉ Even if Americans can't pronounce it, they've always had a penchant for this wine. They knew they were getting a good wine at a good price. Time was. That was when Pouilly-Fuissé was considered a poor man's substitute for those out-of-sight Montrachets. No more. In the last five years, Pouilly-Fuissé itself has zoomed out of sight. Americans have been virtually boycotting the wine.

For a marvelous substitute at within-sight prices, look to Mâcon Blanc or Saint-Veran (see both), though it must be stated that Pouilly Fuissé is superior to both. And, in fact, to a lot of other dry white wines. It's clean, fresh, the ideal companion for fish and shellfish in particular, but also poultry, veal, pork, and hors d'oeuvres. Serve it chilled—if you can afford it—and are a spendthrift. The very best Pouilly-Fuissé comes from such single vineyards as Château Fuissé and Les Vignes Blanches, now selling for $8 and $9, and few Americans are rich enough or dumb enough to pay that kind of money for a little Pouilly-Fuissé.

What is more commonly seen in the U.S. is "plain" Pouilly-Fuissé, without the name of an individual vineyard, with only a shipper's name, such as Joseph Drouhin, Louis Latour, Louis Jadot, Marcel Vincent—reputable shippers, all—but their simple little commune Pouilly-Fuissé wines, now at $7 and $8, are just bad buys, and in these days it's good-bye to a bad buy! If you have any Pouilly-Fuissé on hand, it's at its best within four years of its vintage date.

POUILLY-FUMÉ Don't confuse this with Pouilly-Fuissé (see), though they are quite similar. This is a light, dry white wine, quite respectable, from France's Loire Valley. Compared with its cousin, Pouilly-Fuissé, and its great-aunt, Chablis, it's moderately priced, and if you find it for around $4, do try it. It's got a slightly smoky taste, as the name indicates: Fumé-"Smoke." Château du Nozet is the best, but at $7.50 it's a dubious value indeed. Pouilly-Fumé is not a wine to be consumed on its own, but with fish and shellfish, or poultry when pressed. The American equivalent of this wine is Sauvignon Blanc (see), much more modesty priced. Or if you prefer a French wine, try a Muscadet at half the price. Pouilly-Fumé is at its best when it's between two and four years of age. Don't buy anything over five years old.

(LES) PREUSES: See CHABLIS, FRENCH.

PRITCHARD HILL This sounds like the name of a winery—but ain't. It's a secondary label used by Chappellet Vineyard (Calif.), thus far, only for one wine:

Chenin Blanc The first vintage was in 1969, and it was clearly no big deal, **. The '70 was in like manner, **. The '71 was a step ahead: ***. The '72 is still another step ahead, an extraordinary wine, *****, a dry-type Chenin Blanc, with excellent varietal character: stylish and tasty. The '73 steps in the wrong direction: ***. It's hard to see how the "first run" Chenin Blanc under the Chappellet label could be any better. Serve chilled, as a dry aperitif wine or with light foods, fish, shellfish. Fair value, $4 to $5.

PULIGNY-MONTRACHET Excellent dry white Burgundy wine, rather expensive, but still less than half the price of the great Montrachets, to which it is kin. It is usually good enough to merit careful drinking on its own, but it also goes well with fish, seafood, fowl, veal, pork. The following shippers are eminently trustworthy and their Puligny-Montrachet will merit **** and in the best of years, *****: Reputable shippers include Barton & Guestier (B & G), Chanson, Leflaive ("Clavoillon"), Joseph Drouhin, Sichel, Maufoux, Jaboulet-Vercherre, Louis Jadot, Thevenin.

PULIGNY-MONTRACHET, "CLOS DU CAILLERET": See (LE) CAILLERET.

PULIGNY-MONTRACHET, "LES COMBETTES: See (LES) COMBETTES.

Q

QUINTA DA ROEDA: See under CROFT.

QUINTA DO NOVAL VINTAGE PORT "Quinta do Noval" is the name of the finest Porto made by the esteemed Portuguese firm of A. J. da Silva. The 1931 was a tremendous wine, now a legend: Classic. It's just now reaching its best. The 1941 was not normally a "declared" vintage year, but the firm had a batch of especially promising grapes and they made it into a Vintage Porto. It's superb wine, now at its peak: *****. The 1963 is also exceptional: Near-Classic. How to serve Port: See under PORT.

QUINTA DO VARGELLES VINTAGE PORT Quinta do Vargelles is the name of a second vineyard of the illustrious Port-shipping firm of Taylor, Fladgate & Yeatman (see Taylor's Vintage Port). The wines are of high quality, and half the price of the "straight" Taylors. The 1912 was outstanding (Near-Classic), and the 1935 not far behind. Of current vintages, the 1966 and 1967 were exceptionally fine: *****, and may well ascend to Near-Classic status when mature, around 1990—don't leave.

How to serve: See under PORT.

R

RAUENTHAL(ER) BAIKEN
One of Germany's finest Rhine wines, it tends to be on the expensive side, as it is one of the German people's own favorites. It has a certain spiciness which the Germans call *"würzig."* These wines are regularly ****.

RAY, MARTIN, INC. (Saratoga, Calif.) Martin Ray is the name of an unusual winemaker and some unusual wines: some unusually good, some unusually bad. Nothing's in the middle of the road with Martin Ray! But you won't be finding this name on any wines from here on in, as most of the vineyards are now in the hands of the Mt. Eden Vineyards (see). Ray's name has loomed large in California winemaking for a long time and is held in benediction by some, in malediction, it appears, by others. So also with Ray's wines: all of them rare and extremely expensive, they have been hailed as some of the world's finest on the one hand, and damned as swill on the other.

Whatever else may or may not be said about Martin Ray wines, pro or con, they *are* different and they *are* distinctive. Not necessarily better, much less best, but different.

Ray grew only three grapes—the noblest and greatest: Pinot Noir, Pinot Chardonnay, Cabernet Sauvignon—and produced only those three 100 percent varietals. At their sky-high prices, it would be wholly sinful to savor Martin Ray wines other than without distracting food accompaniment.

Cabernet Sauvignon, 1953—Not recommended At one time Ray declared this to be the finest wine he had ever produced. He seems to have been the only one so convinced. Only one thing is certain—the wine, at twenty-plus years of age, is still immature! But judging from its present state, who wants to wait around? This is not a great wine, and even at maturity, it will be less than great by a "fur piece."

Cabernet Sauvignon, 1963 **** Four stars means very good, but it's not worth whatever the present outlandish asking price happens to be: $15 and upward.

Cabernet Sauvignon, 1964—Not recommended At ca. $25, this may be one of the worst wine values in the world. One critic calls it "terrible." In a blind tasting (labels were hidden), of 23 similar wines, it ranked 23rd.

Cabernet Sauvignon, 1966 **** (With reservations) In a comparative tasting of 50 wines a few years ago, this wine placed 50th. Yet the **** may still prove accurate—or even an underrating, as this wine, "big and gutsy," as one wine writer describes it—was certainly immature at that time

244

(1970). It may even rise to
***** status. It will be at its
best (with slightly crossed
fingers), 1980–1990. Watch for
sediment; if present, decant.

Cabernet Sauvignon, 1968
**** (?) Experts are at total
variance on the future development of this wine, but it seems
that given five or ten more
years, this wine will develop into
something very good, mayhap
even something great, ***** or
Near-Classic. It's a calculated
risk.

Chardonnay It is often said
that Martin Ray's wines are for
connoisseurs, not novices. Of
none of them is this more true
than of his Chardonnay. It's
just as well, though, because
only people who can afford to
become connoisseurs in the first
place can afford these wines.
Almost all agree that this Chardonnay is Ray's finest effort—
perhaps so—but one can certainly question whether these
wines—or any wines, for that
matter—are worth these astro-
nomical prices. Ray gave all
his wines fanciful names descriptive of their individual personality. The names are, indeed, often quite descriptive,
but one cannot help but wonder
why none of them, in view of
their price tags, were named
"Yeeeeeeeeeeeeek."

**Chardonnay, 1966 "Le Fruit
Mur des Vignes Dorées"** ****
"Ripe Fruit from Golden
Vines," the name means: the
grapes were picked late in the
fall, when the leaves had turned
to gold. According to Ray, this
is his finest Chardonnay. A
connoisseur's wine, surely, as
only he can appreciate fully
such a woody, non-fruity wine
—and only he will not choke
on it at today's price of $30 or
more.

**Chardonnay, 1968, Finest
Piece Cask******* All agree that
Ray put it all together with this
one. It's comparable to the
finest white Burgundy (the
world's greatest dry white wine),
but the price is also big-time:
$25 to $45. Whatever that price
is, it certainly is not a *fair* value.

Chardonnay, 1970, Ecrasant
The name means "Overwhelm-
ing," and that can only refer to
the price tag which says $50.
And it's been selling—or rather,
it's sold out. A British expert
says the bouquet is of oatmeal
—guess what it tastes like! It
placed near-dead-last in a blind
tasting in '73. Save your $50
for less prestigious—and better
—more plebeian wines at one
tenth the price.

Pinot Chardonnay: See CHAR-
DONNAY.

Pinot Noir, 1962 The winery rates this their second-best
Pinot Noir, and calls it and
the two succeeding wines, "La
Meilleure Récolte," "The Greatest Vintage." QED!

**Pinot Noir, 1962–1963 Mar-
riage*** Some marriage! And
with a $15 price tag yet!

Pinot Noir, 1963—Not recommended One critic says it's
"plain awful!" Another says it's
very good. All agree it's different and not worth the asking
price, wherever in the stratosphere that may be today. In a
blind tasting (labels hidden) of
18 wines, it placed 16th.

Pinot Noir, 1964** The
winery rates this as their very
best Pinot Noir. Well, at least
nobody's been calling it plain
awful. It will be at its best 1975
through 1985. Again, the price
will almost certainly make it a
poor value.

**RAYNE VIGNEAU, CHÂ-
TEAU DE** Great French Sauternes wine second only to Châ-

teau d'Yquem and one or the other châteaux, and at times, not even second to them. It's a luscious, full, golden wine selling for half the price of Yquem. How to serve it: See under SAUTERNES.

REAL, MONTE: See MONTE REAL.

REAL VINICOLA DÃO TINTO, CABIDO*** A good little red table wine from Portugal. Serve it, enjoy it as you would a Beaujolais or a Chianti. For further detail: See under DAO. A good value at $2.75.

REBELLO VALENTE VINTAGE PORT This is the name of an outstanding Porto—the real thing, from Portugal. Authentic Portuguese Porto is, by common consent, one of the world's great wines, some say the greatest. Rebello Valente has been made since the eighteenth century. The 1935 was especially memorable: Near-Classic. The 1963 was also one of the very best; it placed first in a tasting of some of the world's greatest Portos. It's already good drinking, but not really mature; it will be at its best around 1985. Near-Classic. Another exceptional vintage was the '67: Near-Classic. Drink it starting in 1985. How to serve: See under PORT.

RECIOTO DELLA VALPOLICELLA (or: RECIOTO DELLA VALPOLICELLA AMARONE) This is a special wine, somewhat renowned, a kind of "super" Valpolicella (see) made from the same grapes in the same place, but from special late-harvested grapes which have absorbed extra sunshine and are replete with flavor. If the wine has the word "Amarone" somewhere on the label, it's a dry version; if the word is not there, the wine will have noticeable sweetness and will vaguely resemble a light Port. Either way, the wine is high in alcohol, has a strong bouquet, and is velvety smooth—a superior wine. Recioto deserves to be appreciated on its own, or with cheeses, after a meal. It is a much longer-lived wine than the "straight" Valpolicella and is at its best when it's between five and fifteen years old, though it will live on for another decade or two. There is even a sparkling version, mercifully not often available.

RED PINOT A youngish, fruity red wine (also called Pinot St. Georges), rarely made in the U.S.—or anywhere else —but a rather upstanding wine for all that. It's similar to California Gamay and is listed in the "Comparative Standings" under that wine. Inglenook is the only major American winery to make a Reo Pinot (see).

RED WINE, AMERICAN: See BURGUNDY, AMERICAN (RED).

RENÉ BARBIER Despite the French name, these are Spanish wines, economical enough, but not too impressive. There's a red (Tinto) and a white (Blanco); the Blanco would be too expensive if it were free, but the red (1967), though it's on the rough side, is a pretty good little wine at only $2.40. How to serve these wines: See under RIOJA (though these are not strictly Rioja wines).

RHEINGAU This is the name of a German wine district, not the name of the wine. Look up your wine under its proper name: Steinberger, etc.

RHEINHESSEN This is sometimes the most prominent word on German wine labels. It shouldn't be—it's only the name of the district. Look further, to the name of the wine itself: Liebfrauenstift, or whatever.

RHINE GARTEN: See under GALLO.

RHINESKELLER: See under ITALIAN SWISS COLONY.

RHINE WINE Civilized people—mostly foreigners—are constantly criticizing Americans for some of their outlandish—not to say mendacious—wine labeling. Nowhere is the criticism more justified than here, with this name, Rhine Wine. The wine that is bottled in the U.S. under this name has not the faintest, foggiest resemblance to true German Rhine wine. It could almost be said that of all American white wines, Rhine Wine is the furthest removed from the true German product! The name can only have originated in jest, as the baldest man is inevitably called "Curly"!

What passes by the name of "Rhine Wine" in the U.S. is almost always an innocuous, nondescript, flabby, distinctly sweet white wine with only one thing to commend it—it's cheap. American "Rhine Wine" can be made from any grape on God's green earth—and usually is.

America also makes a "Moselle" —are you quite sure you're ready for all this?—a "Moselle" which, again, is as like unto a true German Moselle as Hi-C is to Chartreuse—or as ol' Hamlet would put it, as a "Hyperion to a Satyr."

America, does, however, produce some genuine "Rhine-type" wines, and generally good wines at that. They're wholly different from their German counterparts, though made from the selfsame grapes, viz., the Riesling and the Sylvaner, Germany's two greatest wine grapes. They're called, not Rhine Wine,

but Johannisberg Riesling and Riesling (see both).

California's Rhine Wine is best utilized as a drink of refreshment, well chilled, of a summer day. Most of it is too sweet to accompany food or to serve as an aperitif.

It will keep a year or two after purchase, won't improve in the bottle, but be of good heart, it can't get much worse!

Below are listed the best of America's Rhine Wines and Moselles, in descending order of excellence. Where wines have the same rating, the least expensive is listed first. Prices are approximate.

American Rhine Wines—
Comparative Standings

***

Good

  San Martin Mountain Rhine ($1.60)

  Paul Masson Rhine ($2)

  Great Western Dutchess Rhine Wine ($2.05)

  Paul Masson Rhine Castle ($2.25)

  Great Western Delaware Moselle ($2.35)

  Concannon Moselle, 1972 ($3)

**

Fair

  Cribari Vino Bianco da Pranzo ($1.25)

  Winemaster's Guild Rhine ($1.40)

  Inglenook Navalle Rhine ($1.90)

  Great Western White Niagara ($2)

  Weibel Rhine ($2)

  Gold Seal Rhine Wine ($2)

  Cresta Blanca Rhine ($2.10)

  Great Western Rhine Wine ($2.10)

  Christian Brothers Rhine ($2.20)

  Widmer Lake Niagara ($2.30)

Concannon Moselle ($3)

*

Passable

Franzia Rhinewein ($1.15)

Italian Swiss Colony Rhine ($1.30)

Italian Swiss Colony Rhine-skeller ($1.30)

Almadén Mountain Rhine ($1.75)

Eleven Cellars Rhine ($2)

Inglenook Vintage Rhine ($2.30)

Not Recommended

Roma Rhine ($1.35)

CK Mondavi Rhine ($1.80)

RHONE: See CÔTES DU RHONE.

RICASOLE, BARONE: See BROLIO CHIANTI CLASSICO and BROLIO RESERVA.

(LES) RICHEBOURG One of France's greatest red Burgundies. It is especially noted for its rich bouquet, its depth of flavor, its velvety smoothness. It's both rare and expensive, the 1970 currently selling for around $42; the '65 is practically a give-away at $16.50. For details on this wine's service and enjoyment: See under RO-MANÉE-CONTI.

Some vintages:

1952 Romanée-Conti: *****
—Good drinking now but will get even better.

1955 Leroy: Near-Classic—Be sure to air it.

1958 Leroy: ****—A great achievement in a difficult year.

1959 Charles Vienots: Near-Classic.

1961 Romanée-Conti: *****

1962 Romanée-Conti: ****

1964 Drouhin: Not recommended.

Romanée-Conti: *****

1966 Vienot: *****

Romanée-Conti: ****

1967 Romanée-Conti: *****

1969 Jean Gros: *****

1971 Remoissenet: ****

Jean Gros: *****

1972 Romanée-Conti: *****

1973 Jean Gros—Will probably be great.

RIDGE VINEYARDS (Cupertino, Calif.) Here's a name inexperienced wine drinkers may be well advised to avoid—but seasoned wine lovers usually bow their heads at the sound. Almost all Ridge wines are expensive, big, rich, powerful. What they lack in delicacy and finesse they make up for in substance and guts. They're not for the faint of heart. Every bottle is an experience—not always a happy experience. But an experience.

Cabernet Sauvignon One of the best of the best: the best of California's best red wine, Cabernet Sauvignon. Ridge's product is near-black, full, intense, strong, has a wholesome taste of the earth, needs lots of aging. It deserves to go with your finest steaks or roasts, rack or leg of lamb. Wine lovers will probably want to savor it on its own or with cheese or nuts. These wines are all very tannic —astringent—and need a long time to mature. Some are virtually undrinkable when first released. One must be patient with these wines—and often, long-lived.

The Cabernets of the 60s should be aired a half hour; those of the 70s, about an hour.

1959 and 1960***** Big rich, deeply flavored wines. Just now becoming ready to drink, and will be at the top of their form for at least another decade.

1963**** Now at its best and should hold there at least until 1980. This is lighter than most Ridge Cabernet Sauvignons.

1965**** Far from mature,

try it starting in '78 or '79. It will live at least until 1990.

*1966**** Will be at its best, 1978 through at least 1985.

*1967**** Very hard at this time. One mustn't even try this wine until 1980. Don't even look at it.

*1968, 1969***** These will probably grow into two of California's greatest—between 1980 and 1990. Relax! Marvelous wines to lay down.

*1970 Monte Bello**** Monte Bello is the mountain ridge whence came the grapes for this wine. Ridge says this wine could be ready to try in '75, but you'd be better advised to wait until about 1977, when it surely will be at its best and where it will remain for at least a full decade. Caution: There are also several nonvintage Monte Bellos (no vintage year given), which should be considerably cheaper (see below). Fair value, $10.

*1971, Monte Bello***** Typical Big Ridge wine, in their distinctive style, some say Near-Classic. It will be at its best 1979 through the 80s. Fair value, $10.

*1971 Eisele**** Eisele is the name of a Ridge Vineyard in the eastern hills of Napa Valley. This wine has scored very high in a number of wine tastings, despite the fact that it is not yet mature. It may well go on to rate ***** in five or ten years. With its present $7.50 price tag, it constitutes a good value—if you can find it.

1972, Monte Bello An early peek at this wine says rich and powerful. Huge potential, though it's much too early for a final assessment, but to all appearances a beauty to squirrel away for the 80s and 90s. Clairvoyantly: **** for a starter.

*N. V. Monte Bello, Bottled 2/71*** This is a blend of '69, '70 and is much softer than most of these Ridge Cabernets. It will be at its best, 1975 through 1980.

*N. V. Monte Bello, Bottled 4/72*** A blend of '66 and '71, this is the only Ridge Cabernet that is ready for present drinking. It will hold at its peak through 1980.

Carignane, 1971*** Only one or the other California winery makes a wine by this name —they all grow (or buy) this grape but usually use it for blending purposes, especially in their "Burgundies." Maybe they should reconsider. This is a good little red table wine, of deep purple color, now at its best and will remain so through '78. Fair value, $3.50 to $3.75.

Chardonnay In California this is usually a dependable white table wine to go with seafood and light foods. In the hands of Ridge it comes out somewhat differently: as a rich, heavy, woody-tasting, highly alcoholic, always expensive and almost always controversial wine. Not everybody, especially wine beginners, will like this wine . . . nor will many experts.

*1967** Highly alcoholic, strong, woody. Not recommended at $8 or more. Nor at $7 or less!

*1969** In one tasting of 13 wines it ranked 13th; in one of 64 wines, it placed 64th. Not recommended at today's $10— or at almost any price. There's also a special bottling, Monte Bello, and it's pretty much more of the same.

*1970 Monte Bello**** Like many of Ridge's wines, this one is unfiltered and will probably throw some sediment in time— decant if you wish. Best drinking, 1976–1980. Fair value, ca. $7.

1970, Vine Hill*** Good, not great. Poor value at $6 or more.

1971, Monte Bello**** A controversial wine—some critics hesitate to award it even *. Try it—you'll like it—or hate it. For the venturesome, a fair value at $6.75.

1971, Vine Hill**** Fair value, $6.50.

1972*** Watch for tartrate crystals in this wine—it's okay, the result of the wine's not having been filtered. Air about an hour, serve it chilled. The Monte Bello bottling, *****, will be at its best, 1975 through 1978. Fair value, $6.75.

Gamay, 1971 York Creek **** Gamay is an Americanized Beaujolais—a young gay red wine that fits in almost anywhere. Ridge has a winner here, but they're not exactly giving it away, at ca. $5. But compared with most of Ridge's out-of-sight prices, this is reasonable. Several critics have called this wine the best Gamay they've ever tasted. It's at its best right now and will hold there for three or four years, though it will never be better than it is right now. The '73 also rates ****, and may be drunk now and through 1978.

Grey Riesling, 1972, Zeni Vineyard**** Not one of Ridge's staples, this flavorful white wine will graciously complement a fine fish or seafood course. The cognoscenti—ugh, them again!—will mostly want to sip it, slowly, philosophically, chilled. Fair value, ca. $4.50.

Johannisberg Riesling: See WHITE RIESLING.

Petite Sirah, 1970 Mendocino*** Good red table wine, perfect with heavy or spicy foods, game, venison, cheese. Fair price, $4.25.

Petite Sirah, 1971 York Creek***** Big robust wine, deserving of its recent gold medal at the Los Angeles County Fair. Fair value, $5. The '73, still in cask, also seems headed for great things.

Petite Sirah, 1972 York Creek***** Another big one, it took a gold medal at the 1974 Los Angeles County Fair. It's already fetching around $6, but it's verily worth it. But don't you dare drink this wine before 1979—or, preferably, 1982, when it will be even better. Remember that patience is the crown of all virtues!

Pinot Chardonnay: See CHARDONNAY.

Pinot Noir, 1970 Coast Range *** It's not yet clear just how this wine is going to develop, but at the moment it augureth well. It's just about ready: drink, 1975 through 1980.

Pinot Noir, 1971** It may gain some stars as it ages, but at the moment it's worth exactly what it bears. Fair value, $4.25.

Riesling*** Riesling is the noble grape of the famed wines of the Rhine. Ridge's Rieslings are rather far removed from those soft and delicate German wines, but the two should not be compared, really. It's rather like comparing apricots and watermelons. The '67 is a good wine, ***, distinctive and substantial. The '69 Select Vine Hill is also a good wine, ***. Watch for sediment in both of these and decant if necessary. There's a question, however, of relative value: neither of these wines seems to be worth today's asking price of ca. $6.

Ruby Cabernet, 1971**** Marvelous flavor, but relax—it needs at least another five years to soften and mature. It will bite you if you try it before 1979! Fair value, sorry, $6.

Sylvaner*** Sylvaner is a tasty white wine too often overlooked in the U.S. It's for summertime enjoyment, chilled, a great thirst-quencher. Recent vintages—1968 through 1973—have been consistently *** and the special Vine Hill merits ****. The older vintages, 1968, 1969, 1970, should be consumed *now*. The '71, '72, '73: Drink now and through 1976.

White Riesling**** Most California wineries call this wine Johannisberg Riesling, but Ridge's terminology is the more accurate. And their wine is also more on the mark than most. Ridge's product is a big-style wine, with full nose and body, on the dry side. Excellent with salmon, pork, ham. It is at its best from three to seven years after its vintage date. All recent vintages, 1968 through 1971, are excellent. The '70 comes in two bottlings, Vine Hill and Santa Cruz Mountains, equally good. The '71 is labeled "Exceptional" and that's accurately said—it really is. It even has a bit of sparkle—a poor man's Champagne. Serve chilled. Fair value, $4 to $5.

White Zinfandel, 1970*** A rare wine in California—or anywhere else in the world. The "regular" red Zinfandel is popular in the U.S.—and it's usually a good wine. Ridge's red Zinfandels are especially famous. This white variety shows good promise. Its flavor, not surprisingly, is quite different from that of the red "Z," but good. On the dry side, use it as you would a Chardonnay: with fish, ham, pork, or as a dry aperitif. Serve chilled. Fair value, $3.50 to $4.

Zinfandel Ridge goes totally bananas over this wine—they love it. They produce, year after year, a bewildering array of bottlings: for every vineyard plot, even for grapes from the same vineyard but from different elevations, every picking, every crush—all of these get separate bottlings and separate labels. No winery in the entire world is as fussy with its Zinfandel—or, for that matter, with any of its wines. Nor is anybody else as explicit and honest in their labeling as Ridge: the entire history of every drop of wine is meticulously set forth on the labels, fore and aft.

Ridge is understandably proud of their "Z"—it's not infallibly a resounding success—but most of the time it's excellent, if expensive. It goes especially well with red meats—it deserves the very best cuts. But as unique and intense as it is, it really deserves to be savored on its own, without distraction. Or with cheese or nuts. Air all bottles at least one hour, and serve at cool room temperature.

1966, 1967 Monte Bello, 1100' *** Fair value: 1966, $5; 1967, $3.75.

1967 Monte Bello, and *1967 Templeton* and *1967 Geyserville***** Some of these wines showed poorly in tastings in '71, but the wines were wholly immature at the time. These are full-bodied, slow-maturing wines and won't be at their best until 1976 or 1977, and they should remain so for at least five years.

1968 Essence, Lodi Grapes ***** The winery says this may be the most unique wine ever made in California, and they may not be too far wrong. The grapes were allowed to become extremely ripe and they even developed some "noble rot," a highly desirable fungus that gives a rich lusciousness to many great European white wines. The wine has its full Zinfandel zing, combined with a Port-like richness. A wondrous mouthful. It's already very drinkable, and it's going to do nothing but improve over the next several years. It should be at its best, 1977 through the 80s. Expensive at $8 or $9, but worth every cent of it. If you can find it, splurge this once!

*1968***** All the "regular" '68 bottlings—Geyserville, Lodi, Jimsomare, Monte Bello—were fine wines. None should be drunk before 1976, and all will hold well into the 80s. The Late Picked bottlings should be given an additional two or three years before they're consumed. Fair value, ca. $4.50.

*1969 Jimsomare***** Very complex wine—it's complexity that elevates a wine into the "great" category—and a fine value (if you can search it out) at ca. $5.

*1969 Monte Bello***** According to Ridge this is the most intense Zinfandel—be sure your fillings are secure!—they've ever made. But relax—it may need twenty years to mature. Fair value, $4.50.

1970 Late Harvest and *1970 Fulton***** Jubilation, here are two Zinfandels you can drink immediately, and they will remain at their best at least until 1985. The Late Harvest has some sweetness—serve it after dinner—or for midnight sipping. Fair value, $5.

*1970 Late Lodi Harvest***** Similar to the '68 Essence, Lodi Grapes (above), though not as intense and rich. Drink it as you would a good Port— preferably after dinner. Fair value, $7.

*1970 Jimsomare, 1970 Occidental, 1970 Monte Bello, 1970 Geyserville****** These are four different Ridge vineyards, and four huge wines which will be at their best, 1976–1986. Fair value, $5 to $6. One critic rates the Jimsomare as perfect: 20 points out of a possible 20.

*1970 Occidental Late Harvest****** High in alcohol, some residual sweetness—serve it with pride after dinner. One could drink this wine now but it would be somewhat treasonous; it will be at its peak, 1976–1990.

*1971 Geyserville**** Surprise, the winery says this wine is now ready to drink. And it will hold for at least ten years. Fair value, $4.50.

*1971 Lodi**** For present drinking and until 1979.

*1971 Lodi Essence**** This is another of those semisweet dessert-type Ridge Zinfandels, but not up to the standards of some of the earlier vintages. Ready for present drinking and will hold for at least a decade.

*1971 Mendocino****** Made from 70-year-old vines, good wine to lay down, will be at its best from 1980 onward . . . Fair value, $7 to $8.

*1971 Monte Bello**** A very different Zinfandel from Ridge's usual product: a light young wine, to be drunk young, in the manner of a Beaujolais. Now ready and will be at its best and freshest through 1978. Fair value, $4 to $4.50.

*1971 Occidental Late Harvest****** Big rich wine, very fruity yet completely dry. Already drinkable and will hold at its best for many years, at least through the 80s. Fair value, $7.

*1971 Primeur*** Departed, Amen.

*1972 Healdsburg*** Healdsburg is yet another Ridge vineyard. Sequester this bottle for a few years before trying it.

*1972 Geyserville***** Not ready; try it first, 1976 or 1977. Fair value, $6.

*1972 Coast Range*** This is the only Ridge Zinfandel priced for the peasantry: ca. $3. It's soft and fruity, already potable but will be better, 1976–1980. A good value.

1972 Lodi and *Lytton Spring* **** Both are very tasty wines. The Lodi is already at its best and will hold at least through 1977. Give the Lytton Spring until late 1975, and enjoy it through 1978. Fair value, $3.50 to $4.

*1972 Zeni Ranch***** Zeni is a little ol' seventy-year-old mountain vineyard. Despite a difficult harvest this year, this wine will undoubtedly soon be meriting its **** and may well ascend, in three to five years time, to *****.

*1972 Essence***** First reports say it's a charmer—should be at $12! It's 14.4 percent alcohol and 6.7 percent sugar—serve it after dinner or of a blustery winter's eve. For a wine lover's evening in paradise, compare this with one of Mayacamas's Late Harvest Zinfandels.

*1973 Lodi***.* Fair value, $3.75.

RIESLING There is nothing in all this mad mad world, nothing whatsoever in the heavens above nor the earth beneath, nothing more illogical than American wine nomenclature.

Witness this simple name, Riesling. It is the name of one of the finest white wine grapes in the world—the name of *the* German grape, the grape responsible for all the great wines of Germany. But nary a single bottle of German wine ever bears that name. (When the word is on the label at all—almost always in small print—it indicates the grape from which the wine was made—it is not the name of the wine.) Millions of bottles of California wine bear the name Riesling in bold type on their labels—but they're not made from the Riesling grape at all. They're made from the Sylvaner grape! California wine made from the true Riesling grape is called, not Riesling, but Johannisberg Riesling (see)—for no good reason—it sounds nicer.

But hear this: California Riesling, though not made from the noble German Riesling grape, can be a good wine, though never a great one. And it's often a good value. Of course it can also be pretty blaaaah . . . Stick with the higher ratings in the list below. At its best, California Riesling is soft and light, even flowery and fruity. And what's more, it's getting better year by year—American expertise.

Perhaps Riesling's noblest service is simply as a thirst-quencher on a hot afternoon. Or as an aperitif wine. But it can also accompany light foods: fish, chicken (simply prepared) sandwiches, macaroni salad. Serve it chilled. Drink all Riesling, California, Alsatian, or otherwise, young: within a year or two of purchase and if it's vintage-dated (it rarely is), within four years of its vintage date.

Below are listed California's

best Sylvaners in descending order of excellence. Where wines have the same rating, the least expensive is listed first. Prices are approximate.

California Rieslings and Sylvaners— Comparative Standings

****

Very Good

Parducci Sylvaner ($3.20)

Robert Mondavi Riesling ($3.30)

Mirassou Monterey Riesling, 1971 ($3.35)

Ridge Sylvaner Vine Hill ($6.25)

***

Good

Gallo Riesling ($1.85)

Sebastiani Sylvaner Riesling ($2.50)

Charles Krug Sylvaner Riesling ($2.85)

Beaulieu Riesling Sylvaner ($3.10)

Mirassou Monterey Riesling, 1972 ($3.35)

Souverain Riesling ($3.50)

Ridge Riesling ($6)

**

Fair

Widmer Riesling ($2)

Paul Masson Riesling ($2.25)

Martini Riesling (Sylvaner) ($2.55)

Christian Brothers Riesling ($3)

*

Passable

Almadén Sylvaner ($2.35)

San Martin Sylvaner Riesling ($2.50)

Inglenook Sylvaner Riesling ($3)

California is not the only one to market a white wine by the name of Riesling: Alsace, Austria, Chile, and surprisingly even Italy also do so. And to muddy the waters even further, these Rieslings are actually made from the true Riesling grape.

Riesling is Alsace's finest wine, and, remember, those folks over there know how to make wine! Alsatians call it the king of wines. It's usually a good value. Some of the best producers are these: Leon Beyer; Dopff & Irion; Gaschy; Hugel; Jos. Meyer (the label says Josmeyer); Sichel; Trimbach; Willm.

Noteworthy bottles of Alsatian Riesling are evaluated under these headings: Riesling, Hugel—Beyer, Leon: Riesling—Willm Riesling—Trimbach Riesling.

RIESLING, HUGEL Riesling is the name of the grape—the noble German grape—Hugel, the name of the prestigious Alsatian wine firm. Together on a wine label they spell an excellent bottle of wine. Some recent vintages:

1966 Cuvée Exceptionnelle: ****. Precisely so! It's still excellent but drink soon.

1969: ****. The Reserve Exceptionnelle rates *****. Both now at their best, drink by 1976.

1970: ***. Drink, 1975–1977.

RIESLING, JOHANNISBERG: See JOHANNISBERG RIESLING.

RIESLING, WHITE: See JOHANNISBERG RIESLING.

RIEUSSEC, CHÂTEAU Marvelous French Sauternes wine—not even remotely related to what sells in the U.S. as "American Sauterne"—sweet and luscious and golden. The vineyard is contiguous with the illustrious Château d'Yquem, which sells for twice the price. How to serve and enjoy this wine: See under SAUTERNES.

RIOJA An important wine district of Spain (pronounced Ree-oh-ha) from whence come (everybody agrees) Spain's finest table wines. These are solid, middle class wines: never great, rarely poor. Always trustworthy. Remember the cartoon of the two grizzled winos brandishing the bottle of wine, observing, "It's not a great wine, but it's a good one." The wine was a Rioja!

Almost everybody agrees that Rioja reds today are the greatest value in red wines in the entire world. That, of course, is a gigantic assertion, but a considered one. Certainly the only competition would be from some of California's best economical reds, such as Burgundies, Gamays, Zinfandels.

Almost all Rioja wines are vintaged, but one need not take these posted years too seriously, at least on the lower-priced wines. They're more like generalizations; *Cosecha* 1967 on a $2.50 wine says: This wine comes from vintages, roughly, 1965 to 1970—it's pretty old—about ready to drink.

Red Rioja is a wide-ranging wine: it fits at the barbecue grill, at a luncheon, at a formal dinner. It can accompany any red meat, turkey, goose, veal, pork. Its specialty is Spanish dishes—logically enough—especially Paella.

White Rioja: when it's good—check carefully, some of it is dreadfully dull—it goes well with light meats (veal, chicken, pork), fish and seafood. Both wines, when at their best, deserve to be consumed on their own or with cheeses, especially Cheddar, Port Salut, Brie, Cantal.

It is well to air Rioja wines: reds at least one hour (unless it is extremely old), whites a half hour. Serve the reds at cool room temperature (ca. 68°F), the whites chilled (45 to 50°F).

Rioja wines are almost always ready to drink when purchased. Only the very best reds will benefit from further aging; this book will advise you when such is the case.

The following Rioja wines are individually evaluated in this book under their proper names: Brillante, Cepe de Oro, Cune, Federico Paternina, Marqués de Murrieta, Marqués de Riscal, Monte Real, Tondonia, Viña Albina, Viña Pomal, Viña Zaco, Yago. Two similar wines but not in the Rioja area are: René Barbier and Torres.

RISCAL: See MARQUÉS DE RISCAL.

RISERVA DUCALE: See RUFFINO RISERVA DUCALE.

RIUNITE LAMBRUSCO: See LAMBRUSCO.

ROBERT MONDAVI: See MONDAVI, ROBERT.

ROCHE, CLOS DE LA: See CLOS DE LA ROCHE.

(LOUIS) ROEDERER One of the largest of France's great Champagne houses. Their "Best of the House" and best-known Champagne is their Cristal ($23), which comes in a clear "crystal bottle," designed a century and a half ago for the Russian Czar. The '59 is a Classic. The '62, *****. The '64 and '67, a mere ****. The '66: Near-Classic. The '69, from here, looks like a full-blown Classic. There are two Bruts, a vintage ($16) and a nonvintage ($13.50). The vintage is a great wine: the '64 rates Near-Classic, but won't be at its best until late '75 or '76. The '66 Brut is ****. The nonvintage Brut is a fine wine, a good value as these things go, a mere $13.50. The "bottom of the line" is the Extra Dry, practically a give-away at $12.50, a fine Champagne.

ROGER, POL: See POL ROGER.

ROMA WINE CO. (Fresno, Calif.) Roma is a huge operation—fifteen miles of vineyards near Delano alone—now owned by Schenley, mostly producing standard, economical jug wines, neither better nor worse than those of their competitors.

Their more important offerings:

Burgundy: A few years ago this wine was consistently receiving very low marks, but recently some have spoken well of it: **.

  Chablis: * At best.

  Claret: Not recommended.

  Rhine: Not recommended.

  Sauterne: ***, a good value at $2.25 to $2.65 a half-gallon.

  Vin Rosé: **, received a gold medal, Los Angeles County Fair, 1973.

  Vino Blanco: *.

  Zinfandel: ***, a good value at $2.50 to $3 per half gallon.

LA ROMANÉE A truly great red French Burgundy, but it's one of the world's scarcest wines, for the entire vineyard comprises a scant two acres. It's adjacent to and a first cousin—or more exactly, a brother—to the illustrious Romanée-Conti (see). How to serve and enjoy such a great red Burgundy: See under ROMANÉE-CONTI.

ROMANÉE-CONTI Probably no two wine experts would agree on which is the greatest red wine in the world, but this Burgundy would certainly be in contention. It's called magisterial, the Burgundy par excellence. It is a rich, heavy wine, extremely expensive—only 500 cases a year are produced. Romanée-Conti suffered at least a partial eclipse for some ten years, after its vines were re-

planted in 1946. From '59 on, however, it had regained its pristine preeminence. You will want to drink your Romanée-Conti—if you are ever lucky enough and/or rich enough to get your grubby little hands on a bottle—you will want to savor it, drop by precious drop, by itself, or, at most with some good cheeses and plain bread rolls. Romanée-Conti will generally be at its best when it is between seven and twelve years old; truly great bottles will live on for decades. Air it one hour, and serve at cool room temperature.

Most of Burgundy's greatest vineyards are owned by a number of different growers, and in referring to a wine of a particular vineyard one must specify the particular grower or shipper who is responsible for the wine. This is not the case with Romanée-Conti, for the entire vineyard—all four acres of it—is owned by the Société Civile du Domaine de la Romanée-Conti. The society also owns substantial portions of other important vineyards—La Tache, for example—and so, on the label of the Domaine's wine from that vineyard, the name Romanée-Conti will appear. Clear? As Harry Belafonte says: "It is clear as mud, but it covers the ground . . ."

ROMANÉE - SAINT - VIVANT One of the greatest of red French Burgundies, a first cousin of and living next door to the renowned Romanée-Conti, La Tache, Richebourg (see all). How to appreciate and serve this splendid wine: See under ROMANÉE-CONTI. Some notable vintages:

  1923 The wines were classic.

  1937 Leroy: Not recommended.

1947 Leroy: Near-Classic—
Still at its peak.
1962 Bouchard: ****
1964 Drouhin: ****
  Noellat: *****
  Bouchard: Not recom-
  mended.
  Romanée-Conti: Not recommended.
1965 Morey-Monge: *****
1966 Romanée-Conti: Not
recommended.
  Morey-Monge: *****
ROSALINE, SAINT: See
SAINT ROSALINE.
ROSÉ Everybody knows rosé
wines—even nonvinously-in-
clined Americans. Housewives
who don't know Manischewitz
Concord from Château Mou-
ton-Rothschild '61 are veritable
authorities when it comes to
rosés. They can tell you what
food to serve it with (almost
any), at what temperature
(chilled, 45–50°F), and can
even rattle off preferred brands
(Mateus, Almadén Grenache
Rosé). How come? For the
good and sufficient reason that
rosé wine is the simplest in the
world: it's found everywhere,
it's cheap, it's readily appreciated, it can be served anywhere, anytime, to anybody.
You don't have to read any
silly books, know any vintages,
or even read the label. There
it is, it's pink, you buy it, and
serve it.
Wine experts and connoisseurs
—not to mention real wine
snobs, of which there happen to
be an abundance in this world
—can be very condescending
toward rosé wines. And truthfully they can be only so good
—they can sometimes stretch
beyond their normal height and
reach ****, very good status,
but never beyond that.
But their virtues are obvious:
simplicity, cheapness, versatility

—and most of all, wonderful
freshness. Of a warm summer's
evening, is there anything quite
as welcome and refreshing as a
glass of chilled sprightly rosé?
None of this is to say that
rosés are all alike—they come
in many shapes and varieties.
They vary in degree of sweetness, from very sweet to bone
dry—in color: from light baby
pink to orange-red—in quality:
from vile to glorious—in price:
from $1 per fifth to $7 and
more.
Everybody makes rosés: from
South Africa to Alsace to Australia to the U.S. But nobody
makes more and enjoys their
rosés more than do Americans.
Europeans drink their rosés
only through the summer
months, as a substitute for their
heavy *vin ordinaire*—Americans drink theirs the year round.
America makes some of the
best in the world—and some of
the worst. But broadly speaking, stick with American rosés
—they're better values than the
imports.
The U.S. makes two distinct
types of rosé: generic rosés,
labeled simply Rosé or Vin
Rosé or occasionally Mountain
Rosé, made from unspecified
grapes. Secondly, varietal rosés:
made predominantly from one
particular grape, which name
will be part of the wine's name:
Grenache Rosé, Zinfandel Rosé.
The generic rosés are generally
less expensive, have less individuality and character, and are
sweeter than the varietal rosés.
Abstracting from personal preferences, one can list American
rosés in the following *roughly*
ascending order of excellence:
(1) "Plain rosé, Vin Rosé,
Mountain Rosé; (2) Zinfandel
Rosé; (3) Grenache Rosé; (4)

Gamay Rosé; (5) Cabernet Rosé.

This is, of course, a broad prospectus: note the *"roughly ascending, etc. . . ."* There will be many exceptions to this hierarchy and a particular winery's "Vin Rosé" may be better than their Cabernet Rosé.

Americans seem to prefer their rosés on the mellow side, medium-sweet—which goes to demonstrate that Americans do know something about wines, for a dry rosé is a kind of contradiction in terms. Rosés, because of their lightness and lack of body, need a touch of sweetness. When they're bone dry, there is no depth, no *wininess* there to sustain them, and they can be simply bitter little wines.

The best rosés are made from black grapes—the stems and skins are removed after a few days of fermentation, when the wine has achieved just the right shade of pink. It can be said, therefore, that rosé is an incomplete wine and this is precisely why a rosé can never achieve true greatness. It simply lacks the body and character.

Who makes the best rosés? The U.S., Portugal, France? Who has the most beautiful women? You'll get as many opinions as you ask people! It's often said that the rosés of Tavel (France) are the world's best, but what about Portuguese rosés, particularly the enormously popular Mateus and Lancers? And no nation on earth offers the vast assortment of rosés that the U.S. does, and more than a few of them rate an impressive ****. But it is also true that an awful lot of rosés of like sweetness are an awful lot alike. There is less individual difference, less distinction between individual bottles of rosé than with almost any other type of wine.

All of which makes price the overriding factor in the selection of rosés. All other things being equal—and they usually are with rosés—buy the cheapest.

It is true that rosés are considered "universal" wines suited to accompany almost any kind of food other than pickles and ice cream, but because of their lightness they're much better suited to accompany light foods. Here are the ideal foods to serve with rosé wines, in exact descending order of appropriateness: (1) Ham (smoked), sweetly cooked (with pineapple and stuff); (2) Sandwiches (lightsome)—not the Reuben's and Chorizo variety; (3) Barbecued chicken—but not with some corrosive sauce; (4) Chinese food—but only the milder types—none of that TNT Oriental mustard; (5) These cheeses: Cantal, Cheshire, Port-Salut, Monterey Jack, Gouda, Hervé; (6) Eggs or egg dishes. Serve rosé chilled, but not frozen—45 to 50°F is sufficient. All rosé should be drunk young, surely within five years, and preferably within three years of its birth. Vintage dates are unimportant except that they tell you how old the wine is.

Rosé wines have a place in the divine scheme of things, even if it's a relatively humble place. They're not the royalty of winedom, not even the aristocracy. But they do belong to the substantial middle class. The sinful part comes when rosés become the only wine one knows and drinks—and most sinful and deadly of all, the only wine one *wants* to know and drink.

Enjoy your sprightly little Mateus—properly pronounced Ma-tay-oosh, but nobody will know what you're talking about —enjoy your "Matoos," but, friend, look upward, ascend from these lowly monotonous plains unto yonder beckoning heights!

What with America's predilection for rosé wines, the nation's wine shops and liquor stores are awash with rosés of every nation and description. One would be well advised to hold a steady course through all the distracting, bewildering array, and *buy only the better known brands that you find in this book*.

Below are listed the majority of American rosés, in descending order of excellence. They're a formidable host. All pink wines are included, even if they don't call themselves rosé. Prices are approximate.

American Rosés—
Comparative Standings

****

Very Good

  Ste. Michelle Grenache Rosé ($2.65)

  Robert Mondavi Gamay Rosé, 1970, 1971, 1972, 1973 ($2.85)—Medium sweet.

  Simi Rosé of Cabernet, 1972 ($3.30)—On the dry side.

  Buena Vista Cabernet Rosé (Rose Brook), 1970 and 1971 ($4.50)—On the dry side.

  David Bruce Grenache, 1970 ($6.50)—Dry.

***

Good

  Gallo Pink Chablis ($1.40) —Slightly sweet.

  Pedroncelli Sonoma Rosé ($1.60)

  Almadén Mountain Nectar

Vin Rosé ($1.70)—Slightly sweet.

Paul Masson Pink ($2)— Slightly sweet.

Great Western Rosé ($2)— Sweet.

Gold Seal Rosé ($2)—Sweet.

Almadén Grenache Rosé ($2) —Slightly sweet.

LaMont Grenache Rosé ($2) —Slightly sweet.

Beringer Gamay Rosé ($2)— On the dry side.

Pedroncelli Zinfandel Rosé ($2)—On the dry side.

Taylor Rosé ($2.10)—Relatively dry.

Christian Brothers Napa Rosé ($2.20)—Medium sweet.

Novitiate Charvet Rosé ($2.20)

Sutter Home Mission Rosé ($2.25)—On the sweet side.

Boordy Rosé Wine ($2.25)— On the dry side.

Beaulieu Beaurosé ($2.30)— On the dry side.

Great Western Isabella Rosé ($2.30)—Sweet.

Sonoma (or Windsor) Vin Rosé ($2.30)—On the dry side.

Beaulieu Grenache Rosé ($2.35)—On the dry side (but sweeter than Beaurosé).

Sebastiani Grenache Rosé ($2.40)—Touch of sweetness.

Sebastiani Vin Rosé ($2.40) —Dry.

Concannon Vin Rosé ($2.50) —Slightly sweet.

Novitiate Grenache Rosé ($2.55)

Sonoma (or Windsor) Grenache Rosé ($2.60)—Medium sweet.

Mirassou Petite Rosé ($2.85) —On the dry side.

Inglenook Gamay Rosé ($2.85)

Louis Martini Gamay Rosé ($2.85)—Relatively dry.

Oakville Gamay Rosé ($3)

Concannon Zinfandel Rosé ($3.10)—On the dry side.

Simi Rosé of Cabernet, 1971 Alexander Valley ($3.30)

Llords & Elwood Rosé of Cabernet ($3.50)

Heitz Grignolino Rosé ($4) —Dry.

Buena Vista Cavernet Rosé (Rose Brook), 1972 ($4.50)

David Bruce Grenache, 1969 ($6.50)

**

Fair

Franzia Vin Rosé ($1.10)— Medium sweet.

Brookside Rosé Suave ($1.10) —Sweet.

Franzia Grenache Rosé ($1.30)

Roma Vin Rosé ($1.35)

Italian Swiss Colony Grenache Vin Rosé ($1.35)

Brookside Vino Rosado ($1.50)

Los Hermanos Mountain Rosé ($1.60)

San Martin Vin Rosé ($1.60) —Medium sweet.

Weibel Classic Vin Rosé ($1.65)—Sweet.

Sebastiani Mountain Vin Rosé ($1.80)—Slightly sweet.

Inglenook Navalle Rosé ($1.90)—On the dry side.

Wente Rosé Wente ($2)— Dry.

San Martin Grenache Rosé ($2)

Paul Masson Vin Rosé Sec ($2)

Pinard Rosé ($2)

Korbel Mountain Rosé ($2)

Simi Grenache Rosé, North Coast ($2.10)—On the sweet side.

Taylor Lake Country Pink ($2.10)

Weibel Vin Rosé ($2.10)

Cresta Blanca Grenache Rosé ($2.20)

Charles Krug Vin Rosé ($2.25)—On the dry side.

Korbel Château Vin Rosé ($2.25)—On the dry side.

Widmer Isabella Rosé ($2.30) —Sweet.

Buena Vista Grenache Rosé ($2.50)—On the dry side.

Parducci Pink Fumé ($2.50)

Brookside Mouvedre ($2.50)

Weibel Grenache Rosé ($2.55)

Bargetto Zinfandel Rosé ($2.70)—On the dry side.

Bargetto Vin Rosé Dolce ($2.70)—Sweet.

Bargetto Grenache Rosé ($2.70)

Bully Hill Rosé Wine, 1971 ($3)

Buena Vista Zinfandel Rosé ($3)—On the dry side.

Mayacamas Zinfandel Rosé, 1972 ($5)—On the dry side.

*

Passable

Cribari Vino Fiamma da Pranzo ($1.25)—Sweet.

Italian Swiss Colony Pink Chablis ($1.70)—Sweet.

Gallo Rosé ($1.70)

Inglenook Vintage Vin Rosé ($1.90)

Not Recommended:

Napa-Sonoma-Mendocino Vin Rosé ($1.70)

Sutter Home Zinfandel Rosé ($2.25)

Just about every wine-producing nation of the world makes a rosé of some kind. The most and the best come (in vaguely descending order of excellence) from: (1) Portugal: marvelously fresh, fizzy rosés; (2) France: especially from Tavel, Anjou, and Provence regions; (3) Italy and Spain: recently have increased their imports to the U.S.

The best of these rosé wines are individually assessed under their individual label-names: Mateus, Lancers, Château d'Aqueria, etc. But if you don't find it specifically listed in this book, don't buy it.

ROSÉ, CRACKLING: See CHAMPAGNE, PINK.

ROSÉ DES ANGES (CHANSON) This "Rose of the Angels" is trustworthy and good, even if it isn't quite up to its celestial nomenclature. It's clean, fresh, lightly on the sweet side. It's from the Anjou region of France. Serve it on its own, or with a not-too-sweet dessert. Fair value, $2.90.

How to serve it: See under ROSÉ

ROTHSCHILD This is a name that looms large among Bordeaux (French) wines. The name Rothschild, the famous banking family of France, is part of the name of a number of Bordeaux châteaux, owned by various branches of the family. In descending order of excellence, these are the principal Rothschild wines: Château Lafite, Château Mouton, Château Mouton-Baron-Philippe, Château Duhart-Milon-Rothschild, Château Clerc-Milon, Château Mouton Cadet (see all). From the Baron Philippe's cellars also come some lesser—though uniformly reliable—regional red Bordeaux: Barsac, Graves, Médoc, St. Emilion, Sauternes, Pomerol. These are all regularly ***, at least.

ROYAL HOST A brand name owned by East-Side Winery of Lodi, Calif., a huge farmer's cooperative, with a capacity of some 40 million gallons. These are inexpensive wines, many of them good values. Deserving

of special mention are the following. All of these wines are ready for immediate drinking upon purchase and none should be kept more than a year or two.

Burgundy ** and Claret** (Good with those grilled hamburgers, pasta, stew).

Chenin Blanc** Recently introduced (sip it of a warm summer's evening).

Gold** A soft semi-dry white wine made from a new grape variety produced by the University of California (try it as an aperitif wine).

Grey Riesling** (To go with your seafood, barbecued chicken, chicken salad).

Ruby Cabernet** (Save for your steaks and roasts); this may even improve with a year or two in the bottle.

Zinfandel** Better than no Zinfandel at all.

RUBAN ROUGE: See MÉDOC.

RUBION: See under (PAUL) MASSON.

RUBY CABERNET Here's a purely American wine—it's produced nowhere else in the world, and even the grape was created in the U.S.—at the University of California, Davis: a cross between the Cabernet Sauvignon and the Carignane.

The Ruby Cabernet grape produces some good red wine in the western U.S., not of the noble stature of Cabernet Sauvignon, but a full and fruity wine, and almost always a good value. It has some of the enviable taste characteristics of the Cabernet Sauvignon but lacks its depth and complexity.

Ruby Cabernet will go well with all red meats, from hamburgers or even hot dogs, to Chateaubriand or a rack of lamb. It can also serve admirably to accompany cold cuts, poultry, sausage, eggs, and, of course, cheese and cheese dishes. Serve it at cool room temperature, 68 to 72°F.

Listed here are California's most notable Ruby Cabernets, in descending order of excellence. Where wines have the same rating, the least expensive is listed first. Prices are approximate.

****

Very Good
    San Martin Ruby Cabernet— It occasionally merits this rating. See text, p. 269 ($2.50)
    Ridge Ruby Cabernet ($6)

***

Good
    Gallo Ruby Cabernet ($1.85)
    Royal Host Ruby Cabernet ($1.85)
    LaMont Cabernet ($2)
    Paul Masson Rubion ($2.30)
    San Martin Ruby Cabernet ($2.50)
    Heitz Ruby Cabernet ($3.50)

**

Fair
    LaMont Burgundy Cabernet ($1.70)
    Inglenook Navalle Ruby Cabernet ($1.90)
    Novitiate Ruby Cabernet ($2.80)

*

Passable
    Bargetto Ruby Cabernet ($2.50)

(LES) RUCHOTTES. See CHAS-SAGNE-MONTRACHET (WHITE).

RUDESHEIM(ER) Rudesheim is a picture-postcard Germany village on the Rhine, and a Rudesheimer is a wine from Rudesheim. Generally a rather good wine, fruity and flowery. If it just says "Rudesheim," without a vineyard name, it's a regional wine, not of the very highest category, usually ***.

(Anheuser, though, makes an excellent one, regularly ****; it sells for around $5.) The best wines of Rudesheim are those from these individual vineyards: Rudesheim(er) Burgweg; Rudesheim(er) Rottland; Rudesheim(er) Berg Schlossberg; Rudesheim(er) Bischofsberg.

RUFFINO BARDOLINO** Lovely flavor, mellow in every sense, a bargain at $3.

RUFFINO CHIANTI It's in *fiasco*—not a disaster, but the traditional straw-covered flask. The I. L. Ruffino firm of Florence, Italy, exports three grades of Chianti to the U.S.: this is the lowest and a good wine, at a good price. The '69 rates ****. The current vintages, 1970 and 1971, are both clean, tasty fresh red wines: ***, to be enjoyed through 1975 and '76. A large 59-ounce bottling of this wine, called a "Misura," (the word is on the neck label) a 1971 vintage, is a fine value at around $5.50. Serve your Ruffino at cool room temperature, with red meats, casseroles, pasta. Fair value, $3.85 per quart, $3.25 per 24 ounces.

Ruffino Riserva Ducale Excellent red Chianti wine, even though it is not "Classico"— notice that it does not have that word on the label nor does it have the classic seal, the black cockerel, on the neck label. Some notable bottles:

1957: It was remarkable but now past its peak.

1959: Selling today, ca. $10, but not worth it.

1964: Non-great, ungood.

1966: *****—Marvelous wine, now at its best, drink during '75.

1967: ****—Glorious wine, soft and mellow, fully mature

—Good drinking through 1978. Besides the regular Riserva with a white label, there is a "super" Riserva with a gold label, selling for almost $3 more, ca. $7.50 vs. $4.75—it's fine wine but not always worth the price difference.

RUFFINO DEL MAGNIFICO: See DEL MAGNIFICO.

RUFFINO VALPOLICELLA: See VALPOLICELLA.

S

SACRAMENTAL WINES This is wine used by many Christian churches, notably the Roman Catholic, Anglican, and Orthodox Communions, not for the "Sacraments," plural, but for *the* Sacrament, singular, the Sacrament of the Lord's Body, the Eucharist. Contrary to much popular belief, Sacramental wine need not be a "special" wine. The only strict requirement is that it be "natural" wine, the fermented fruit of the grape. (Annie Green Springs Peach Creek won't do —it's an apple wine, with fruit flavors.) Individual bishops do at times give their blessing to a particular brand of wine, a certification that such wines are "natural," valid material for Sacramental use.

Generally speaking, Sacramental wines can be red or white, sweet or dry, expensive or cheap. Ironically—and/or ecumenically—many Christian churches use sweet Kosher wines such as Manischewitz Concord Grape. Others use a sweet California wine such as Muscatel or Angelica.

Some wineries, such as California's Novitiate (see), owned by the Jesuit Fathers, make an entire line of Sacramental wines, with their own names, but the wines come from precisely the same barrels as the commercial products.

During the days of American Prohibition (1920-1933) there was a noticeable increase in the fervor and piety of American priests, which was detectable solely from the clergy's suddenly increased consumption of Sacramental wine, which, of course, could only have been due to the huge number of "Sacraments" that were suddenly being dispensed. One winery received federal approval—you will not believe this—to make "Sacramental" Champagne!

SAINT AMOUR *** to **** Excellent red Beaujolais wine, one of the lightest of them, fresh and soft. It's being increasingly shipped to the U.S. and can be a good value, at least for a French wine these days. The name Beaujolais is not always on the label, but the quality is in the bottle. How to serve it: See under BEAUJOLAIS. The most reliable shippers are also listed there.

SAINT DENIS, CLOS: See CLOS ST. DENIS.

SAINT-EMILION France's Bordeaux area contains lots of Saints—not necessarily the virtuous kind but the wine-district kind—there is Saint-Julien, Saint-Estephe, and this one. The very best wines go to market under the name of a château: Château Cheval Blanc, Ausone, etc. Lesser wines, though still good and reliable—go simply under the name of Saint-Emilion. They range in price from $4 to $6, which has often been more than they're worth! As of late 1974, however, prices of Bordeaux wines have begun to level off and actually to descend in some places—as well they might after their wild rise in the early 70s. How to serve this wine: See under BOR- DEAUX.

1967—Some good ones: Si- chel, B & G, De Luze, Ginistet, Calvet. All ****. Now good drinking, but don't hold these.

1969—Look for these: Cruse, Baron Philippe de Rothschild, Marson & Natier, Ginistet. Now at their best and good drinking through 1980.

1970—Some good ones: Florent Bruneau, Dreyfus Ash- by. (Not recommended: Gini- stet and Armand Roux.) Best drinking: 1975 through 1985.

SAINT-ESTEPHE A wine dis- trict of the Bordeaux region, France. Most of the wines, and all of the best ones, go to mar- ket under their own names: Château Calon-Ségur, Château Montrose, etc. If you find a wine going simply by the name of Saint-Estephe (with no Châ- teau Such-and-Such), be aware that you are dealing with a lesser red wine, though by no means a poor one. Generic Saint-Estephes are now selling for $4 to $7, but happily these prices have leveled off and are now beginning to decline. How to serve Saint-Estephe wines: See under BORDEAUX.

SAINT JACQUES CLOS: See GEVREY-CHAMBERTIN, CLOS ST. JACQUES.

SAINT-JULIEN This is not the name of a medieval saint— it's the name of a Bordeaux wine district and the name of a good red wine from there. The best wines from this excel- lent area go to market under the name of their châteaux:

Château Beychevelle, Château Léoville, etc. The lesser wines —though still excellent in their own category—will not say Château Such-and-Such, but will say simply in bold letters, Saint-Julien. If they once were, these are no longer economical wines or good values. Of all Bordeaux's "regional" wines (grapes are from the entire area, not from a specific vine- yard) the Saint-Juliens are the most expensive: $6 to $9. They're excellent wines and very safe, but such price tags put them into competition with the great "classed" (officially classified) growths of Bordeaux. These are regularly **** wines. Look for one of these: B & G, Cruse, Jouvet, Johnston, Ar- mand Roux.

STE. MICHELLE VINE- YARDS (Seattle, Wash.) Most people think of all wineries as centuries-old, moss-encrusted, moldy. But new wineries spring up almost every month in Cal- ifornia. And here's one that's sprung up recently in a new state, Washington. These are the only state of Washington wines nationally distributed. The first wines were bottled only in 1970 and the signs are auspicious.

Cabernet Sauvignon, 1968*** Here's a wine that will set your teeth on edge, grrrrrrr, if you try it today; it's extremely tan- nic, astringent. But this wine will soften with time and fully merit its *** and perhaps ascend to **** status. Stash it away at least until 1979 or 1980. Then bring it out for your best steaks, grilled lamb chops, or that prime rib roast. Air one to two hours. Serve at cool room temperature. Fair value, $4.

Cabernet Sauvignon, 1969

**** This is in the same style as the preceding. Don't be in a hurry. Squirrel this away until 1980. A good value at $4.50 to $5.

Chenin Blanc, 1972**** Graceful and charming wine. How to serve it: See under CHENIN BLANC. A fine value at $4.

Grenache Rosé**** Even wine critics, who almost unanimously have an aversion for rosé wines, extoll this one. It surpasses many of its European counterparts. Excellent value at $2.50 to $3.

Johannisberg Riesling
1971 If it's still around, award it ******.
*1972*********
*1973******** Fair value for all, $4.

Sémillon, 1968, 1969, 1970 and 1972**** This was once a popular wine in the U.S., but today it's out of style. Few wineries make it at all. The more's the pity, for the Sémillon is an excellent grape and makes some wonderful wine. Ste. Michelle's version is semi-sweet—good with medium-sweet dessert, or with fresh fruit, or by itself as a sipping wine. All of these vintages are at their best right now; don't hold them beyond 1975. Fair value, $2.75 to $3.

ST. ROSALINE, CHÂTEAU *** This is the best rosé wine made in the Provence area of France. Provence rosés tend to be dry and rather bitter, but St. Rosaline comes only from the first light pressing of the grapes, and it's a lovely, light, barely-on-the-dry-side pink wine, perfect as an aperitif on a warm day, or for refreshment purposes. It's more expensive than the run of rosés, around

$4. How to serve it: See under ROSÉ.

SAINT VERAN*** This is a dry white Burgundy wine, small, tasty, relatively inexpensive. It makes a good substitute for out-of-sight Pouilly-Fuissé. It's a brand-new name, a brand-new wine, for the name has only recently been given official recognition by the French government. It will go especially well with fish and shellfish. It sells for $3.25 to $5.

SANDEMAN APITIV SHERRY**** Sandeman is a huge and venerable British wine firm (with offices in both Portugal and London) producing fine authentic Ports from Portugal and sherries from Spain. This Apitiv is an extra dry Fino, fresh and clean, correctly named, for it makes an elegant aperitif wine. For more on how to serve it: See under SHERRY. Fair value, $4.50.

SANDEMAN DRY DON SHERRY**** This is a medium dry Amontillado, rich and tasty. It's an all-purpose sherry: goes before, during, or after meals. For more on serving: See under SHERRY. Fair value, $5.

SANDEMAN FINE RICH CREAM SHERRY**** Charming sweet sherry, for after-dinner enjoyment. It can even accompany a not too sweet dessert. It vies with Harveys Bristol Cream, at $3 less. A good value, this, at ca. $4.80. How to serve it: See under SHERRY.

SANDEMAN'S THREE STAR TAWNY PORT Sandeman offers a range of fine Ports—from the very best, their Vintage Port (see, below) to this Tawny, one of their least expensive. This Three Star Tawny is the best of Sandeman's lower-priced Portos, a good value at $5.25. At least ****.

SANDEMAN VINTAGE PORT Sandeman Portos, although always reliable, tend to be a trifle on the sweet side. Maurice Healy, the famous Irish wine critic, said of the 1897, that it was the finest Port he ever drank—and he drank a lot of it before he came to die! Other notable vintages were the 1934, 1945, 1958, all a healthy *****, and all for present drinking. Don't dilly over the '34. The '62 is presently bringing about $15.

SANGRE DE TORO: See TORRES SANGRE DE TORO.

SANGRIA Every country in Europe has its own summertime wine punch. Sangria is Spain's, the best known of them, and the best. You just take some light red wine, add some crushed fruit, some sugar, and perhaps some ice (to placate those ice-happy Americanos), and, olé, Sangria!

Wine punch may even go back to Old Testament times. Jeremiah tells the gang, "But as for you, gather wine and summer fruit . . ." (40: 10)

With the rise of "Pop" wines in the U.S., Sangria was a natural. American wineries began to bottle it under such names as Spañada and Sangrole (see under Gallo and Italian Swiss Colony, respectively). These are bottled wine punches, nothing more nor less, and if you like bottled wine punches . . .

The Spanish also knew a good thing when they saw it—or a profitable one—and everybody and his *tio* is now bottling a Sangria to export to the U.S. The first, and probably still the best, is Yago Sant'Gria (see). Lope de Vega and Señor Fama are also good.

But the best Sangria, by eleventeen kilometers, is the one you make yourself with a young red wine (or even an old flabby one) and some fresh fruit. Leave those bottled Sangrias to uninformed wastrels. Here's the world's best Sangria recipe, bar none:

> Boil ½ cup of water and 1 cup of sugar with ¼ teaspoon of cinnamon for five minutes and let the syrup cool. Cut 1 lemon, 2 bananas, peeled, and 1 orange, peeled, into thick slices and cover the fruit with the cooled syrup. Chill the fruit for several hours. Put ice in a glass pitcher and add the sliced fruit, ½ cup of the syrup, and 1 quart of red wine. Stir the mixture thoroughly, mashing the fruit slightly. Serve the Sangria in well-chilled tumblers, garnishing each glass with some of the sliced fruit.
>
> (*Gourmet,* September, 1967)

SANGROLE: See under ITALIAN SWISS COLONY.

SAN MARTIN WINERY (San Martin, Calif.) Despite their size—San Martin has storage capacity of more than three million gallons—these folks make some very creditable wines, and lots of reliable standard ones. Lots of wine for sure: approximately fifty of them at last count, including fruit and berry wines. (These latter are not included here, as wine is the fermented juice of the *grape*—not the pomegranate or artichoke: cf. Webster's Third International.) The peasantry will be well advised to speak well of San Martin wines; these are some of the best wine buys in America. They are made for now-consumption; except where noted below, all San Martin wines are ready to drink when you bring them home and you should not keep them more than a year or two.

Burgundy** The name "Burgundy" covers a multitude of sins in the U.S.—everything from pure bile to some excellent red table wine. This Burgundy is quite average, smooth and dry, will pick up those grilled hamburgers.

Caution: There is also a Mountain Burgundy (see), a cheaper and lesser wine.

Cabernet Ruby: See RUBY CABERNET.

Cabernet Sauvignon*** This red table wine, one of San Martin's best, is a bit thin but still has good flavor. Ordinarily it's nonvintaged (no vintage date on the bottle) but nevertheless will improve with a year or two in the bottle. It will go well with almost any kind of food, especially meat, red or white. Or enjoy it by itself, with cheese, nuts, fruit. Fair value, $3.50. (There was a special bottling, Limited 1968 Vintage: **** but not worth $9.)

Chablis: See PETITE CHABLIS.

Champagne, Brut** San Martin makes a host of sparkling wines, with rather mixed results. This is one of the better ones, but it's highly questionable with this wine, as with almost all of San Martin's sparkling wines, whether it's worth its relatively high price. There are many bulk-fermented California Champagnes at half the price, which are much more than half as good as the San Martin products.

All sparkling wines are served well chilled. They go well al-most any time, anyplace. Fair value, $5.

Champagne, Extra Dry—Not recommended.

Champagne, Pink* It won a gold medal at the Los Angeles County Fair, 1973, but one wonders what constituted the competition. Medium-sweet. Fair value, $4.75 to $5.

Champagne, Rouge—Not recommended.

Chenin Blanc*** How to serve: See under CHENIN BLANC.

Cold Duck* Not the ugliest duckling in the skies these days but not the prettiest either. For summer evening's sipping—if you're not too fussy. It's medium-sweet, clean, and fresh. Fair value, $4.

Cream Sherry: See SHERRY.

Dry Sherry: See SHERRY.

Emerald Riesling*** Tasty white wine, slightly sweet, made from a California-invented grape of the same name. Marvelous for warm weather refreshment, chilled.

Gamay Beaujolais** Light red wine, small flavor. There are better Gamays lurking about at this price. Not a good value at ca. $3.

Gran Spumante: See MALVASIA, GRAN SPUMANTE.

Grenache Rosé** You can do better elsewhere at the same price. Fair value, $2.

Grignolino*** An unsual Italian-type red wine, light and dry. It will go well with any full-flavored food, especially pasta, red meats. Fair value, $2.50. There was a special bottling, Limited 1970 Vintage: ****, light and fresh.

Hostess Emerald Riesling: See EMERALD RIESLING.

Hostess Sémillon: See SÉMILLON SAUTERNE.

Malvasia Bianca*** Be careful here: there's also a Malvasia, Gran Spumante (see), a sparkling wine, more expensive. If you like sweet wines, you'll like this. It's smooth, perfumy, not syrupy-sweet. It will go well with almost any kind of dessert. Or enjoy it as an 11:00 wine— A.M. or P.M. Fair value, $3.

Malvasia, Gran Spumante*** This is an Italian-type Champagne—*bello, bello!* (It used to be called Spumante Moscato.) Perfect with dessert of whatever description—or with that birthday cake. Fair value, $4.

Mountain Burgundy ** to *** Those who like an edge of sweetness in their red table wine will rank this ***; those who don't, will rank it **. It has some substance and fruit. An excellent value at $1.60 to $1.75.

Mountain Rhine***

Muscato Canelli, 1973 Marvelous dessert wine. Fair value, $4.

Petite Chablis*** This name is borrowed from France, but it's not very complimentary, as France's Petite Chablis, as the name proclaims, is a smaller wine than simple Chablis. This Petite Chablis, however, is not all that small; it's of good size, dry and flinty, like it's French progenitor. Excellent with seafood, poultry, fowl, ham. Fair value, $2.
Be careful, though: there is also a Mountain Chablis—it's extremely *petite*—avoid!

Petite Sirah*** Nice little red wine for the table; it will ennoble your humblest fare. Serve at cool room temperature. Fair value, $2.80 to $3.

Pinot Chardonnay*** It's not Le Montrachet—though it's made from the same grapes— but neither is the price. And it's an honest dry white wine that will be a credit to your table,

especially when it accompanies your fish or seafood course. Fair value, $3.30 to $3.50.

Pinot Noir*** It's not Le Chambertin—though it's made from the same grapes—but it's a savory red table wine. Save it for your Saturday evening steaks, Sunday holiday fare, or Boeuf Bourguignon. Fair value, $3.25 to $3.75.

Rare Sherry: See SHERRY.

Ruby Cabernet *** to **** Fresh young red wine, very flavorful. Some batches are a little better than others, though none have descended below *** in recent years. The '72—it's not on the label, look at the bottom of the bottle, if there's a '74 there, it's a 72, as it was bottled in '74—is especially good, ****.

Sémillon Sauterne*** Fresh, medium-sweet white wine, makes for excellent summertime sipping, especially around 11:00 —A.M. or P.M., or sorta in-between times too.

Sherry*** (Castlewood) San Martin makes three: all very good values, at $1.80 to $2.25. *Dry:* not as dry as it sounds, but their driest, good aperitif wine. *Rare:* Medium-sweet, serve it before dinner or after. *Cream:* Received a gold medal, Los Angeles County Fair, 1973. Serve it after dinner.

Spumante Moscato: See MALVASIA, GRAN SPUMANTE.

Sylvaner Riesling*

Vin Rosé** Medium-sweet.

Zinfandel** For manner of serving: See under ZINFANDEL.

SANMINATELLI, CONTESSA ELENA: See VIGNAMAGGIO.

SANTA CRISTINA This is the lowliest grade of Chianti made by the reputed Italian firm of Antinori (Florence). It is a good little red wine, consistently *** vintage after vintage. The current bottling, 1970, is already good drinking but will improve further if you lay it down for a couple of years. Fair value, $3.50.

How to serve this wine: See under CHIANTI.

SANTA REY DÃO* An economical little table wine from Portugal—it comes in both Tinto (red) and Branco (white); both are well made and excellent values at less than $2. How to serve these wines: See under DAO.

SANTENAY Good red wine of France, light, smooth, can be very fruity—never great, but always dependable and usually a good value. It can be served and enjoyed in exactly the same way as Beaujolais (see), which it resembles.

If it says *"l^er (Premier) Crû"* on the label, with the name of a vineyard—Clos (de) Tavannes, Les Gravières, La Comme —it's even better. Santenay is at its best when it's from three to seven years old. Air it at least an hour. Especially recommended are: Joseph Drouhin ($6, a bit steep), Pierre Olivier (an excellent value at $3.75), J. Faiveley ($5.25).

SANTENOTS, CLOS DES: See VOLNAY.

SAUTERNES AND SAUTERNE If it's spelled without a final "s," it's certainly a California white wine, and almost certainly a dry and inexpensive one. If it's spelled with a final "s," it's almost certainly a white French wine, very probably a sweet and luscious one.

Clearly, someone is misusing the name, and as Pogo says, we've discovered the enemy and he is us! Properly speaking, Sauternes, a sweet wine, is only the wine produced in the Sauternes district of Bordeaux (France). American vintners do violence to the name when they use it for some of their gutless concoctions. Call it simply "California White," or after the grapes from which it's made, but not Sauternes, with or without an "s."

French Sauternes is probably the finest sweet white wine on earth. For some reason such wines are out of fashion today, and hence are often excellent values. Sauternes is a naturally sweet wine, it is not sugared. The grapes are picked very late, when they are fully ripe and even overripe, having been attacked by the "noble rot," which renders the wine even more luscious. Pickers will go over the vineyards up to a dozen times—once they were still picking on Christmas Day. These wines are necessarily expensive, but they are like no others on this earth—dessert wines par excellence. But at least a little goes a long way here; pour your Sauternes grudgingly and stingily, well chilled (40 to 45°F).

Sauternes is one of the very few fine wines that can stand up to a sweet dessert. But it shows to even better advantage when it accompanies melon (with honeydew—heavenly!) or fresh fruit (especially peaches). A century ago it was fashionable to serve Sauternes with hors d'oeuvres and even with fish and white meats. Most Americans, however, presented with such combinations, might be in danger of suffering from *mal de mer*. But Sauternes is recommended, even by the most conservative and sober-sided, to accompany pâtés and caviar. As the ancient philosopher saith, "Don't knock it till you've tried it."

But fine Sauternes reaches its full stature only when it is sipped, carefully and lovingly, on its own, in the company of upstanding wine-loving friends.

The best French Sauternes will have the name of a specific château in bold print on the label—and often a picture of it as well—the word "Sauternes" will usually be secondary. The very best are these, listed in roughly descending order of excellence: Château d'Yquem; Château Climens; Château Coutet; Château Filhot; Château de Rayne-Vigneau; Château de Suduiraut; Château Rieussec; Château Lafaurie-Peyraguey; Château La Tour Blanche.

Bottles that say Sauternes in bold letters and do not say Château Such-and-Such are the lowest grade of French Sauternes, but usually pretty good wine and a good value. They'll range in price from about $4.50 to $6.50.

Recent Sauternes Vintages:

1966: Good wines. Drink, 1975 and 1976.

1967: Excellent year, fine, well-balanced wines. Drink, 1975 through 1978.,

1968: Terrible—drink never!

1969: Fine wines. Best drinking, now and to 1980.

1970: Great year—exceptional wines. Will be at their best, 1976 through 1985.

1971: Superb vintage. Best drinking, 1976–1985.

Note, however, that the real big ones, Château d'Yquem and that ilk, will not only keep for fifteen years and more, but will mellow and deepen in both color and intensity.

American Sauterne American Sauterne, however, is a whole new ball game. It drops more than a mere final "s"—from Sauternes to Sauterne—it also drops most of what serves to make French Sauternes a great wine. To start with, French Sauternes is always sweet—the American product rarely is. Saddest of all, a great deal of Sauterne (American) is a cheap, nondescript jug wine—Hamlet would have described it as "weary, stale, flat, and unprofitable . . ." Well, he might have left off that last adjective.

Some of this cheap white wine might just as well be labeled Chablis or White Mountain, or whatever. Indeed, it is said that wine from one and the same vat has sometimes been labeled Sauterne, sometimes Chablis.

America does produce some respectable Sauterne, however—it is still several light-years removed from the real French article, but it can be quite commendable in its own right. The best of it will have the distinct aroma and taste of the Sémillion grape: a perfumy kind of earthiness. In fact, the wine sometimes goes by that name: Sémillon.

Listed below are the best of California's Dry Sauternes, in descending order. When wines have the same rating, the least expensive is listed first. Prices are approximate.

California Dry Sauternes
Comparative Standings

****

Very Good

   Korbel Dry Sauterne ($2.25)
   Wente Dry Sémillon, 1968 and 1969 ($2.65)

***

Good

   Gallo Sauterne ($1.30)
   Roma Sauterne ($1.35)
   LaMont Sémillon ($2)
   Cresta   Blanca   Sauterne ($2.10)

Krug Dry Sauterne ($2.25)

Almadén Dry Sémillon Sauterne ($2.35)

Cresta Blanca Dry Sémillon ($2.45)

Assumption Abbey Vertdoux Blanc ($2.50)

Concannon Dry Sémillon ($2.50)

Wente Dry Sémillon, 1970, 1971, 1972 ($2.65)

Inglenook Dry Sémillon, 1969 and 1970 ($2.75)

Krug Dry Sémillon (2.85)

Fetzer Sémillon ($5)

**

Fair

Franzia Sauterne ($1.20)

Gold Seal Sauternes ($2)

Eleven Cellars Sauterne ($2)

Great Western Aurora Sauterne ($2)

Masson Dry Sauterne ($2)

Weibel Sauterne ($2.05)

Martini Dry Sauternes ($2.10)

Novitiate Dry Sauterne ($2.15)

Christian Brothers Sauterne ($2.20)

Beaulieu Dry Sauterne (Sémillon) ($2.75)

Inglenook Dry Sémillon, 1971 ($2.75)

Boordy Sémillon Sec ($2.80)

*

Passable

Italian Swiss Colony Sauterne ($1.30)

Winemasters Sauterne ($1.40)

Dry Sauterne should be served chilled (50°F). It goes well with chicken, simply cooked fish and seafood; it's excellent at a luncheon or buffet. The better bottles (*** and ****) will serve well as an aperitif wine.

America does make some Sweet Sauterne, but like its French progenitor it is not very popular at the moment. It lacks the richness and complexity of the French original, but it can be quite acceptable. It goes by all manner of different names, and the wines are not of equal sweetness. Some are actually semi-dry. The sweetest are those called Château Whatever. Listed below are America's best Sweet Sauternes, by whatever name they go, listed in descending order of excellence. Where wines have the same rating, the least expensive is listed first. Prices are approximate.

*American Sweet Sauternes—
Comparative Standings*

****

Very Good

Ste. Michelle Sémillon ($2.85)

***

Good

Eleven Cellars Haut Sauterne ($1.90)

LaMont Sémillon ($2)—Semisweet.

Bargetto Haut Sauterne ($2.50)

San Martin Sémillon Sauterne ($2.50)

Wente Château Wente (formerly Château Sémillon) ($2.75)

Concannon Château Concannon ($3)—Quite sweet.

Oakville Sauvignon Fleur ($3.25)

Beaulieu Château Beaulieu (Sauvignon Blanc) ($3.60) —Sweeter than their Haut Sauternes.

**

Fair

Novitiate Château Novitiate ($2.10)

Assumption Abbey Haute Sauterne ($2.15)

Christian Brothers Haut Sauterne ($2.20)

Beaulieu Haut Sauternes (Sweet Sémillon) ($2.70)

Krug Sweet Sauternes ($2.85) —Medium dry.

Note: Christian Brothers' Château La Salle (**—$2.30) is quite different from the above "Château" wines, has a distinct Muscat flavor.

SAUVIGNON BLANC This is the noble grape that teams up with the Sémillon to produce the great white wines of Graves (see) and Sauternes (France) (see), and by itself it is responsible for the delightful white wines of France's Loire Valley. In America it finds its way into the best of our American Sauternes—would that they could all claim its presence—but it's at its best when on its own, bottled under its own name or under one of its French names, Blanc-Fumé (or, bass-ackwards, Fumé-Blanc, as some American vintners insist on it).

This is a full-bodied white wine, fruity, almost herblike, with a wholesome earthiness. It can be used as a dry aperitif wine, but its best service will be to accompany light foods: fish, seafood, poultry, veal, casseroles with light sauces, pork, ham; excellent also to grace your luncheon buffet. Serve chilled (45 to 50°F).

California's finest and poorest in roughly descending order of excellence. When wines have the same rating, the least expensive is listed first. Prices are approximate.

****
Very Good

Sonoma (or Windsor) Sauvignon Blanc—Dry ($2.75)

Sterling Blanc de Sauvignon, 1970—Dry ($3.50)

Robert Mondavi Fumé Blanc —Slightly Dry ($4.75)

Oakville Sauvignon Blanc—Dry (1971) ($4.75)

Concannon Sauvignon Blanc,

Ltd. Bottling, 1971—Dry ($5)

Cuvaison Sauvignon Blanc, 1972—Dry ($5)

Fetzer Dry Sauvignon Blanc, 1970 ($5)

Van Loben Sels Sauvignon Blanc, 1972—Dry ($5)

Spring Mountain Sauvignon Blanc—Dry ($6)

***
Good

Wente Sauvignon Blanc, 1971 and 1972—Dry ($2.80)

Cresta Blanca Sauvignon Blanc—Very dry ($3.20)

Beringer Fumé Blanc—Dry ($3.50)

Concannon Sauvignon Blanc, 1968, 1969, 1971, 1972— Dry with touch of sweetness ($3.50)

Oakville Sauvignon Blanc, N.V.—Dry ($3.50)

Sterling Blanc de Sauvignon, 1971—Dry ($3.50)

Charles Krug Pouilly Fumé —Dry ($3.85)

**
Fair

Gallo Sauvignon Blanc—Dry ($1.85)

Almadén Sauvignon Blanc— Dry ($3)

Christian Brothers Sauvignon Blanc—Semisweet ($3.20)

Concannon Sauvignon Blanc, 1970—Dry, touch of sweetness ($3.50)

Fetzer Dry Sauvignon Blanc, 1971 ($5)

Wente Sauvignon Blanc, 1966, 1967, 1968, 1969—Dry ($5)

*
Passable

Eleven Cellars Sauvignon Blanc—Dry ($2.70)

Eleven Cellars Fumé Blanc —Dry ($2.85)

SAVIGNY-LES-BEAUNE Good red Burgundy wine, though not of the top echelon.

The wines are similar to and somewhat overshadowed by those of Beaune (see), making them good values. Louis Latour, Moillard, Poulet, Jadot make fine Savignys.

SAX'S NATURAL ARKANSAS GRAPE WINE It has finally been revealed: this is the original wine long sought by historians, a sample of which, when sent to the University of Arkansas for a chemical analysis, was returned with this report: Your horse has diabetes.

SCHARZBERGER Superb Saar (Germany) wine, first cousin to the more famous Scharzhofberger (see). Vintages are very important here—see under Scharzhofberger for the ones to look for. A famous Eiswein was made in 1961: Classic. How to serve: See under MOSELLE.

SCHARZHOFBERGER If somebody gives you a bottle with this name emblazoned across the label, embrace the person gratefully, or more appropriately, fall down and at his (her) feet and worship, for you've been given a bottle of one of the world's finest white wines—some say simply *the* finest. This is a superb wine from Germany's Saar region (the label says Mosel-Saar-Ruwer) with tremendous flavor, yet elegant and fragrant. It sometimes goes by the name of Dom Scharzhofberger. Note that there is also a Scharzberg (see), an adjoining vineyard. As regal as this wine is, you will want to appreciate it wholly on its own, without food accompaniment. Serve it chilled. Vintages are extremely important here, for Scharzhofberger in poor years is hard. Look for these:

1953—Superb wine.

1959—Ditto.

1961—Marvelous wines.
    Auslese Eiswein (Muller): Famous: Classic.

1962—Excellent year.

1966—Good to Very Good.

1967—Excellent year— "Plain" Scharzhofberger has begun to fade—Auslese and above: Now at their best.

1969—Magnificent wines.

1971—Great year—Look for Von Volxem wines in particular.

SCHLOSS BOKELHEIM(ER) "Schloss" means "Castle," but this is actually the name of a German village. It's a good white wine. A '63 Auslese (Plettenberg) is a glorious wine just now fully matured, but don't keep it: *****. A "straight" 1970 by Plettenberg is weak: **. A '72 by Deinhard is much better, a fine, fresh, elegant wine: ****.

SCHLOSS JOHANNISBERG-ER Probably the most famous vineyard in all of Germany—the wine is world-renowned. Unhappily, fame and price usually ascend in direct proportion. Schloss Johannisberger has become prohibitively expensive, and excellent as it is, it is almost always overpriced. You can often obtain an equally fine wine at half the price from one of the adjacent vineyards, particularly Johannisberger Klaus (see—other excellent names are also listed there). The Schloss has an elaborate system of colored capsules, and this "rank" is also indicated in print on the label. In ascending order of excellence: Rotlack (Red capsule); Grünlack (Green); Weisslack (White); Rosalack (Pink).

Some notable vintages—if you can find them—and afford them —or choose to afford them:

1950 Spätlese Eiswein—Priceless, a classic.

1953 One of the Schloss's greatest vintages: *****

1959 A disappointment, despite a great vintage year; also: it's past its peak, and certainly not worth its present asking price, in the vicinity of $25 . . . $2.50 would be too much.

1966 It has departed this world, Amen.

1967 Rotlack—Now at the top of its bent, but don't keep it.

1969 Rotlack—Disappointing.

1970 Rotlack—****

1971 Grünlack Spätlese: *****—It will be even better if you keep it until 1976.

SCHLOSS VOLLRADS One of the finest and best known of all German Rhine wines; incredibly the vineyard and its wine date back some 750 years, to 1211! Vollrads is noted for its elegance and its remarkable bouquet. It has an elaborate system of colored capsules which indicate the grade of the wine. In the old system (before the new German wine laws, 1971) there were a full fifteen different capsules and grades of the wine—Germanic thoroughness!—but with the new simplified system there are a mere eleven of them! In simplified form, in ascending order, the capsules are:

Green—Lowest grade but still a Qualitätswein (original-Abfüllung in the old system).

Red—Schlossabzug: estate-bottled, in old system (not often used in new).

Blue—Kabinett wine.

Pink—Auslese in old system; Spätlese in new.

White—Beerenauslese in old system; Auslese, new system.

White-gold plus Vollrads neckband—Trockenbeerenauslese, old system.

Gold—Beerenauslese, new system.

Gold with Vollrads neckband:—Trockenbeerenauslese, new system.

Some famous vintages:

1920—Trockenbeerenauslese: One of the most famous German wines of all times—Classic.

1937—Trockenbeerenauslese —One of the greatest. One critic said it may last forever: Classic.

1947—Trockenbeerenauslese —Tasted in 1973, still has many wonderful years ahead: Classic.

1959—Trockenbeerenauslese: Classic.

Some recent vintages:

1969—Good, well-balanced wine—Not extraordinary, has developed slowly—now at its best—Even a green capsule (lowest grade) of Graf Matuschka rates ****, a Kabinett of the same (blue capsule), *****.

1970—Delightful wines, fast-maturing—Drink before 1978.

1971—Fabulous vintage—If you can find and afford them, buy, buy! Just getting to their best, will remain at the top of their bent through the 70s and beyond.

SCHOONMAKER FRANK Frank Schoonmaker has been one of the most important names on the American wine scene for forty years, and when you find his name on the neck label of a wine saying he selected the wine, it's *prima facie,* though not infallible, evidence that you're looking at a good bottle of wine.

SCHOONMAKER, FRANK— SELECTION: PINOT CHARDONNAY Most of the Pinot Chardonnay you see in the U.S. is from California. This one is

from France (Burgundy, to be exact), selected and endorsed by the eminent American wine authority, Frank Schoonmaker. A good selection, a good wine, a good value at ca. $3.50. ***
SCHRAMSBERG VINE-YARDS (Calistoga, Calif.) These ancient Champagne cellars vaulted to sudden fame in 1972 when then President Richard Nixon picked up thirteen cases of Schramsberg Champagne (at approximately $1,300) when he stopped over in California en route to Peking. He was well advised—Schramsberg probably makes the finest Champagne in America today.

Blanc de Blancs The name means simply white wine from white grapes, for much white wine (Champagne included) is often made from dark grapes. In itself the name does not connote superior quality, but it does in this instance, for here you're ascending to the vinous heights. This is certainly one of America's finest Champagnes, sometimes conceded to be *the* finest. Be cautioned however, that such delicate and austere Champagne, made extremely dry, is not to everyone's tastes, especially beginners in matters winey.

To ascend even further into the stratosphere, there is a special, superior blend of this wine made each year, a Reserve *cuvée*, from the very choicest grapes and aged longer; this receives no *dosage* (sweetening) at all, and only 200 cases are made. Of California Champagnes, this is surely the *crème de la crème*. Schramsberg says it goes beautifully with seafood, soups, poultry, or sauté dishes —surely true enough, but at the price, $8.50 or more, most of the bourgeoisie will consume it

on rare and splendid occasions, as an aperitif or tasting wine.

1966: Near-Classic A California classic. It possessed marvelous freshness in its youth, was pleasantly yeasty, and probably still has and is. Drink it soon—as who wouldn't?

1967 and *1968:* ******** Excellent drinking now and until whenever.

1969: ******** and reaching for ********* This was the toasting wine former President Nixon took to Peking—no wonder the Chinese were mollified.

1970: ******** Drink now—and whenever.

1971: ******** Schramsberg makes some of America's greatest Champagne, but the '71 was not quite up to their usual high standards.

1972: ******** Already great drinking and it will be even better, 1976–1978.

Blanc de Noir This white Champagne made from black grapes is a fuller-bodied wine than the Blanc de Blancs, but still very dry.

1967 ******** Drink now and through 1979.

1968 ******** Not for long-time keeping—drink it during '75 and '76.

Cremant (Demi-Sec)**** "Cremant" means "Creaming," a word the French use to describe a wine that is not fully sparkling. Schramsberg thought this style of Champagne would be appealing as a dessert wine —they're right. Here's a soft, rich dessert Champagne, something America's been needing. The label also says Demi-Sec, literally half-dry, but in Champagne terminology that translates to "Pretty Sweet," making this an ideal dessert wine.

Cuvée de Gamay**** Here's one of the most elegant pink bubblies you're going to encounter on this good earth. (In heaven, however, you will do even better.) It's even bottled in clear glass, so's you can admire the delicate rose color and the effervescence. For that special anniversary, birthday. Or, if $$$ are only a minor consideration, here's some luxurious sipping, with fresh fruit, fine cheese. Fair value, $6 to $7.50.

SCHWARZE KATZ: See ZELLER SCHWARZE KATZ.

SEBASTIANI VINEYARDS (Sonoma, Calif.) Sebastiani grows larger year by year—current capacity: some two and a half million gallons—but to date they're still a family operation, praises be! No spectacular or great wines have ever issued from the Samuele Sebastiani casks and vats, but millions of gallons of good and above-average wines have flown therefrom, lo, these seventy years. The wines are not all equally good, of course, but over the long haul, Sebastiani is a name to be trusted. A few of the wines are not good values, but there is no such thing as a bad Sebastiani wine.

Amore Cream Sherry**** Very rich, definitely sweet, silky soft. One of California's best creams. Fair value, $3.75 to $4.

Arenas Dry Sherry*** Ideal aperitif wine. Fair value, $3.75 to $4.

Barbera***** This Italian-type red wine has always been one of Sebastiani's mainstays and showpieces. It can't stop winning gold medals, from the 50s to the present. Some say it's California's best Barbera, bar none. It's robust, hearty, very tasty—excellent with red meats, stews, pasta. Or sip it tenderly, with cheese or nuts. It can be consumed young, but it's big enough to improve with age. It's at its best five to ten years after its vintage date. Serve it at cool room temperature. A good value at $3 to $3.25. The '69 took a gold medal at the 1974 Los Angeles County Fair. The '67 (Bin 15) is ****, sells for $5.

Burgundy*** It's too bad the U.S. uses borrowed (stolen?) names such as "Burgundy" for so many good American wines, for "Burgundy" comes only from the Burgundy region of France, and this wine doesn't even remotely resemble a fine French red Burgundy. This is not to say that this is not a good wine. It is, but it's not "Burgundy." It's a tasteful, hearty red table wine, deserving of recognition in its own right. Fine accompaniment for those grilled hamburgers, steaks, roasts, stews, it's ready to drink when you buy it, and though it won't improve with age, it will keep well for three or four years. Serve at cool room temperature; a good value at ca. $2.25.

Note: There is also a Mountain Burgundy (see), also a good wine and less expensive.

Burgundy, 1967, Bin 24**** It's rare that you'll find a simple "Burgundy" with a vintage date on it, but this is a notable wine, well balanced and flavorful, worth looking for. It's now at its best and will hold there at least through the decade. A good value at $3.75 to $4.

Cabernet Sauvignon*** Cabernet Sauvignon is the grape that makes the greatest red wines in the world—Sebastiani's isn't the greatest red table wine in the world by a large measure, but it's an honest and reliable wine. Save it for your more elaborate dining: it's ready for drinking when you buy it and it will even improve for two or three years in the bottle. Serve at cool room temperature. Fair value, $4 to $4.25. There have been a number of special bottlings through the years, most of them excellent wine.

Cabernet Sauvignon Bin 32 (1966), but the year isn't on the label**** Will be at its best starting in 1976. Fair value, $6.

Cabernet Sauvignon Bin 34 (1967)**** Will reach its peak, 1977 through 1985. Fair value, $6.50.,

Cabernet Sauvignon Bin 190 (1964, not on label)—Not recommended.

Cabernet Sauvignon, 1968— **** for a starter. "Spectacular," one writer calls it; the wine was released only in late 1974. Fair value, $6.50.

California Sherry: See SHERRY.

Chablis** Note that there is also a Mountain Chablis (see), a cheaper wine. Sebastiani whites are not yet up to the standards of their reds. They'll make it, but this one's not there yet. Fair value, ca. $2.25.

Chenin Blanc** Showing improvement in recent years, but not quite there yet. Anon, anon . . . Fair value, $2.30 to $2.60.

Chianti** You (consumer) and they (winery) can do better.

Cream Sherry: See SHERRY.

Gamay Beaujolais**** Sam Sebastiani loves this wine—it shows. Young and soft, with a grapelike flavor, this should be everybody's favorite. It will fit in almost everywhere: luncheon, outdoor barbecues, for-

mal dining. Or, most fun of all: sip it lovingly, on its own, or with cheese, nuts, fresh fruit, at cool room temperature. It's ready to drink upon purchase and won't improve in the bottle, but will keep three or four years. A good value at $3 to $3.25.

Gamay Beaujolais, Bin 192— Not recommended. Produced in 1966 (not on the label), and past its peak.

Gamay Beaujolais, 1968**** May be on decline.

Gamay Beaujolais, 1969, Bin 71**** Drink it *now*.

Gamay Beaujolais, 1971**** It will never be better.

Gamay Beaujolais, 1972*** Drink now and through 1977.

Gamay Beaujolais, 1973 **** It took a silver medal at the 1974 Los Angeles County Fair.

Gamay Beaujolais, Nouveau *** Sebastiani was the first American winery to make this kind of an infant, sappy wine. It's truly a baby, bottled at six weeks—not months—of age, and on the shelves at six months. The French do this annually—it's a ritual with them—with some of their Beaujolais. It's different from any other wine you'll ever taste: totally simple, grapey, very light, youthful. For your picnic or luncheon, with sandwiches or hot dogs. The '72 and '73 were equally good. Serve cool (50°F), not chilled. Fair value, $3 to $3.25.

Gewürz Traminer Sebastiani's version is light and softly spicy. It goes well with fish, seafood, fowl. Drink it when it's young and fresh: within five years of its vintage date. Fair value, $3 to $3.25.

1969 (Bin 82)***
1970***

1971**
1972***

Green Hungarian This oddly-yclept wine "grows" only in California. Some say Sebastiani's is the best in the state. It's a pleasant little white wine with a trace of sweetness. It's perfect, chilled, at a luncheon or at a summer's evening sipping session. Drink it young: within four years of its vintage date. Recent vintages ('70, '71, '72): ***. Fair value, $2.30 to $2.50.

Grenache Rosé*** Recent vintages have been improvements—avoid anything before 1971. Drink it young (before its fourth birthday), chilled, with light foods. Touch of sweetness, the ladies will like it. A good value at $2.15 to $2.35.

Johannisberg Riesling This California Rhine wine has some of the virtues of its German counterpart, but it's tarter and more suitable to accompany light foods: poultry, fish, chicken salad. Serve it chilled, with pride—it's an elegant wine. Fair value, $3.50 to $3.75.

1967**** A beautifully balanced wine. At its best right now but don't keep beyond 1975.

1969***

1970 Auspicious omens but no certainty yet.

1972***

Kleinberger Riesling, 1969** This was probably the only wine by this name ever produced anywhere. It was made only in '69 and is no longer available. You may find it on some retailer's cobwebby shelf and if you like oddities, okay. Treat it as you would a Johannisberg Riesling, don't keep it. Fair value, $3.50.

Mountain Burgundy*** The winery calls this the teen-age brother of their "straight" Burgundy (see). It's at least that, and may even be the adult brother, though not the older brother. It lacks entirely the phony sweetness of so many cheap California Burgundies. It's Burgundy in the light style, but it has some character. Serve it as you would the straight Burgundy; it's for immediate enjoyment, don't keep it more than a year or two. An excellent value, at $1.75 to $1.90.

Mountain Chablis** The price is right, $3.30 to $3.50 per half-gallon, but the quality's not.
Note: There is also a "plain" Chablis (see), but it's not much of an improvement.

Mountain Red: See MOUNTAIN BURGUNDY.

Mountain Vin Rosé ** Drier than the Grenache, but still no big deal. One writer says it tastes like Juicy Fruit gum. . . . Fair value, $1.65 to $1.75.
Note: There is also a "plain" Vin Rosé (see).

Pinot Chardonnay White wines are not Sebastiani's strong suit, and this white Burgundy-type wine, despite its relatively high price, $3.50 to $3.75, is just not worth the money. The best batch thus far, 1971: ***. 1972: ** only.

Pinot Noir Sebastiani had some trouble getting the combination of this difficult grape at first, but recent vintages have all been fine. The 1967, ****, is now at its best and will hold there at least until 1978. The 1968, also ****, is likewise at its peak and the winery says it will remain there until around 1983. The 1969, also ****, will be at its best from 1976, at least through 1979. These three wines were offered in a wooden case for Christmas giving in 1974 at a cost of around $16.50.

Bin 185 (Produced '63–'64) **

Bin 121 (Produced, '61–'63): Sebastiani's best effort thus far: ***. (Bottled February '68).

Sherry** Sebastiani has long made the standard three types of sherry—dry, medium, and sweet—by standard California methods—which is to say, the wines are not very well made. Happily, all three have been recently discontinued. Some bottles, however, may still be lurking about on some retailers' shelves . . . be forewarned. They are: Pale Dry, California Sherry, Cream Sherry.

Sebastiani has recently introduced two new sherries, made in the true Spanish manner and aged in outdoor wooden casks: Amore Cream and Arenas Dry (see both), commendable beverages.

Sylvaner Riesling*** Sebastiani's most interesting and promising white. Sylvaners are never great wines but this is a clean, fresh wine, a perfect thirst-quencher. Serve it chilled, before dinner. Drink it young, before its fifth birthday. Fair value, ca. $2.30.

Vin Rosé Note that there is also a Mountain Vin Rosé (see), a cheaper wine. This is a dry-type rosé, with good flavor and character. Recent vintages, 1971 and 1972, ***. Avoid earlier vintages. It's ready for immediate enjoyment, don't hold it more than a year or two. A good value at ca. $2.20.

Zinfandel**** The label boasts of a "unique bramble flavor" and they're right and it has. Honest, gutsy, full-flavored wine, to go with those barbecued steaks or hamburgers, roasts, stews, even spicy Italian dishes. Serve at cool room temperature. A good value at $2.30 or $2.50.

Nonvintage, Bin 182 and *184* *** Ready for present drinking, will keep at least five years after purchase.

1970**** There was a "plain" and a Vintage Reserve bottling this year. Even the "plain" was excellent, with fine flavor. The Vintage Reserve received extended aging in redwood and was released only in 1974. It's now ready to drink and will keep for many years to come.

1972**** Excellent drinking now and for many years ahead.

SECCO: The word simply means "Dry" in Italian, but sometimes it's so prominent on the label that it looks like the name of the wine. Look up your wine under its proper name, e.g., Recioto.

SEDIMENT IN WINE: See DECANTING.

SELS, VAN LOBEN: See VAN LOBEN SELS.

SÉMILLON This good white grape does well in both France and the U.S. In France it is partially responsible for the success of the great white wines of Graves and Sauternes (see both). In the U.S. it gets into the act in the best Sauternes, which are mostly dry. America also produces some sweet Sauterne, and there is more of the flavorful Sémillon grape in it than in the dry. In fact it is usually called not sweet Sauterne at all, but Sémillon.

For a listing of the best Dry Sémillons, see listing of Dry Sauternes, pp. 271–2. For a listing of the best Sweet Sémillons, see the listing of Sweet Sauternes, p. 272. For an evaluation of individual bottles (e.g., Krug's Sweet Sauternes), see under the name of the winemaker (e.g., Krug).

(Conti) SERRISTORI This is the name of a dependable producer of Italian wines, especially Chiantis. Their best is their Machiavelli. Most commonly seen in the U.S. is their Chianti Classico, which has not always been up to "classic" standards. The current vintage, 1973, merits ***, but is nowhere near ready to drink; allow it to sleep in some quiet, darkened nook at least until 1979. There is also a large-size offering, a full 59-ounce bottling of "plain" Chianti, ***, selling for around $4.50, an excellent value.

SERVING WINE The rules are simple and logical: White wines before reds—dry before sweet—young before old—light before heavy. With wines of the same type, heed the Scriptural injunction: "Every man at the beginning doth set forth good wine; and when men have well drunk, then that which is worse." (John 2: 10) Don't fuss with baskets or cradles for serving wine—baskets are for weaving and cradles for babies. It is quite proper for the host to serve himself first, a small portion only, so that he gets all the cork and crud. Older wines may need decanting (see under DECANTING).

SHERRY Sherry is one of the world's greatest and most versatile of wines. The British have always appreciated it, and Americans who know not sherry are "the lesser breed without the law," and the poorer for it. The very finest sherries rank, along with just a handful of other wines, among the world's truly great classic wines.

Sherry probably has a larger "spread" than any other single wine—it ranges in taste from bone-dry to luscious-sweet; in color, from almost colorless to near-black; in price from something like $1 per fifth for some California horrors to $25 and more for some treasures. In quality, sherry ranges from infernal bilge to celestial elixir.

A couple of centuries ago sherry was made only in Spain—some people think that's still the case —but today "sherry" comes also from the U.S., South Africa, Australia. Until just a few years ago these imitation sherries were usually pretty abominable stuff. Today, some of these "foreign" sherries, particularly American, are excellent wines, not up to the very finest of Spanish sherries certainly, but honest sherry, made in the true Solera method of Spain, and, *ciertamente, muy sabrosos.*

You'll find a lot of British names—Duff Gordon, Williams and Humbert, Harveys, Sandeman—on sherry labels. The British have been in the trade for centuries; though the wine may have been bottled in Spain, it was blended according to the specifications of the British firm. The following Spanish sherries are individually treated in this book, under their proper names: Findlater; Gonzalez Byass; Harveys; Magigal; Palomino; Pedro Domecq; Williams and Humbert; Wisdom & Warter.

British and Spanish imaginations run wild on sherry labels: El Cid—Santa Maria—El Sabio (The Wise One)—Dry Sack— A Winter's Tale—Guitar—La Ina—Brown Beauty—Double Century—Tio Pepe—La Majestad—Ambrosia—Brown Bang—Dry Don—Golden Jubilee—Tio Paco—Shooting Sherry—Soldado (Soldier)—

Bristol Cream—Dry Fly—Christmas Carol.

Sherry is the world's easiest wine to drink, not only because it slides down so easily and deceitfully, but also because, for all its diversity, it's a simple, not a fussy wine to drink. There are no vintages to worry about—it's ready to drink when you buy it, and it won't get any better. (Don't keep it too long, though—two or three years is okay.) The label will usually tell you whether it's sweet, medium, or dry. And you can drink it either at room temperature or chilled, though most experts recommend the dry types slightly chilled, the sweet types at cool room temperature.

Enjoy sherry in large tulip-shaped glasses or in Spanish *copitas*—never in those miserable little glasses bars sometimes use. If you're so served, send back glass and wine with high indignation and deep regrets. Sherry keeps well even after it's been opened, especially sweet sherries. Even a dry sherry will keep for several days after the cork's been pulled, particularly if you'll refrigerate it and put it in a smaller bottle, eliminating extra air space. A sweet or medium sherry will keep so for weeks.

There are a few sherry terms that may need clarification:

1. Fino: Dry light sherry. Most people say it is the finest of all sherries.

2. Manzanilla: The Fino of Finos. It's very delicate, very dry, with a touch of saltiness, for it's grown by the sea. It makes an ideal aperitif.

3. Amontillado: A medium sherry, softer and darker than a Fino. A good Amontillado should have a distinctly nutty flavor.

4. Oloroso: Full, dark, sweet sherry. Olorosos are usually the oldest sherries generally available and the most expensive. They are called—and these are the words you'll see on the labels—Brown, Cream, or East India.

5. Milk: The term is usually used of sherries shipped to Bristol, England, and implies sweetness and softness, though the wine is lighter and less sweet than Cream.

6. Golden: Usually interchangeable with Cream.

There is a sherry for every food, for every occasion, for every mood and exigency. Dry Sherry (called Cocktail or Fino or Manzanilla) makes one of the best of all aperitif wines—it's especially suitable if there is to be a lavish dinner with a variety of table wines. Most people prefer dry sherry chilled. Medium Sherry (called Amontillado or milk, but in the U.S. usually goes by "plain" sherry, without any adjectives or modifiers) is called all-purpose sherry: it can precede the meal, can even be served during the meal (with soup), or can follow the meal (with a not very sweet dessert, or with coffee). But perhaps its best employment is on its own, for refreshment, resuscitation, rehabilitation, just about any time.

Sweet or Cream Sherry (sometimes called Oloroso, on Spanish labels) is a wondrous after-dinner wine. It has a satisfying nutty richness all its own.

Some specific recommendations by experts and plain ol' sherry-lovers alike: Dry Sherry: With Chinese food—smoked salmon—smoked oysters—olives—cheeses: Bleu, Gouda, Edam, Caerphilly (semi-hard from Wales).

Medium Sherry: With clean soup or turtle soup or any soup for that matter—Macademia nuts and all nuts—melon —cheeses: Gjetost (don't ask how to pronounce it, just how to eat it: with medium sherry!), Cheddar, Longhorn, Gouda.

Sweet (Cream) Sherry: Not too sweet desserts—fresh fruit —nuts.

Sherry Timetable

Noon: Fino (Dry) Sherry, especially Manzanilla—ante- or cum-lunch, or both

3:00 P.M.—Medium Sherry for between-meals picker-upper or slower-downer.

6:00 P.M.—Cocktail (Dry) Sherry—Note that an hour and a half is allowed for this exercise.

7:30 P.M.—Amontillado (Medium) Sherry, with the soup course.

9:00 P.M.—Cream (Sweet) Sherry, after coffee.

11:00 P.M.—Oloroso (Cream, Sweet) Sherry—Nightcap.

2:00 A.M.—Ah ha—NONE! Get to bed!

7:00 A.M.—Medium Sherry, eye-opener, but permitted only on rare occasions: vacations, hegiras, Holy Years, Jubilees, Sundays, holidays, holy days, saints' days (psst, you can find one almost every day if you look closely), most weekdays.

11:00 A.M.—Medium or Sweet Sherry, wine for the "elevenses."

Noon—Proceed to Noon, above . . . if you pass "Go" . . . Note that the above schedule is not absolutely iron-clad—one may alter times up to three or four minutes. Also, one need not observe *all* the appointments *every* day—one or the other of the "observances" may be omitted once or twice a month.

Nicotine addicts, be of good heart—before you die!—even the meanest, grumpiest, narrowest of wine purists will allow you to smoke while you sip your sherry. You may also pray while you sip your sherry. A Franciscan and a Jesuit were once discussing this matter and the Franciscan said he had been denied permission by his superiors to drink sherry while saying his Divine Office, while the Jesuit had been granted such permission. "How did you ask?" said the Jesuit. "I asked if I could have a little sherry for my lumbago while I said my breviary." "Ah, ha," said the Jesuit, "that was your mistake. I asked if it would be all right if I prayed while I drank my sherry."

Individual bottles of sherry, both Spanish and American, are evaluated under their producers' names: Harveys, Almadén, Findlater, Williams and Humbert, Taylor, etc. Don't buy any sherry unless you find your specific bottle listed in this book.

Below are listed America's better sherries, in three categories, according to sweetness, all in descending order of excellence. Where wines have the same rating, the least expensive is listed first. Prices are approximate.

American Cocktail Sherry— Comparative Standings

****

Very Good

Gemello Pale Dry Sherry ($1.85)

Almadén Flor Fino Sherry ($2)

Inglenook Vintage Pale Dry Sherry ($2.30)

Weibel Dry Bin Sherry ($2.60)

Cresta Blanca Dry Watch Sherry ($2.85)

Concannon Dry Sherry Prelude ($3)

Los Amigos Sherry Sack ($3)

***
Good

San Martin Dry Sherry ($1.90)

Beaulieu Pale Dry Sherry ($2.10)

Korbel Cocktail Sherry ($2.10)

Christian Brothers Cocktail Sherry ($2.15)

Christian Brothers Dry Sherry ($2.15)

Taylor Pale Dry Cocktail Sherry ($2.20)

Heitz Dry Sherry ($2.45)

Widmer Cocktail Sherry ($2.50)

Buena Vista Ultra Dry Sherry ($2.60)

Martini Dry Sherry ($2.85)

Cresta Blanca Palomino Sherry ($2.85)

Paul Masson Rare Flor ($3)

Llords & Elwood Great Day D-r-ry Sherry ($3.50)

Sebastiani Arenas Dry Sherry ($3.80)

**
Fair

Gallo Cocktail Pale Dry Sherry ($1.15)

Winemasters Guild Pale Dry Sherry ($1.20)

Gallo Very Dry Sherry ($1.30)

Beringer Fino ($2)

Eleven Cellars Pale Dry Sherry ($2)

Assumption Abbey Sherry Palido ($2.30)

Charles Krug Pale Dry Sherry ($2.35)

Novitiate Flor Sherry ($2.80)

Vin de Biane Fres Flor Sherry Sec ($3.25)

Not Recommended

Franzia Cocktail Sherry

Franzia Very Dry Sherry

American Medium Sherry— Comparative Standings

****
Very Good

Almadén Golden Sherry ($2)

Inglenook Vintage California Sherry ($2.30)

Llords & Elwood Dry Wit Sherry ($3.50)

***
Good

Winemaster's Guild Sherry ($1.20)

Gemello Sherry ($1.85)

San Martin Rare Sherry ($1.90)

Beaulieu Sherry ($2.10)

Korbel Sherry ($2.10)

Christian Brothers Golden Sherry ($2.15)

Taylor Sherry ($2.20)

Assumption Abbey Sherry de Oro ($2.30)

Novitiate Sherry ($2.30)

Widmer Special Selection Sherry ($2.50)

Weibel Classic Sherry ($2.60)

Masson Old Rare Sherry ($3)

**
Fair

Beringer Club Sherry ($2)

Eleven Cellars Sherry ($2)

Charles Krug Sherry ($2.35)

Not Recommended

Franzia Sherry

American Cream Sherry— Comparative Standings

****
Very Good

Inglenook Vintage Cream Sherry ($2.30)

Cresta Blanca Triple Cream Sherry ($2.85)

Llords & Elwood Judges Secret Cream Sherry ($3.50)

Sebastiani Amore Cream Sherry ($3.80)

Christian Brothers Melosa Cream Sherry ($4)

***
Good
> Winemaster's Guild Cream Sherry ($1.20)
>
> Gallo Livingston Cream Sherry ($1.30)
>
> Gemello Cream Sherry ($1.85)
>
> San Martin Cream Sherry ($1.90)
>
> Beringer Velvet Cream Sherry ($2)
>
> Eleven Cellars Cream Sherry ($2)
>
> Masson Rare Cream Sherry ($2)
>
> Beaulieu Cream Sherry ($2.10)
>
> Korbel Cream Sherry ($2.10)
>
> Christian Brothers Cream Sherry ($2.15)
>
> Taylor Cream Sherry ($2.20)
>
> Widmer Cream Sherry ($2.50)
>
> Weibel Amberina Cream Sherry ($2.60)
>
> Martini Sweet Sherry ($2.90)

**
Fair
> Almadén Cream Sherry ($2)
>
> Buena Vista Golden Cream Sherry ($3)
>
> Vin de Biane Fres Flor Sherry Creme ($3.25)

*
Passable
> Charles Krug Cream Sherry ($2.35)

Not Recommended
> Franzia Cream Sherry

SICHEL A huge international wine firm centered principally in Germany (where it originated more than a century ago), France, London, and New York. Millions of bottles of wine, mostly German and French, bear the name of Sichel, sometimes in huge bold print, sometimes in tiny, almost illegible type. On German wines the name is H. Sichel Sohne (Sichels' Sons), on French,

Sichel & Fils Frères (Sichel & Sons, Brothers). Sichel specializes in the more economical wines, frequently inventing names for them, such as "Blue Nun" (see), and Wan Fu, a Bordeaux-produced wine with a Chinese name! Sichel wines are often very good values.

SICHEL ET FILS, GEWÜRZTRAMINER: See GEWÜRZTRAMINER SICHEL.

SICILIAN GOLD MANDOCREMA*** A lovely after-dinner Italian wine from the island of Sicily. (It's actually a Marsala, which see.) What's more, it's almond-flavored. You can sip it carefully, straight, or even serve it "on the rocks" or over vanilla ice cream. For more on this type of wine: See under MARSALA.

SIMI WINERY (Healdsburg, Calif.) Over the years this has been a roller-coaster kind of operation: now up, now down. Right now it's up, and getting upper. The winery was completely renovated, physically and spiritually, in the early 70s, and now at the helm are some of the most knowledgeable wine people in the state of California. The wines, already on the plus side, are certain to improve even more.

Notice that all Simi labels bear one of the following designations: North Coast, Sonoma, Alexander Valley; these are the respective areas where the grapes are grown. In general they are in ascending order of excellence: from the most generic place name (North Coast) to the most specific (Alexander Valley). From henceforth all wines will be vintage-dated.

Burgundy, North Coast*** Generic wines such as this (wine made from no single grape but from a variety of grapes) are usually not top-flight. Simi's Burgundy is a happy exception: not a great wine by any means, but a tasty, full-bodied red table wine to enhance your humblest fare or complement your *haute cuisine*. By way of exception for a California Burgundy, this wine will improve in the bottle; it will be at its best 1975–1980. Serve at cool room temperature. A good value at $2 to $2.25.

Cabernet Sauvignon, Alexander Valley. This noble grape of France does nobly for Simi also. Rich red table wine of some complexity—save it for your finer cuts of beef. Or, if you would make like a connoisseur and enjoy your noble Cabernet to the fullest, sip it lovingly on its own, or with bits of cheese, nuts, fresh fruit. Serve at cool room temperature. Air one hour. It's ready for immediate consumption and will keep for at least five years after purchase, and may even improve slightly in the bottle. The nonvintage (undated) rates at least ***.

*1935**** Some of this ancient brew is still available and in its original bottle. It's still in hale shape and will hold at least until its fiftieth birthday. Interesting wine, surely, but the price tag may cause abrupt loss of interest: $30 to $42. Stand it upright for twenty-four hours, then decant, and serve at cool room temperature.

*1970**** From this vintage forward all Simi's Cabernet Sauvignon will be vintaged. Gold medal winner, Los Angeles County Fair, 1973. Will be at its best, 1976–1985. Air one to two hours.

*1971**** It took a silver medal at the 1974 Los Angeles County Fair.

Carignane, North Coast** Simi is one of the few wineries in California—or the world—to make a wine by this name. That's why it's a favorite, a kind of pet at Simi, because it's so unusual, even an underdog, for the Carignane is a lowly grape. Simi turns it into a mellow red wine with good flavor. Use it as you would a California Burgundy: with steaks, hamburgers, barbecued chicken, pasta, stew. It is ready to drink now and will keep for at least five years. Serve at cool room temperature. Fair value, $3 to $3.25.

Chablis, North Coast** True Chablis comes only from France, but California's Chablis is a wine in its own right. Simi's Chablis goes especially well with oysters and shellfish. It's ready to drink upon purchase, shouldn't be kept more than two or three years. Serve chilled. Fair value, $2 to $2.25.

Chenin Blanc, Alexander Valley** Light, tasty white wine—it almost sparkles. A faint embroidery of sweetness, just right. Ideal for summer sipping. Ready for immediate enjoyment, don't keep it more than three or four years. A very good value at $2.50 to $2.75. *Caution:* There's also a Chenin Blanc Sec (see).

Chenin Blanc Sec, Alexander Valley** "Sec" means "Dry," and that's just what this wine is, a nonsweet variation of the above wine. At this stage it doesn't come quite up to the quality of its sweeter twin. Ideal with light food, such as creamed chicken, fish, sandwiches. Ready for immediate consumption, don't keep it more than three or four years. Serve chilled. Fair value, $2.75 to $3.

Gamay Beaujolais** This

wine is no longer being made —it's a pity, really—but it's still on many retailers' shelves. It's very pleasant young wine, serve it at your outdoor barbecue. Don't horde it—it calls for early consumption: within two years. Serve at cool room temperature, a good value at $2.80 to $3.

Gewürztraminer, North Coast **** A spicy Alsace-type white wine with excellent richness, ideal (say the Alsatians) with sausage, seafood, poultry. Drink it young and fresh: within four years of purchase (or vintage date). Serve chilled. One could wish it weren't selling for $4 to $4.25.

1972***** First batch to be vintage-dated. It follows the nonvintage (above) style: full, rich, spicy. Now ready, enjoy it through 1976 or 1977.

Grenache Rosé, North Coast ** Very average, on the sweet side. Best use: Chilled, summer-evening sipping, or on a picnic.

Johannisberg Riesling, Alexander Valley**** Another Simi winner . . . white Rhine-type wine, though heavier than the German originals, well suited to accompanying light foods (seafood, fowl, ham, pork). This is one of the best of this variety you're going to find. Serve it chilled; it's ready for immediate enjoyment and should be drunk within about five years of purchase or vintage date. Fair value, $4 to $4.50.

Pinot Chardonnay, Sonoma *** Dry white wine to accompany your chicken in cream sauce, barbecued guinea hens, baked ham, veal cutlets. Slight oakiness, just right. Serve chilled. Ready for immediate drinking and will keep for five years. Fair value, $4.50 to $4.75.

1971**** Air 30 minutes, serve chilled. Will remain at its best through '78.

1972***—Fair value, $4.50.

Pinot Noir, Sonoma*** Red table wine vaguely similar to the great red Burgundies of France. At the price, $4.50, save this wine for your finer cuts of beef or your supreme culinary feats. Serve at cool room temperature. Ready to drink when purchased, it will hold well for at least six or seven years.

Rosé of Cabernet, 1971, Alexander Valley*** Drier than their Grenache Rosé. Excellent for that buffet luncheon, or your picnic-cum-hot dogs. Elegant wine. Serve chilled. Fair value, $3.25 to $3.50. The 1972: ****.

Zinfandel, North Coast**** One of the best of California's many fine "Z's," full-flavored, delicately woody. Zinfandel can accompany almost any food but it shows off best with red meats, pasta, chicken. It's ready to drink when you buy it, and this one will even improve with a few years of bottle age. A good value at $3 to $3.25.

1935**** Another of those unusual old bottles (see also the '35 Cabernet Sauvignon, above), miraculously preserved, lo, these forty years. Like the Cabernet, it's hale and fit, still zesty, and will see its fiftieth birthday in fine fettle. If you can find it, *you* decide whether it's worth $22.50 to taste a forty-year-old California red. Sip it, as porcupines make love, carefully.

1970, 1971**** Soft, silky smooth.

SIMON, ANDRÉ Simon was one of the most important people in the entire world of wine for a half century and more. His name is still found on some bottles of wine: "Selected by André Simon." But the good man's been departed this world for some five or six years now, and unless somebody knows Simon's present address or phone number . . . best disregard these unearthly recommendations.

SIRAH, PETITE: See PETITE SIRAH.

SOAVE Good little Italian white wine, some say like Chablis, but the resemblance is rather remote. But with Chablis and Pouilly-Fuissé priced out of sight these days, Soave can be an admirable substitute. It is dry, light, mild, goes well with fish, abalone, crab—and it's cheap. Drink it very young, preferably one to two years old. Serve it well chilled. Some dependable names: Amici; Antinori; Bertani (fine wine); Bolla (dependable, $3.60 per 24 ounces); Fabiano; Folonari (a good value); Gancia; Lamberti (a nonvintaged wine, it's fine); Mirafiore (one of the best; $3.85 per 32 ounces); Ricasoli; Ruffino.

SOLAR DO MINHO VINHO VERDE*** Fresh young white wine from Portugal—the name literally means "Green Wine," a reference to its youthfulness, not its color. It's a delightful little wine, chilled, for a summer's afternoon's enjoyment. How to serve it: See under VINHO VERDE. A good value at $2.75.

SONOMA VINEYARDS (or: WINDSOR) (Windsor, Calif.) You can't buy a bottle of this wine in California—not because it's outlawed, but because it goes by the name of Windsor in California, and by Sonoma

in the rest of the country. But it's exactly the same wine. And if you want to give your wine-loving friend who has everything an unusual Christmas present, you can give him a case of Sonoma wine inscribed with his very own name on the label, and if that doesn't impress him, nothing this side of heaven is apt to!

In summary, Sonoma (or Windsor) Vineyards may not do too much with their wines, but they sure do a lot with their printing. They do, in fact, have a printing shop on the premises. And it is, indeed, true that three fourths of Windsor's wines are sold with personalized labels through mail subscription. It is not precisely accurate, however, to say that Windsor's printing is better than their winemaking. Windsor does make some good wines, and also some pretty average stuff—but "average" in wine language means kind of awful.

Burgundy*** A light and young Burgundy, with good flavor and depth. It's versatile: goes with almost any kind of food, and especially hamburgers, steaks, pasta. Serve at cool room temperature; fair value, ca. $2.40.

Cabernet Sauvignon*** Almost everyone agrees that Cabernet Sauvignon is California's best red wine, but it wasn't Windsor's version that so convinced them. Which is not to denigrate the wine but only to say that it's a good, not a great wine. Serve it pridefully with your best cuts of beef or roast leg of lamb. It's ready to drink when you buy it and will get even better if you lay it down in some dark cool corner for a few years. Sonoma recently cut the prices of all its wines, with its Cabernet Sauvignon enjoying the biggest reduction of all: from $4 to $3, a fine value at that price.

*1970***** This was a special bottling; it's already good drinking and it will be even better, 1976–1985. This was a good wine for cellaring when it was first released at $4, but it's already listed at $6.25 and more. Keep it for your most elegant dining, especially if your meal features beef or lamb. Serve at cool room temperature.

Chablis** Dry white wine, for immediate drinking, best with fish, shellfish (especially oysters), chicken. Serve chilled. Fair value, $2.30 to $2.50.

Champagne Sparkling wines are one of the things Sonoma does best. Their winemaker (Rodney Strong) says they're trying to get some of the wine back in Champagne. It's not just bubbles. It's wine, supposedly good wine, with bubbles. (Plain water with bubbles is called club soda!) Windsor's best is its Brut, Blanc de Blancs, Blanc de Noir (see all). Sadly, they're all expensive.

Brut***** Windsor takes special pride in this wine and it's not misplaced. One cannot question the quality of the wine but one can certainly question the price: $7.50. The wine is made by the painstaking classic "Champagne method." There are a number of different *cuvées* (101, 102, etc.), all equally superb. It's an ideal wine for an aperitif on a momentous occasion. Serve well-chilled.

Chardonnay Blanc de Blancs and Blanc de Noir***** Both are new wines, and, in fact, were released only in late 1974. Both are elegant, dry, expensive, ca. $7.50.

Chenin Blanc*** This fresh young white wine seems to vary noticeably from vintage to vintage. At its best it's good enough to be sipped by itself. And it's best while it's young: within two or three years of purchase. Serve it chilled. Fair value, $2.70 to $3.

French Colombard*** This rather unusual white wine is light, tart, very dry; serve it with light food, chilled. Fair value, $2.50 to $3.

Gamay** to ******* Another of Sonoma's nonvintage "variables": it's ahh one year, blaaah the next. Best advice: Proceed with due caution. At its best, it's a marvelous fresh young red wine. It goes anywhere: on a picnic, to your outdoor grill, to your veranda (how's that?) for summer evening's sipping. Serve cool, not chilled. Fair value, $2.70 to $3.

Grenache Rosé*** It's medium-sweet, can be sipped casually on its own of an evening or accompanying light foods. Drink it young and fresh: within a year or two of purchase. Fair value, $2.50 to $2.75.

Grey Riesling*** This light white wine, rather dry, is best employed at your dining room table, chilled, to accompany light foods: chicken in white sauce, fish, seafood, pork. Ready to drink when you buy it, drink it within a year or two of purchase. Fair value, $2.70 to $3.

Johannisberg Riesling** This classic German grape is not always up to its full potential at Sonoma. Serve it, chilled, with light foods, especially fish. In good conscience, this nonvintage version cannot be recommended at $4 and more. However, Sonoma did put it all together at least once, with:

Johannisberg Riesling Spätlese, 1972***** Everybody and his uncle has acclaimed this wine, the happy result of an unusual attack of "noble rot," a rare phenomenon in California, upon the late-picked Riesling grapes. It's a soft, luscious wine, deserves to be drunk on its own. A true collector's item, the winery has been admirably restrained in not raising the price out of sight. Serve well chilled. A good value at $5.

Johannisberg Riesling Auslese, 1972 At least ****

Petite Sirah** This red table wine has been consistent with Sonoma: consistently average, or at least in this non-vintage version. It has shown poorly in every tasting in which it has been entered over the past few years. But the moment one says something like that of a Sonoma wine, they rise to the occasion and to the heights, and so here again, behold:

Petite Sirah, 1971 and *1972* **** "Glycerine fatiness around a slightly earthy center," says one wine publication—that means it's good—we hope.

Pinot Chardonnay*** Over the years this dry white wine has had a very mixed press . . . like so many Sonoma wines! In some tastings it has placed first, in others, dead last. But it's the kind of wine that appeals variously to various people, not an unusual thing with Chardonnay. The overall consensus, however, must be: ***, but if your taste buds say **** or *, so be it. Serve it chilled; it's ready to drink upon purchase, and will be good drinking for at least five years thereafter. Fair value, $4 to $4.50. There have been two special bottlings:

1970**** Best drinking, 1975–1976.

1971**** Drink now and through 1977.

Pinot Noir A new wine for Sonoma, and final word is not in yet. The winery is optimistic —wineries always are, at least in print—saying that the word for this wine is *velvet*. They also tell us that this is a wine with "an abundance of things to say." Listen ye! Tentatively: ***.

Sauvignon Blanc**** Not one of Windsor's best sellers, but one of their best wines. It's a delicate white dinner wine. Drink it within three years of purchase. Serve it chilled. It's an excellent value at $2.50 to $2.75.

Sonoma Red and Sonoma White** Good everyday wines, to accompany common fare. Serve the red at cool room temperature, the white, chilled. Good values, both, at ca. $1.50.

Vin Rosé*** On the dry side, has good clean taste. Serve it chilled, whenever and with whatever. Not for keeping, drink it within a year or two. A good value at $2.30 to $2.50.

Zinfandel*** "Z" is one of California's best reds—it's also one of Sonoma's best efforts. They claim it has a raspberry-ish flavor. Fits well at the barbecue grill, luncheon, picnic, informal dining table. It's ready to drink when you buy it and it keeps well—for five years anyhow. Fair value, $2.50 to $3.

SOUVERAIN CELLARS (St. Helena, Calif.) The name means "Ruler," "Sovereign," and the winery's new label is surmounted by a royal crown. It's symbolic of what the winery has been trying to do since 1943: reign supreme with quality wines. And they've been at least partially successful. Under the supervision of a very competent winemaker (Lee Stewart), who still oversees the operation, some fine wines have flowed from Souverain's oak barrels.

The winery recently underwent a huge expansion program under its new owner, the Pillsbury Company. Wine people have their fingers crossed, trusting that none of that cake mix will be getting into the vats. *Videamus!*

Burgundy**** In keeping with the winery's regal name, this is a royal kind of Burgundy, made from some of Napa Valley's finest grapes. The wine shows its regal lineage: rich and tasty, one of California's finest Burgundies. This is no hamburger wine, but a steak and prime rib wine. You may drink it upon purchase but you'll be much wiser and more responsible if you let it age for a couple of years; it will improve measurably. Serve at cool room temperature. A good value at $3.75.

Cabernet Sauvignon California's noblest wine, and Souverain does nobly by it. It's the counterpart of France's great Clarets. Reserve it for your most elegant dining—ideal with lamb (rack, leg, chops), the finest beef. Or, to accentuate the positive even further, sip it lovingly on its own, or at most, with cheese, nuts, fresh fruit. Air all the following wines, especially the younger ones, at least one hour, and serve at cool room temperature.

1961***** If this shows up on some restaurant wine list, skip the dinner, order all they've got.

1964**** If you stumble across this wine, don't hesitate, procure! Great drinking today and will improve further over the next couple of years.

1965, 1966, 1967*** At their peak and will hold there through 1979.

1968***** It's going to be marvelous, but not yet. Best drinking: 1976–1985. Marvelous value, ca. $7.

1969**** Has had some bad reviews but the best judgment says ****, if not now, then from 1976 through 1985. Fair value, $5.75 to $6.25.

1970**** This is going to be great, perhaps Souverain's best ever. It will be at its best 1976 through 1985. Look for it—it's going fast. Fair value, $6.50 to $7.

1971 Mixed reviews. Wait, see.

Chablis** True Chablis from France has a dry, steely taste, and so does this, though it's minuscule. Will go well with light foods, especially seafood. Fair value, $2.50.

Chardonnay This most aristocratic of all grapes helps produce France's finest Champagnes and all of its great white Burgundies. It's scarcely less aristocratic in California, Souverain's version being a good example. Here's an elegant wine, deserving of your most elegant seafood: broiled lobster, Coquilles St. Jacques, cracked crab. Serve chilled. It will be at its best from three to seven years after its vintage date. Fair value, $6.

1968, 1969*** Both are for present drinking.

1970**** At its best now and until 1976.

1971***

1972****

Flora A new hybrid grape ("invented" by the University

of California), Souverain is the first winery to make this wine. They won't be the last. This is a fruity, slightly spicy white wine; it will go well with a variety of foods: chicken, ham, pork, fishy fish, fondue. Serve chilled (50–55°F); it's ready for immediate drinking and will keep for four or five years. Fair value, $3.50 to $3.75.

*1969, 1970*** *
*1971*** ** *

Green Hungarian This white wine of the strange name—it's named after a grape, not a weirdly-hued native of Hungary —is found only in California. Souverain makes one of the best. It's a small dry wine with just a trace of sweetness, best at your table with light foods, especially fish (particularly salmon) and pork. Serve it chilled. Fair value, $3.25.

*1970, 1971, 1972*** * All for present drinking; will keep five years beyond their vintage dates. Avoid the earlier vintages.

Johannisberg Riesling Souverain and Stony Hill (see) make two of the finest Johannisbergs in California. Souverain's has a distinct touch of sweetness, making it a delightful sipping wine. It would also go well with light foods, especially seafood. Serve it chilled. It sells at the winery for $5.

*1968, 1969*** ** * They even have a slight sparkle—drink immediately.

*1970*** ** * Consume before 1976.

*1971*** * At its best now and through 1976.

*1972 Napa Valley*** * Doesn't seem to warrant its $4.50 price tag.

*1972 Alexander Valley** * Disappointing—not recommended at $4.50.

*1973*** ** * Fruity and delicious. Best drinking, 1975–1978.

Mountain Zinfandel One of the winery's specialties. It's made wholly from Napa Valley grapes (note the label), the finest. "Z" is one of California's best red wines, a good value. It shows off best with red meats, pasta, good casseroles. The better vintages (see below) demand to be appreciated on their own, or with Cheddar cheese or nuts. Serve at cool room temperature. Air recent vintages one to two hours. Fair value, $4.50.

1967 * Long gone.
*1968*** * Drink now.
*1969** * Drink soon.
*1970*** ** * Best drinking, 1975–1978.
*1971*** ** * Enjoy it from '75 through '79.
*1972 *** ** * and reaching for *** ** ** * It's already great drinking but it will be even better, 1978–1982.

Petite Sirah Souverain pioneered with this wine in California and it's always been their special pride. It's one of California's finest, though it does vary from vintage to vintage. It's a hearty, full-bodied, spicy wine, a big mouthful; it can enhance almost any food, but particularly hearty dishes: Italian foods, even Mexican food (if not totally incendiary), stews, roasts. It's ready to drink immediately upon purchase but it will improve with a few years in the bottle. Souverain's Petite Sirah will keep at least fifteen years after its vintage date. Fair value, $5.

*1966** *
*1967** * Uncharacteristically, this wine is beginning to decline.
*1968*** *

1969**** It's in short supply —buy it if you can find it, and lay it down peacefully for at least five years. It will be at its best through the 80s.

1970**** Big, mouth-filling wine, already marvelous drinking, but shame on you if you drink it before 1980; it will be ***** by then.

Pineau Souverain This used to be called Chenin Blanc. It's America's answer to that altogether lovely wine of France's Loire Valley, Vouvray. Souverain is noted for this wine, but it does vary from vintage to vintage. It will go well with very light foods (chicken in white sauce), but it is so delicate and fruity that it is best appreciated on its own, sipped carefully, before dinner, or after, or with fresh fruit. Drink it young and fresh, chilled, before its fourth birthday. Fair value, ca. $4.

1969, 1970***

1971**** A gem—look for it, and drink it soon.

Pinot Chardonnay: See CHARDONNAY.

Pinot Noir, 1971 ** and 1972 **** A new wine with Souverain, only two vintages to date, and you can't say that it hasn't shown consistent improvement. It will go well with grilled meats, fowl, cheese dishes. Serve at cool room temperature. Best drinking, 1975–1978. Fair value, ca. $5.30.

Riesling*** This name, in California, can mean almost anything; in this case it means a blended light white wine, remarkably similar to German Rhine wine. It can be enjoyed on its own before dinner—or with light food at a luncheon. Drink it young and fresh, before it's five years old. Serve chilled; a good value at $3.50.

Zinfandel: See MOUNTAIN ZINFANDEL.

SPALETTI (CHIANTI): See POGGIO REALE.

SPAÑADA: See under GALLO.

SPARKLING BURGUNDY This festive red wine is made in both France and the U.S. (White sparkling Burgundy is not considered here, as it is almost never seen in the U.S.) The French rather despise sparkling Burgundy, and with good reason: theirs is usually poor wine. Fine red Burgundy wine is so good and so precious that it is never made into a sparkling wine. It is the inferior brews that are used.

Still and all, some rather good sparkling Burgundy does find its way to our shores from France, but considering what's available from our domestic vineyards, it must be said that French sparkling Burgundies are overpriced.

One British wine writer says that a sparkling red wine is incongruous—like a fat old man dressed up like a fairy.

But a lot of people and a lot of experts disagree. They call this pure wine snobbery. And most would agree that America, by and large, makes better sparkling Burgundy than does France.

Our best sparkling Burgundies are not made from wine too poor to sell otherwise; they're made from excellent base wines, and they're made by the true "Champagne method," fermented in the bottle. Some are made by the "bulk process," it is true, but it seems that this treatment is particularly successful in the case of sparkling Burgundy, helping to preserve the fruitiness of the wine. Good sparkling Burgundy is a huge improvement over its distant cousin, Cold Duck.

Sparkling Burgundy is a festive, a "celebracious" wine—for one thing, it's so pretty—perfect to accompany that Thanksgiving turkey. Or it can serve as an aperitif wine, or even as an after-dinner wine, though not with a sweet dessert. Some British wine snob said it's ideal for *unsophisticated* parties! Humph!

France's Best Sparkling Burgundies

They are listed in order of ascending price. None of these wines are good values.

B & G (Barton & Guestier) Sparkling Burgundy ($5.50)

Leonce Curial Sparkling Burgundy ($6)

Chauvenet Red Cap ($7)

Cruse Sparkling Burgundy ($8)

Sichel Sparkling Burgundy ($8.50)

American Sparkling Burgundies— Comparative Standings

Wines are listed in descending order of excellence. Where several wines have the same rating, the least expensive is listed first. Prices are approximate.

****

Very Good

Korbel Rouge (Sparkling Burgundy) ($5.70)

Mirassou Sparkling Gamay Beaujolais, 1970 ($5.75)

Beaulieu Rouge Champagne ($6.10)

***

Good

Le Domaine Sparkling Burgundy ($3.10)

Great Western Sparkling Burgundy ($5.10)

Cresta Blanca Champagne Rouge ($5.50)

Weibel Sparkling Burgundy ($5.70)

Kornell Sparkling Burgundy ($5.75)

Mirassou Sparkling Gamay Beaujolais, 1969 ($5.75)

**

Fair

Mission Cellars Sparkling Burgundy ($2.70)

Gallo Sparkling Burgundy ($3)

Lejon Sparkling Burgundy ($3.25)

Cook's Imperial Sparkling Burgundy ($4.50)

Masson Sparkling Burgundy ($5)

Heitz Sparkling Burgundy ($5.35)

Almadén Sparkling Burgundy ($5.40)

*

Passable

Franzia Sparkling Burgundy ($2)

Calwa Sparkling Burgundy ($2)

Jacques Bonet Sparkling Burgundy ($2)

André Sparkling Burgundy ($2)

Christian Brothers Sparkling Burgundy ($5.05)

Not Recommended:

San Martin Champagne Rouge

SPÄTLESE When you see this word on a German wine label, know that you're dealing with a superior grade of wine. The word means "late picking," indicating that the grapes were allowed to ripen beyond the normal picking time (with the concomitant danger of damage from frost and freezing). Such wines will always be more expensive, richer, fuller, and a mite sweeter than the "straights." Also, a Spätlese will often be double the price of the "plain."

After the Spätlese, there can be later and later pickings, with the grapes becoming riper and riper, sweeter and sweeter with each successive picking. They may also be attacked, hopefully, with "noble rot," which makes them even sweeter and more luscious. The resulting wines are progressively sweeter, richer, and forbiddingly expensive. Here is the ascending hierarchy of these special pickings of these great German wines:

Spätlese

Auslese—Often three times the price of the "regular" wine.

Beerenauslese—Ranges in price from about $25 to $90—per bottle.

Trockenbeerenauslese—From around $50 to over $100.

SPRING MOUNTAIN VINEYARDS (St. Helena, Calif.) A

small, lustrous winery that enjoys making high-class wines. A law of inverse proportion seems to function among California wineries: the smaller the winery, the bigger the wines. Nowhere does the law operate more predictably than at Spring Mountain: they produce just three wines, all of them big by anybody's standards, but rather untouchable, by most people's standards, because of price. They *are* dear, dear. These wines are so intense, so expensive that they demand to be served on their own, or at most, with innocent tidbits, so that you can enjoy every dollar's worth of richness.

Cabernet Sauvignon This noble grape of the great French Clarets is nobly used by Spring Mountain, producing big, rich, gutsy wines—the kind of wines, the French say, you can chew.

Sadly, you may choke on the price tag: $6.50 to $8.

1968–1969 Marriage (Lot II, 68-69)***** Big, deep wine, still immature. Will be at its peak 1978 or 1979 and will hold there for at least a decade. By then it may well rise to Near-Classic. Air one hour, serve at cool room temperature.

1970**** Best drinking, 1977 onward. Air one to two hours, serve at cool room temperature.

1972 Not yet released, but it's already looking beautiful. Watch ye . . . These wines have a sneaky way of becoming collector's items very quickly. It's going to merit at least ****.

Chardonnay

1969**** Another huge wine, full of flavor and spice. But be careful: somebody said it finishes like a young colt. Serve it chilled. Best drinking, present to 1977.

1970**** Now at its best and will hold through 1977 at least. Fair value, $7.50.

1971***** Limited supply— but if you find it, buy it. It will be at its superlative best, 1976 through 1980.

1972 It's already looking like *****—or better. Some say this is the best Chardonnay Spring Mountain has ever made. You'll have to hurry to catch some. Present price is $7.50, and a good value at that.

Pinot Chardonnay: See CHARDONNAY.

Sauvignon Blanc White table wine with a wholesome earthiness, softly spicy, good enough for sipping on its own, but perhaps best used to accompany shellfish. Current vintages are A-okay. The '67 (if you can find it): **** The '72 looks like their best yet: *****. Serve chilled.

SPUMANTE, ASTI: See ASTI SPUMANTE.

STEINBERGER One of Germany's—and the world's—greatest vineyards and greatest white wines. It is so famous that the wines are allowed to go to market wholly on their own, without the name of town of origin. Steinberger is a huge wine for a white: big-bodied, big bouquet, powerful, overflowing with flavor. It is aged in the ancient cellars of the Kloster (Monastery) Eberbach, and that name often appears on the label. Steinberger is as superb in good years as it can be bad in poor years. Be very vintage-conscious here:

1951—Avoid.

1953—Outstanding.

1954—Avoid.

1959—Marvelous wines.
Beerenauslese (Staatsweinguter): *******
Trockenbeerenauslese (Staatsweinguter): Near-Classic.

1966—Riesling Spätlese (Staatsweinguter): Not recommended at $8.

1967—Fine year.

1968—Bad news—Avoid.

1969—Better than '68 but not by much—Best avoided.

1970—A good year—Wines now at their best and through 1978.
Riesling (State Domain): Excellent value at $3.80. *******.

1971—Superb vintage—At their best, 1975 through 1980.
Riesling Spätlese (Staatsweinguter): *******
Riesling Auslese (Staatsweinguter): *******

1972—Very good year—Will be at their best, 1975–1978.

STERLING VINEYARDS (Calistoga, Calif.) One of the newest and surely *the* most unique winery in California today. This glistening-white brand-new six-million-dollar plant atop what is now called "Mount Sterling," looks for all the world like a Greek monastery overlooking the Mediterranean. The wines are of a piece: bright, new, top-flight. Among California's better wines (called varietals), Sterling's wines already have established themselves as some of the best values in the land. And recall that these wines are their first offerings—think of what future glories may be forthcoming . . . these folks are just learning.

Blanc de Sauvignon There are a half dozen different names for this wine around California, but Sterling is the only winery using this one. By whatever name, it's a tasteful white table wine, with a lot of character. Sterling's version is on the dry side and will go particularly well with shellfish; also with veal, chicken, salmon. It's ready to drink when you buy it and will remain so for at least five years after its vintage date. Serve chilled. A good value at $3.50.
1970****
1971***

Cabernet Sauvignon, 1969 **** This noble red table wine is made in frank imitation of France's great Clarets, and the resemblance is striking. Most of California's better Cabernets take an unconscionable length of time to soften and mature. This one's already soft, in a mere six years. It's the perfect accompaniment for barbecued steaks, beef rib roasts, lamb (chops, rack, or leg). But a true wine lover will want to slurp this wine, slowly and tenderly, on its own, or with cheese. (*Slurp* is the correct verb: one should suck up one's wine audibly, mixing it with the maximum amount of air—it's not at all uncouth among wine-knowledgeable folks—dribbling or slobbering, however, is forbidden, if detected.) Fair value, $4.50; best drinking, 1975–1980. There is also a nonvintage available (actually a blend of '68 and '69), very similar to the '69 and also meriting ****. Hold it until 1976 for first sampling.

Chenin Blanc This is Napa Valley's most popular white wine, and it's usually made with a sweet edge, which makes it delightful indeed. Sterling's Chenin Blanc, however, defies the traditional: it's dry and austere. It's also elegant and complex—beautiful adjectives to hang on any wine. Serve it chilled with your finest seafood entree (Coquilles St. Jacques, broiled lobster, scampi). Or if you like a dry aperitif, this is fastidious elegance.

1971 and *1972**** Best drinking, 1975–1980. Good value at $4.

Gamay Beaujolais, 1972* Made by a new process—new to California, at least—which accentuates youthfulness and freshness in a wine.

Gewürztraminer* Sterling's Gewürz is in a different style from most California Gewürz. It's not as spicy as most, but it's nonetheless clean, crisp, flavorful. It is also in short supply. Try it of a summer's evening, on your trellised veranda, at your poolside—or in your cluttered living room or grubby kitchen. Serve chilled.

Merlot* Some wine lovers, when they first encounter this wine label, are going to shake their heads in disbelief. They know the Merlot grape all right, but it's always, always used in blending. Well, here it is on its own, and doing handsomely. This is a charming young red wine, soft, flavorful. It's good enough, in fact, to serve as an aperitif wine, with cheese. It's been well aged when you buy it, so it's ready to drink. It will remain at its best for six or seven years beyond its vintage date. Fair value, $4.

Merlot Primeur, 1973** This is a quickie wine: quickly made, quickly consumed. In fact, it's already past its lowly peak. Six months is about maximum life span for such "Nouveau" wines. Look for the 1974, the crystal ball says it's going to be ***—but drink it up, immediately, if not sooner. At cool room temperature or slightly chilled.

Pinot Chardonnay White table wine, soft and tasty. It's not the precise equivalent of France's great white Burgundies, but Sterling's working at it . . . Chardonnay is the classic wine to accompany fish, seafood, fowl simply prepared. It will benefit from a year or two in the bottle after purchase, and should not be kept more than six or seven years beyond its vintage date. Serve chilled.

*1969*** Perhaps a bit too oaky. Drink through 1975.

*1970**** Best drinking 1975–1978.

*1971***** It sells for $6 and is worth that and something more. This wine has placed at the very top in every blind tasting it's been in, ahead of a host of $15 and $20 French white Burgundies. Best drinking, 1975 through 1979.

*1972**** It took a gold medal at the Los Angeles County Fair, 1974.

Pinot Noir, 1971** Sterling doesn't make this wine every year—if the wine from their Pinot Noir grapes develops in a different style, they give it a different name. They call 'em like they see 'em.

Sauvignon Blanc: See BLANC DE SAUVIGNON.

Zinfandel California "Z" gets better with each passing year, as American vintners continue to bestow more attention and affection upon this once lightly esteemed grape. Sterling, ditto. Theirs is a rich, deep red wine, excellent at an outdoor barbecue or for indoor formal dining. Serve it at cool room temperature. Fair value, $5 to $6.

*1968*** Drink now and through the decade.

*1969**** Best drinking, 1978–1985.

1970 and *1971**** The '70 won a good medal at the 1974 Los Angeles County Fair. Best drinking for both, 1976–1985.

*1972***

STONY HILL VINEYARD (St. Helena, Calif.) A small, splendent operation in the Napa hills—the name tells you about the vineyards. Stony Hill makes only three wines, all white, all aristocratic, rare, expensive. The wines are sold only by subscription, if you can get on the crowded mailing list. They're often collector's items and almost all are connoisseur's wines.

Gewürztraminer By Stony Hill standards this is a rather plebeian wine, similar to much California "Gewürz," but even then it's distinctive and pronouncedly spicy. It will be the perfect accompaniment, as it is in Alsace, for sausage or cheese fondue.

*1967, 1969**** Drink soon.

*1971**** Best drinking, present through 1976.

*1972**** Best drinking, present through 1977.

Johannisberg Riesling: See WHITE RIESLING.

Pinot Chardonnay Almost everybody agrees that this is one of California's best Chardonnays—some say *the* best. But it's often a connoisseur's wine, with a very pronounced and distinctive oakiness (from the aging barrels). Even the winery acknowledges that they sometimes get carried away with the woodiness, and as somebody said: "If I wanted woodiness, I'd chew on a shingle."

1964 and *1966***** Don't go looking for these, however —they may be gone. If you possess some, consume now.

*1968***** At its peak but don't hold it, drink it.

*1969**** At its best, 1975 through 1976.

1970 Near-Classic Some have called this a masterpiece. In one blind tasting it placed first over $15 and $20 French Burgundies (inluding Le Montrachet, the greatest). Best drinking, 1975 through 1980.

*1971**** Front runner in a number of tastings. May rise to ***** status. Best drinking, 1975 through 1980.

*1972**** It's still in the barrel, but it's already got all the earmarks of becoming a fine, perhaps great, wine.

White Riesling (Johannisberg Riesling) Most California wineries call this Johannisberg Riesling. It's one of California's best whites; Stony Hill's is on the dry side, making it ideal for the table, especially to accompany light foods.

*1970*** Drink soon.

1971 and *1972*** Best drinking, present through 1976. Fair value, $4.50.

STORING WINES You can spend thousands of dollars on a ready-made refrigerated wine vault—one brand *starts* at $1,550, contains from 174 to 2,028 bottles—but unless you have an awful lot of Richebourg, Lafite, and Montrachet, or an awful lot of money—or both—you can keep your wines in good condition until ten years after you depart this world with a few simple precautions. Rule One is store your wines on their side, so that the cork remains moist and thus will not dry up and allow too much air to get to the wine. The only exception is wines with metal caps (they're beyond redemption) and those with high alcoholic content (they're beyond changing) such as Ports, sherries, Tokay. Of course none of these will be harmed in any way if you store them on their sides. Also important is temperature: 55°F is ideal, but if you can keep your wines between 45°F and 70°F, you'll be in good shape. A normally summer-refrigerated and winter-heated American home will do nicely. But if you live in a tent, tree, or igloo, you have problems. Consult your wine broker, pastor, or landlord. Also, keep your wines in a dark, airy place, free from vibration—not in the boiler room, not in the mop closet. Be nice to your wines. Handle them gently, treat them with care. They're delicate, need lots of love.

STRAVECCHIO: See MELINI.

SUMNER, GEORGE C. When the neck label of your wine says that it was selected by George C. Sumner, you're off to a good start. Sumner is a knowledgeable wine man. Still it's only a start, not an infallible guarantee, so check your wine under its proper name in this book.

SUTTER HOME WINERY (St. Helena, Calif.) A small, family-operated winery, producing a remarkable number of wines (listed below are only the more important ones), and some remarkable wines. They place special emphasis on their Zinfandel.

Barbera*** Full, robust Italian-style red wine to go with red meats, Italian dishes, outdoor barbecue. Drink it within three years of purchase. Serve it at cool room temperature.

Burgundy*** Good hamburger wine, with a light freshness; it might even improve with a year or two of further aging after purchase. An excellent value at $2.30 to $2.50.

Cabernet Sauvignon, 1971 **** Tasty red table wine, a California "Claret," serve it with your best cuts of beef or roast lamb. It will be at its best, 1977–1985. Serve it at cool room temperature, having aired it for one hour. An excellent value at around $4.

Chablis*** Good little wine, big value at $2.

Chianti*** It has a touch of sweetness, a tasty and fruity little *vin ordinaire*, a good value at $2.

Mission Rosé*** Named after the first grapes planted in California by the Franciscan missionaries, it's surely the only wine so named in all the world. It's on the sweet side; serve it with dessert or fresh fruit. A good value at $2.50.

Nuovo Zinfandel: See ZINFANDEL, NUOVO.

Petite Zinfandel: See ZINFANDEL.

Pinot Chardonnay, 1971**** A California white "French"

Burgundy, excellent with sea-food, fish, ham, pork, veal. Drink now and through 1976. Serve chilled. Fair value, $5.

Sauvignon Vert*** An unusual wine, very rare anywhere. It's a white wine to accompany light foods. Serve chilled, and drink it young: within two years of purchase.

Zinfandel This is Sutter Home's specialty—and it shows. "Z" is, in fact, one of California's specialties, and it's usually a good value. Sutter Home's is especially so. Serve it, at 65°F, with pride, at your outdoor barbecue, at poolside with cheese and nuts—or at your most formal dinner. Air one hour.

1968***** This was Sutter Home's first Zinfandel, what a way to get started! The wine has even become something of a collector's item. It is rich, with a Port-like quality, luscious enough to be served after dinner. Or before dinner, with cheese and nuts. Delightful right now, but will get even better, 1976 through the 80s. An excellent value, if you can find it at $6 or $7.

1969**** Similar to the '68 but not quite as huge. Use it as you would the '68. A good value at $5 or $6.

1970**** There were a number of different bottlings of this wine ("Deaver Vineyards," Lots 1, 2) but disregard these designations: all the 70s were basically alike. The wine is not yet mature; best drinking will be from 1976 onward for a decade or more. Check the bottle for sediment; if present, stand it upright for twenty-four hours, then decant. Serve at cool room temperature. Fair value, $4 to $5.

1971**** Fine wine, soft, mature, with a kiss of sweetness, but it lacks acidity. Drink, 1975–1980. Fair value, $5.

Petite Zinfandel, 1971** It's what the name says—small. Fair value, $3.25.

Zinfandel, 1972**** There were two Zinfandels made this year: a "plain," from the winery's vineyards in Amador County, and a Dickerson Vineyard which is in Napa Valley. These are two distinct types of wine—California vintners continue to marvel at "Z's" myriad manifestations—it makes a different wine every few hundred yards! Both are substantial wines of upright character. They are already good drinking, but they'll be better, 1976 through 1980. By that time they may well merit *****.

Zinfandel, 1973, Dickerson Vineyard: ***

Zinfandel, Nuovo, 1973*** "Nuovo" is Italian for "New," and that's what this wine is: new and young and fruity. It should be drunk that way, while it's young and fresh: 1975 through 1976. The winery says it's a quaffing wine, not a sipping one, and should be served chilled, they say. But quaff discretely—or you may collapse indiscreetly. All good wines deserve to be sipped—appreciatively.

Zinfandel Rosé—Not recommended.

SYRAH, PETITE (or Petit): See PETITE SIRAH.

T

(LA) TÂCHE One of the very great red Burgundies. Like Romanée-Conti, it's entirely owned by the Society of Romanée-Conti, so you won't be seeing the names of various growers and shippers on the label. There is only one La Tâche—and praise God for such singular excellence! For details on the serving of this wine: See ROMANÉE-CONTI.

Some notable vintages:

1904 Classic—One of the greatest of wine critics said it was "beyond all description."

1923 Near-Classic—It's still in excellent condition.

1942 Near-Classic

1945 Near-Classic

1949 Near-Classic

1951****

1953*****—Despite an indifferent year—may be beginning to decline.

1956*****

1957*****—Great wine in a difficult year.

1958***—Poor value.

1960***—Drink soon.

1961***** Now at its peak and until 1980 will remain so.

1962*****—Good drinking now—Don't keep.

1963*****—Good drinking now, but it won't hold.

1964 Near-Classic—Now at its peak.

1966*****—Now at its peak.

1972*****—Drink it from 1980 on.

TAITTINGER One of France's greatest Champagnes—it comes in two versions: Comtes de Champagne Blanc de Blancs ($25.50) and La Française, a *Brut* Champange ($13). The Comtes is a truly great wine—remember how James Bond ritually ordered it on his annual return to Casino Royale? The 1964 is marvelously soft, fragrant, elegant: Near-Classic. The '66 is even better: Classic. The La Française, at half the price, is nonvintaged, and one of the best values to be found in all of French Champagne.

TALBOT, CHÂTEAU Fine red Bordeaux (French) wines, it has a rather low official rating but everybody agrees that it is better than its classification, and, in truth, it consistently sells at prices far above its ranking. It's a full, fruity wine (owned by the Cordier family), consistently above average. How to serve it: See under BORDEAUX.

1934—*****—May still be available—recently sold at auction for $23.

1959—****—Fair value $10.

1961—****—Fair value $12.

1962—****—Fair value $8.

1964—****—Fair value $7.50.

1967—****—Fair value $7. All the above, good drinking now and to 1985.

1969—****—Will be at its best, 1976–1986.

1970—****—Will be at its best, 1977–1990.

TASTING WINE This may

seem like a needless entry, but it is perhaps the most important in this entire book. Surely everyone knows how to taste wine! But do they? They know how to consume wine, yes, but to really taste it? A billy-goat can consume wine. To taste wine means to appreciate it wholly and fully, every beguiling drop—to delight in its length and breadth and depth, to savor its myriad complexities, to exult in its subtle nuances. There is no other beverage given to man on this earth that comes in such a wide, wild assortment of shapes and flavors, grades and types, from Ripple to Tokay Eszencia, and there is no earthly beverage as complex as a fine wine.

To *really* taste your wine sip it noisily, slurpingly, combining it with as much oxygen as possible. Yea, verily! Swirl the wine about in your mouth, hold it in your mouth and inhale—be careful not to choke—one authority suggests you gargle it, but at a formal banquet that might raise a quizzical eyebrow or two. But know that among wine-loving folks it's not one bit boorish to slurp your wine —they'll be impressed, think you're a real aficionado. Try not to slobber or drool though.

TAVEL ROSÉ For an evaluation of individual bottles of this French rosé, see under the name of the producer: Domaine des Roches, Chapoutier, Château d' Aqueria, etc.

Some people hail Tavel Rosé as the best in the world. A few damn it as the worst. It is neither—this is gospel!—it's a decidedly dry rosé, and that's not everybody's cup of wine. Dry rosé, indeed, is virtually a contradiction in terms, for rosé, by its very nature, is meant to be light, refreshing, slightly sweet—for hot-weather sipping. Yet some wine lovers truly dig dry rosés—one expert says Tavel Rosé has the taste of a rock warmed by the sun. So if sun-warmed rocks are to your taste . . .

TAVOLA RED, (Guild) VINO DA** This simple wine may not be in the best Italian style, as the name tries to suggest, but it's in the American style: mass-produced, inexpensive, standard, consistent, successful. The red-checkered label has almost become a trademark for the Guild Wine Company which owns the brand name. A good value at ca. $2.10 per half-gallon.

TAVOLA WHITE, (Guild) VINO DA*

TAYLOR WINE COMPANY (Hammondsport, N. Y.) The Taylor label is one of the best known in all America—in the dingiest, sorriest package liquor store where there may be only one brand of table wine offered, it will invariably be Taylor's. It's a trusted name; it spells consistency and dependability to people who know nothing whatever about wines. Taylor is a huge operation, producing almost four million . cases of wine annually, none of it among America's best. Its best seller is its Champagne. But Taylor wines are sound, inexpensive, and wholly New York State. They possess that distinctive wild taste of native grapes which is called "foxy." Impossible to define or describe, it is impossible *not* to detect. Most enophiles (wine lovers to the unlettered) abhor the taste, but Easterners who were weaned on New York wines like it; some prefer it. In this matter it is most important to recall that first law of all wine appreciation: If you like it, drink it—it's good. Taylor feels the same way. They don't apologize for their New York flavor and heritage. They emblazon it on their labels. On their Champagne "New York State" is so prominent that it appears to be the name of the wine.

Burgundy This may not be the world's worst red wine, but to those who dislike musky foxiness in a wine (or foxy muskiness, if you don't get the picture) then this would certainly be in the running! Yet some people, born and bred to the flavor of Eastern grapes, will prefer this wine to Le Chambertin. And to each his own. *Salud! Prosit! Sante!*

Champagne* Champagne is what Taylor does best of all, and their Brut (Yellow label) is the best of their best. There is also a Dry (White label), slightly sweeter than the Brut, and a Pink Champagne, the sweetest of the three. And of course there's a Cold Duck.
All Champagne is served chilled or iced, in tall tulip-shaped glasses (not in wide-mouthed sherbet glasses—ach!). Champagne, white, yellow, or pink, fits in anywhere. Connoisseurs say it's *the* breakfast beverage—we used to think coffee or orange juice was—those hot cakes will never be the same again!
All Taylor Champange has a faint tinge of native grapes, but it's not at all offensive; in fact, it enhances the wine when it's subdued, as it always is with Taylor. Fair value, $4.50 to $5.50.

Claret* A light, soft, red dinner wine which will appeal to those who appreciate just a hint of foxiness. The price is right: $2.05.

Cold Duck: See CHAMPAGNE.

Lake Country Red, Lake Country White, Lake Country Pink* Honestly labeled and honestly made. The Catawba "native" taste is detectable here, in all three of these wines, especially in the red.

New York State Champagne, Sherry, etc.: See under name of the wine: Champagne, Sherry, etc.

Pale Dry Sherry: See SHERRY.

Pink Champagne: See CHAMPAGNE.

Rosé* Fresh and pleasant, relatively dry. Fair value, ca. $2.

Sherry* Taylor makes three: a plain *Sherry* which is medium-sweet; a *Pale Dry Cocktail*, and a *Cream Sherry*, a sweet dessert wine. These are well-made wines. Sherry, with its manifold variations, is one of the world's most versatile wines; it fits anywhere: before dinner (Cocktail Sherry, and the plain Sherry), the soup course (Cocktail Sherry); after-dinner (Cream Sherry); or 11:00 A.M. sipping-hour (any of the three). All sherry can be served slightly chilled.

TAYLOR FLADGATE LATE BOTTLED VINTAGE RESERVE This Taylor is not to be confused with Taylor wines of New York State. This Taylor is Taylor, Fladgate & Yeatman, of London and the Oporto region, Portugal. The finest Portos invariably bear British names, as Porto has always been one of England's favorite wines and the British have been in the Port wine business for centuries. Most of these fine Portos, in fact, are aged and bottled in Britain.

This "Late Bottled" Porto is the nearest thing to a true Vintage Port that there is—at less than half the price. The 1965 was exceptional, took a precious gold medal recently, and it's now at its best. It's *****. The current 1969 seems to rate ****, sells for ca. $6.

TAYLOR FLADGATE TWENTY-YEAR-OLD TAWNY PORT Superb wine and ready to drink, *now*. It's drier than the Vintage Porto (below), sells for around $11, rates a confident *****. Drink within two or three years of purchase.

TAYLOR FLADGATE VINTAGE PORT Taylor is probably the most prestigious name in fine Port—meaning, of course, Portuguese Port. It's a name you can trust universally and unhesitatingly. Their Vintage Port is their very finest, the *crème de la crème*. Here you're at the heights.

Taylor has a secondary vineyard, the Quinta do Vargelles (see), also fine wine.

Some outstanding Taylor Vintage Portos:

1920: Fine wine, near perfection—Though now more than fifty years old, this wine shows no sign of enfeeblement—It sold, at Christie's wine auction, London, for $11 in 1971, for $27 in 1973. Near-Classic.

1924 and 1927: Superb vintages, both wines are near-perfect—Incredibly, the 1927 just a few years ago still seemed too young! Near-Classic.

1935: Tremendous wine—Drink now—Near-Classic.

1945: Many have declared '45 the "vintage of the century" and some have called this wine perfect—It's now at its very best—You may not find it at Harry's Horrible Liquors, however—it fetches around $45. Classic.

1950: Though not one of the very best "declared" vintages, Taylor's was superb: Near-Classic—Now at its best.

1966: Superb wine of a superb vintage: Near-Classic— Don't touch it for at least another decade!—It sold for ca. $11 at Christie's in 1973—If you find it for $15, don't hesitate!

How to serve fine Port: See under PORT.

THANKSGIVING DAY WINES On this festive American holiday even non-wine-drinking Americans go "Continental"—or bananas, according to some—and drink wine with their holiday fare. In the most summary fashion, here are some general suggestions. The presumption throughout these recommendations is that roast turkey constitutes the *pièce de résistance*.

BEFORE THE MEAL:
    California Champagne—
      or:
    Cocktail sherry (California or Spanish)

WITH THE MEAL:
    California red: Zinfandel, Burgundy, Pinot Noir, or Cabernet Sauvignon—
      or:
    California sparkling Burgundy—*or:*
    True French Burgundy

AFTER DINNER:
    Cream sherry (preferably Spanish)—*or:*
    French Sauternes—*or:*
    Tokay Aszu—*or:*
    Tawny or Vintage Porto (from Portugal, not California)

Specifically, according to one's means or largesse:

For Clergymen and Other

Peasant Types—Wines, $2 to $4 per bottle:

BEFORE DINNER:

California Chenin Blanc: Simi—Charles Krug—Robert Mondavi—Mirassou—Sterling—Christian Brothers Pineau de la Loire (see p. 76 for complete listing).

or:

Le Domaine Brut or Extra Dry Champagne or Henri Marchant Brut or Extra Dry Champagne (other California Champagnes listed, pp. 61–4).

WITH DINNER:

A good California Burgundy: Beaulieu (1970 or 1971, preferably)—Souverain—Sebastiani—Concannon Red Dinner Wine (others, pp. 42–3).

or:

A good California Zinfandel: Inglenook (1968)—Fetzer (1968)—Sutter Home (1968)—Davis Bynum—Sebastiani—Louis Martini—Beringer—Christian Brothers—Kenwood—Mirassou 1968, 1969 (others, see pp. 331–3).

or:

A California sparkling Burgundy: Le Domaine—Gallo—Lejon—Cook's Imperial (others, see p. 294).

or:

A white California dinner-type wine: Sebastiani Johannisberg Riesling (1967)—Louis Martini Johannisberg Riesling (1969)—Pedroncelli Johannisberg Riesling (1971, 1973)—Simi Johannisberg Riesling (others, see pp. 148–9).

AFTER DINNER:

A California muscat wine: Novitiate Muscat Frontignan—Beringer Malvasia Bianca—San Martin Muscato Canelli (others, pp. 213–4).

or:

A nice California sweet Sauterne: Ste. Michelle Sémillon (from the state of Washington actually)—Eleven Cellars Haut Sauterne—LaMont Sémillon—Wente Château Wente—Bargetto Haut Sauterne—Concannon Château Concannon (others, see p. 272).

For the Comfortable Middle Class: Doctors, Bishops, Attorneys, Monsignori, Artisans, Wheeler-Dealers, Entrepreneurs, Most Texans—Wines from $4 to $7:

BEFORE DINNER:

A fine American Champagne: Korbel Natural or Brut—Gold Seal Blanc de Blancs—Almadén Blanc de Blancs—Great Western Brut—Korbel Brut—Beaulieu Brut (1968, 1969)—Inglenook Brut (1967)—Mirassou Brut—Masson Extra Dry—Llords & Elwood Extra Dry.

or:

A good German Moselle: Bernkasteler Badstube—Bernkasteler Graben—Brauneberger Juffer—Erdener Treppchen—Urziger Wurgarten—Zeltinger Himmelreich—Wehlener Sonnenuhr—Graacher Himmelreich.

or:

A fine Spanish Fino sherry: Harveys Tico Cock-

tail Sherry—Pedro
Domecq Guitar—Pedro
Domecq La Ina—Wil-
liams & Humbert Cedro
—Wisdom & Warter
Amontillado Fino—Pal-
omino & Vergara Don
Juan.

WITH DINNER:

A fine California red.
Either a Pinot Noir: see
listing, pp. 234–6 or a
Cabernet Sauvignon, see
listing, pp. 47–9.

or:

A great California white
such as: Heitz Pinot
Chardonnay ('69, '70,
'71)—Sterling Pinot
Chardonnay—Ridge
Pinot Chardonnay
(1972)—Louis Martini
Pinot Chardonnay
(1968)—Wente Pinot
Chardonnay—Christian
Brothers Pinot Chardon-
nay—Parducci Pinot
Chardonnay ('71) (oth-
ers, see pp. 232–3).

or:

One of California's finest
Johannisberg Rieslings:
Llords & Elwood Cuvée
6—Freemark Abbey Jo-
hannisberg Riesling
(1971, 1972)—Sonoma
Riesling Spätlese (1972)
—Château Montelena
Johannisberg Riesling
Spätlese—Wente Ries-
ling Spätlese.

or:

A good California spar-
kling Burgundy: Korbel
Rouge—Mirassou Spar-
kling Gamay Beaujolais
—Beaulieu Rouge
Champagne.

or:

A true French Burgundy—
this would be the best
choice of all, funds
permitting: a Pommard

—Clos des Mouches—
Gevrey-Chambertin—
Vosne-Romanée—Cor-
ton Grancey—Les
Cailleret.

AFTER DINNER:

A lovely French Sauternes:
One of these châteaux:
Climens—Coutet—
Filhot—Rayne-Vigneau
—De Suduiraut—Rieus-
sec.

or:

A German Auslese

or:

Tokay Aszu

or:

A real Portuguese Porto:
Croft Distinction—Croft
Fine Ruby—Cockburn
Aldouro Tawny—Cock-
burn's #25—Harveys
Gold Cap Ruby—Sande-
man Three Star Tawny.

For Millionaires, Industrial-
ists, Heirs & Heiresses, Royalty
(Rich), Big Wheels, Plumbers
(White House variety, and
"plain"), Tycoons, Big-Time
Rectors (Episcopalian), Big
Spenders—Wines from $7 and
up, up, up. . . .

BEFORE DINNER:

California's finest Cham-
pagne: Schramsberg
Blanc de Blancs—Kor-
bel Natural—Windsor
Brut—Kornell Sehr
Trocken.

or:

A great French Cham-
page: Moët et Chandon
Brut Imperial—Dom
Perignon—Mumm René
Lalou or Cordon Rouge
—Charles Heidsieck Cu-
vée Royale or Blanc de
Blancs—Perrier-Jouet
Special Reserve (others,
see pp. 59–60).

or:

Spain's finest Finos: Gonzalez Byass Tio Pepe—

Harveys Tico Cocktail Sherry—Williams & Humbert Dos Cortados —Williams & Humbert Dry Sack—Williams & Humbert Pando.

WITH DINNER:

One of Bordeaux's great Premiers: Châteaux Marguax, Lafite-Rothschild, Mouton-Rothschild, Pétrus, Latour, Haut-Brion, Cheval Blanc.

or:

One of France's great Burgundies: Chambertin— Romanée-Conti—La Tâche—Richebourg— Musigny—Clos de Vougeot. For a complete listing, see p. 44.

AFTER DINNER:

The greatest of all French Sauternes: Château d'Yquem.

or:

A German Beerenauslese or Trockenbeerenauslese.

or:

A genuine Portuguese Vintage Port: Croft—Cockburn's—Taylor Fladgate —Sandeman.

TIBURON VINEYARDS: See SONOMA VINEYARDS.

TIO PEPE: See GONZALEZ BYASS.

TOKAJI ASZU Luscious golden dessert wine from Hungary, pronounced Toe-Kie, rather than Toe-Kay. It has a distinct and satisfying *gout de terroir* (taste of the earth). The sweetness and the price of the wine ascend according to the number of *puttonyok*, or baskets of overripe grapes, that are used —it's on the label—three or four or five *puttonos* (or *puttonyos*). Five *puttonos* is a very luscious wine, almost a liqueur. Here's one place you don't

have to worry about growers', shippers', producers' names—all Tokay (Anglecized spelling of Tokaji) Aszu is shipped by the state-controlled firm of Monimpex. Tokay Aszu comes to the U.S. in pint bottles—a little goes a long way—and should sell for around $4.50 for the three Putts (as it's sometimes abbreviated) to around $5.50 for the five. It's easily always at least **** wine.

TOKAJI ESZENCIA (or ESSENCE) As the name indicates, this wine is the concentrated essence, the quintessence, of the finest, richest Tokaji Aszu. It is incredibly luscious, difficult to come by, and expensive, $50 to $500 for 16 ounces. Of old it was sipped by dying monarchs to prolong their life. It is related that Pope Leo XIII subsisted on Tokaji Eszencia for the last two weeks of his life, before he died at the age of ninety-three.

TOKAJI SZAMORODNI (DRY) Don't try to pronounce it—just drink it. It's a nice white wine of Hungary, a good value at $3.20. This is the "straight" version of the sweet Tokaji Aszu (see), made from normal grapes, not overripe ones.

TOKAY: See TOKAJI.

TONDONIA This is the "given" name of some excellent wines, both red and white, produced by the firm of Lopez de Heredia of the town of Haro, in Spain's Rioja region. The red is a wonderful wine with lots of character, already well matured when you buy it. Don't take the vintage year too seriously, though, these are generalizations saying that the wine is "young," or "old," or "very old." Some important generalizations:

1934: The '34 on the label says it's a very old wine—and a very good one. One expert says it's better than Bordeaux '34 . . . that may be a bit much, but it's a sure *****.

1947: Old wine, assertive wine: ****. Fully mature.

1954: Now at its best, marvelous flavor, fair value, ca. $6. ****

1958: Mark it "omit."

1960: ***

1964: **** At its best.

1966: *** Fair value, $3. It will be at its best, 1977 on.

How to serve these wines: See under RIOJA.

TORRES CORONAS* A hearty, economical red wine made by the Miguel Torres firm of Spain. Torres wines have become quite popular in a modest kind of way over the U.S. these past five years or so, for the good and ample reason that they are good wines (though a bit rough at times) at reasonable prices. Torres is not actually in the Rioja (northern Spain) region, where the best table wines are made, but in Catalonia (easternmost province, Barcelona area). All Torres wines are vintage-dated, but particularly with the cheaper wines this means only that *some* of the wine is of that particular vintage. Serve and drink these Torres wines as you would the reds of Rioja (see). Air the reds one to two hours, except the 50s (fifteen minutes is sufficient for them).

TORRES GRAN CORONAS This red wine is a distinct notch above the plain Coronas, above. It's another hearty wine, but with more body, and smoother. It's worth the additional dollar. Note that there is a "super" Gran Coronas with a black label—it's about $2 additional

(ca. $5.75) but it can be a glorious wine. Some vintages:

*1955—****

*1959 Black Label—*****—* Gorgeous wine, truly Burgundian, soft, fully matured, lovely flavors.

*1961, 1962—****

*1961 Black Label—*****

TORRES SANGRE DE TORO This "Blood of the Bull" (that's what the name means) is the cheapest of Torres' reds, lighter and younger than the preceding wines, but a remarkable wine for the money, $2.75 to $3. It's a vintaged wine, but you need not bother about vintages here—all the current Sangres, 1964, 1966, 1969, 1970, are a healthy ***, sometimes pushing ****.

But, *cuidado,* there is also a Gran Sangre de Toro, ****, a Reserva (always superior), which sells for about 75¢ (ca. $3.50) more than the "straight," and is worth the difference. There is even a Tres Torres Sangre de Toro—the name does not mean three bulls (that would be Tres Toros) but "Three Towers," a play on the firm's name. The 1966 recently received a prestigious British gold medal: *****.

TRAMINER: See GEWÜRZTRAMINER.

TRES GRAND COLD DUCK (Guild Wine Co.)** It's a seemingly never-ending flock of ducks that's plaguing us, though a few of them have been shot down this past year or two. This one by Guild is just one more of them: sweet, light, adequate, if Cold Duck's your thing. At least it's cheap, $2.25 to $2.50.

TRES TORRES: See TORRES SANGRE DE TORO.

TRIMBACH CLOS SAINTE HUNE: See CLOS SAINTE HUNE.

**TRIMBACH GEWÜRZTRA-
MINER and TRAMINER**
F. E. Trimbach, in Ribeauville,
Alsace, is a reputable shipper
of Alsatian wines. They've been
around for a respectable 350
years—that ought to make
them a bit dependable. Some
recent bottlings of their
Gewürztraminer:

1967 Traminer *** but done
gone.

1970 Gewürztraminer: ***

*1971 Gewürztraminer Re-
serve:* ***

*1971 Gewürztraminer Cuvée
des Seigneurs de Ribeaupierre:*
****

TRIMBACH RIESLING De-
pendable white wine of Alsace
—Trimbach is the venerable
firm who made the wine. This
Riesling is made from the same
noble grape that's responsible
for Germany's greatest wines.
Trimbach's very best Riesling
goes by the name of their best
vineyard: Clos Sainte Hune
(see). How to serve Riesling:
See under RIESLING. Recent
vintages of Trimbach's "plain"
Riesling: 1970 is *** and the
'71 ****

TROCKENBEERENAUSLESE
Taken literally the name doesn't
really sound very appealing:
"The Late Picking of the Dried-
up Grapes." But every human
being born of a woman should
be allowed to taste one of these
wines at least once before he
comes to die. This is the highest and most expensive category
of German wines. The grapes
are literally picked, not cluster
by cluster, but grape by grape,
at the fullness of maturity.
(Just a step below this wine are
the Beerenauslesen, also marvelous wines). Trockenbeerenauslesen are extremely rare
and expensive wines (from $50
to over $100 per 23.5 ounces),
rich and luscious beyond all
description. These are like no
other wines of this earth. One
sips them, well chilled, very
very slowly, very carefully,
very gratefully, all the while
praising God's bounteous creation. Happily, a little goes a
long way here: one bottle can
serve ten or twelve people—
provided you keep most of
them chained to their chairs.
You don't have to worry about
Trockenbeerenauslesen spoiling
on you: they are at their best
when they're between ten and
fifty years of age.

U

UNITED STATES—WINES
The inevitable question: Does
the U.S. make wines as good
as those of France? The inevitable answer: Yes and No.
Yes, some American wines are
better than some French wines.
No, the U.S. does not make as
many great wines as does
France. But if you are asking
about the overall average quality, the "average" bottle of
French wine vs. the "average"
bottle of American wine—as
though there were such a thing
—then you would have to say
that American wines are probably the better of the two, over
all. (That sentence may earn
this book the undying enmity
of 51,921,400 Frenchmen!)
Only in the last decade or two
has the U.S. been consistently
producing great wines, but
they're fast getting the hang of
it—it takes lots of time, skill,
and money—and the number of
great wines produced in America increases every year. And
Americans are finally beginning
to appreciate their own wines.
H. G. Wells's statement of fifty
years ago is no longer true:
"You Americans have the loveliest wines in the world, you
know, but you don't realize it.
You call them *domestic* and
that's enough to start trouble
anywhere."
Perhaps—just perhaps—American wines have not quite
reached the ultimate status of
great classic wines but they are
clearly within a hair's breadth
of that noble goal. Finally what
distinguishes a great wine from
a merely fine one is its complexity—a great wine is a sym-
phony of tastes, aromas, sensa-
tions. A great wine does not
merely strike a single beautiful
note, it strikes a chord—even
a chorus.
But in a certain sense American
wines should not be compared
with French wines at all—in
fact, in this sense no wines can
be compared. Because every
wine stands on its own merits—
is it good or is it bad? Not, how
does it compare with such-and-
such? No two wines in the
world are the same—no more
than any two human beings are
identical. Even wines from the
same area, with the selfsame
label, can vary widely. How
much more, then, will a Cabernet Sauvignon made in California differ from a Cabernet
Sauvignon made in France?
The valid question, therefore, is
not: How does California Pinot
Noir compare with France's red
Burgundies, or California's Johannisberg Riesling compare
with Germany's Rhine wines;
the valid question is: How good
is California Pinot Noir and
how good is California Johannisberg Riesling?

ÜRZIGER   WÜRZGARTEN
It may be difficult to pronounce,
but it's easy to drink, is this
fine wine of Germany's Moselle
Valley. These wines tend to be

expensive, especially the '71s, but they are among the finest, some say even better than those of Bernkastel. The Spätlese and Auslese (see both) wines are particularly good. Vintages are very important here. Some recent ones:

1961—Riesling Spätlese Eiswein: Famous—Classic.

1964—Auslese (Christoffel): *****

1967—(Jos. Berres): *****

1969—Feinste Spätlese (Graff): ****

Spätlese (Nicolay): ****

1971—Auslese (Priesterseminar): *****

How to serve this wine: See under MOSELLE.

V

VAILLON(S): See CHABLIS, FRENCH.

(P. J.) VALCKENBERG, WORMS AM RHEIN A large, important, and reliable German wine shipping firm located in the city of Worms, or more accurately, Worms-am-Rhein: Worms-on-the-Rhine. Look up your particular bottle under the name of the wine: Madonna, Liebfrauenstift, etc.

VALLE DE ORO RED, VALLE DE ORO WHITE** The name means "Valley of Gold," referring to the Livermore Valley where Wente Bros. produces these two *vins ordinaires*. The wines were originally intended only for employee consumption, but then the public got wind of them. Even today they're sold only at the winery. They are sound, unpretentious wines for everyday quaffing. Fair value, $2.75 per half-gallon.

VALMUR: See CHABLIS, FRENCH.

VALPANTENA: See VALPOLICELLA.

VALPOLICELLA Fine red Italian wine, dry, soft, fruity. It's a youthful kind of wine, at its best when between two and five years old. It goes with almost any food, almost any time, under whatever pretext. It's regularly a good value, well worth looking for. Serve Valpolicella at cool room temperature or slightly chilled, ca. 60° F. Sometimes you'll find the word "Valpantena" on the label, sometimes by itself but more often following "Valpolicella." This wine comes from an adjacent area, but it's the same wine.

Some vintages:

1969 Excellent year—Drink soon.

    Lamberti: ***
    Mirafiore: ****
    Antinori: ****

1970 Excellent year, fine wines—Drink during '75.

    Petternella: ***
    Cantina Sociale di Soave: ***
    Bolla: ****

1971 Good wines—At their best, 1975 through 1976.

    Cantina Sociale di Soave: ***
    Leonardo: ***
    Ruffo: **
    Bolla: ****
    Fedeschi: ****

1972 Sanzeno: ***
    Ruffino: ***
    Bolla: ****

VAN LOBEN SELS, SAUVIGNCN BLANC, 1972**** This soft, silky white wine is the only wine thus far made under this label, the property and the product of Oakville Vineyards (see), where Bud van Loben Sels presides. It's a good omen, is this wine. One winemaker says it possesses "indigenous sweetness," yet it's totally dry. Perfect with shellfish. In late '74 the winery reduced the price from $5 to $4, making this an excellent value.

VAUDESIR: See CHABLIS, FRENCH.

VERAN, SAINT: See SAINT VERAN.

VERRAZZANO This is the "given" name of a fine red Italian Chianti made by the firm of Luigi Cappellini. It is a "Classico" Chianti, made in a specific delimited area—notice the guarantee of a "Classico," the black cockerel on the neck of the bottle. The '69 was a beauty: ****, full-flavored and clean—one American critic rated it "perfect"—an excellent value at around $4. The '71, recently come to market, is a solid **** and may well reach ***** when fully mature. It's already good drinking but it will be much better if you will restrain yourself and allow it to age for another two or three years. It will improve in the bottle until about 1980. Be sure to air this wine at least one hour, preferably more.

VEUVE CLIQUOT PONSAR-DIN It's named for the stalwart and formidable Widow Cliquot—you should see her picture—frighten little boys!—one of France's greatest Champagnes. "Best of the House" is called—what else?—La Grande Dame, regularly *****, and the price tag is equally formidable: $23.50. There is a Gold Label Vintage Brut ($15.75) and the current vintage, 1966, is round and fine, ****, now at its best. But the nonvintage Yellow Label Brut is a better value ($13.75), a very dry Champagne, regularly ****.

VIGNAMAGGIO This is the "given" name for a fine Chianti Classico (the best kind) made by the Italian firm of Contessa Elena Sanminiatelli (Florence).

The 1967 deserves ****, and the '68, ***.

How to serve this wine: See under CHIANTI.

VILLA ANTINORI This is the best Chianti made by the distinguished Italian firm of Marchesi L. & P. Antinori (Florence). It is noted for its elegant "balance," its perfect proportion of sweetness and tartness.

Besides its Riserva and "plain" Chianti Classico, Antinori also makes a Santa Cristina, their humblest grade of Chianti. It is a good little red wine and you can trust it. See it under its own name.

How to serve Villa Antinori: See under the general heading CHIANTI.

Some notable bottles:

1955: Chianti Classico Riserva: *****—A great one but don't keep it, drink it!

1964 Chianti Classico: **** —At its best, 1975–1978.

1967 Chianti Classico: **** —Has brownish tinge (a sign of aging) but it's still at its peak—But don't tempt fate, drink it soon.

1967 Chianti Classico Riserva: *****—Now at its best —Enjoy through the 70s.

1969 Chianti Classico: **** —"Graceful" is the word for it —Mellow, fully matured, drink it now and through the decade ahead.

For value for current vintages: Chianti Classico: $4 (24 ounces) —Riserva: $6 (24 ounces).

VILLE FONTAINE (Geyserville, Calif.) Another of those sparkling (yeah!) new California wineries, this one owned by Souverain Winery (see), which in turn is owned by Pillsbury.

Chenin Blanc, North Coast Counties, 1972* Fresh, rather dry white wine, recommended, chilled, for summer's evening sipping. Drink it during '75, '76. Fair value, $2.75.

Gamay Rosé, Sonoma Valley, 1972*** See Chenin Blanc, above—exactly the same words apply here—except for one: "white." Delete it, and substitute "pink."

Grey Riesling, Mendocino County, 1972*** See Chenin Blanc, above—exactly the same words apply here.

VIÑA ALBINA Fine red wine from Spain's best district, the Rioja. It's made by the same people who make Monte Real (see), is somewhat drier, and equally good. The '66 Reserva was especially commendable, and an excellent value at ca. $3.25. How to serve it: See under RIOJA.

VIN (or Vins) D'ALSACE This means simply, "a wine (or wines) of Alsace," and it's an official designation. For an assessment of bottles so labeled, see under next most prominent word on the label—Riesling, Hugel, or whatever.

VIÑA POMAL**** A trustworthy, mellow little red wine from Spain's Rioja (see) region; it's got a big bouquet and a good, mouth-filling flavor. It's made by the Bodegas Bilbainas (it's on the label), the biggest shipper in the Rioja. Viña Pomal always bears a vintage date: *Cosecha* 1967 (or whatever), but pay it scant mind, for vintage years are rather loosely applied in Spain. Thus *Cosecha* 1967 on a wine of this type says mainly that the wine has been properly aged and is now ready to drink. It's a good value at ca. $3.25. There is also a Viña Pomal Reserva, *****, at twice the price, an excellent wine, forsooth, but

not twice as good as the "straight." How to serve Viña Pomal: See under RIOJA.

VIÑA REAL: See CUNE.

VIÑA TONDONIA: See TONDONIA.

VIÑA VIAL: see (FEDERICO) PATERNINA.

VIÑA ZACO**** A substantial red Spanish table wine, a first cousin to the Viña Pomal (above), made by the same people, and equally as good—or better. It's a clean, dry wine and will be even lovelier if you will keep the bottle you buy today until 1976 or 1977. Fair value, $4. How to serve it: See under RIOJA.

VINHO VERDE The name means "Green Wine" in Portuguese, a reference to the wine's youthfulness, not its color. It's best of all in Portugal, right from the barrel, but if you're not going to be in Lisbon this week, look for Casal Garcia or Gatao or Casal Mendes or Moura Basto or Solar do Minho (see all), at your local wine shop. Vinho Verde is one of the world's most delightful little wines: frizzy on the tongue, wonderfully fresh. Serve it well chilled (40 to 45°F) of a summer's afternoon. It also goes admirably with fish and seafood.

Vinho Verde is low in alcohol —they say that in Portugal it's common to drink an entire bottle with one's luncheon—small wonder they have those three-hour siestas. Don't keep it, drink it within a year of purchase. It's always an excellent value.

VINIFERA WINE CELLARS: See FRANK, DR. KONSTANTIN.

VINYA ROSÉ A decent little Portuguese rosé, refreshing, on the sweet side. Trustworthy. A rather nice value at ca. $2.20:

a small wine at a small price.
How to serve: See under ROSÉ.

VOLLRADS, SCHLOSS: See
SCHLOSS VOLLRADS.

VOLNAY One of the lightest,
freshest, most delicate of all
fine red Burgundies. Volnay is
not of the superstar category
like Romanée-Conti or Chambertin, but an excellent, dependable wine, a joy to behold
—it's a brilliant red—and a
delight to drink. The most important vineyards are these:
(Les) Caillerets; (Les) Champans; Clos des Santenots; (Le)
Clos de Chêne.

When the label says only "Volnay" without naming a specific
vineyard, it is the lowliest grade
of Volnay, but still fine wine,
rarely below **** status.

Volnay goes well with beef, but
especially with lamb, also with
poultry, game, smoked ham. It
will show off best of all, however, on its own or with cheeses
and bread. Volnay is at its best
when it is between four and
eight years of age.

VOSNE-ROMANÉE This is
the name of one of the greatest
—perhaps the greatest—wine-
producing districts in the world.
From here come some of the
world's greatest red wines:
Romanée-Conti, La Romanée,
La Tâche, Richebourg, Ro-
manée-Saint-Vivant. Here, as-
suredly, we are on holy ground.
Wine writers seem to run out
of superlatives: incredible balance—velvety warmth—Oriental opulence. But the most
famous and most descriptive
phrase of all is 200 years old:
"Bottled velvet and satin."

The greatest wines of the district are those mentioned above,
but a lot of fine wine goes to
market under the name of
Vosne-Romanée. In fact, it is
said to be one of France's best

"commune" or "village" wines
for the money. It still isn't
cheap, however, hovering between $8 and $12. These are
long-lived wines—don't rush
them.

Some vintages:

    1962 Violland: ****
      Louis Latour: *****
    1964 Leroy: ***—Poor value.
    1966 Fine wines, full-bodied
and fruity.
    1969 Leroy: ****
    1970 Drouhin: ****
      Jean Gros: *****
      Clos des Reas (Gros):
      *****

    1971 Clos Des Reas (Gros):
****

      Engel: Not recommended.
    J. Henri: *****

VOUGEOT, CLOS DE: See
CLOS DE VOUGEOT.

VOUVRAY Here's a marvelous wine for beginners, soft
and light, fruity and flowery,
with just a touch of sweetness.
Wine novices are invariably en-
chanted with this charming—
that's the adjective everybody
uses—wine from France's Loire
Valley. Vouvray actually is a
far-ranging wine and can be
very dry, or even very old, but
these types are not seen in the
U.S. Vouvray should be drunk
young: from two to four years
old is ideal. It's a fine wine—
chilled, of course—for sitting
and sipping and chatting—
morning, afternoon, evening, or
nighttime. Some names to look
for: Château Montcountour;
Château Gaudrelle (Monmous-
seau); Clos le Mont (Acker-
man Laurance).

Vintages are important here—
they can change the very nature of the wine. Some recent
ones:

    1969 Great year—Drink up
and soon.

1970 Excellent—Drink soon, up.

1971 Again excellent—Drink during '75 and '76.

1972 Good wines, not exceptional—Best drinking, 1975 through 1976.

1973—Fine wines—At their best, 1975 through 1977.

W

WEHLEN(ER) SONNENUHR
One of the very finest of
Moselle wines, especially those
made by the Prüm family.
These are wines of tremendous
balance and elegance—exquisite
is the word—with a suggestion
of honey, some say. Some vintages:

1959—Feine Auslese (J. J.
Prüm): *****

1966—Feinste Auslese (Berg-
weiler-Prüm): *****

1967—Auslese (J. J. Prüm):
****

1969—(S. A. Prüm): This
"straight" '69 (of no special
picking) is an excellent wine,
at least ****, a good value at
around $4.

    Spätlese (S. A. Prüm Er-
    ben): ****

    Auslese (Peter Prüm):
    *****—Best drinking,
    1975–1978.

1970—Kabinett (J. J. Prüm):
****

    Spätlese (J. J. Prüm):
    ****

1971—Marvelous wines—
Will be at the very top of their
bent, 1976–1978.

1972—Good, not spectacular
—At their best: 1975–1977.
How to serve these wines: See
under MOSELLE.

**WEHLEN(ER) - ZELTING(ER)
SONNENUHR:** See ZELTING-
(ER)-WEHLEN(ER) SONNENUHR.

WEIBEL VINEYARDS (Mission San Jose, Calif.) The Swiss
are noted more for their yodel-
ing and holey cheese than they
are for their wines. But they
are very much a wine-loving
nation, and the Swiss family
Weibel, upon coming to America, carried on the tradition.
And well. In some thirty-five
years they have earned a solid
vinous reputation, especially for
their sparkling wines, though
they also make a dizzying assortment of still wines, all the
way from Amberina (some-
body's maiden aunt?) to a wild
brew made with tangerines and
citrus, called Tangor (ugh!).

    **Amberina Cream Sherry (So-
lera Flor)***** The words
"Solera" and "Flor" denote
that the wine was made in the
true Spanish manner, and you'll
find these words on all three of
Weibel's fine sherries. "Amberina" is descriptive: the wine is
a deep amber color, with good
flavor. It's for after-dinner
drinking. An excellent value at
$2.50.

    Black Muscat: See CREAM
OF BLACK MUSCAT.

    Blanc de Blancs, Crackling:
See CRACKLING BLANC DE BLANCS.

    Cabernet Sauvignon*** This
is not the greatest Cabernet
ever produced in California, by
a rather wide margin, but it's
an honest if minor version of
this classic red wine. It will go
especially well with barbecued
steaks (or chicken), lamb, egg
dishes, fondue. Or savor it on
its own with cheese. It's soft
enough to be enjoyed when
purchased, but it will improve

with a year or two of bottle age. A good value at $3.40.

Chablis, Classic: See CLASSIC CHABLIS.

Champagne, Brut*** Note that there is also a Champagne, Chardonnay Brut (see): this Brut is a bit sweeter than the other, and will cost you $2 less. It's a well-made Champagne, serve it with pride.

Champagne, Chardonnay Brut**** Weibel was known for their sparkling wines long before most people even knew that they produced still wines! This is the finest of their variegated array of sparkling wines. In blind tastings (labels hidden) over the years this wine has always done well; in one tasting in 1973 it placed above a host of $15 to $20 French Champagnes. All Champagne should be served well chilled—and pull that cork gently and slowly, don't decapitate anyone —or what's worse, don't lose any of that precious liquid. Champagne fits in almost anywhere: before, during, after meals—A.M. or P.M.—even on Mondays. But this is such a delicate and lovely wine that it deserves to be sipped, drop by exquisite drop, all by itself. Fair value—sorry, after all that build-up: $7.50. *Caution:* There is also a plain Champagne Brut (see), without the Chardonnay in there, a less expensive wine.

Champagne, Extra Dry*** For most people this wine may well be more appealing than either of the two Bruts, above, for it has a little more sweetness to it; it's not quite as austere. Fair value, $5.25.

Champagne, Pink: See PINK CHAMPAGNE.

Champagne, Sec—Not recommended.

Chenin Blanc*** Fresh light white wine with an edge of sweetness. Goes well with light foods, but to enjoy it fully, sip it, chilled, slowly and lackadaisically of a summer's evening—or any carefree evening. Fair value, ca. $2.50.

Classic Burgundy, Classic Chablis, Classic Vin Rosé**, but price and attractive decanter considered: *** Weibel has long produced standard versions of these three wines, but in 1973 they introduced these "Classic" versions, aimed at the young and the neophyte wine drinker. These are light, mellow wines, more readily palatable— though, in effect, they are thereby less truly "winey." They're inexpensive, ca. $1.65, which will appeal to young and old, novice and veteran wine drinker alike. For daily unpretentious enjoyment.

Classic Sherry (Solera Flor, California Medium)*** All purpose, medium-dry (therefore also medium-sweet, marvelous!) aperitif wine, or a with-soup wine, or an after-dinner-with-cigars wine. A good value at $2.50.

Crackling Blanc de Blancs** This sparkling wine is not superior but still a fair value at $4 to $4.60.

Crackling Duck** Is this duck crackling or only quacking? Anyhow, it's sweet and bubbly—if that's your kind of duck. Fair value, $4 to $4.60.

Crackling Rosé** Medium-sweet—it's festive in color, if not in flavor. Fair value, $5.40.

Cream of Black Muscat*** Weibel says it's "heart-warming"—which it is, if one enjoys the distinctive Muscat flavor. It may be hard to find, though, as it's in limited supply. Serve it, chilled, with dessert. Fair value, $2.50.

Cream Sherry: See AMBERINA CREAM SHERRY.

Dry Bin Sherry (Solera Flor, California Cocktail)**** The best of Weibel's good sherries. It's dry, with a deep-down nutty flavor. A perfect aperitif wine and an excellent value at $2.50. Weibel says to serve it slightly chilled or over ice—but be warned: Some say that the latter process constitutes a punishable crime.

Duck, Crackling: See CRACKLING DUCK.

Gamay Beaujolais*** Young, fruity red wine: perfect at your outdoor barbecue, on a picnic, or, for the matter of that, anyplace, with any red meat. It's ready to drink when you bring it home, will probably improve with six months of additional age. Drink it young and fresh, however: not beyond two years of purchase. Fair value, $3.

Green Hungarian**** One of California's best wines by this name. The winery says it's like a Liebfraumilch, which it is, with its definite edge of sweetness, but it's something even more, in its own right. A perfect wine, chilled, fresh and flavorful, for leisurely sipping of an evening—around the fireplace or around the pool. Ready to drink upon purchase and will keep well for four years after purchase. Fair value, $2.50.

Grenache Rosé** Dollar for dollar, you will do better with their Classic Vin Rosé (see). But if you prefer a really dry rosé, then this is your wine. Fair value, $2.50 to $2.75.

Grey Riesling and Johannisberg Riesling*** The winery pushes both these wines as "Rhine-types." Which they are, in a vague sort of way. But that's selling them short, for they're individual wines in their own right: dry white, well-balanced wines, best served with light foods. Ready to drink when purchased, they will keep well for at least four years thereafter. Fair value, Grey Riesling, $2.50 to $2.75; Johannisberg Riesling, $3.50 to $4.

Moscato Spumante*** If you like the Muscat flavor, you'll like this sparkling, medium-sweet wine. It's for after-dinner consumption. Fair value, $3.50 to $3.75.

Pink Champagne*** Fruitily flavorful—and if you can say that you may have another glass. It's pretty besides, a party beverage. Fair value, $5.40.

Pinot Chardonnay*** Trite or not, the best way to describe this wine is to say that it's good but not great. Pinot Chardonnay is the grape responsible for the great white Burgundies of France and partially responsible for France's fine Champagnes—well, Weibel doesn't quite make it to those dizzying heights with their Pinot Chardonnay, but you might say that this is a reasonable facsimile. It's on the dry side, fragrant, slightly aromatic. The perfect accompaniment for fish, poultry, veal, sweetbreads. This nonvintage wine is ready to drink when you buy it and will hold at its best for a full five years thereafter. Fair value, $3.25 to $3.50.

Note: There is also a vintage-dated "Estate Bottled" version of this wine, at around $5: 1967, 1968, 1969. Say Nay. Sometimes the "E.B." product is inferior to the "plain," and never (thus far) worth the extra money.

Pinot Noir**** This noble red table wine may occasionally descend to *** status but it almost always deserves its four-star rating. Serve it with fine red meats, or as a true wine lover you may prefer to appreciate it on its own with Cheddar cheese. It's already good drinking when you buy it, but will get even better if you lay it down for two or three years. Serve at cool room temperature, after airing it about an hour. Fair value, $3.40.

Pinot Noir, Estate Bottled "Estate Bottled" means that the entire winemaking process took place at the winery itself: grapes were not brought in from elsewhere, it wasn't bottled by somebody else, etc. This localized attention almost always means a superior wine. And this "E.B." Pinot Noir is somewhat above their "plain" Pinot Noir, though whether it's sufficiently superior to warrant the price difference, is open to question. Fair value, $5.50.

1966***, reaching for **** May well be the best red wine Weibel has ever produced. Best drinking, 1975 through 1980.

1967*** Now at its best and will remain there through 1978.

1968****, and aspiring to ***** At its best, 1975–1982.

Port: See RARE PORT.

Rare Port (Solera Cask)*** It's cask-aged, which is good, not too sweet, also good, and it's mellow, and that ain't bad. A good value—you could have guessed it—at $2.50.

Rhine and Sauterne** Price is right ($2) but not much else is. Both wines are on the dry side. Serve them—if you must —chilled, with fish or fowl simply prepared. For present consumption; don't keep.

Rosé, Crackling: See CRACK-LING ROSÉ.

Royalty*** This red table wine, made from a rare grape

species of the same name, is unique to California. It's a robust wine with just a touch of sweetness—it's sure to be appreciated by novice wine drinkers. Chill it slightly. Good for summertime sipping or to go with your grilled steaks, hamburgers, chicken. Or on a picnic with hot dogs. A good value at $2.50.

Sauterne: See RHINE and SAUTERNE.

Sherry: See AMBERINA CREAM SHERRY—CLASSIC SHERRY—DRY BIN SHERRY.

Sparkling Burgundy*** Slightly sweet but with some fullness and body. Sparkling Burgundy goes equally well before, during, or after meals. Fair value, $5.40.

Vin Rosé** There is a new version of this wine, called Classic Vin Rosé (see), and dollar for dollar you'll do better with it.

WENTE BROTHERS (Livermore, Calif.) Wente is one of the most honored names in the history of California winemaking. It all got started back in 1883 when Carl Heinrich Wente hiked from the Napa Valley (where he'd been working for the Krug Winery) out to the Livermore Valley to make the first Wente wines. The family has been doing a good job ever since, especially with their white wines.

Blanc de Blancs*** Here's a lovely, light, refreshing wine, good enough to deserve and delicate enough to demand being served on its own, not at a meal to be overwhelmed by abominations like sauerkraut or chili con carne! This wine deserves to accompany the likes of fresh fruit, cheese, broiled lobster. Fair value, $2.50 to $3.

Chablis*** One of California's more "authentic" Chablis: more like its French progenitor than most; it's crisp, dry, clean. Excellent with oysters, crab, fish, or your favorite chicken recipe (provided it isn't overly spicy).

Château Sémillon*** This wine was replaced by Château Wente (see) in 1973, but there is still some around. It's a fairly sweet wine, and can be served, chilled, after dinner. Or you might prefer to use it for informal entertaining. Let it breathe a half hour before serving. Fair value, ca. $2.85.

Château Wente*** This was formerly called Château Sémillon, though the wines are not precisely identical. This one is slightly sweeter and heavier-bodied than the Château Sémillon. 1971 was the first vintage.

Dry Sémillon One of Wente's very best and one of California's best by this name. The "Dry" is deliberate, for there is also a sweet version; Wente calls theirs "Château Wente" (see). Here's an ideal white table wine, at a reasonable price, to accompany cheese dishes, pork, ham, chicken. A good value at $2.50 to $2.85.

1968 and *1969***** Now at their best—drink soon.

1970, 1971, 1972*** Best drinking, now and through 1976.

Gamay Beaujolais Wente has always been known for its white wines, but it now makes four reds. This is not their best nor their worst. It's pretty average and somewhat irregular from vintage to vintage. It's light and fresh—just right for your outdoor barbecue, light luncheon, picnic-cum-hot-dogs. Serve it cool, not chilled. Fair value, $2.80 to $3.10.

1966*** Probably departed this world—don't chance it.

1967** May be over the hill.

1969** Drink soon.

1970*** Best drinking, through 1975.

1971 and 1972*** Drink now and through 1976.

Gewürztraminer, 1972**** A new wine for Wente, and they're off to a flying start with it. "Gewürz" is originally an Alsatian wine, and Wente's version is not as mouth-filling as its Alsatian progenitor, but it's almost as spicy and it's softer. Excellent with sausage, fish, delicatessen. Serve chilled. Sadly, it's more expensive than most Gewürztraminers: $4.50.

Grey Riesling*** Wente's most popular wine, it's soft, dry, slightly spicy, ideal to accompany fish, chicken, light entrees. One good reason for the wine's popularity is its reasonable, pedestrian price: $2.50 to $2.75. Serve chilled. It's nonvintaged, ready to drink when you tote it homeward, and it's best drunk within four years of purchase.

Johannisberg Riesling: See RIESLING SPÄTLESE.

Le Blanc de Blancs: See BLANC DE BLANCS.

Petite Sirah, 1969, 1970, 1971, and 1972** A new wine for Wente. Petite Sirah is supposed to be hearty and robust, but most of Wente's comes through as thin and tart. The '72 is the best of the lot: a hesitant ***.

Pinot Blanc Some people say that Wente makes the best Pinot Blanc in California. Could be. Pinot Blanc is not a very popular wine in California, and it deserves wider acceptance, for as a white table wine it is second only to Pinot Chardonnay, and is always considerably cheaper. It's ideal with chicken, fish, shellfish, and for a real treat, says Wente, enjoy it with crab and sourdough French bread. Serve chilled. Fair value, $2.75 to $3.10.

1968**** It's almost certainly past its peak.

1970**** Drink soon.

1971*** Drink, 1975 through 1976.

1972*** Drink, 1975 through 1977.

Pinot Chardonnay Today Pinot Chardonnay is universally acclaimed as America's finest white wine, offering competition to the great white Burgundies of France. It is always in demand and, in fact, often hard to find. And it was largely Wente that started it all, back in the early 60s. Some French experts extolled the Wente product, and *Life* magazine picked up the story. Everybody and his uncle has been copying Wente ever since. In some cases, the pupils have certainly outdistanced their teacher, and truth to tell, the teacher has not been all that consistent of recent years.

There is no finer wine than Chardonnay to accompany turkey, pheasant, lobster, veal, cold cuts. Serve it chilled. Fair value, $3.75 to $4.10.

1964**** Either going fast or gone.

1966 and 1967*** Consume now!

1968**** Drink soon.

1969*** Best drinking, present through 1976.

1970*** At its best, now and through 1976.

1971*** Has fared poorly in blind tastings; some rate it below average. Drink now and through 1976.

1972**

1973*** It may deserve **** by '76 or '77.

Pinot Noir One of Wente's better reds. Pinot Noir is the classic grape of Burgundy, and though the American version is rarely as satisfying as the French original, it can be a pretty big wine, as Wente's often is. The best vintages deserve to accompany choice red meats: rib roast, steaks. Or, truly to appreciate this wine, drink it on its own, with Cheddar cheese or fruit. Serve it at cool room temperature. Fair value, $3.30 to $3.60.

1964 and 1965*** Both at their peak, but don't hold them.

1966**** Excellent drinking now and through 1976.

1968**** Best drinking, 1975 through 1980.

1969*** Drink now and next two or three years.

1970**** Best drinking, 1975 through 1982.

Riesling Spätlese, 1969 and 1972 and 1973***** Wente doesn't ordinarily make a wine by this name, but in '69 and again in '72, the grapes were late-picked (that's what Spätlese means), having been attacked by the "noble rot," a beneficial fungus which rarely occurs in California, and which gives added richness and depth to the wine. This fine wine deserves to be sipped carefully and gratefully on its own, chilled, with some wine-loving friends. Unhappily it's rich in more ways than one; selling price: $6 to $7. The '69 and '72 are for present drinking, and the '69 should be consumed within a year or two; the '72, by 1978. The '73 will be at its best, 1975 through 1979.

Rosé Wente** A decidedly dry rosé, not the kind of wine to appeal to the American masses, who prefer their rosé with a sweetish edge. It has some character, but it's also a bit harsh. If your taste runs to dry, assertive rosés, this will surely be worth trying at its bargain-basement price of $2 to $2.25.

Sauvignon Blanc This wine has been particularly fickle over the past decade, ranging from beautiful to horrid, from aaaah to uuugh! At its best it's a dry, aromatic wine, excellent with shellfish. Serve it chilled. Fair value, $2.75 to $3.

1963**** Just for the record; it's long gone.

1966, 1967** Departed; no great loss.

1968, 1969** Consume immediately.

1971*** Drink now and through 1976.

1972*** Tasty enough to serve as an aperitif. Best drinking, through '75.

1973**** Drink, 1975 through 1978. A good value at less than $3.

Zinfandel*** Some consider this wine outstanding, but you won't ordinarily be finding it in your local wine shop, as most of it is sold to major airlines. It sells at the winery for $2.50.

WHITE BURGUNDY: See BURGUNDY.

WHITE PINOT: See CHENIN BLANC.

WHITE RIESLING: See JOHANNISBERG RIESLING.

WHITE ZINFANDEL: See ZINFANDEL.

WIDMER'S WINE CELLARS (Naples, N.Y.) Widmer's variegated labels are seen across the face of the U. S., and their very standard wines are better known than those of any and all California premium wine producers. The sheer diversity

is staggering: Widmer's produces almost sixty different wines, at a rate of almost 5,000 cases daily. One sure reason for their wide acceptance is their price, most of them selling for around $2 per fifth. Good clean water costs almost that much!

Widmer's wines are clearly "eastern," made from native American grapes, most of them displaying at least a touch of foxy "wildness." But millions of people who were weaned on Widmer wines will swear by them unto all eternity. For these, the slight pungency is a plus, not a minus. And that's all as it should be—they're right. The best wine in all the world is the wine in all the world that you like best!

Widmer is now owned by the R. T. French Company, the mustard people. One can only pray most fervently that the produce of the two concerns will remain forever separate, if equal—and may the twain never commingle. Amen.

Widmer's *best* include:

Catawba, Sweet: See SWEET CATAWBA.

Cocktail Sherry: See SHERRY.

Cream Sherry: See SHERRY.

Delaware**: A rather fragrant dry white wine made from the red Delaware grape.

Isabella**: A light red; in its production the skins are removed early, thus lessening the foxiness.

Isabella Rosé**: Quite sweet, but has some flavor and fruitiness.

Lake Niagara**: A sweet white wine, one of Widmer's best sellers, and in fact, one of America's best sellers.

Moore's Diamond**: A dry white wine with a touch of

spiciness, goes well with fish, chicken, ham.

Naples Valley Red**: Classed as a dry red, but it has a definite fruity sweetness.

Naples Valley White**: Sweetest of Widmer's "dry" whites.

Riesling**: A dry white, with a distinctive flavor, says the winery.

Sherry*** A native of Jerez, Spain, where the only *real* sherry comes from, might not wax poetic or ecstatic over this New York sherry, but sherry is one of the things Widmer does best, and that ain't bad. In fact, it's quite good, with very little of the pungent foxiness of native grapes. Widmer makes a *Cream* (sweet) and a *Cocktail* (dry) and a *Special Selection*, which is aged, of all places, on the winery roofs, for at least four years. Somehow it seems to benefit from those extremes of New York's harsh climate.

Sweet Catawba***, conditionally A dessert wine. The *** is on the condition that you like Catawba.

Vergennes**: A dry white wine, the driest of Widmer's varietals; serve it with chicken, fish, seafood.

WILLIAMS & HUMBERT CANASTA CREAM***** Williams & Humbert, a British shipper of Spanish sherries— the only real sherry, purists insist—is one of the oldest around and one of the most reliable. The firm blends its sherries exactly to suit British tastes, and American tastes must be very similar, for these sherries are among America's most popular imported sherries. This Canasta Cream is a fine after-dinner (sweet) wine, an easy rival to Harveys well-known Bristol Cream, at a substantial saving. It's nutty and rich, and that's high commendation for a Cream sherry. A good value at around $5.75. How to serve this wine: See under SHERRY.

WILLIAMS & HUMBERT CARLITO SHERRY**** This is a pale Amontillado (medium) sherry, and a fine one. A good value at $4.25. How to serve this wine: See under SHERRY.

WILLIAMS & HUMBERT CEDRO SHERRY**** This is a mite drier than Carlito (above), a true cocktail sherry, less expensive than the Carlito but still an excellent Spanish sherry. A great value at $3.50. How to serve this wine: See under SHERRY.

WILLIAMS & HUMBERT DOS CORTADOS SHERRY— Near-Classic Here's a unique wine, well worth looking for, and not outrageously priced, considering its uniqueness and distinction: $9.50 to $10. Some say it's purely a connoisseur's wine, "Caviar to the general," but with a little urging one could learn quickly! This is a full rich wine, yet it's totally dry—it must be experienced to be appreciated. Nutty and pungent are the best adjectives. How to serve this fine wine: See under SHERRY.

WILLIAMS & HUMBERT DRY SACK SHERRY**** It's not as dry as it may sound —it's more like a medium sherry. (It's actually a Palo Cortado, a cross between an Oloroso and a Fino—if that means anything to you!) Dry Sack is a very popular Spanish sherry—the sack in which the bottle comes may have something to do with that—from a well-known shipper: good wine with good uses: aperitif, refreshment, with soup, after dinner. For more details on how to serve it: See under SHERRY. Fair value, $5.75.

WILLIAMS & HUMBERT PANDO SHERRY***   A fine, very dry Spanish Fino sherry, soft yet crisp and full. It recently took a prestigious British gold medal. How to serve this wine: See under SHERRY. Fair value, $5.30.

WILLM RIESLING This is a German-type white wine made by the giant firm of A. Willm, of Alsace. It is usually fine wine and considerably cheaper than its German counterpart. How to serve: See under RIESLING. Some recent vintages:

1964: ****—Very fruity and very good. Drink soon.

1969: Not recommended.

1970: ****—Now at its best and through 1978.

WINDSOR VINEYARDS: See SONOMA VINEYARDS.

WINE AND FOOD: See FOOD AND WINE.

WINE ETIQUETTE: See ETIQUETTE, WINE.

WINE GLASSES: See GLASSES, WINE.

WINE, SACRAMENTAL: See SACRAMENTAL WINE.

WINE SERVING: See SERVING WINE.

WINE STORAGE: See STORING WINE.

WINE TASTING: See TASTING WINE.

WINEMASTER'S   GUILD This in a brand name owned by Guild Wine Company, a huge California cooperative. Most of the wines are of a rather decent sort (as a British wine critic might say), inexpensive, everyday wines; even good values, some of them. All are for now-consumption, within a year or so of purchase. The reds (Burgundy and Zinfandel) go with grilled hamburgers, steaks, pasta, stew, hearty casseroles.

The whites (Gold Chablis, Sauterne) go with fish, seafood, poultry, light casseroles.

Burgundy* A good value at $4.40 to $5.20 the gallon (fifths: $1.30 to $1.50). Serve at, cool room temperature.

Gamay Beaujolais*   It even took a medal (bronze) at the 1974 Los Angeles County Fair.

Gold   Chablis   Serve chilled; fair value, $3 the half-gallon.

Rhine

Sauterne* Serve chilled. Fair value, $5.30 per gallon.

Sherry The standard grades of varying sweetness are made: *Pale Dry Sherry,* **: the driest of the three, an aperitif wine. "Plain" *Sherry,* ***: medium-sweet, can be used before or after meals. *Cream Sherry,* ***: the sweetest, for after-dinner consumption. It took a silver medal at the 1974 Los Angeles County Fair. All three are very good values at the unbelievable price of $1.10 to $1.25.

Zinfandel   Serve, cool room temperature. Fair value, $5.70 per gallon.

WISDOM & WARTER AMONTILLADO   SHERRY**** The name alone should sell this Spanish sherry: it's got cadence and class. And it's a real name, not invented. *Punch* once said that "Wisdom sells the wine, Warter makes it." Which is about right: Wisdom stayed in England, Warter in Spain. They were both rather shadowy characters—we don't even know Wisdom's Christian name. But they made good sherries—that was back around 1855—and their successors still do. Wisdom and Warter sherries are among the most economical authentic sherries you're going to encounter on this side of the Atlantic.

This Amontillado is a fine cocktail sherry, very flavorful, crisply dry. It's an excellent value at around $3.25. The Extra Amontillado is even better, *****, a bit sweeter, just off-dry, and richer. It's an excellent value at $3.75 to $4. How to serve these wines: See under SHERRY.

WISDOM & WARTER DELI-CATE CREAM SHERRY**

Like the label says: It's delicate —not as sweet as the Golden Cream. And the price is as sweet as the wine: $3.25. How to serve it: See under SHERRY.

WISDOM & WARTER GOLDEN CREAM SHERRY**

Beautiful, soft, full-bodied sweet sherry. After dinner with fruitcake, nuts, fruit. A good value at $4.50. How to serve it: See under SHERRY.

Y

YAGO CONDAL RESERVA 1944 and 1949**** A red Spanish wine, soft and mature, but don't take the vintage years too seriously. The price, unhappily, has skyrocketed in the past year: from $3.50 (a good value) to $6.25 (a very dubious one). How to serve this wine: See under RIOJA.

YAGO SANT'GRIA** Bottled wine-punch is what this is, and in that category this Yago is quite good—put it this way: there are worse. It's a bit much if taken straight; try pouring it over some ice cubes, add some slices of fruit and perhaps some club soda.

Yago Sant'Gria is said to be the largest-selling imported wine in America. As improbable as it sounds, it's almost certainly true. Almost two million cases sold over the past ten years. (The weird bottle probably had something to do with it.) It sells for around $2. But the best Sangria is the one you make at home—all you need is a bottle of red wine, some fruit, a little sugar. See under SANGRIA for the world's best Sangria recipe.

YGAY: See MARQUES DE MURRIETA.

YORK HOUSE TAWNY PORT You'll find it only in New York—only in Macy stores, to be precise. It's their own special label, and one they can be proud of. At $3.75 it's a good value, smooth and tasteful: ****.

How to serve Port: See under PORT.

YQUEM, CHÂTEAU D' The wine of gold—the greatest sweet wine on earth, say many. Wine critics, for some reason, wax more rhapsodic over Yquem than over any other of the world's great wines. One famous writer said that Yquem is the "most beautiful wine God ever allowed man to make, and so ought never to be drunk profanely." He was also convinced that the wine Jesus made at Cana of Galilee was a precursor to modern d'Yquem. It is often overlooked that in the famous official classification of French wines in 1855, Yquem received the highest ranking of all—it was the only wine to be classified *grand premier crû*. Yquem is the perfect dessert wine, and Americans may be surprised to learn that the cognoscenti also recommend it to accompany caviar and *pâté de foie gras*. Serve d'Yquem well chilled, 40–45°F. It is an extremely long-lived wine, and bottles 100 years old have been found in excellent condition. Keeping it a century is not ordinarily recommended, however, unless you're figuring on an extremely long stay. Yquem is ordinarily at its very best between fifteen and twenty-five years old, though it is already a beautiful wine when it's only six or seven years old.

1869—Classic—It was still available in 1973—at $160 (24 ounces).

1890—Near-Classic—It sold for a mere $25 in 1973.

1893—Near-Classic—In '39 it was still "lively and delicious."

1900—Classic—Available at $50.

1921—Classic—Some say the greatest of all Yquems—It sold (at auction) in '73 for $102 (24 ounces). In '45 it was at the top of its form and is still holding.

1928—Near-Classic—Fair value, $65.

1929—Near-Classic—Said to be still "fresh and fragrant." Fair value, $65.

1945—Classic—Still in marvelous shape. Fair value, $50.

1949—Classic—Still at its very best and more reasonably priced than most: around $30.

1950—Near-Classic—And, lo, a good value, around $12.

1953—Near-Classic—Now at its best but don't keep it beyond 1980. Fair value, $20 to $25.

1955—*****—May be beginning to fade. Fair value, $20.

1958—*****—Good despite vintage. Fair value, $10.

1959—Classic—Now at its best and will hold until 2000! You may find it for around $25, a good value these days!

1961—Classic—At its best now and through 2001! Fair value, $35, and you may find it around.

1962—Near-Classic . . . or better. Some say it's better than '61! It's certainly worth looking for, especially at $10 to $15, which is what it's been bringing at auction. It's marvelously drinkable right now and will be even better from 1976 through 2002!

1969—*****—Not ready. Hold at least until 1980.

YVERDON WINERY (St. Helena, Calif.) Another new California winery, a tiny operation high in the hills overlooking the Napa Valley. The first wine was made in 1971, and all the wines are still in short supply. Judging from early results, here's a name and here are wines that bear watching.

Cabernet Sauvignon, 1970, Cask 152 Forget the whole thing: **.

Chenin Blanc A gracious little white wine that deserves to be sipped on its own, chilled, when it is well made, as was Yverdon's in 1971—***—and when it is below average, as was Yverdon's in 1972, it deserves to be left on the retailer's shelf. Fair value, $2.75 to $3.

Gamay Beaujolais, 1971 Lot 530**** Young fruity wine, now ready to drink, don't keep it beyond 1976. Worth looking for. Gamay Beaujolais is versatile: it can accompany any decently palatable food, but best fun of all: sip it tenderly, with cheese and fresh fruit. Fair value, $3.

Johannisberg Riesling, 1970 and 1971**** This was Yverdon's first wine and the experts have been watching it closely. Thus far, with satisfaction. It's rich, flowery, soft—best with fish or seafood. Serve chilled, a good value at $3.50 to $4.

Z

ZD WINES (Sonoma, Calif.) They're springing up like mushrooms these days—or like young vine shoots—new wineries in the prestige areas of California. Here's one of the latest. And as with so many of these small family-operated wineries, it mostly bodes well. The only place where ZD wines trail is in the alphabet.

Chardonnay ZD lavishes a lot of TLC on their Chardonnay, and it's usually appreciated. The '71, though rather acidic, is a very fruity wine, fully mellow: ***. The 1972, *****, is a triumph. One writer says it has "hairy legs," but be not dismayed—that's good! (Gracious, how would they describe it if they didn't like it?) Chardonnay is the best wine in the world—well, the New World at least—to accompany fish, shellfish, pork, veal, ham. Serve it chilled. Both these wines are now at their best and will hold so at least until 1977. Fair value, both wines: ca. $6.50.

Gewürztraminer** ZD has not yet gotten the combination of this fine Alsatian grape. At the price, $4.50 and more, alas, not recommended.

Pinot Noir ZD's most interesting wine thus far. The 1969 (***) is a youthful sort of wine; light and fresh. And so should it be consumed: while it's fresh and youthful, before 1976 rolls around. The

'70 (****), however, is more in the classic European style: heavy, full-bodied, requiring aging. It will be at its best, 1975 or 1976 through 1980 and beyond. The '71 (***) is less forceful than the '70, and it also needs cellaring. Try it first, 1976. Air these wines at least one hour, serve at cool room temperature, with fine beef roast, game, stew. Fair (?) value, ca. $7.

White Riesling** Most California wineries call this wine Johannisberg Riesling, but ZD is more knowledgeable than most: this is the more accurate terminology. It's a well-made wine with good varietal character. Serve it chilled, with fowl, fish, seafood. Fair value, $4.50 to $5.

ZELLER SCHWARZE KATZ The name—the Black Cat—and the label with him right there —have usually been the most intriguing—and best—thing about this wine. Stricter laws have brought about some improvement in the product in recent years, but broadly speaking this wine has been extremely nondescript, technical language for yukkkkk-blaaaaaah. Famous, it's been, even world-renowned, and cheap also, but good, it has not been. The Zeller on the label means a wine from the town of Zell. The best Black Cats are good examples of Moselle wine:

light, flowery, delicately balanced between sweetness and acidity. Here are some of the most trustworthy names among the myriads of Black Cats swarming over the land: Anheuser (one of the most expensive, at $4.80); Beameister; Deinhard; Export Union; Guntrum; Hallgarten; Havemeyer; Kayser; Kendermann; Kreusch (a good value); Langguth; Madrigal; Sichel; Steigenberger.

ZELTING(ER) HIMMELREICH Good German Moselle wine, often one of the most economical of fine Moselles. A '71 Kabinett (H. Ehses) is a beautiful wine, ****, and a good value at around $3.50. But a Spätlese by the same is not recommended at $5. Another '71 Kabinett, by Winzer, is also ****. A '71 Spätlese (Casino), at $4.50, is easily ****.

ZELTING(ER) SCHLOSS-BERG ROTLAY Fine Moselle (Germany) wine, often a good value. One of the fullest-bodied of Moselles. For recent vintages, and how to serve this wine: See under MOSELLE.

ZELTINGER (or: ZELTING (ER)-WEHLEN(ER) SONNEN-UHR) Some say this is the finest wine of this area of the Moselle (Germany).

Some vintages:

1949—Wehlener-Zeltinger Trockenbeerenauslese (J. J. Prüm): Classic. Notice that it's Wehlener-Zeltinger instead of Zeltinger-Wehlener—but it's the same wine—it's just to confuse innocent Americans! Some of this wine is being kept until 2000.

1961—Auslese, Eiswein—Famous: Classic.

1969—Feine Auslese (Von Schorlemer): *****

1971—Auslese (Berres): *****

Spätlese (Ehses-Berres): ****

Kabinett (Prüm): ****

Note that there is also a Wehlener Sonnenuhr (see); it's the same wine; part of the vineyard is in Zelting, part in Wehlen.

ZINFANDEL Big "Z" is one of those rare critters, a native Californian—well, almost. Everything, everybody, and certainly every wine in California seems to have been imported from somewhere else. But zesty "Zin" is indigenous to California in that it's grown nowhere else (as far as is known), and it's very nearly the most widely planted grape in the state (surpassed only by Carignan, a grape used almost exclusively for blending purposes: "Burgundy," "Chianti" and that motley crew).

Zinfandel comes in two styles today: a young fruity red wine, light-bodied, zestful—many say it has a taste of rasperries or brambles—had any brambles lately? Such "Z" is to be consumed young, when it's two to four years old. If it's nonvintaged (undated), drink it within two years of purchase. This "Z" has been called California's "Beaujolais."

The very best Zinfandel, however, is grown where the vintner prunes back the vines severely to limit production and thus increase flavor—these "Zins" are big, rich wines, aged some years in wood before they're bottled, and they will continue to improve in the bottle for another five or more years. These aged "Z's" are, in fact, so hearty and tasty that they are often virtually indistinguishable from lordly Cabernet Sauvignons.

Some of these big Zinfandels are made from late-picked, sugar-laden grapes, and are high in alcohol and residual sugar. With time these can become magnificently luscious wines, incredibly similar to fine Vintage Port!

The youthful type of Zinfandel goes best with all manner of beef, lamb, veal. It's perfectly at home at the barbecue grill —steaks, hamburgers, shish kebab—and will be appreciated most of all when sipped tenderly and languidly with fruit, cheeses, nuts. "Zin" has a special affinity for these cheeses: Camembert, Gorgonzola, Gruyère Parmesan, Stilton. The elderly type of "Z" demands more aristocratic accompaniment: a prime rib roast, a Chateaubriand, Boeuf Bourguignon, Filet of Beef Wellington.

There is also a White Zinfandel—it's actually light orange in color—made by only two wineries, David Bruce and Ridge (see both). It's truthfully more of a curiosity than anything else, though both wines are rated ***, good.

Zinfandel, red or white, is served at cool room temperature, 65–70°F. Air your "Z" at least an hour before serving, particularly the younger wines. Listed below are California's best Zinfandels in descending order of excellence. Where wines have the same rating, the least expensive is listed first. Prices are approximate.

American Zinfandels—
Comparative Standings
Near-Classic
  Mayacamas Zinfandel, 1972 Late Harvest ($12)
  Mayacamas Zinfandel, 1968 Late Harvest ($17.40)

*****
Exceptional
  Inglenook Zinfandel, 1968 ($3.10)
  Fetzer Zinfandel, 1968 ($3.75)
  Sutter Home Zinfandel, 1968 ($3.85)
  Ridge Zinfandel, 1969 Late Harvest and 1971 Occidental Late Harvest ($7)
  David Bruce Zinfandel, 1970 ($8.50)
  Ridge Zinfandel, 1968 Essence ($8.50)
  Ridge Zinfandel, 1970 Occidental Late Harvest ($8.75)
****
Very Good
  Davis Bynum ($2.25)
  Sebastiani Zinfandel (N.V.) ($2.50)
  Louis Martini Zinfandel, 1968 and 1970 and 1971 ($2.85)
  Sutter Home Zinfandel, 1972 ($2.85)
  Charles Krug Zinfandel, 1971 ($2.85)
  Beringer Zinfandel ($3)
  Christian Brothers Zinfandel ($3)
  Kenwood Zinfandel, 1970 and 1971 ($3)
  Simi Zinfandel (North Coast) ($3)
  Inglenook Zinfandel, 1969, 1970 and 1972 ($3.10)
  Parducci Zinfandel, 1968 ($3.25)
  Mirassou Zinfandel, 1968, 1969, 1971 ($3.40)
  Parducci Zinfandel, 1964, 1966, 1967 ($3.40)
  Davis Bynum Reserve Zinfandel ($3.50)
  Sebastiani Zinfandel, 1970, 1972 ($3.75)
  Sutter Home Zinfandel, 1969, 1970, 1971 ($3.85)
  David Bruce Zinfandel, 1967, 1968 ($4)

Louis Martini Zinfandel, 1963 ($4.50)

Ridge Zinfandel, 1968, 1969 Monte Bello ($4.50)

Souverain Mt. Zinfandel, 1970, 1971 ($4.50)

Sterling Zinfandel, 1969, 1970 ($4.50)

Fetzer Zinfandel, 1972, Lolonis-Stafford & Ricetti Vineyards ($4.80)

Buena Vista Zinfandel, 1967 Cask 140, 1968 Cask 160 ($5)

Ridge Zinfandel, 1970 Late Harvest, 1970 Fulton ($5)

Louis Martini Zinfandel, 1962 ($5)

Ridge Zinfandel, 1969 Jimsomare ($5)

Ridge Zinfandel, these 1970s: Geyserville, Jimsomare, Monte Bello, Occidental ($5.50)

Louis Martini Zinfandel, 1962 Private Reserve ($6.50)

Ridge Zinfandel, 1970 Late Lodi Harvest ($7)

Ridge Zinfandel, 1972 Geyserville ($7)

Louis Martini Zinfandel, 1956 Private Reserve ($7.50)

Louis Martini Zinfandel, 1955 Private Reserve ($8)

Ridge Zinfandel, 1971 Mendocino ($9)

Simi Zinfandel, 1935 ($25)

***

Good

Italian Swiss Colony Zinfandel ($1.55)

Roma Zinfandel ($1.65)

C. K. Mondavi Zinfandel ($1.70)

Gallo Zinfandel ($1.85)

Davis Bynum Barefoot Zinfandel ($1.90)

Pedroncelli Zinfandel ($2.50)

Paul Masson Zinfandel ($2.60)

Wente Zinfandel ($2.60)

Eleven Cellars Zinfandel ($2.70)

Bargetto Zinfandel ($2.75)

Sonoma (or Windsor) Zinfandel ($2.75)

Heitz Zinfandel ($2.80)

Krug Zinfandel, 1970 ($2.80)

Louis Martini Zinfandel, 1967, 1969 ($2.85)

Sutter Home Zinfandel, 1973 ($2.85)

Korbel Zinfandel, 1972 ($2.90)

Louis Martini Zinfandel, 1965, 1966 ($3)

Inglenook Zinfandel, 1964, 1965, 1966, 1967 ($3.10)

Cresta Blanca Zinfandel ($3.15)

Mirassou Zinfandel, 1966, 1967, 1970 ($3.40)

Parducci Zinfandel, 1969, 1971 ($3.40)

Buena Vista Zinfandel, 1967, 1969, 1971 ($3.50)

Fetzer Zinfandel, 1969, 1970 ($3.50)

Oakville Zinfandel, 1970, 1971, 1972 ($3.75)

Ridge Zinfandel, 1967 ($3.75)

Buena Vista Zinfandel, 1970 ($4)

Robert Mondavi Zinfandel, 1966 ($4)

Fetzer Zinfandel, 1971, 1972 Mattern and Barra-Cinquinni Vineyards ($4)

David Bruce Zinfandel, 1965, 1966 ($4)

Ridge Zinfandel, 1972 Coast Range ($4)

Fetzer Zinfandel, 1972 ($4.15)

Ridge Zinfandel, 1971 Monte Bello ($4.25)

Souverain Mt. Zinfandel, 1968 ($4.50)

Sterling Zinfandel, 1968 ($4.50)

Ridge Zinfandel, 1966 ($5)

Ridge Zinfandel, 1971 Geyserville ($6)

Louis Martini Zinfandel, 1960 Private Reserve ($6)

**

Fair

Franzia Zinfandel ($1.35)

Winemaster's Zinfandel ($1.45)

Almadén Zinfandel ($2.35)

San Martin Zinfandel ($2.50)

Inglenook Vintage Zinfandel ($2.60)

Charles Krug Zinfandel, 1966, 1967, 1968, 1969 ($2.80)

Inglenook Zinfandel, 1971 ($3.10)

Sutter Home Petite Zinfandel, 1971 ($3.85)

Heitz Zinfandel, Lot 63-79 ($4)

Souverain Mt. Zinfandel, 1969 ($4.50)

*

Passable

Buena Vista Zinfandel, 1966

Mayacamas Zinfandel, 1966, 1967

Not Recommended

Pierrot Zinfandel

ZINFANDEL ROSÉ A California rosé wine made entirely or principally from Zinfandel grapes. The wine tends to be on the dry side. Only a half dozen wineries make it—which may be just as well, for it seems, somehow, a prostitution of good "Z" grapes, for the grapes' true characteristics simply do not come through in such a light-bodied wine. Concannon's and Pedroncelli's (see both) are the best, and for a complete listing, see the "Comparative Standings" under ROSÉ.

INDEX